Illustrated Dictionary of Archaeology

Illustrated Dictionary of Archaeology

Triune Books

Contributors: Nick Balaam, Iris Barry, Warwick Bray, Elizabeth Carter, Christopher Davey, Jennifer Foster, George Hart, Tony King, Jane MacIntosh, Mike Pitts, Jane Siegel, Percival Turnbull

PICTURE CREDITS

We should like to credit the following people and agencies who supplied us with photographs for this book:

Aero Pictorial Ltd; Paul Almasy; Nick Balaam; Tom Blagg; The British Academy; British Museum; Bury Peerless; Jane.Brown/*Observer*; Cambridge University Collection of Aerial Photography; Camera Press; Elizabeth Carter; Peter Clayton; Cleveland Museum of Art; Christopher Davey; Ray Delvert (SPADEM); Donnington Photographics; Elliot and Fry; Werner Forman Archive; Dr I. C. Glover; Robert Harding Associates; Michael Holford; Italian State Tourist Office; Paolo Koch; London Museum of Anthropology; Lowie Museum of Anthropology; Museum of the American Indian, New York; Museum of Fine Arts, Boston; Musée Guimet; Mansell Collection; Mary Evans Picture Library; Ministry of Works; National Portrait Gallery; Pitt Rivers Museum; Mike Pitts; Picturepoint; Photoresources; Josephine Powell; R. Schoder; Sheridan Photo Library; Snark International; Percival Turnbull; Winchester Excavations Committee; Ziolo (Roland).

Line drawings are by Mike Craig.

First published in Great Britain in 1977 by Triune Books, London, England.
Created, designed and produced by Trewin Copplestone Publishing Ltd, London

Printed by New Interlitho, Italy

ISBN: 0 85674 030 6

How to use this book

This dictionary contains over 1500 entries; approximately half of them concentrate on sites and their findings, the other half on the techniques and disciplines of the science which have grown up over the past 150 years.

All major world-regions are featured – for example, the Americas, the Indus Valley, Egypt, etc – together with the finds, terms and pioneer archaeologists linked to them. It is best to approach archaeology by beginning with the entries on the largest areas sharing distinct and recognisable cultural features. The reader can then move on from these to finer detail. Technical terms are included in the articles so that the layman can easily understand them in context. This same identifying aim also governs the selection of finds.

This dictionary is devised to present material in an easy-to-understand way. The cross-referencing system enables the reader to find the meaning of any technical term appearing within an entry. Visual aids include time-charts, regional indexes where sites of archaeological interest all over the world are indicated on a series of maps, line drawings of artefacts, and numerous photographs in colour as well as black and white.

Throughout the book, each illustration or diagram has been carefully tied to its text by means of a symbol. Thus the symbol ▲ next to an illustration relates to ▲ in the text nearby.

Pot from the Nasca Valley

Meroe sculpture

The Eye of Horus

What is Archaeology?

Penny with head of Offa, King of Mercia

Dark museum rooms with dusty cases full of shattered pottery tended by equally dusty curators; dedicated explorers fighting deep into tropical rain forests to seek out lost cities; skin-divers picking gold treasure from long-forgotten shipwrecks. All these are images – more or less untrue – of what archaeology is about. Above all, archaeology suggests digging, and the wonders the spade has revealed. Excavation is part of archaeology, but (as we shall see) only one part.

Archaeology is the systematic study of material remains in order to reconstruct the human past. Its scope is very wide, for the material remains of the past range from massive masterpieces of architecture – such as Egyptian pyramids and Mayan temples – to everyday household rubbish, broken pots and pans, chewed bones and ash. Archaeology covers many millions of years; it studies the roughly-split stones which were the tools of the earliest people, and also the cottages of medieval villagers, the settlements of seventeenth-century European colonists in New England, and the factories and foundries of the Industrial Revolution. And in a century or two it will investigate the buildings we are constructing and the refuse we are dumping today.

As a systematic study archaeology is little more than a century old; it has its origins in three overlapping traditions.

The first of these was the interest, which began in the Renaissance and has flourished ever since, in ancient Greece and Rome. Scholars read the Classical authors, and began to look closely at the surviving Classical monuments (temples, aqueducts, theatres, baths and so on) in the Mediterranean lands.

A second source was the florescence of the natural sciences in the nineteenth century, and especially the discoveries of archaeology's sister-disciplines, geology and palaeontology (which study the natural, rather than human, remains of the past). At this time archaeological discoveries of ancient stone tools, together with the bones of the people who made them and of the animals they hunted, provided key evidence for Darwin's theory of evolution. It was realized that human origins were to be found not in a literal reading of the Book of Genesis but in a long succession of hominid ancestors over millions of years, and archaeologists began to search for and study their fossilized remains.

The third source was the natural interest of intelligent men everywhere in the ancient buildings, earthworks and objects of their native lands. So in Britain they dug into burial mounds – the most obvious of ancient monuments – in search of the

Ancient Britons, in France they looked for the Gauls, and in America no less a man than President Jefferson investigated ancient Indian remains.

All these traditions were absorbed into archaeology, which by late Victorian times had established itself as a separate field of study. By then many of its modern methods had been established in a rudimentary way.

A key development of the mid nineteenth century was the discovery of *prehistory* (a word first used in 1833): the period before writing was invented and therefore of which no records survived. As long as human history was taken to be a matter only of ancient manuscripts and inscriptions it was impossible to discover what had gone on before there was writing; until scholars learned to glean information from the 'silent stones', prehistoric times were lost in a fog of uncertainty and speculation. Gradually chance discoveries of ancient objects, deliberate excavations and the study of antiquarians' collections cleared the fog.

By the 1860s the outlines of prehistory were clear. Early people during the *Palaeolithic* period used stone tools and lived on wild plants and animals during the alternating ice ages and warm spells of the Pleistocene era. After the final retreat of the ice about 12,000–10,000 BC men continued this way of life until *Neolithic* times when polished (rather than chipped) stone tools, pottery and agriculture all made their appearance. Later came the successive use of metals, first the *Bronze Age*, and then the *Iron Age* which covered the centuries immediately before historical times. This sequence, first worked out in Scandinavia, was found to apply, with modifications, elsewhere.

The later nineteenth century saw the first of a string of brilliant discoveries all over the world, from Siberia (where entire woolly mammoths were found frozen and perfectly preserved in the ice) to the tropics (where whole civilizations, such as the Olmecs and Maya of Central America and Zimbabwe in southern Africa, were discovered). There are many great and romantic tales of archaeology in those days. Heinrich Schliemann, a German banker, for instance, went to what is now Eastern Turkey to find the ancient city of Troy. Using the *Iliad*, the Classical Greek poem which dates from several centuries before Christ, as if it was a modern guide-book, he decided that a mound called Hissarlik was Troy and set about excavating it. He found there a whole series of cities, and a great golden treasure which was smuggled off the site in his wife's voluminous skirts.

Archaeology today is more organized but no less exciting. There are many specialisms within archaeology, but the general approach is common to all.

First comes surveying, the collection of information without actually excavating. A prehistorian, for instance, studies the landscape acre by acre and field by field for signs of ancient occupation which may be revealed by the slightest trace of ancient earthworks, or by flint, pottery and bone brought up by the plough. The medievalist searches ancient records for clues as to how a town grew. The underwater archaeologist surveys with echo-sounder and aqualung.

Then comes excavation of selected small areas. They are small for two reasons. First of all, excavation requires an enormous quantity of painstaking labour (it is done not with spades but with masons' trowels, and delicate work with tools such as dental picks). Secondly, excavation is destructive. Each layer is uncovered, plotted and photographed, then removed to reveal the next deposit: once removed it can never be replaced. So the archaeologist must record in great detail and with great accuracy all he finds. (This is why holes made by 'treasure-hunters' do such damage, for even if nothing of value is taken, part of a precious site is destroyed without record.)

Finally comes work in the laboratory and library. All the material is conserved against decay, compared with finds from elsewhere, and subjected to scientific tests which enable the archaeologist to extract the maximum information from his excavation work.

Archaeology, then, is a curious business. It uses a great many scientific methods and tests, yet is not a science itself. It studies ancient art, but not because of its beauty. It expands the information historians find in documents, and it does much more: wherever the historian for lack of material cannot go – and that is most of human history – archaeology is the key witness. Writing is only a few thousand years old, yet archaeology discovers what men were up to more than a million years ago. Archaeology fills in the silences in the past, from the religions of prehistory to the sinister and shadowy barbarians outside the Classical world and the techniques of medieval plumbing.

ABBASIDS The second dynasty of the Moslem empire after the death of Mohammad. Descendants of Mohammad's uncle al'Abbas skilfully used propaganda to gain the support of the Arabs and Iranians. In AD 747 Abu Moslem was able to lead a revolt against the ruling OMAYYADS, defeating them at the Battle of the Great Zab River in about 750 and proclaimed Abu al-Abbas as-Saffah, the first Abbasid caliph. His successor Abu Jafar in 762 decided to build a new capital on the site of a SASSANIAN village, Baghdad. The city he constructed was 2700m in diameter and was very much a world of its own; its mystery and power are reflected in *The Thousand and One Nights*. The power of the army considerably weakened the caliph after *c* AD 900, and 1055 the SELJUKS took his political power leaving the caliph as religious leader only. The Abbasid caliphate was finally destroyed by the Mongol invasion in 1258.

○ **ABBEVILLEAN** The oldest HANDAXE-using culture in Europe, characterized by rough handaxes, as opposed to the much finer specimens of the later ACHEULEAN. The stone industry also includes FLAKES and heavy, coarse CHOPPING TOOLS. The TYPE-SITE is Abbeville in the Somme valley. Various deposits in the Somme gravels date the Abbevillean to the Mindel interstadial (*see* GLACIATIONS).

ABRI PATAUD, France A recently excavated site in the Dordogne, with a rich Upper PALAEOLITHIC sequence of AURIGNACIAN, Upper PERIGORDIAN and Proto-MAGDALENEAN industries.

ABU SHAHRAIN, Tell
see ERIDU

● **ABU SIMBEL, Southern Egypt,** downstream from Second Cataract. Originally on bank of Nile, the site of two temples cut into mountainside under Ramesses II (Dynasty XIX). These are:

(1) The Great Temple to Amun-Re, Re-Horakhty, Ptah and Ramesses himself. Four colossal statues of Ramesses (20m high) on the eastern-facing façade. The Main Hall (18m deep) contains pillar-statues of Ramesses as Osiris. Its reliefs show Ramesses at Battle of Kadesh (1285 BC) against the Hittites. The Sanctuary at the rear contains statues of Ramesses and the three gods – lit up at dawn twice a year (equinoxes) by the sun's rays.

(2) The Temple of Hathor and Nefertari (Ramesses's queen). Buttresses alternate with standing statues of Ramesses and Nefertari as Hathor. Sistra (sacred rattles of Hathor) on supporting pillars of main hall and statue of Hathor-cow in sanctuary.

One of the world's largest archaeological rescue operations was mounted on an international scale when the construction of the Aswan High Dam threatened to drown the temples. The sandstone temples were cut up into over 1000 blocks and re-erected on a new site above the water level.

ABUSIR, Egypt Necropolis (south of MEMPHIS) for the pharaohs of Dynasty V. The pyramids are in a poor state of preservation – the best belonging to King Sahure. His funerary temple used granite, basalt, limestone and alabaster and had a drainage system for rainwater. Abusir shows the power of the sun-cult and the pharaoh's strength as the sun-god's son. King Niuserre's sun temple possibly imitates the great temple at HELIOPOLIS, the sun-god's cult centre. An OBELISK about 36m high, symbol of the sun-

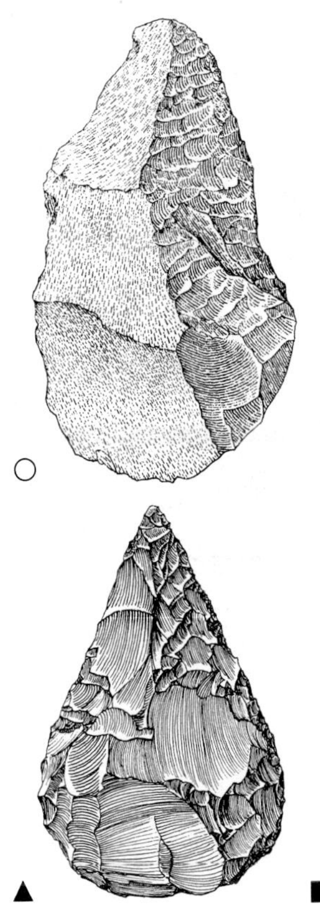

god, stood on a blunt pyramid rising out of a man-made platform. Reliefs in the temple emphasize the sun as the source of Egypt's prosperity and commemorate the occasion of the obelisk's construction on the pharaoh's jubilee. A boat for the sun's journey made of rock and brick has been discovered.

ABYDOS Sacred site in Upper Egypt, necropolis for This, hometown of the southern rulers who united Egypt *c* 3100 BC. Its ancient local god was a dog-deity, lord of the dead, called Khenti-amentiu (Foremost of the Westerners, i.e. those in the cemeteries). The cult of OSIRIS from the Delta spread to Abydos, absorbed the local god, and made this site its major sanctuary. MARIETTE found many STELAE from the Middle Kingdom – votive gifts from visitors to the 'tomb' of Osiris.

The excavations of PETRIE revealed royal monuments (possibly cenotaphs rather than tombs) of the Archaic period. *See also* MEMNONIUM, OSIREION, UMM el QAAB.

ACHAEMENID Persepolis in southern Iran was the capital of the Achaemenid (or Persian) empire from *c* 518 BC, when it was built by Darius I (522–486 BC), until it was destroyed by ALEXANDER THE GREAT *c* 330 BC. Cyrus II (the Great) began the Achaemenid empire when he defeated the MEDES *c* 553 BC and made Pasargadae his capital. The vast empire which extended as far as the Aegean was ruled liberally, permitting people to keep their own religion and language. It was divided into provinces, each ruled by a Persian called a 'satrap', and it was the first empire to base its economy on money rather than barter. Persepolis reflects the wealth and diversity of the empire. The great palaces and columned reception halls (apadana) were built on terraces, the walls of which were decorated with reliefs of various court scenes.

▲ **ACHEULEAN** A Lower PALAEOLITHIC HANDAXE tradition identified throughout much of the Old World. In Europe, it succeeds the ABBEVILLEAN, whose rough handaxes are distinguished from the finer, soft-hammer (*see* FLAKING) products of the Acheulean. In Africa, all bifacial handaxes are referred to the Acheulean, which consequently there has a greater span of existence than in Europe; a similar situation exists in India. The TYPE-SITE (Saint Acheul, Amiens) is one of a number of important Palaeolithic sites on the Somme river terraces.

■ **ACROPOLIS** The general name for the citadel or defended centre of a Greek town. It is also the name of the citadel at ATHENS.

The Acropolis was the original nucleus of Athens in MYCENAEAN times and must have resembled that of MYCENAE or TIRYNS. It was a royal palace until the 11th century BC when it became a public sanctuary. Temple foundations of *c* 700 BC have been found. The first Parthenon was built in 561 only to be destroyed by the Persians in 480. The existing Parthenon was built, mainly by Phidias, 447–438. The Propylea or entrance was built 437–432, the temple of Athena Nike (or Victory) in 421, and the Erechtheum 421–*c* 410. These temples are the major monuments on the hill. Others, such as the Asclepion (dedicated to the god of healing) and the theatre of Dionysus, are later works.

The Parthenon was dedicated to Athena (the goddess of wisdom and the patroness of Athens), to whom there was a gigantic gold and ivory statue in the temple. The

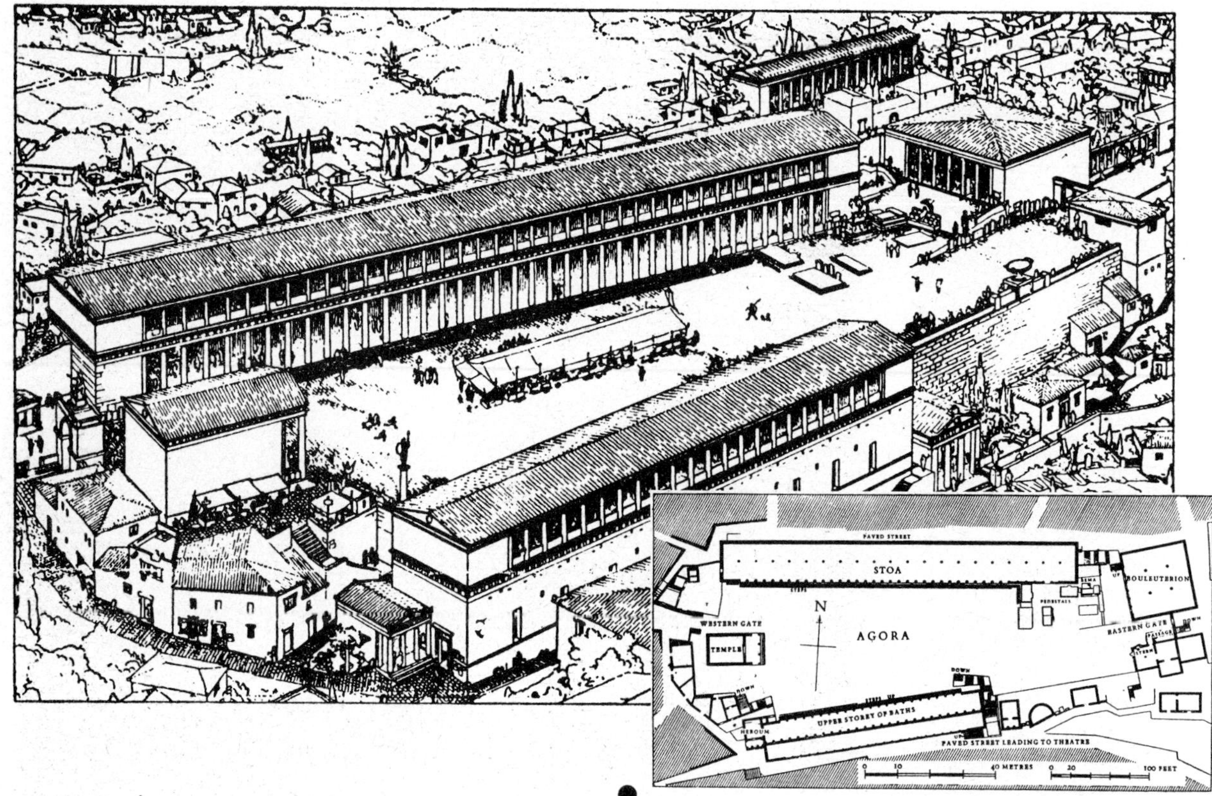

Erechtheum was the spiritual centre of Athens and many holy relics were kept there. The east end was dedicated to Athena and the west end to Poseidon (the god of the sea). A feature of the building is the south entrance whose porch is supported by caryatids (columns in human form).

Remains of the acropolis are on the hill itself, but can also be seen in the British Museum, where the Parthenon frieze now is kept (the Elgin Marbles).

ADAD (Canaanite – Hadad) the weather god of the Near East. He was both the giver and destroyer of life, and was also the god of oracles and divination. His symbol was a cypress tree and his sacred number was 6.

ADENA In the Ohio valley, North America, it represents the initial phase of the WOODLANDS tradition emerging *c* 1000 BC, and is characterized by large burial mounds and earthen enclosures. Settlements were small villages with large circular houses; craftsmanship was of a high standard and included the carving of stone tablets, cold-hammering metal into ornaments, textile manufacture and the production of rather plain cord-impressed pottery. The Adena culture was ancestral to HOPEWELL in this region.

ADOBE The term given in the New World to the MUD-BRICK building material used in the construction of houses, PYRAMIDS and PLATFORM MOUNDS.

ADZE A woodworking tool with the blade set at right angles to the handle. *See also* AXE.

AFGHANISTAN The small amount of excavation has not given very much historical knowledge of this area. The Persians (*see* ACHAEMENID Empire) had satrapies here in the sixth century BC; ALEXANDER THE GREAT campaigned through the area in 326 BC and his administration was later overthrown by the PARTHIANS. People from central Asia, the KUSHANS, drove the Parthians out of Afghanistan in the 1st century AD and seem to have continued in the area in spite of an invasion of White Huns *c* AD 480. Finally Moslems over-ran the country in the 11th century. Mundigak, a TELL near Kandahar, was excavated 1951–8. The occupation of the site began a little before 3000 BC and finished *c* 800 BC. The earliest occupation has similarities to JEMDAT NASR in Mesopotamia. Later there are parallels with the INDUS CIVILIZATION although Mundigak would seem to be earlier. Surkh Khotal, BAGLAN, BEGRAN and Old Kandahar are other sites that have been excavated.

AGGER
see ROMAN ROADS

● **AGORA** The Greek word for the market-place of a town where business was conducted, where the administration was centred and, often, religious activity was based. There are many exceptions, especially in early towns: ATHENS has its religious centre on the ACROPOLIS above the agora, while several towns had their administration away from the agora. However, in HELLENISTIC and Roman times the agora was truly the heart of the town. STOAS were covered markets in agoras and the *bouleuterion* was the council's assembly hall. The agora was in general more haphazardly planned than its Roman counterpart, the FORUM.

AGRICOLA, Gnaeus Julius (*c* AD 40–93) The most famous, and one of the most able, of the Roman governors

▲ 

of Britain, known best from the TACITUS biography. He served in Britain as a military tribune and as a legionary commander before becoming governor in AD 78. He began at once by taking Anglesey, stronghold of the DRUIDS, and safeguarding the conquest of Wales. He fought six campaigns in the north of Britain, subduing the Brigantes and pushing well into the Highlands of Scotland (*see* INCHTUTHIL), defeating the Caledonian states at Mons Graupius. His Scottish victories were not consolidated. He was also responsible for the peaceful romanization of southern Britain. He is said to have sailed around the coast of Britain, and to have sighted Ireland.

AGRIGENTO A Greek colony in Sicily, founded 581 BC chiefly by Rhodians. There is an ACROPOLIS with the town stretching below it, at the farthest end of which are several temples. The largest, to Zeus, has been levelled but the temple of Concord (5th century BC) is one of the best examples of Doric architecture. *See* COLUMNS; CAPITALS.

AHRENSBURGIAN One of three late GLACIAL hunter–fisher–gatherer groups of the north European plain (*see* LYNGBY and SWIDERIAN cultures). As with the HAMBURGIAN, the main hunting quarry seems to have been the reindeer. At Stellmoor, Schleswig-Holstein, Germany's favourable conditions resulted in the preservation of such objects as antler harpoons and wooden arrow-shafts. Evidence from the site also indicates that the Ahrensburgian post-dates the HAMBURGIAN.

▲ **AIR PHOTOGRAPHY** Viewing archaeological sites from the air provides a new dimension and a lot more information. This was quickly realized in the 1920s when aeroplanes became fairly common, and air photography has developed ever since. Four types of sites can be photographed: standing buildings, earthworks, crop marks, and soil marks. Not much need be said about standing buildings but an aerial view of an earthwork, usually thrown into relief by low shadows, clarifies the nature of the remains and provides an overall picture difficult to obtain on the ground.

This is even more the case with crop and soil marks, where the site may not even be visible from ground level. Soil marks are produced in ploughed areas where the top-soil is thin and the substratum is in a different colour, e.g. on chalklands. Ditches dug into the subsoil and then filled in will show up dark on light soils, and ploughed-out banks will show up lighter. Crop marks are produced mainly on light, well-drained soils. They show only in ripening crops or parched pasture, usually in a dry period after a good shower of rain. They are formed by variations in crop growth: the richer soil in ditches causes slower growth, and the thinner soil over walls causes faster growth and earlier ripening. Other methods of detection include the observation of differential drying of dew and frost and snow.

AJANTA
see ROCK-CUT ARCHITECTURE

AKKAD, Akkadian [Agade] A term used by the SUMERIANS to refer to the north of Sumer, near Babylon. The area was inhabited by AMORITES who with their king, Sargon (Sharru-kin), gained control not only of the rest of Sumer but also the whole of MESOPOTAMIA and northern Syria from the Persian Gulf to the Mediterranean. Sargon, who reigned 2371–2316 BC, was always remembered for his

greatness and may be the person depicted in a bronze head from Nineveh. The Akkadian empire was beset with revolts when Sargon died. Sargon's grandson, Naram Sin reigned 2291–2255 BC over a similar empire which ended with an invasion by the little-known Gutiums. From this time Akkadian applies to the Semitic language of the Amorites which was written in CUNEIFORM script and develops into the language of ASSYRIA and BABYLON.

ALACA HÜYÜK, Turkey A TELL in central Anatolia which has been inhabited since *c* 4000 BC. While it was only a modest agricultural community *c* 2450 BC, tombs show that at that time there was a wealthy aristocracy. Fine gold jewellery, weapons and furniture inlaid with gold were found together with 'sundisks' and standard mounts of deer and bulls. The most spectacular architectural period came 1,000 years later when the HITTITES built fortifications and a temple. The site continued to be occupied until Ottoman times in the 15th century AD.

ALALAKH [Modern Tell Atchana] Syria TELL on the river Orontes near the Turkish-Syrian border. It was excavated by Woolley 1937–49 who found the city gate, a series of temples used between 2000–1200 BC, the palace of Yarim Lim and a HILANI. It was soon after Yarim Lin's reign, *c* 1660 BC, that Alalakh lost its independence to the HITTITES for whom it became a provincial capital, although there was a period of relative independence under King Idrimi (about 1550 BC) whose statue was found at the tell.

ALCANTARA, Spain The Roman road from MERIDA into Lusitania (Portugal) is carried across the river Tagus on a bridge 300m long and 50m high. The bridge is built of rough-faced granite ashlar, erected without mortar. An arch over the roadway commemorates the construction of the bridge by 11 cities of Lusitania under the direction of the Emperor Trajan in AD 106.

ALEXANDER THE GREAT Born in 356 BC at Pella, Macedonia, north-eastern Greece. After a classical education under the philosopher Aristotle, he became king of Macedonia at the age of 20. Two years later he began his Persian campaign which marks him as one of the greatest generals of all time. He wrested Asia Minor from the Persians, captured the island of Tyre (*see* PHOENICIANS) and subdued Egypt. In the east he occupied BABYLON, destroyed Persepolis (*see* ACHAEMENID Empire) and captured the Iranian plateau, controlled the SCYTHIANS in northern Afghanistan and invaded India. On his return to Babylon he died at the age of 32 after ten days' illness in 323 BC. His kingdom was divided between four of his generals: Cassander ruled Macedonia, Lysimachus controlled Thrace, Antigonus held Asia Minor and Syria, and Ptolemy ruled Egypt and Palestine. Later another general, Seleucus, took control of Babylon and the East. A mosaic ▲ found at POMPEII depicts Alexander defeating the Persian king, Darius III, at the Battle of Issus in 333 BC. Wherever Alexander gained control he imposed Greek culture. He founded over 18 cities and assisted in the rebuilding of many others in Greek style. This policy was continued vigorously by his generals.

● **ALEXANDRIA** Western Nile Delta, founded by ALEXANDER 332 BC was the main commercial centre for Egypt. The Island of Pharos acted as breakwater: its lighthouse was

■ 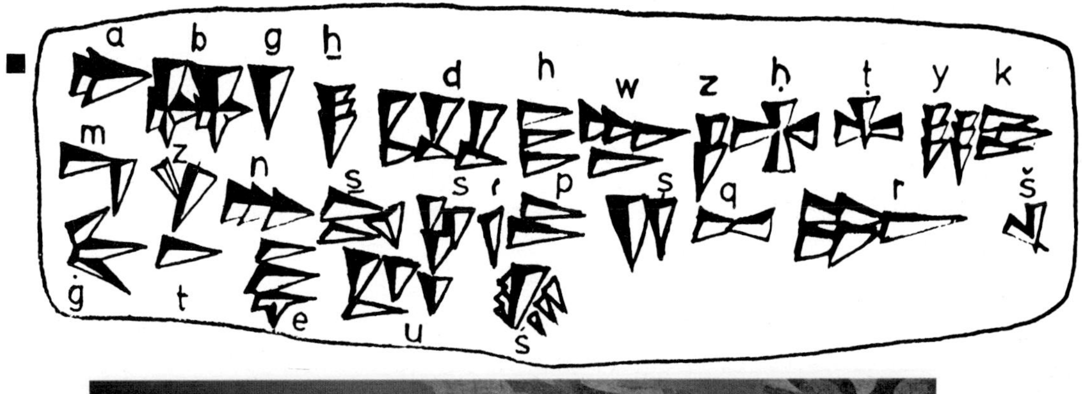

▲ 

totally destroyed by the 13th century AD. The city was roughly rectangular with intersecting streets. Its Library and Museum attracted scholars like Euclid and the geographer Eratosthenes. The monuments have been much looted or destroyed. Archaeologists have discovered a marble Roman amphitheatre and baths of Tiberius. 'Pompey's pillar', granite 30m high – actually in honour of Diocletian – formed part of a temple of Serapis, god of the Ptolemaic royal cult.

Excavations revealed a huge underground funerary complex of the early Christian era; architecture and decoration with Egyptian and Graeco-Roman motifs.

ALFRED King of WESSEX AD 871–99. During the earlier part of his reign he resisted the Danish incursions on Wessex and defeated their army at Edington in 878. In a treaty of 886 the DANELAW was recognized, and a period of comparative political stability ensued during which many far-sighted reforms were instituted. A permanent naval force and constitutional military levy were created, laws codified, military boroughs and strongpoints established. Although there was great growth in town life, trade and prosperity, Alfred lamented the decay of English learning and arts and personally encouraged writers and craftsmen.

ALIGNMENT
see MEGALITH

ALMERIAN CULTURE A south Spanish WESTERN NEOLITHIC culture of *c* 4500–3500 BC. Agricultural communities lived in settlements of round or oval houses (as at El Garcel, Almería) storing farm produce in underground pits. Almerian round-based pottery is found in small round drystone tombs 2–3m across, containing one or more human burials. These tombs were probably ancestral to the larger corbelled tombs of the later LOS MILLARES culture.

ALPHABET A system of WRITING in which each sound is represented by a symbol. The advantage of this system over others is its simplicity, in that only 20 to 30 symbols are required. The ordinary person can read and write an alphabetic script without great difficulty whereas other more complex systems require a specialist. The first examples appear in the LEVANT *c* 1500 BC. A tablet from ■ UGARIT, probably a school text, uses CUNEIFORM signs to represent single sounds. Different signs were used further south and it was the PHOENICIANS who disseminated this system. Vowels were not written until the Greeks adopted the alphabet in the 8th century BC. They used as vowels some of the existing signs for which they had no corresponding sound.

ALTAMIRA, Spain The site of some caves near Santander in north-east Spain, discovered in 1879 to contain paintings in several colours of deer, bison and wild boar. Altamira played a part in the early debate surrounding the supposed age of cave paintings in France and Spain, and it is now accepted that the majority of the art at this particular location is of MAGDALENEAN origin.

AMARAVATI, India This STUPA is of a somewhat different design from the northern examples. The use of limestone instead of sandstone gives greater delicacy to the decorative scenes. The stupa spans a considerable period from 2nd century BC to 2nd century AD. Until the late 1st century AD, as at other Buddhist sites, the Buddha was here

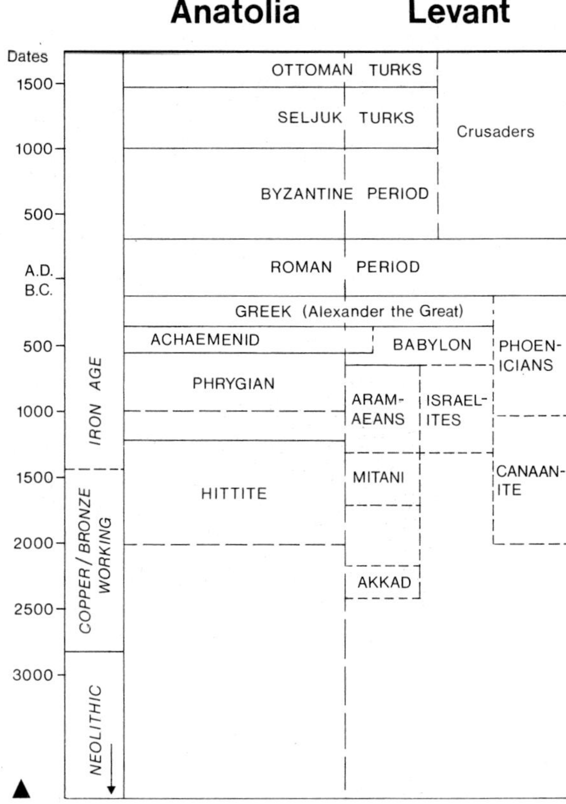

represented by symbols, but thereafter at Amaravati he is shown in human form. *See also:* GANDHARAN ART; MATHURA ART.

AMARNA A semicircular desert tract bounded by cliffs on the east bank of the Nile in Middle Egypt. Site of the new capital and centre of sun-worship under Amenophis IV-Akhenaten. The town, called Akhetaten (Horizon of the sun-disk), had been devastated by later pharaohs after the return to orthodoxy. They demolished the buildings for materials for their own monuments. However, the digs of PETRIE, a German expedition and the Egypt Exploration Society have recovered the plan of the city. There were several palaces, and a Great Temple to the Aten notable for the courtyards open to the sky. Pictures of the palace and temple in the rock tombs of Akhenaten's courtiers have helped archaeologists immensely. The ground plan of the palace was preserved due to the technique of the ancient Egyptian architects in covering the flooring with layers of sand. Amarna is one of the few archaeological sites in Egypt from which we can see how a town was organized – streets, quarters for nobles, sculptors' workshops (from one of which came the polychrome bust of Queen Nefertiti). The tombs of the courtiers in the cliffs behind the town show the preoccupation with worshipping the Aten through the royal family. The royal tomb situated in a blind wadi is extensively ruined, but its reliefs are significant in any attempt to understand this complicated pharaoh.

AMERINDIAN Peoples of Asiatic Mongoloid type who entered the New World probably by 28,000 BC across the Bering landbridge when Asia and Alaska were linked during WISCONSIN glaciation in the PLEISTOCENE period. All native American Indians excepting the ESKIMO are of this racial group, sharing blood groups A and O and totally lacking B. Sites such as OLD CROW FLATS and ONION PORTAGE demonstrate the early passage of these first colonists from Asia on their way south. They had reached the tip of South America by *c* 10,000 BC. *See also:* FELL'S CAVE.

AMORITES A SEMITIC people who migrated from the desert into SUMER during the 3rd millennium. They were assimilated within the culture, and eventually certain Amorites were to be found in high administrative positions from which they dominated MESOPOTAMIA particularly during the dynasty of AKKAD. In the west they captured cities in Syria and Palestine *c* 2000 BC and settled with the CANAANITES in that area.

AMPHITHEATRE A type of Roman building with an arena surrounded by tiers of seats for spectators to watch games and circuses. It was developed from the COLOSSEUM and became a standard feature of all large towns. There was often an elaborate system of underground passages and trap doors in the arena for moving scenery and animals.

AMPHORA A storage jar with two handles, often with a spiked base. Amphorae are very common finds on sites of the Roman period, being used for the export of oil, wine and GARUM; huge quantities of amphorae were used for shipping cargoes from Spain.

AMPURIAS, Spain A colony of the Phocean Greeks near Barcelona, closely related to MASSILIA and probably founded at about the same time in the early 6th century BC.

The first settlement was on an island close to the coast but soon the population expanded onto the mainland to found the Neapolis ('new town') of Ampurias. The local tribe lived in an annexe to the main town which was replaced by a COLONY of JULIUS CAESAR, who rebuilt the annexe along Roman lines. The Greek neapolis was subordinated to the new colony. Late Roman and Visigothic Ampurias was on the outskirts of the Roman town and the site was deserted after the Arab invasions.

AMRI, India Like most pre-Harappan sites Amri is situated well above the flood plain, suggesting that the problem of coping with the annual inundation of the Indus river had not yet been solved. The earliest occupation lacks structures which appear in later periods, first as mud-brick houses with stone footings, then as stone and mud-brick dwellings raised above the ground on platforms. There is continuity in the material culture, in which Harappan pottery increases in proportion throughout. By phase III a full Harappan culture is found here. *See also* INDUS CIVILIZATION.

AMUDIAN A Middle PALAEOLITHIC industry of south-west Asia, named after Wadi el Amud in Galilee. It is well represented at MOUNT CARMEL and Jabrud (the TYPE-SITE of contemporary JABRUDIAN). A similar industry has been recognized further west at HAUA FTEAH, Cyrenaica, Libya. Because of its ancestral relationship with the later Upper Palaeolithic industries of south-west Asia, the Amudian is sometimes referred to as the 'pre-AURIGNACIAN'.

AMULETS (Egyptian) A plethora of figurines and inanimate articles from ancient Egypt (discovered in burials of predynastic date and occurring thereafter throughout pharaonic civilization) witnesses the population's reliance on devices believed to contain supernatural power. Magic and superstition played considerable part in the Egyptian approach to religion and medicine. Amulets worn during a person's lifetime were meant to ward off diseases and avoid lethal contact with dangerous animals (lions, crocodiles, scorpions, snakes) or mythical creatures possibly living in the desert regions. Some amulets in the shape of a god or divine symbol are requests for assistance, e.g. to Thoueris the hippopotamus goddess, who ensures a smooth pregnancy. Some endow a person with the protection of a pharaonic godhead e.g. those in shape of royal crowns or the URAEUS. Others are more general appeals for good fortune and happiness e.g. a kneeling figure with a palm branch, symbol of longevity. Amulets adorned the corpse in large quantities to give similar protection and benefits in the afterlife – some naturally developing more specialized funerary symbolism.

Materials for amulets varied, ranging from gold and semi-precious stones (e.g. carnelian) to the ubiquitous FAIENCE. *See also* ANKH, CIPPI, DJED, EYE OF HORUS, GIRDLE OF ISIS, HYPERCEPHALI, MAGICAL KNIVES, MENAT, SCARAB.

AMUN Ancient Egyptian god whose origins seem to have been as one of the OGDOAD at HERMOPOLIS. His name means 'invisible one' or 'wind'. Before the reunification of Egypt and territorial expansion by the pharaohs of the Middle Kingdom, he was on Theban soil as a relatively minor local deity – in keeping with the then insignificance of Thebes itself. His rise to kingship of the gods matched the political fortunes of the Theban princes. By the New Kingdom his position as chief god in the pantheon was paramount and his priesthood was by far the wealthiest in Egypt. (The only setback during this period was the interlude of the reign of the pharaoh Amenophis IV-Akhenaten (Dynasty XVIII), whose passion to establish the sole worship of the sun's disk involved moving the religious nucleus of Egypt from THEBES to AMARNA.)

The great temple complex of KARNAK had sanctuaries for Amun, his wife the vulture-goddess Mut and their falcon-headed son Khons the moon god. The processional way from Karnak to LUXOR was lined with rams sacred to Amun. His anthropomorphic appearance shows him wearing the crown of a solar disk with the two tall plumes stemming out from it. The pharaohs also constructed growing monuments south of the First Cataract, e.g. Amenophis III (Dynasty XVIII) at SOLEB, Ramesses II (Dynasty XIX) at ABU SIMBEL. Amun was also the national god of state around the Fourth Cataract whose rulers invaded Egypt itself and became Dynasty XXV (*see* NUBIA).

ANASAZI A culture of the SOUTH-WESTERN tradition evolved from earlier DESERT antecedents in parts of Arizona, New Mexico, Utah and Colorado beginning *c* 100 BC and continuing through five developmental periods until historic times. Later sites were characterized by the building of enormous PUEBLOS. Maize agriculture became increasingly important and artefacts include painted pottery, elaborate basketry, textiles, chipped and ground stone tools. Many important sites are located in the Chaco Canyon and include the Pueblo Bonito. Contacts were maintained with the contemporary MOGOLLON and HOHOKAM peoples. The culture was already declining before the time of Spanish contact and, later, pressures by nomadic Apache and Navajo tribes further restricted settlement. A few pueblos are still occupied to the present.

▲ **ANATOLIA** The modern name given to the area of Asiatic Turkey. It derives from the Turkish name. Our history of Anatolia begins with ÇATAL HÜYÜK and Hacilar, and continues with Troy (*see* SCHLIEMANN) in the west and ALACA HÜYÜK and KULTEPE in the centre. The HITTITES who migrated from the Caucasus were the main power in the 2nd millennium BC, although the HURRIANS in the east influenced a wide area. In the 1st millennium BC the PHRYGIANS and the Lydians of SARDIS dominated the centre until the Persian invasion. The Greeks settled on the Aegean coast at such places as EPHESUS, and later in the Roman empire this area was administered from PERGAMUM.

■ **ANGKOR, Cambodia** From the 9th to 15th century AD the capital of the Khmer empire was situated in north-west Cambodia, at Angkor. Strong Indian influence is evident in the magnificent monumental architecture instituted by the rulers of the period. The city complex included reservoirs, irrigation canals, and massive structures serving as kingly mausoleums and temples. The temple remains are the best known of the Angkor complex, especially Angkor Wat, built in the 12th century by Suryavarman II. Its laterite and sandstone buildings cover three square km, with the central sanctuary reaching a height of 40m. Later in the same century Jayavarman VII built the royal city of Angkor Thom, surrounded by a vast defensive moat and wall. The temple he built (known as the Bayon) is decorated with huge statues displaying Indian and local motifs. With ▶

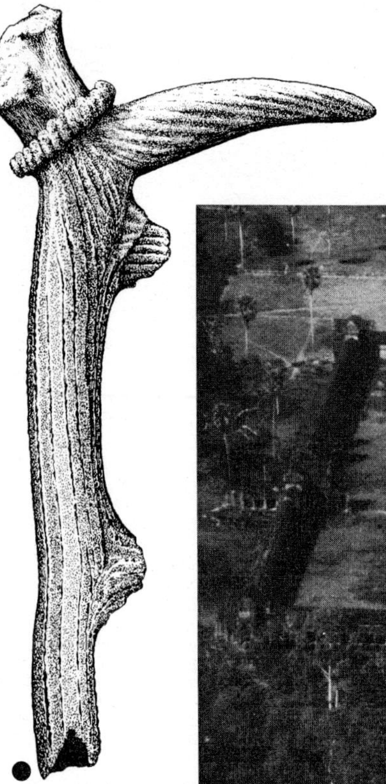

the decline in the kingdom's power, the city of Angkor was abandoned, and the capital shifted to Phnom Penh in 1434, leaving the jungle to encroach on the monuments of Angkor until they were 'rediscovered' in the 19th century by French archaeologists.

ANGKOR THOM
see ANGKOR

ANGKOR WAT
see ANGKOR

ANGLES One of a group of Germanic tribes which came to England as FOEDERATI in the 5th century AD and later became settlers. Their Continental homeland was in southern Jutland, north of the river Eider. According to BEDE they populated the areas of England later known as EAST ANGLIA, MERCIA and NORTHUMBRIA. Before the time of the migrations the Angles had probably already become mixed with the SAXONS, FRISIANS and JUTES, resulting in an equally mixed archaeological assemblage.

ANIMAL ORNAMENT From the end of the 5th into the late 6th century AD the commonest ornament on metalwork is a CHIPCARVED animal which has lost its zoological reality and has been reduced to a mere pattern. Heads, legs, tails and teeth are mixed with a charming confusion which covers every square centimetre of the surface of the object. Called 'Style I' in Salin's typology of continental animal ornament, it has been found throughout Germany, Scandinavia, Hungary and eastern Europe as well as in England. Style II develops as a much quieter and simple ribbon-like INTERLACE pattern.

ANKH Ancient Egypt amuletic symbol, still fashionable in contemporary jewellery. Its shape is the knotted tie of a sandal-strap. In the hieroglyphic system it represents the sound-value of the word for 'life'. Often occurs in inscriptions as part of formulae following the name of the pharaoh to indicate his eternal existence. The ankh also symbolizes the arbitrary power of the pharaoh to extend mercy to conquered enemies or tribute principalities: scenes on monuments show Middle Eastern and African rulers on their knees or prostrate begging the king for the breath of life to be given to their nostrils. The ankh sign is frequently found in the hands of deities as a reminder of their power over human life, e.g. seated statues of the ferocious lioness-goddess Sekhmet. During the reign of Akhenaten (Dynasty XVIII) the sun-god Aten with many rays emanating from his disk proffers the ankh to his son the pharaoh and the queen – emphasizing that the welfare of Egypt depends on the cult upheld by the royal couple. The ankh occurs as decorative features on furniture: TUTANKHAMUN's ornate four-legged cabinet exhibits ebony ankh sign between its lower rails. It can also, rather amusingly, be animated as on Tutankhamun's ostrich feather fan where an ankh with human arms and legs marches carrying a sun-shield behind the king hunting from his chariot, protecting his life. The ankh was one of few pharaonic motifs to find its way into the art of Coptic Egypt where it forms a distinctive version of Christ's cross.

● **ANTLER PICK** Unshaped Red deer antlers were used in the Neolithic in north-west Europe as digging tools and are especially common at sites on chalk. Picks recently excavated at GRIMES GRAVES still had the finger-prints of their last users on the shafts.

▲ 

■ 

▲ 

ANTONINE WALL A turf wall built across the Scottish Forth–Clyde isthmus following the abandonment of HADRIAN'S WALL after the death of Hadrian. The new wall was constructed under the Emperor Antoninus Pius in the governorship of Lollius Urbicus, *c* AD 138; it is 58km long and fronted by a broad ditch. The foundation of the walls is stone. The wall, with the 19 new forts along its line, was the focal point of a new frontier policy in Britain, the conquest of Southern Scotland having apparently been necessitated by dissent among the tribes there. Between 154 and 158 the wall was abandoned and the frontier moved back south, presumably because of revolts in this buffer zone; a second period of occupation began in 161 and ended *c* 180 following another Roman campaign against the northern tribes.

ANTONINIANUS The Roman double-DENARIUS piece, characterized by the head with the radiate crown, after which it is often called a 'radiate'. Introduced by Caracalla in AD 215, the coin quickly became very debased, its silver content falling to almost nothing. Large numbers of unofficial copies known as 'barbarous radiates' were struck to meet the demand caused by massive inflation.

ANYANG, China The site in North Honan of the last capital city 'Great Shang' of the SHANG dynasty. Written accounts state that P'an Keng, the 19th king, founded the city *c* 14th century BC, moving from the earlier capital of CHENG CHOU. Excavations in both regions have revealed the remains of this first literate, metal-using civilization of China. *See also* HSIAO-T'UN.

ANYATHIAN The Burmese regional variety of the Lower PALAEOLITHIC tool tradition.

APHRODISIAS, Turkey A site in western Turkey named after the goddess of love. It was occupied as early as the 4th millennium although most interest is in the extensive ▲ classical remains. Most spectacular of these is the stadium where athletic contests and festivals were held. The temple of Aphrodite, an odeum (small theatre), a palace and a theatre are among other notable remains. An inscription in ▲ the wall warns that whoever throws rubbish there would incur the curse of the bishops (who met at Nicaea in AD 325).

APIS One of the earliest animal gods in ancient Egypt, worshipped under the form of a bull throughout pharaonic civilization. His palatial quarters were at MEMPHIS, where he was the manifestation of PTAH, the god of the capital of Egypt. The bull symbolized strength and fertility and was a fitting symbol of the pharaoh's power. The Apis absorbed the solar disk of Re and the URAEUS, which are carried between his horns. While alive, the Apis enjoyed a regal existence in his palace, viewable by the public on festival days. The cow that produced him ('Isis, the mother of the Apis') was also given privileged treatment. On his death the priests followed elaborate procedures, burying the god in the vast underground catacombs at SAQQARA. The bull symbolized OSIRIS with whom he was identified at death. The succession of a new Apis, specially chosen by the priests from his body-markings, was the signal for general rejoicing in that Ptah was again incarnate at Memphis. *See also* MARIETTE; SERAPEUM.

■ **AQUEDUCT** Designed to carry water into a town from a frequently distant source, aqueducts are perhaps the most impressive feats of Roman engineering. A detailed treatise on their design and use was written by FRONTINUS. At their

▲

most impressive, aqueducts are free-standing structures supported on several tiers of arches to carry the conduit across a river-valley, such as the PONT DU GARD; at their simplest they consist of a pipe or channel following the natural contours down to the point of delivery; the Raw Dykes at Leicester may be an example of this. Some aqueducts were considerably over 50km in length. ROME is known to have had at least 20 aqueducts.

● **AQUILEIA, Italy** A Roman colony founded in 181 BC at the head of the Adriatic. Its position gave it a key role in the defence of Italy against attack from the east and it was used as a base for campaigns into Noricum, Pannonia and Dalmatia in the early Imperial period.

The city was prosperous, having a famous glass and INTAGLIO industry, and probably a population of up to 100,000. It became important as a Christian centre in the 4th century AD, and there are a large number of Early Christian mosaics. It was destroyed by Attila the Hun in 452 and thereafter RAVENNA was the chief town of the area.

ARAD, Israel A TELL in southern Palestine which is mentioned in ancient records from *c* 1400 BC until *c* AD 350. Excavations undertaken since 1962 have uncovered a large city which was destroyed *c* 2700 BC. Later occupation from *c* 1000 BC until *c* AD 650 has also been found and the most notable building from this period is a small temple. OSTRACA found in the temple show that it was used by the ISRAELITES.

ARAMAEANS A SEMITIC people who infiltrated almost the entire FERTILE CRESCENT from the desert during the 2nd millennium BC. They gained control of many states at the beginning of the 1st millennium BC and were the main opposition to the westward expansion of the ASSYRIANS. An ▲Assyrian RELIEF illustrates tribesmen related to the Aramaeans and their camels in battle with Assyrians. The extent of their influence can be seen in the fact that their language Aramaic became the international language of the Near East replacing AKKADIAN.

ARAWAK AMERINDIAN group occupying the Greater Antilles in the West Indies and parts of Venezuela at the time of European contact. Linguistic evidence, supported by local pottery styles, point to a South American origin for these people, who practised a settled agricultural economy and elaborate religious ceremonies. They also occupied parts of the Lesser Antilles until ousted by the CARIBS in late prehistoric times.

ARCHAEOMAGNETISM Many rocks and clays contain magnetic oxides of iron, which, when heated above a temperature known as the Curie point, lose their previously-held magnetism and acquire fresh magnetic orientation. This new magnetization is aligned with that of the earth's magnetic field (provided there is no other magnetic influence on the subject). When the clay or rock cools, the iron oxides retain their newly-acquired 'thermoremanent magnetism' and as long as the oxides are not reheated beyond the Curie point, the direction of magnetic alignment is preserved.

When a kiln or other object containing suitable iron oxides is found *exactly* in the position in which it was last heated beyond the Curie point, the date of the last heating can be calculated. In theory, this can be done quite simply by comparing the direction of alignment of the magnetic

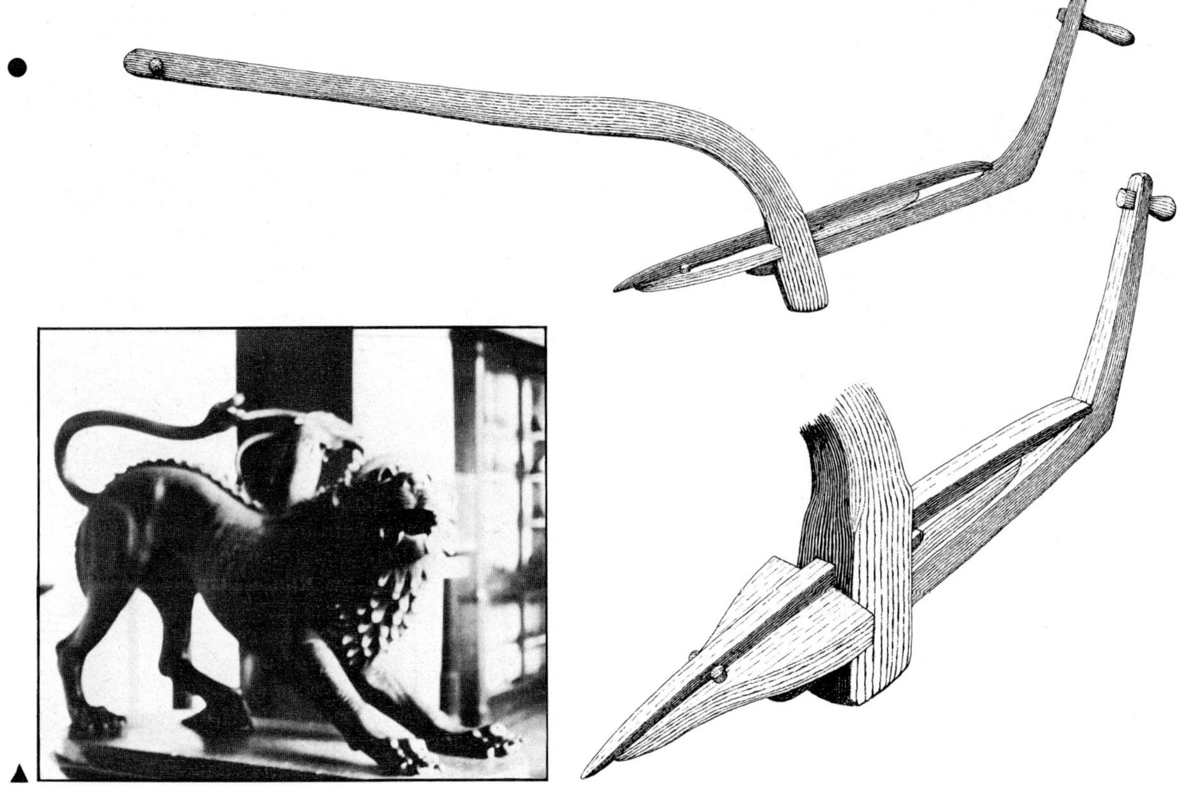

fields of the iron oxides with the known fluctuations of the earth's magnetic field in antiquity. There are however a number of ways in which this technique may fail. Further research is needed before it can be widely used on archaeological material.

ARCHAIC MASTABAS EMERY was able to assign fourteen mastaba tombs at SAQQARA to Egypt's Dynasty I. A problem exists in that these mastabas contained seals and inscriptions giving names of rulers who also have a smaller tomb-like structure at ABYDOS. Possibly the northern tomb was the burial place and the southern tomb a cenotaph in the locality where the ancestors of the archaic pharaohs originated.

The name mastaba is an Arabic description for the bench-like effect of these tombs with a rectangular mud-brick superstructure over underground chambers cut into the rock. Usually the outer wall imitates the façade of a royal palace with projecting and recessed panels. Subsidiary tombs might indicate the practice of killing servants to accompany their pharaoh after death – not found in later dynasties.

ARCHAIC TRADITION Cultures in the eastern woodlands of north America stretching from the Gulf Coast north into Canada and westward to the edge of the Plains, which adapted to the temperate forest and river conditions with an economy based on hunting, fishing and collecting. The tradition emerged by *c* 8000 BC lasting in many areas until *c* 1000 BC when it gave way to the WOODLANDS and MISSISSIPPI cultures. After *c* 5000 BC, polished stone axes and adzes become characteristic, together with the older forms of tools like notched stemmed stone points and a great variety of bone implements. The Archaic blends in the far north with Arctic traditions and in the west with the NORTHWEST COAST cultures, whilst in the south-west there are contacts with the farming and DESERT traditions.

● **ARD** A primitive PLOUGH, usually of wood and pulled by oxen. It has no wheels, coulter or mould-board. Sometimes the share was tipped with stone or metal. Ard ploughs are still used in some parts of Europe. *See also:* DONNERUPLUND ARD.

AREZZO, Italy This city midway between Florence and PERUGIA has a few surviving monuments of the Etruscan period. The remaining stretches of city wall are notable for being built partly of brick (elsewhere the Etruscans invariably used massive stone blocks for this purpose). Numerous terracotta votive figures have been found on the ▲ site. The famous bronze *Chimaera* was also found in the neighbourhood. From the 3rd century BC Arezzo was noted as an industrial centre and during the Roman empire it became famous for the manufacture of ARRETINE WARE.

ARGISSA, Greece A TELL site near SESKLO in Thessaly. The earliest levels, dating from before 6000 BC contain evidence for domesticated plants and animals (the latter mainly sheep, but also including pigs, cattle and dogs), but no pottery. The settlement continued to exist well into the BRONZE AGE.

ARIKAMEDU, India The village of Arikamedu on the Madras coast was an important Roman trading post. From small beginnings when a modest foreign quarter existed, it developed into a substantial brick-built town

with a warehouse and well-built industrial quarters, sometime after the mid 1st century BC. Roman material from the site includes ARRETINE WARE, Mediterranean AMPHORAE and Roman lamps as well as many Roman coins, especially of Augustus and Tiberius. *See also:* PERIPLUS, MONSOON, COIMBATORE.

ARLES, France The earliest Roman town to be founded in Gaul (in 46 BC, after JULIUS CAESAR's conquest), Arles was instituted as a COLONIA for veterans of the Sixth Legion. It is a river port near the mouth of the Rhône, and was sufficiently prosperous to support the fine public buildings which can still be seen. There is a large and well-preserved ■ AMPHITHEATRE, built in the second half of the 1st century AD and a fine theatre near by, also noteworthy for its statuary. To the west is a large underground structure, perhaps built as warehouses for grain and constructed in the 1st century BC. Traces of a CIRCUS and of a large temple also survive.

ARMANT, Egypt Major town of Egypt (also called Hermonthis). Cemeteries from the predynastic period indicate its antiquity. Its falcon-headed war-god Montu had strong adherents at THEBES. During Theban domination Armant acted as an important suburb. Following the decline of Thebes, it became the main metropolis for the region. Its monuments are now in ruins or destroyed (e.g. Cleopatra's temple). EMERY discovered the Bucheum, the Graeco-Roman subterranean burials of Buchis-bulls (sacred to Montu), also the necropolis for cow-mothers. Excavations revealed the outline and stone-blocks of Temple of Montu (restored by Tuthmosis III, Dynasty XVIII).

ARRAS The Arras CULTURE of Yorkshire is one of two IRON AGE cultures in Britain that are termed LA TÈNE (*see also* BELGAE). On the whole the Iron Age in Britain is a mixture of introduced and native elements. The Arras culture is called after a BARROW cemetery of 100–200 INHUMATION graves at Arras, first excavated in 1815. Several other cemeteries, one containing 500 burials, are of the same culture. The earliest grave goods (*c* 4th century BC) have very close parallels in northern France; these graves seem to represent a first-generation immigrant group. Carts and harness fittings were included in the richer burials, as well as personal ornaments. The cart fittings are local copies of French types, but some of the ornaments are direct imports from La Tène Europe. The culture still retained its Continental style of burial about the 1st century BC.

ARRETINE WARE A high-quality Roman fired pottery, manufactured around Arretium (modern AREZZO) in northern Italy, and traded as far away as India (*see* ARIKAMEDU). The fabric is pale red, coated in a slip of glowing orange. Shapes are very standardized, based upon the more prestigious metal vessels, and include flagons, cups, dishes and craters for mixing wine. Moulded decoration is a common feature, showing figures, foliage, etc, often in mythological scenes. The SAMIAN wares of Gaul were a development of the Arretine tradition. The manufacture of this ware died out by about the beginning of the 1st century AD.

ARROWHEAD The earliest evidence for the use of the bow and arrow comes from the Upper PALAEOLITHIC in the form of SOLUTREAN points in Europe. The absence of arrowheads in an archaeological deposit need not mean that bows were not used, as arrows can be completely made of wood (some have been found in MAGLEMOSEAN contexts in Europe). Wooden arrows are particularly effective if the points are hardened by fire.

● **ARTILLERY, Roman** Siege equipment, notably the BALLISTA and ONAGER, was adapted by the Roman army from HELLENISTIC models, and was used also as field artillery. In sieges it was deployed on rolling wooden towers to match the height of the defences; later it was used in defence, mounted on the walls and towers of forts and towns.

ARYANS The Aryans, or INDO-EUROPEANS, were a people whose existence is known from historical sources and from their legacy in both east and west, notably the Indo-European language, but of whom the origins and archaeological traces are obscure and uncertain.

The end of the INDUS CIVILIZATION may be connected with their arrival in India since their literature claims the destruction of the *pura* ('strongholds of the natives') a word that suggests the Indus cities. The burning of whole villages in Baluchistan seems to indicate the passage of the Aryans, while the upper levels at MOHENJO-DARO contain objects with Iranian affinities.

The site of HARAPPA shows the development in the Punjab. The upper levels are composed of decadent structures of re-used brick. The pottery in these levels seems to represent an amalgam of the two cultures, Indus and Aryan, at this site *c* 1750–1400 BC.

A picture begins to emerge of successive waves of invasion into India from Iran and the Caucasus in the second millennium BC. It is roughly in that area that the domestication of the horse occurred; also the development of iron-working took place there *c* 1800 but remained the monopoly of the HITTITES until *c* 1200 BC. The earliest Aryan invaders used the horse and it is probably that the later waves, around the turn of the millennium, introduced iron to India. Aspects of the Aryan way of life are portrayed in the RIGVEDA, in which the Aryan area of settlement is largely centred in the Punjab. In later Vedic literature, the focus passes to the Ganges–Jamuna Doab, indicating movement in this direction, and iron is now mentioned as the material used for tools and weapons.

The earliest Iron Age in India is characterized by PAINTED GREY WARE, the distribution of which coincides largely with the area of the late or post-Harappan cultures. Beyond this to the east, in the central Ganges valley, contemporary cultures continued to use BLACK-AND-RED WARE. The Painted Grey Ware culture shows a marked contrast to earlier cultures in this area. The material culture includes iron arrow and spearheads from the earliest levels, but copper is less frequent. Bone points are common but there is no stone blade industry. Glass beads and bangles are also known. The houses were generally of wattle and daub with mud floors. Plough agriculture was now practised, though the economy was still based on cereals and rice, cattle and horses as in earlier times.

Evidence from the Puranas, a rambling combination of legends, myths and religious material, gives a picture of warring village states in this period, as does the Mahabharata epic, committed to writing in the 4th century BC to 4th century AD, but referring back to this period. Certain events in the narrative have now been confirmed by archaeological evidence (*see* HASTINAPURA). Further evidence comes from the Upanishads and from later Vedic literature, in which methods of forest clearance and cultivation are described, as well as details of religion and social organization, which foreshadow the caste system.

About 500 BC the Painted Grey Ware culture was replaced by the urbanized NORTHERN BLACK POLISHED WARE culture (*see* GANGES CIVILIZATION).

See also: ATRANJIKHERA, KAUSAMBI, RAJAGRIHA, RAJGHAT, RUPAR, UJJAIN.

ARYBALLUS A diagnostic INCA pottery vessel for carrying liquids. The jar had a pointed base, broad body and tall neck with a flaring rim and was carried on the back by straps which ran through two small handles low on the body and across a small nubbin on the shoulder of the vessel. The name derives from the small classical Greek oil or perfume jar of similar shape.

ASMAR, Tell
see ESHNUNNA

▲ **AŚOKA** King of MAGADHA in northern India *c* 273–232 BC. Shocked by the brutality of warfare when he conquered Kalinga in 260 BC, he vowed henceforth to abstain from bloodshed, and adopted Buddhism. Thenceforth his life was devoted to the propagation of Buddhist principles both throughout his kingdom (*see* AŚOKAN PILLARS; AŚOKAN ROCK EDICTS) and abroad. His foreign missions travelled as far as Egypt, Syria and Macedonia as well as to South India. Legend credits him with the building of 84,000 Buddhist STUPAS (*see* BHARHUT SANCHI). He was responsible for the development of Buddhism as a world religion.

■ **AŚOKAN PILLARS** In 249 BC AŚOKA made a pilgrimage to the most holy Buddhist sites, Kusinagara, PATNA, SARNATH, LUMBINI, Sravasti, KAPILAVASTU, SANKISA, and BODH GAYA. At each he set up a commemorative pillar of highly polished sandstone, an animal capital, of which the splendid Sarnath lion capital is the finest. In 243 BC he set up a further seven pillars bearing inscriptions reiterating his former teachings (*see* AŚOKAN ROCK EDICTS). The design of the pillars show a subtle blend of tradition with imported ACHAEMENID art.

AŚOKAN ROCK EDICTS A series of edicts proclaiming the general rules of conduct of Buddhism, inscribed by orders of the Indian emperor AŚOKA, *c* 252 BC and carved on rock faces at various places in his empire.

ASSART A medieval term for the practice of clearing small areas of forest to provide fresh agricultural land.

ASSEMBLAGE A group of artefacts found in close association. If containing a variety of objects of different material, an assemblage may be typical of a CULTURE; if a limited range (e.g. flint tools), then of an INDUSTRY.

ASSUR [Pronounced **Ashur**], **Iraq** A large TELL on the bank of the Tigris River in northern Iraq. As the religious capital of ASSYRIA during the 1st and 2nd millennia BC, it was endowed with many temples. Excavations have uncovered the temples of ISHTAR and Assur the chief god of the city. Double temples of SIN and SHAMASH, and Anu and ADAD, were also found together with a palace and many fortifications.

ASSYRIA The name of the country in northern MESOPOTAMIA which, although it was originally the city-state of ASSUR, came to include the area around modern Mosul. This area underwent the same cultural development as the rest of Mesopotamia but at the same time it was influenced by nomads from the desert and non-semitic people from the northern mountains. The kings of AKKAD built cities in Assyria *c* 2300 BC, and trade with neighbouring kingdoms prospered (*see* KULTEPE, for example). After a period of decline Shalmaneser I and Tiglathpileser I campaigned vigorously, but their achievements were not followed up by their successors and Assyria again declined. From the accession of Ashurnasirpal II, Assyria became the major power in the FERTILE CRESCENT and eventually under Ashurbanipal controlled the entire area from Elam (*see* SUSA) to Egypt. This empire was too large to maintain and Assyria soon ended when tribes from the north-east, MEDES and SCYTHIANS, as well as cities in revolt such as Babylon, besieged and captured the capital cities of Assyria. The Assyrians are remembered largely because of their sophisticated weapons and sheer brutality which are recorded in their palace reliefs. The library at NINEVEH reveals that they had some interest in the arts although it was in architecture and sculpture that they made their achievements. The large human-headed winged bulls guarded the gateways of all their palaces are an example of their sculpture.

ASWAN Called also Syene and Elephantine, it was Egypt's natural frontier at the First Cataract of Nile. Rock Tombs of powerful local princes date from the last years of the Old Kingdom until Dynasty XII. Harkhuf's tomb has a lively biography: three expeditions into Nubia and a request from king Pepi II (Dynasty VI) to take extra care of a pygmy being sent to the palace.

Granite quarries supplied (by river) the pyramid-builders about 805km to the north. The technique of extracting granite blocks can be seen from the abandoned OBELISK (36m high).

The Nilometer consists of gradations beside the river to measure the extent of inundation. *See also* PHILAE.

ATCHANA, TELL
see ALALAKH

ATERIAN A Middle PALAEOLITHIC INDUSTRY of north-west Africa, named after Bir-el-Ater, Tunisia, and notable for its stemmed points.

ATHENS, Greece The ACROPOLIS was the centre of MYCENAEAN occupation in this town which was strong enough to resist the DORIAN invasions of the 12th century BC.

The Early Iron Age is mainly documented by the Kerameikos cemetery (11th–8th centuries BC). During this period there was a rule of kings, replaced in the 7th century by an oligarchy and, ultimately, in 507 by a democracy. Pericles is commonly associated with this period, during which the plays of Aeschylus, Euripedes and Sophocles were written and the acropolis temple built.

Athens played a major part in resisting Persia 490–449 BC but was much weakened by a rift and war with SPARTA and the Peloponnesians from 460. Sporadic warfare continued into the 4th century (during which Aristophanes, Plato and Aristotle were writing) until Philip of Macedon in the 350s subdued Greece. ALEXANDER, his successor, was more

▲

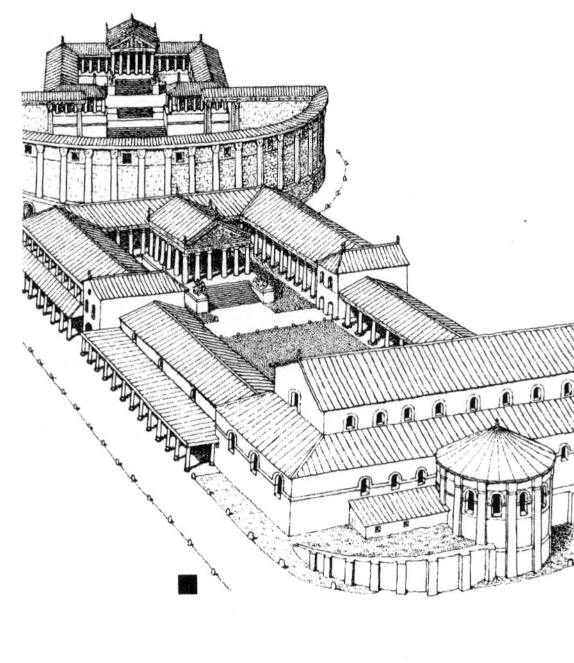

■

concerned with Asia Minor than with Greece, and Athens thereafter lost its former splendour. The HELLENISTIC age saw it as a centre of learning and culture. It survived the Roman takeover in the 2nd century BC (CORINTH did not) and enjoyed a brief renaissance under Hadrian in the 120s AD. Its pagan teaching was unable to survive the coming of Christianity and the schools closed in 529.

The main archaeological sites are the ACROPOLIS, the AGORA, several temples and the restored stadium.

ATLANTIC
see POSTGLACIAL PERIOD

ATLANTIS Plato's *Timaeus* and *Critias* were responsible for the myth of Atlantis. He described a Utopian island of vast dimensions which sank beneath the sea as a punishment. The measurements could only put it in a large ocean. However, it is most likely that the island is a philosophical abstraction whose details were unimportant but which perhaps preserved memories of the destruction of Crete and the MINOANS by the explosion of THERA.

ATLATL The New World word for SPEAR THROWER.

ATRANJIKHERA, India The earliest deposits at this Ganges valley site contain OCHRE-COLOURED POTTERY, followed in the later 2nd millennium BC by BLACK-AND-RED WARE, with hearths, copper artefacts and stone MICROLITHIC and FLAKE tools. The painted grey ware occupation, 1200–600 BC, has wattle and daub structures. From 600–200 BC NORTHERN BLACK POLISHED WARE pottery marks a fully urban settlement, with mud-brick bastions and intensive building activity. Periodic flooding breaks the essential continuity of the site, which shows constant and gradual development. *See also* ARYANS, GANGES CIVILIZATION, GANGES COPPER HOARDS.

▲ **AUBREY, John (1626–97)** One of the leading English antiquarians, Aubrey keenly described, and attempted reconstructions of STONEHENGE and AVEBURY. He wrote a survey of English antiquities, the *Monumenta Britannica*, but this was never published. Main books (posthumously published): *Natural History of Wiltshire* (ed. Britton 1847); *Perambulation of Surrey* (in *Natural History and Antiquities of Surrey*, 1719).

■ **AUGST, Switzerland** A Roman colony founded in 43 BC, known in Roman times as Augusta Raurica. The FORUM (which was closed to traffic), the BASILICA, the THEATRE and the baths have been excavated. The council-chamber is almost circular and is unique in this respect. The town was planted to romanize the wild people of Helvetia, modern Switzerland, and was also a base for the Roman advance into Germany. A complete town-house is on view today.

AUGUSTINE Sent by Pope Gregory to England in AD 596, St Augustine went to the court of King Aethelbert of Kent where Queen Bertha, the Christian daughter of the FRANKISH King, had re-established an old Roman church served by a chaplain. Within the year Aethelbert was converted to Christianity, and in 601 Augustine was created first Archbishop of Canterbury. The Roman mission was rapidly successful and sees were established at Rochester and London. Augustine himself died *c* 606, but the mission continued less dynamically in EAST ANGLIA and in NORTHUMBRIA under PAULINUS.

AUGUSTUS, Gaius Julius Caesar Octavianus (63 BC–AD 14) The first Roman Emperor, and adopted son of JULIUS CAESAR, whose murderers he defeated with the help of Mark Antony. He fell out with Antony, and after the latter's defeat at Actium in 31 BC found himself the sole real power in Rome. He became emperor in 27 BC: his reign was a period of security and prosperity, as can be seen in the remains of the fine towns which flourished in Italy and Gaul. More than any other man he was the founder of the Roman empire. He died in AD 14, and was then deified.

AUNJETITZ Another name for UNETICE.

AUREUS The gold piece of the Romans: its full name is *denarius aureus*. Despite the grotesque fluctuations in value of the silver coinage of the empire, the value of the aureus remained fairly stable. The weight was fixed by AUGUSTUS at 42 to the pound of gold, and it did not fall far below this. The artistic level of the designs on gold coinage was consistently high, and aurei, can be strikingly beautiful.

AURIGNACIAN An Upper PALAEOLITHIC INDUSTRY dating from 40–30,000 BC, named after a cave at Aurignac near Toulouse, southern France. The Aurignacian is considered by some to lie chronologically between the CHÂTELPERRONIAN (or Early Perigordian) and the GRAVETTIAN (or earliest Upper Perigordian), while others see the PERIGORDIAN and Aurignacian as contemporary. Animals and signs engraved and painted on stones from Aurignacian layers at La Ferrassie, France, represent the earliest known art in the west, and perhaps in the world. At Petersfels, Germany, were found bone whistles. *See* CRO-MAGNON.

AUSTRALOPITHECUS (literally 'southern ape'). The earliest known form of man. His remains have been found in south and east Africa in deposits *c* 2–3 million years old. There were two main types. The first, whose remains have been found at Taungs, Sterkfontein and Makapansgat, was a small, light-bodied creature, inhabiting the plains and living off a meat diet. The second, found at Swartkrans, Kromdraai and OLDUVAI Bed I (where it has been called *Zinjanthropus* 'east African man'), was larger and more heavily built, and moved about in a forest environment eating mainly plant foods. The large jaw of this second variety has resulted in the nickname 'Nutcracker man'.

● **AVEBURY, Marlborough, Wiltshire** The best surviving of four large HENGES in central southern England, *c* 2500 BC (*see* DURRINGTON WALLS). A circular ditch (still nearly 4m deep, but containing up to 10m of silt) and outer bank, with a diameter of well over 400m are crossed by four entrances. Just inside the ditch was a circle of about 100 SARSEN MEGALITHS, which in turn enclosed two smaller circles of standing stones, each about 90m in diameter. Two parallel rows of similar stones (known as the West Kennet Avenue) ran from the south entrance for nearly 4km ending at 'the Sanctuary' on Overton Hill, a round structure (similar to WOODHENGE but without a surrounding ditch) whose timber posts were eventually replaced by two stone circles. A second 'avenue', of which little trace now survives above ground, ran from the west entrance.

The Avebury circle and its surrounding monuments (including SILBURY HILL, the WEST KENNET chamber tomb and a major concentration of BARROWS) is one of the most impressive archaeological sights in Europe, and testimony to a complex society.

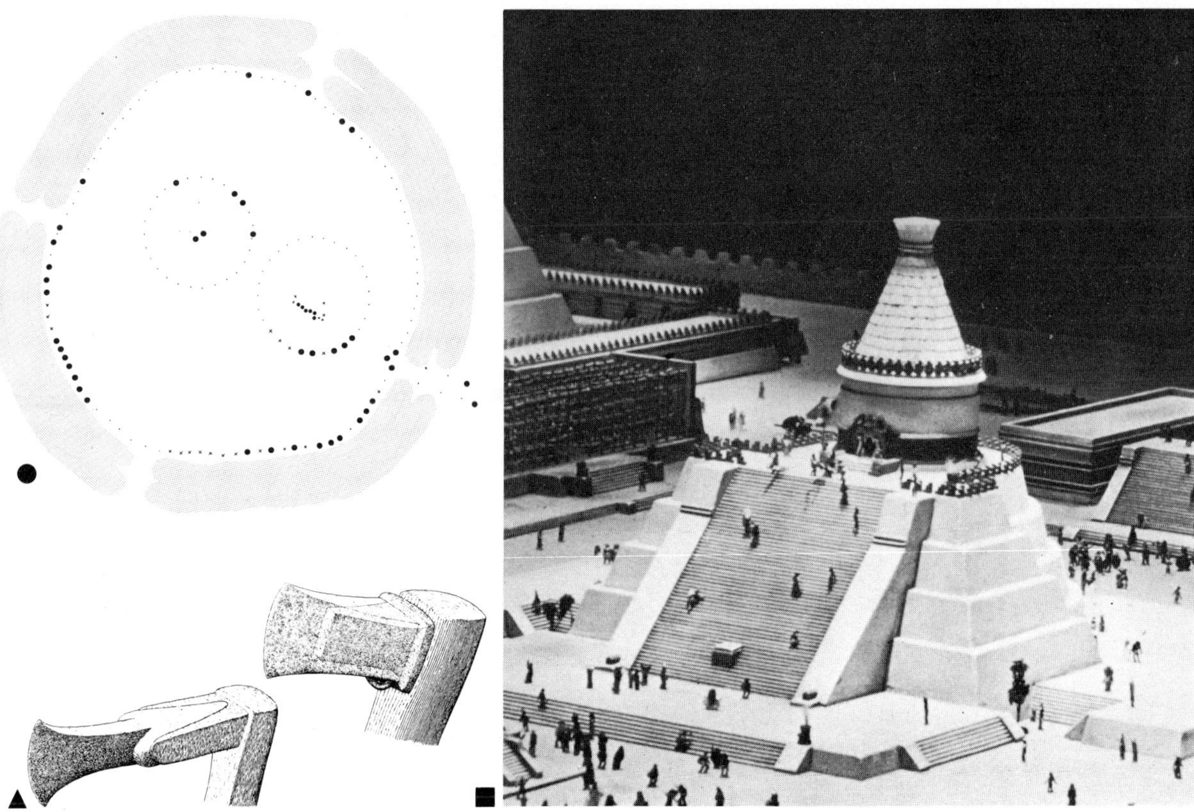

▲ **AXE** A heavy implement generally used for cutting wood, although some kinds were used in battle, attained ritual status or even became a form of currency. The axe is distinguished from the ADZE mainly by its hafted position, the blade being set parallel to the handle; an adze blade is at right angles to the haft.

AXE FACTORY Ground and polished stone axes, mainly NEOLITHIC in date, are widely distributed in Britain and north-west Europe. By studying thin slices of stone from such axes under a microscope (*see* THIN SECTIONING) and relating them to parent rock outcrops, it has been shown that many of these implements were carried over considerable distances, probably by some form of trade. A number of production centres or 'axe factories' have been identified at sites with outcrops of suitable rock. The term does not imply industrial organization in the modern sense; most outcrops were probably worked by small communities during certain parts of the farming year. Important factories include Langdale (Lake District), Graig Llwyd (north Wales) and Tievebulliagh (Northern Ireland).

AYACUCHO, Peru Located in the south-central Highlands, it is an intermontane basin which has yielded important evidence of the evolution of crop plants and animal domestication together with settled village life. Sites within the valley, e.g. Flea Cave (Pikimachay), have long accumulations of human occupation going back to 14,000 BC and earlier, when hunting peoples with stone-age technology killed animals now extinct in that region, such as the horse, elephant and a species of giant ground sloth. *See also* TEHUACAN.

AYLESFORD, Kent A CREMATION cemetery of BELGIC date, *c* 50–10 BC. Three burials contained extremely rich grave goods including buckets, imported Italian bronze vessels and AMPHORAE. Around these were arranged poorer cremations. All the graves were accompanied by fine wheel-made pottery, a characteristic of the Belgic graves in Kent, Essex, Herts., and Bedfordshire. The cultural group is named the Aylesford–Swarling CULTURE, after this cemetery and another series of rich graves at Swarling in Kent.

AZILIAN The final Upper PALAEOLITHIC culture in north Spain and south-west France, succeeding the MAGDALENEAN. Adapted to a late glacial forested environment, the flint industry is MICROLITHIC in character. The Azilian is noted for its flat bone HARPOON heads and in particular for its pebbles painted with simple linear designs as found at the TYPE-SITE (Mas d'Azil, Ariège, France).

AZTECS NAHUATL speakers calling themselves the Mexica or Tenochca, who arrived in Mesoamerica during the 12th century AD, last of a wave of CHICHIMEC invasions of which they had been a part. They wandered for a while in the Valley of Mexico and were eventually driven to an island in Lake Texcoco by other more powerful inhabitants of the region. Here they founded their capital ■ TENOCHTITLAN in 1345 and during the next century became a political power in their own right, initiating the Triple Alliance with two other city states around the shores of the lake – Texcoco and Tlacopan. Under the influence of such emperors as Moctezuma Ilhuicamina and his grandson Ahuitzotl, the Mexica engineered their great expansion which eventually gave them dominion from the Gulf Coast to the Pacific and the borders of Guatemala. They did not

▲

govern a tightly knit and politically unified empire, but depended on their military supremacy to exact a ruthless tribute of foodstuffs, raw materials, luxury items and human beings for sacrifice from conquered tribes who were otherwise allowed to administer themselves. At its height, Tenochtitlan had a population estimated at 150–200,000 persons, most of whom were engaged in political, religious or craft-specialist pursuits. These latter produced the fine turquoise mosaics, stonework and sculpture for which the Aztecs are renowned. The city centre contained the large ceremonial complex – temples built on tall PYRAMIDS around PLAZAS and dedicated to such important deities as Huitzilopochtli, the supreme Aztec god of war, whose worship led to the Aztecs' main purpose in life – war and the capture of prisoners for sacrifice. Archaeologically, the Aztecs are known for their stone and ADOBE buildings (square flat-topped pyramids with a double stairway at one side), their distinctive style of stone sculpture and pottery with black geometric decoration on an orange base. They also adopted and developed the pictographic writing systems known in Mexico, largely of MIXTEC origin (*see* CODEX), and used complex CALENDARS (Calendrics) for religious computations.

● **BAAL** A god worshipped particularly by the CANAANITES. The name is a SEMITIC word meaning 'lord', 'owner' or 'husband'. He was god of fertility, the sender of rain and also the storm god who rode in the clouds. A temple to Baal has been found at UGARIT, with a large number of TABLETS relating various myths associated with the pantheon.

BAB EDH DHRA
see JORDAN

BABYLON (Babylonia), Iraq A city in the River Euphrates 80km south of modern Baghdad, capital of Iraq. Little is known of its early history except the story of the Biblical Babel and a reference in a text from a king of AKKAD *c* 2250 BC both of which are concerned with a ZIGGURAT there. Our knowledge increases with the commencement of its first dynasty *c* 1894 BC. The 6th king of this line, HAMMURAPI, established a short-lived empire which extended from the Persian Gulf to MARI. After the HITTITES raided Babylon *c* 1595 BC, an INDO-EUROPEAN group of peoples from the mountains of western Iran – the Kassites – took control. ASSYRIA was first established there *c* 1200 BC and dominated Babylon despite numerous revolts until *c* 626 BC. Nabopolassar became king in Babylon in 626 and quickly threw off Assyrian overlordship. With the help of the MEDES and SCYTHIANS he captured the Assyrian capitals. He then began conquests in Syria. Nebuchadnezzar, the crown prince, continued the attack, sacking Carchemish in 605 BC, defeating the Egyptians at HAMA and over-running the rest of Syria and coastal Palestine. Judah revolted against Babylon, and in reply Nebuchadnezzar destroyed Jerusalem in 587 BC, having deported its nobles some years before. Cyrus, after taking over the Median empire (*see* ACHAEMENID empire), captured Babylon 16 October 539 BC, and ended the Babylonian Empire. The Persians ruled Babylon until 331 BC when ALEXANDER captured it, beginning Greek rule. This was in turn followed by the PARTHIANS in about 64 BC. After its conquest by the Moslems in AD 641, Babylon fell into ruin. Little remains today of the city which once contained the Hanging Gardens, numbered amongst the Seven Wonders of the ancient world. Best preserved is the Ishtar Gate ▲ showing figures of bulls, lions and dragons in relief.

BADARIAN CIVILIZATION Archaeologists encountered its artefacts in the necropolis at Badari, an Egyptian village upstream from Asyut. It forms the first of the major southern predynastic cultures (*c* 5th–4th millennium BC). Badarians had technically advanced industries: of pottery – delicately rippled with thin fabric, as well as utilitarian pots for storage and cooking – and of flint weapons and tools (especially winged arrowheads). Copper working was still in primitive stages; only beads requiring piercing and glazed with copper colour. Ornaments were made of ivory, bone and pebbles. Slate palettes (later highly decorated) provided surfaces on which to grind mineral ore into eye paint. The earliest terracotta figures of people belong to this period.

BAGLAN, Afghanistan A site in north Afghanistan composed of numerous small shrines with a central temple. Dating from the period of the KUSHAN emperor Kaniska, in the early 2nd century AD, Baglan contains numerous examples of provincial GANDHARAN ART, including a Kushan figure in boots and belted trousers which may represent Kaniska himself.

BAHRAIN An island in the Persian Gulf believed to be a place often referred to as Dilmun by seafaring merchants from SUMER. Excavations have uncovered a number of temples of the 3rd millennium, and these contain evidence of trade between MESOPOTAMIA and the Indus Valley. There are also an estimated 100,000 burial mounds containing tombs of the 2nd millennium BC on the island.

BALA HISSAR
see CHARSADA

BALLANA [QUSTUL], Egypt Downstream from the Second Cataract, now under Lake Nasser, tumuli on both banks of Nile were excavated by EMERY. Tombs belonged to Nubian X group rulers – probably about fifth century AD.

At Qustul on the east bank were plundered vaulted chambers tunnelled into by robbers, but a trench cut into the mounds revealed a ramp descending to the entrance. Miscellaneous objects in a mound: iron axeheads, cruel silver horse bit, wooden saddles and silver-trappings, pottery of X-group typology (3rd–6th centuries AD).

The Ballana tumuli were more sand-locked and overgrown. Archaeologically they were more difficult to excavate because water had caused the mud brick used in constructing the tombs to solidify into an alluvium mass, obliterating walls and making it necessary to cut objects by knife from congealed mud. In royal burials, some of which were undisturbed, were silver crowns and jewellery showing mixture of Egyptian and Byzantine art, iron weapons and tools, slaughtered horses, camels and donkeys with grooms, queen and slaves killed to accompany the king in afterlife.

■ **BALL COURT** Originated in MESOAMERICA and basic to its cultural tradition. Ball courts were a prominent feature in any important CEREMONIAL CENTRE or town, and archaeology records their existence as far back as the 1st millennium BC OLMEC culture. Figurines from this time sometimes represent ball players in their typical outfit of helmet, padded belt and cloth padding for the knees and elbows; the game was rough, played with a solid rubber ball 25–50mm in diameter and prohibited the use of the hands or feet during play. The ball court was shaped like a

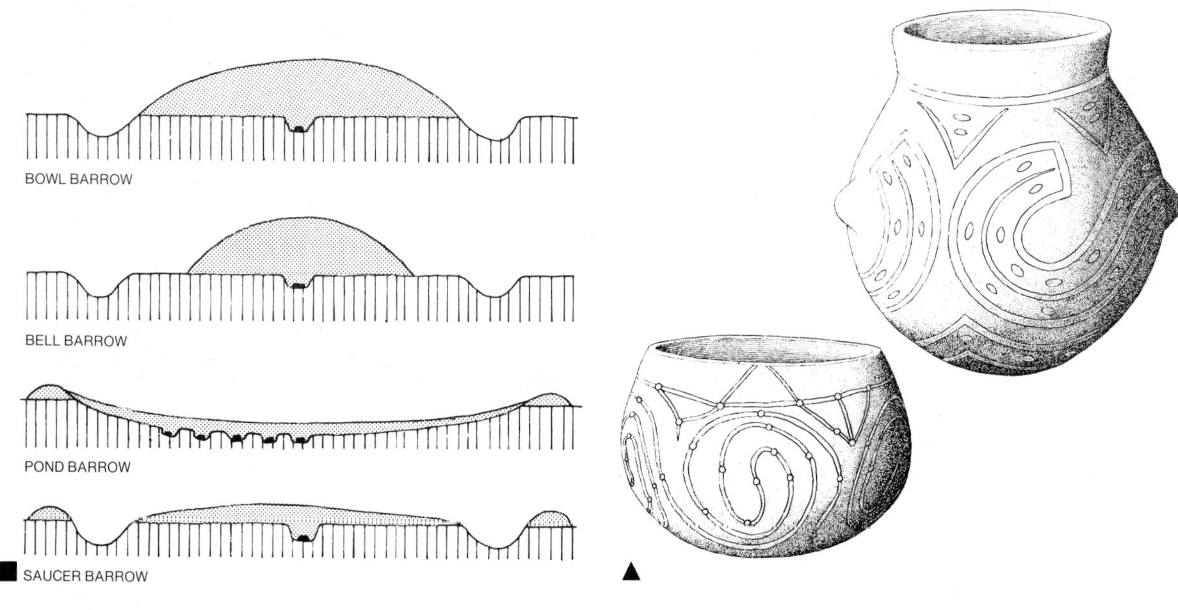

capital I. In the middle of the side walls, set high up, were stone rings through which, should any player be adroit enough to pass the ball, his team won outright, whereupon they had the right to claim the clothes and jewels worn by the spectators – if they could catch them. Ball players were generally professionals and drawn from the nobility. The game was a highly popular sport.

BALL GAME
see BALL COURT

BALLISTA A piece of Roman ARTILLERY equipment of a form akin to a crossbow. Its power was derived from two arms drawn back in tension against resistant cords of gut. A metal bolt, some 200mm long, was projected; its effectiveness is well demonstrated by a defender's vertebra from MAIDEN CASTLE (Dorset) with such a bolt embedded in it (preserved in the Dorchester Museum).

BALSA RAFTS and BOATS Small vessels (sometimes provided with a sail) made from bundles of reeds with a long tapering prow. They date from prehistoric times in both Egypt and South America and continue in use in such areas as lake Titicaca, Bolivia, down to the present. The word is also used for the large sailing rafts made of balsa logs, which were employed at the time of the Spanish conquest along the coasts of Ecuador and north Peru.

● **BAN CHIENG, Thailand** A burial mound in north-east Thailand, where excavations since 1967 have yielded abundant remains from periods from Neolithic to Iron Age. Dating, if accurate, places the use of the site from *c* 4500 BC to AD 1000. The site's most characteristic feature is its wealth of painted pottery, generally red on buff. Similar pottery has also been noted from other early bronze-using sites in the area, such as NON NOK THA, though Ban Chieng remains the richest source of the painted pottery. Designs on these wares are usually geometric or spiral motifs.

▲ **BANDKERAMIK** Literally from the German, 'ribbon-pottery'. It refers to the pots made by the LINEAR POTTERY cultures. The various bowls and jars are usually round-based, and their characteristic feature is the incised linear decoration, frequently consisting of spirals and meanders of parallel lines.

BAN KAO, Thailand A burial and habitation site in west central Thailand excavated in the 1960s. The 'Bang' site is the most important of those in the complex. Extended burials, with grave goods including pottery, stone adzes and animal bones were typical. Though no bronze was found, two of the burials contained iron implements. Pottery was especially abundant, and more than 150 pots have been fully reconstructed from sherds. The ware was often black or red; amongst the forms were tripods, 'fruit-stands', jars, pedestal bowls, footed vessels and round-bottomed, necked vessels. Cord-marking and burnishing were frequently employed. The excavator interpreted the remains as Neolithic, with later iron-age burials. Others suggested that the site may really be a late cemetery, cutting into an earlier site dating probably to mid second millennium BC; this view explains the polished stone adzes as talismans placed with the late burials.

BARABAR HILLS
see ROCK-CUT ARCHITECTURE

BARBARICUM, India A market town at the head of the Indus mentioned in the PERIPLUS as an outlet for PARTHIAN trade with the west. Imports from the latter included thin clothing, figured linens, topaz, coral, frankincense, glass vessels, gold and silver plate, and wine. From the east, often from a considerable distance, came many spices and medicines, silk yarn, muslin, turquoise, lapis lazuli, indigo and east Asiatic skins.

BARBOTINE A type of pottery decoration in which a slip is trailed from a bag or pipe onto the surface of the vessel; it is common on Roman pottery, especially the beautiful colour-coated beakers made in Britain and elsewhere.

■ **BARROW** A mound raised over one or more burials, sometimes, as in the KURGAN culture of Russia, containing a wooden mortuary house. The earliest barrows in Britain are NEOLITHIC, *c* 3000–2500 BC; these are earthen long mounds found in eastern England. In the highland zone, barrows of earth were raised over stone CHAMBER TOMBS or GALLERY GRAVES (*see* BOYNE VALLEY). The long mounds were replaced in the Early BRONZE AGE by BEAKER round barrows. Barrows are most commonly dated to *c* 2200–1600 BC, although burials under barrows were occasionally made from the IRON AGE to the Saxon period (*see* SUTTON HOO). Barrows were often reused for secondary burials, sometimes at a much later date. The 'bowl' barrow is the most usual bronze age type in Britain; other types of bronze age round barrow are restricted to the WESSEX CULTURE. 'Pond' barrows are not always connected with burial: one excavated at WILSFORD turned out to be the top of a shaft. Barrows in the Bronze Age were often arranged in cemeteries, such as the BUSH BARROW group.

BARYGAZA
see BROACH

BASILICA A building usually found adjoining the FORUM or market-square of a Roman town. It takes the form of a roofed hall, generally rectangular, and acted as a meeting-place and a centre for the administration of justice: one end usually includes a tribunal for this purpose. The basilica is an obvious development of the colonnade which had usually surrounded the forum. The earliest known true basilica is the Basilica Porcia in ROME, built in 184 BC. By the 1st century AD most Roman towns of any significance included such a building; a fine and well-preserved example exists at TRIER. The term also came to refer to Christian churches built in basilica-like form, Christians in the 4th century having met in the fora, and later designed their churches in the same form.

BAT CAVE, New Mexico, USA COCHISE culture. In 1948 tiny maize cobs measuring 20–30mm long were discovered here and yielded RADIOCARBON date of 3600 BC. They were shown to be ancestral to the primitive cultivated variety (Chapalote) and are important for their implications in the origins and domestication of maize (*see also* TEHUACAN).

BATH [Aquae Sulis], Avon Bath began as a small Roman town based on a spa: the modern name comes from the series of monumental baths begun during the late 1st century and extended several times; these were particularly magnificent and, with the temple of Sulis Minerva (the goddess of the spring), formed the focus of the town. A lovely head of the goddess in gilt-bronze probably came from this temple. Bath fell to the Saxons *c* AD 577.

BATHS, Roman A suite of rooms for bathing in dry heat and in water. They varied in size from small domestic ranges of a few rooms to the public baths of cities, such as the vast Baths of Caracalla in Rome, 140,000 square metres in area. There was a regular sequence to be followed: from the undressing rooms, exercise area and cold bath, via a cold room to the warm room, then the hot room. Heating was usually by HYPOCAUSTS and hot water was provided in plunge baths. Because of the fire risk, baths were nearly always of masonry, often concrete.

● **BÂTON DE COMMANDEMENT** The name given to objects of unknown use of the European Upper PALAEOLITHIC. They consist of a length of antler, with a hole at the thicker end. They are frequently covered with engraved designs, particularly in the MAGDALENEAN.

BATTERSEA SHIELD A bronze REPOUSSÉ shield of the 1st century AD, dredged from the river Thames at Battersea. Decorated in the CELTIC ART style, with inlaid panels of red glass. Obviously ceremonial, not practical, it may be a ritual deposit like numerous other fine IRON AGE objects from the Thames.

BAYON
see ANGKOR

BEAKER PEOPLE A group of peoples in late neolithic Europe named after the pottery beakers that they put into their INHUMATION graves; the early bell-shaped beakers vary little in their range from France to Hungary. Other objects associated with the beakers show that the people were archers – they had stone wristguards and flint barbed-and-tanged arrowheads. There were also gold ornaments, buttons pierced with a U-shaped perforation, and copper pins and knives. The Beaker people spread the knowledge of copper and gold metallurgy across Europe *c* 2000 BC. Coming originally from Portugal or Spain, they moved quickly through France, Central Europe, and as far as Hungary. By 1800 BC or earlier they had reached Britain. They can be distinguished from the earlier British population because they are BRACHYCEPHALIC (or round-headed). Very few Beaker settlements or houses are known. These people have therefore been thought of as nomads, but were probably traders who copied the earlier Neolithic types of houses. In central Europe the Beaker phase was followed from 1500 BC by the UNETICE Bronze Age.

BEDE Born *c* AD 673, he was sent as a child to Benedict Biscop's new monastery at Wearmouth from which he was transferred to Jarrow in 682. There he began the most important of his works, his *History of the English Church and People*, completed in AD 731, and one of the earliest accounts of the Anglo-Saxon settlement of England. It is by far the most important of surviving histories, since although written from a NORTHUMBRIAN viewpoint it is not a mere chronicle or hagiography. Bede examined all available records and living authorities, recorded local traditions and stories and critically assessed them. Because of his critical attitude and use of sources he has been called the 'father of English history'. He died in AD 735.

BEDSA
see ROCK-CUT ARCHITECTURE

BEER SHEBA, Israel The name (which means 'seventh well' or 'well of oath') is identified with a TELL in southern Palestine 4km north-east of the present town of the same name. It is often referred to in the BIBLE and has been excavated since 1969. A number of structures near the gate were identified as store-houses. Similar structures have been found at HAZOR and MEGIDDO, and were used by the ISRAELITES. A Roman fortress, numerous buildings and fortifications have also been found. An ancient culture contemporary with, and having many similarities to, the GHASSULIAN culture has been found in the Beer Sheba area.

BEGRAM, Afghanistan Situated *c* 75km north of Kabul. The old town, built by Graeco-Bactrian kings, dates from the 2nd century BC, while the new Royal Town was probably built by Indo-Greeks and occupied from the 1st century BC to the 5th century AD. In the 2nd and 3rd centuries AD the site must have been an important *entrepôt* or customs depot where passing caravans left dues in kind, which survive today as the Begram treasure. This includes carved ivories probably from MATHURA, Mediterranean ▲ glass vases, bronzes and plaster plaques from Alexandria, western bronze bowls and steelyard weights, lacquer bowls from China and KUSHAN coins. The trade route with the far east via Begram and the Peshawar plain, TAXILA and the Indus was important to the west due to the semi-permanent hostility of the PARTHIAN empire which straddled the most direct route from east to west. This Indian detour was the main route for the export of Chinese silks to the west; it lay within the well-organized and liberal Kushan empire.

BEHISTUN, Iran A rock face in the range of Zangers in western Iran. In 516 BC, Darius I of Persia chose this site to record the victories which enabled him to rule the ACHAEMENID empire. The monument consists of a RELIEF and an inscription in three languages carved into the rock face, which was made inaccessible by the removal of the ■ rock below. The relief shows Darius followed by two officials, with his foot on one of the enemy and nine rebel chiefs before him. Over their heads is the symbol of the god, Ahuramazda. The inscription is in CUNEIFORM script in the languages of Old Persian, Elamite and Babylonian. Between 1835 and 1847 Rawlinson copied the inscription by lowering himself down the cliff face on a rope. His persistence was rewarded when these copies of the inscription gave him the key to decipher cuneiform script.

BEIDHA
see JORDAN

BEIT EL-WALI, Egypt Originally just downstream from Kalabsha, now moved from the floodwaters of Lake Nasser to just above Aswan High Dam. A temple cut into mountainside by Ramesses II (Dynasty XIX). Reliefs show deities of the First Cataract – Khnum and wives Satis and Anukis – as well as Isis and Horus of BUHEN. Other depictions show the king in his chariot or on foot defeating Middle Eastern, Libyan and African armies. There is a propaganda element in representation in the southern temple of a strong pharaonic presence via the royal son of Kush (Egyptian prince) and of presentation to the pharaoh of gold, weapons and African products.

BELGAE [adjective **Belgic]** From 250 BC onwards, large numbers of people arrived in southern Britain, bringing

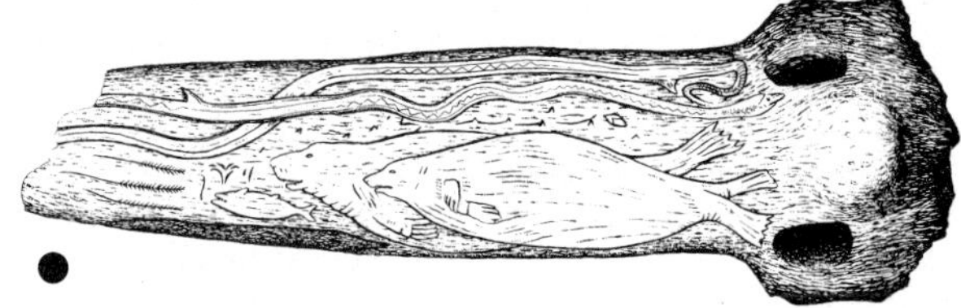

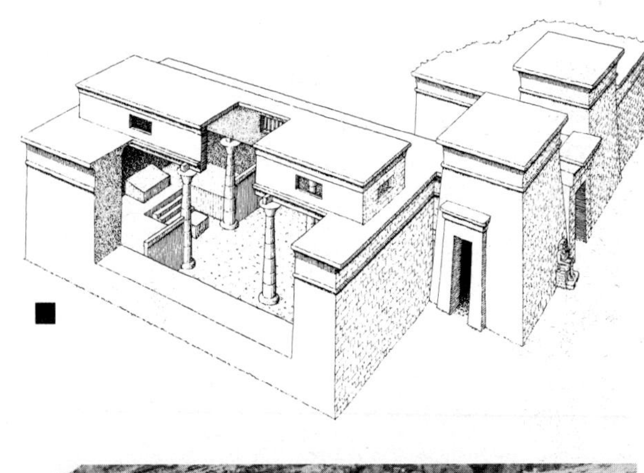

their traditions and CULTURE with them. JULIUS CAESAR called them the Belgae, a CELTIC tribe from Gaul. The invasion can be recognized in the AYLESFORD – Swarling culture in Kent, Essex and Hampshire, and by the presence of different types of coins (*see* GALLO-BELGIC). When Caesar landed in 55 BC the whole of Britain was divided into tribal territories. In south-east England the Belgic tribes were the Catuvellauni, Trinovantes, Cantiaci, Coritani, Iceni and Atrebates.

● **BELZONI, Giovanni Battista (1778–1823)** Italian antiquity-hunter and discoverer. By modern standards an archaeologist's nightmare (e.g. in his negligence to bodies and objects in pursuit of papyri in some Theban tombs), he deserves respect for attempting to apply more sophisticated techniques than most of his contemporaries. Financed in some of his work by Henry Salt, British Consul-General in Egypt, Belzoni was helped also by his immense physical strength. The British Museum owes its colossal two-tonne granite head of Ramesses II to Belzoni's removal of it from the RAMESSEUM. Two of his greatest achievements were the discovery of the tomb of Seti I (Dynasty XIX) – reproduced with great success in 1821 at the Egyptian Hall, Piccadilly – and the reasonably scientific opening of the temple at ABU SIMBEL, recording measurements and position of statues.

He died searching for the source of the river Niger.

Main book: *Narrative of the operations and recent discoveries within the Pyramids, Temples and Tombs, and excavations in Egypt and Nubia* (1820).

▲ **BENI HASAN, Egypt** Although possibly the birthplace of the builder of the Great Pyramid, its archaeological importance stems from role as necropolis for the nomarchs (*see* EGYPT) of this district of Middle Egypt. The series lasts from Dynasty XI till the absolute centralization of authority in Dynasty XII. The tombs provide vital historical sources in informative biographies of these politically powerful princes as well as lively painted scenes. The tombs are cut into the hillside, usually having an open portico and sometimes with fluted columns mistakenly called proto-doric. The wall-scenes painted onto a plaster surface reflect daily life under a feudal system. For example the tomb of Khnumhotep, hereditary prince and overseer of the eastern desert, shows a hunt, fishing scenes, a boat with harem-quarters, and a caravan of bedouin.

BENTY GRANGE, Derbyshire The only known Anglo-Saxon helmet, other than that from SUTTON HOO, was found in a grave in Benty Grange in 1848. It is a very elaborate piece of armour, consisting of a framework of flat iron bands built up spherically to form a cap. The gaps between the bands were filled with horn. An inlaid silver cross decorates the noseguard. The crest is particularly interesting: a boar decorated with silver gilt plates, with the eyes of garnets set in gold FILIGREE. The boar crest is very similar to one described in BEOWULF.

BEOWULF Probably composed in the 8th century AD by a Christian poet for a Christian audience, this is the only surviving epic poem in Old English. The hero Beowulf, a Scandinavian warrior, struggles against Grendel and other monsters in a story whose main theme is the conflict of good and evil. The poem is not only a great work of literature but also reveals much of the wealth and magnificence of Anglo-Saxon and Scandinavian society

during the Pagan period in which it is set. The picture of a rich and sophisticated court has been verified by archaeological finds from SUTTON HOO and from BOAT BURIALS in Norway, and by the great HALLS excavated at YEAVERING and at CHEDDAR. The unique copy of the text is in the British Library, London.

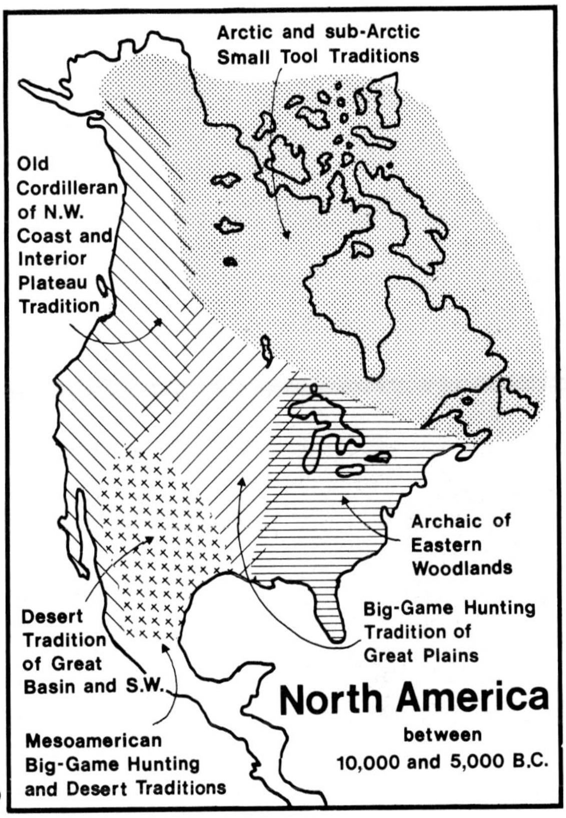

BETH SHAN [modern Beisan], Israel A high TELL in the Plain of Esdraelon of northern Palestine mentioned in Egyptian texts from about 2000 BC. Excavation by the University of Pennsylvania in 1921–33 revealed that the site was occupied from the 4th millennium BC. A series of CANAANITE temples were found dating from about 1400 BC These were Egyptian in style and one dating from about 1000 BC may be the 'house of Ashtorath' (*see* ISHTAR) mentioned in I Samuel 31:10. A Greek temple and Byzantine church represent a time when Beth Shan was a provincial capital. Cemeteries nearby had burials of all periods – the most notable finds being some anthropoid SARCOPHAGI.

BETH YERAH
see KHIRBET KERAK

BHAJA
see ROCK-CUT ARCHITECTURE

BHARHUT, India The original STUPA at Bharhut was probably constructed in the reign of AŚOKA but the earliest known remains are the reconstruction, dated *c* 150–100 BC. Buddhist JATAKA STORIES decorate the railing pillars. Their style shows artistic development from the art of the AŚOKAN PILLAR CAPITALS of the previous century.

Arctic and sub-Arctic Small Tool Traditions
Old Cordilleran of N.W. Coast and Interior Plateau Tradition
Archaic of Eastern Woodlands
Big-Game Hunting Tradition of Great Plains
Desert Tradition of Great Basin and S.W.
North America between 10,000 and 5,000 B.C.
Mesoamerican Big-Game Hunting and Desert Traditions

BHIR MOUND
see TAXILA

BIBLE The holy book of the Christian faith. The Old Testament is also the Jewish holy book and contains a history of the world which begins with creation and centres on God's relations with the ISRAELITES before *c* 500 BC. It was written mainly in Hebrew by many writers, probably on papyrus or hide. The New Testament was written in Greek; the earliest surviving fragments are from the 2nd century AD. *See* QUMRAN.

BIG GAME HUNTING TRADITION Cultures whose economic activities were based on the pursuit of large game animals on the Great Plains of north America. The distribution of diagnostic tool types, especially CLOVIS, FOLSOM and other bifacially flaked lance points, indicates that this tradition spread into eastern north America and parts of the south-west and Mesoamerica where 'kill' and camp sites have also been found. In western north America, where diagnostic projectile types are sometimes found, there is some intermingling with the OLD CORDILLERAN tradition. Origins are obscure, but the tradition seems to have emerged before 10,000 BC and began to change or die out after 8000 when the waning of the PLEISTOCENE brought climatic change which initiated the extinction of such big game herd animals as the horse, camel, mammoth and some bison species.

BIGNOR, England A Romano-British villa in Sussex. This large building was not begun until *c* AD 225. Starting with a simple range of rooms, buildings were added gradually so that a courtyard plan came about in the early 4th century.

▲

The building continued in use until the early 5th century, probably after the end of the Roman Britain. It is best ▲ known for its mosaics of Venus, Ganymede, Medusa, the Seasons, and Cupids dressed as gladiators.

BIRKA, Sweden Situated on an island in Lake Malar, Birka was one of the most important Baltic ports in the VIKING age. It was a famous fur market and attracted much international trade from as far away as Arabia. Although the oval fortress and ramparts can still be seen, the richest archaeological finds have been made in the 'Black Earth' area of the town where deep layers of charcoal, ashes and organic material have accumulated. BARROW cemeteries surround the town, and the grave goods from thousands of burials provide evidence of everyday life in Viking Scandinavia.

BISKUPIN, Poland An URNFIELD site in Poland of 6th–5th century BC. The defended settlement was built on a peninsula jutting into a lake. Later flooding preserved the wooden construction of the site, which included a corduroy ring road and adjoining cross streets of oak timbers, and TIMBER-LACED RAMPARTS. The 80–100 houses are all of the same plan, built of oak and pine timbers, with wooden beam floors and stone hearths.

● **BLACK-AND-RED WARE** An Indian pottery type found in sites of the central Ganges valley and throughout the Deccan, contemporary with PAINTED GREY WARE and sometimes preceding it in sites of the Doab, e.g. ATRANJIKHERA, while at Son near Mathura the two are reputedly found together. It shares with Painted Grey Ware and NORTHERN BLACK POLISHED WARE their two major vessel forms, a shallow tray and a deeper bowl. *See also:* ARYANS; SOUTH INDIAN MEGALITHS.

BLACK FIGURE
see GREEK POTTERY

BLACKWATER DRAW New Mexico, USA An early 'kill' site, important for the finds of CLOVIS fluted projectile points associated with the remains of extinct camel, horse, bison and mammoth in the grey sand level. The brown sands above the grey stratum contain FOLSOM fluted points associated with bison bones. RADIOCARBON dates average 9200 BC for the Clovis and 8300 for the Folsom strata.

BLADE A long parallel-side FLAKE, usually of flint, chert or obsidian, removed from a specially prepared CORE. Blades, particularly characteristic of Upper PALAEOLITHIC INDUSTRIES, could serve as blanks for a great variety of implements (e.g. BURINS or SCRAPERS). *See also:* FLAKING.

BOADICEA
see BOUDICCA

BODH GAYA, India Scene of the BUDDHA's enlightenment. A sandstone railing, dating from the 2nd century BC or earlier, surrounds the tree beneath which Buddha sat. There is also an AŚOKAN PILLAR.

BOG BURIAL
see TOLLUND

BOGHAZKOY
see HITTITES

BONAMPAK, Mexico Located in the dense rainforests of the Rio Usumacinta, Chiapas, a late Classic MAYA CEREMONIAL CENTRE dating from AD 450 to 750, famous for its unique and realistically painted frescoes which depict elaborate processional, ritual and sacrificial scenes. The paintings were executed in green, yellow, dark red, orange and turquoise on several layers of lime plaster.

BONDI POINT A variety of Australian MICROLITHIC BLADE which is asymmetrically backed. While their occurrence seems to show a coastal tendency, with a special concentration in New South Wales, their distribution extends to other Australian regions as well. The earliest dated specimens are earlier than 3000 BC.

BOOK OF THE DEAD Modern title for a collection of about 200 Egyptian spells (also called 'chapters') which from New Kingdom become a popular insurance-policy against possible hazards in afterlife. Some spells clearly derive from Middle Kingdom Coffin Texts, but many additions of amuletic nature reflect diverse superstitions and fears. Usually a selection (perhaps about 50) from these spells was commissioned for a scribe to write (in cursive hieroglyphs, heiratic or demotic) on a PAPYRUS roll placed in tomb in proximity to corpse. Brightly-painted vignettes often supplement a particular spell, making it more efficacious via illustration. Fine polychrome illustrations can be seen in the papyrus belonging to the scribe Ani, and the priestess Anhai. Later dynasties more frequently produce copies where the vignettes are sketched in black ink. Vital spells are responsible for deceased being free to leave the tomb at will, and for passing a crucial scrutiny of his past life at the ceremony of weighing the heart. Others act as passports to get through gateways guarded by ferocious armed demons who (it is hoped) give way at recitation of the spell naming them. There was an immense variety of dangers to avoid, e.g. being irreversibly positioned on one's head, or dying a second time. Invocations to OSIRIS and Re, secured survival in two different hereafters – in the underworld and in the boat of the sun-god.

Under the Saite dynasty the Book of the Dead underwent extensive modifications.

BOREAL
see POSTGLACIAL PERIOD

BOUCHER DE PERTHES, Jacques (1788–1868) It has been said that when EVANS and Prestwich accepted the authenticity of Boucher de Perthes' finds on the Somme, prehistoric archaeology came of age. His finds, made in the gravel pits of Menchecourt and Moulin-Quignon near Abbeville, France, consisted of some rough flint FLAKES associated with the bones of extinct animals. These finds were crucial in arguing the case for the antiquity of man. Until the championing by Evans and Prestwich, de Perthes' views were widely scorned. Eager to convince, he offered a reward of 200 francs for any fossil human remains, and a skull was duly 'found' by a workman in the Moulin-Quignon pit in 1863. This time Prestwich and Evans were sceptical, and in fact the bones were soon shown to be faked. The original finds, however, were undoubtedly authentic.

Main books: *De la Création: essai sur l'origine et la progression des êtres* (5 vols, 1838–41); *Antiquités Celtiques et Antédiluviennes* (3 vols, 1847ff.).

BOUDICCA [or BOADICEA] The wife of Prasutagus, king of the CIVITAS of the Iceni of East Anglia. She was flogged and her daughters raped by Roman soldiers taking over the kingdom (and thereby denying her the succession) after her husband's death. Her reaction was, in AD 60, to lead a rebellion against the Romans: the Iceni were soon joined by the Trinovantes, a tribe which also nursed grievances against the Romans. CAMULODUNUM, VERULAMIUM and LONDON were burned by the rebels before Suetonius Paullinus led an army against them, and defeated the Britons with considerable slaughter, carrying out savage reprisals. Boudicca is said to have killed herself.

BOULDER CLAY A deposit of glacial origin, consisting of material which ranges in size from clay particles to fairly large boulders. Large areas of northern Europe and north America are covered by such deposits left by various GLACIATIONS.

BOYNE, Ireland In the Boyne valley, County Meath, north-west of Dublin, is a remarkable group of prehistoric monuments. At least 25 PASSAGE GRAVES include the well-known sites of Dowth, KNOWTH and New Grange. New Grange is similar to MAES HOWE in plan, and consists of a chamber and passage built of ORTHOSTATS which support a CORBELLED roof, the whole covered with a mound nearly 90m across. Around this was a circle of some 35 standing stones. Recent excavations at New Grange have shown that a large number of the flat stones used in the construction of the tomb were covered with pecked designs of great variety. Motifs on these and on stones from other tombs from the area have been compared with contemporary (Late NEOLITHIC) design from tombs in Brittany and Iberia, as well as with decoration on some GROOVED WARE pots. A Boyne culture has been defined, which as well as tombs is characterized by its pottery, distinctive 'poppy-headed' bone pins and perforated stone beads.

BRACHYCEPHALIC
see CEPHALIC INDEX

BRAK, Syria A TELL near the Khabur River in eastern Syria. Excavations in 1937–8 unearthed occupation extending from the 4th millennium to about 1500 BC. The remains of temples of the Jemdat Nasr period (*c* 3000 BC) were found. These are called 'eye' temples because of a large number of 'eye' figurines made from flat alabaster which were associated with them. Brak was later a border town of the kingdom of AKKAD and contained a palace during that period built by Naram Sin of Agade in about 2280 BC. It was reconstructed in about 2050 BC.

BRIDGE AND SPOUT POT A closed vessel with two projecting spouts connected by a ceramic bridge or strap handle. One spout was often replaced by a small moulded figure which might contain a whistle. This form was common in ancient Peru and is sometimes found elsewhere in the New World.

BRIQUETAGE Debris of salt-making, usually fragments of porous unfired clay troughs and cups used in evaporation of seawater (*see* RED HILLS) or in preparing rock salt (*see* HALLSTATT).

BRISTLECONE PINE (*Pinus aristata*) An exceptionally long-lived conifer, native to the south-west of north

▲ 

America. The archaeological importance of this tree rests on the fact that a TREE RING sequence has been built up from living and dead trees, extending back to *c* 5000 BC. By using RADIOCARBON to date selected pieces of bristlecone pine timber, it has been possible to check and correct radiocarbon dates from various sites. The 'Bristlecone pine correction curve' can be applied to radiocarbon dates throughout the world, as it reflects changes in the world's atmosphere and not regional climate variation.

BROACH [Ancient Barygaza], India Situated on the Gujurat coast of India, Broach was an important trading centre exporting ivory, precious stones, spices, medicines, muslin and silk, and importing wine, metals, coral and topaz, gold and silver coin, and glassware. It enjoyed great importance due to its favourable position for trading with central India and the north. It seems to have been in use since the time of Solomon, when ivory, apes and peacocks were its reputed exports. *See also* MONSOON; PERIPLUS.

▲ **BROCH** Circular drystone tower-forts, 5–9m in diameter and over 8m high. They are found only in Scotland, where 510 sites are known. Brochs were used as fortified refuges; the width of the walls ensured that they were rarely forced. The only entrance was a tunnel with a single door and a guard chamber to one side. There were no windows on the external face. The walls were hollow with stairways leading to galleries. The internal court sometimes had a hearth and may have been roofed. Brochs date from the 2nd century BC to the 1st century AD. *See also* JARLSHOF.

BRONZE AGE Copper, and its alloy with tin, bronze, were worked in MESOPOTAMIA by 2500 BC. In Europe bronze was not used until after *c* 2000 BC, following the introduction of copper-working by the BEAKER people. Despite the scarcity of tin ore, bronze, being harder, rapidly replaced copper for tools. The early bronze age centres of metal-working were the MYCENAEAN civilization in the Aegean; the UNETICE in Central Europe; and also Spain and southern Britain. There are few early or middle bronze age settlements known from Europe, and archaeological finds are chiefly burials and grave goods. At one time, the lack of settlements was thought to indicate that bronze age people were nomadic, but this is unlikely, especially as settled farmers thrived before 2000 BC and after 1000 BC. The widespread trading which brought amber from northern Europe to Unetice, WESSEX and Mycenae is more likely to be the result of gift exchange than of nomadic journeys. The later Bronze Age in Europe is given the name URNFIELD after the cemetries of urned CREMATIONS found throughout Europe. More settlements of this period are known, some of which are fortified in the fashion of later HILLFORTS. The Bronze Age in Europe ended with the coming of the HALLSTATT Iron Age, *c* 750 BC. Knowledge of metal working was introduced into Britain by the Beaker people *c* 2000 BC. Important early bronze age finds come particularly from the graves of the Wessex culture. They are rich burials in comparison with the majority and are probably those of a ruling aristocracy. Metal-working innovations however came not from Wessex, but from Ireland. The bronze age chronology is ■ based on TYPOLOGIES of its tools and weapons, as shapes ▶ and manufacturing techniques evolved. Principal tools in the COPPER AGE were copper flat AXES and HALBERDS; these were followed by the flanged axes, CAMERTON–SNOWSHILL daggers and spearheads of the Early Bronze Age. This

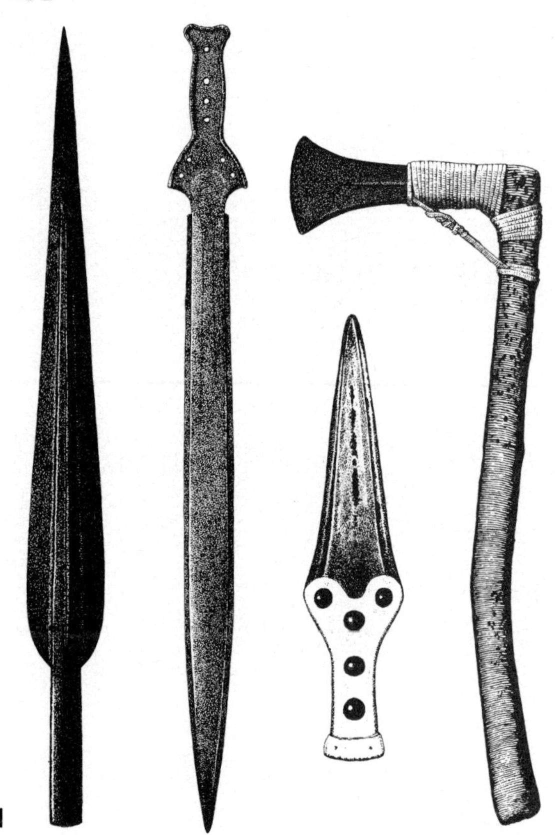

■ period ended with the influx of new metal types from the continent (RAPIERS, PALSTAVES and socketed spearheads). Areas such as Wessex which had been wealthy in the Early Bronze Age now appear backwaters, with centres of manufacture in the Thames valley and the Fens. Settlement evidence continues to be scanty, although palisaded farmsteads of the DEVEREL–RIMBURY culture in southern Britain are now attributed to this period (*c* 2000–1000 BC). The Urnfield burial rite was introduced into Britain in the Middle Bronze Age; Rimbury is the site of a cremation cemetery. The Late Bronze Age is divided from the earlier phase by another metallurgical change: the introduction of bronze with a high proportion of lead. The used of leaded bronze began in the 10th century BC in southern Britain but only in the 8th century became common in northern England, Scotland and Ireland. Hoards of metalwork, e.g. from HEATHERY BURN, became very numerous in the Late Bronze Age. Very few burials are known (a trend which continues into the IRON AGE), and the period is known largely through settlements. Many of the hilltops fortified in the Iron Age (e.g. IVINGHOE BEACON) were already occupied in the Late Bronze Age by undefended farmsteads. The Bronze Age ends *c* 500 BC with the coming of iron; iron-working is known from the Late Bronze Age deposit at LLYN FAWR, though it did not become common until at least 100 years later.

BUBASTIS In the eastern Nile Delta it was a cult centre for the cat-goddess Bastet. The site has produced numerous bronze statuettes of Bastet, thought to represent the sun's beneficial powers. Excavations in the cemetery found charred cats and ovens, proof of the cremation preferred to mummification in this sanctuary. Archaeologists have found support for Herodotus' awe at the size of the Great temple. Its granite blocks show the names of the pyramid-builders Cheops and Chephren. The Middle Kingdom pharaohs enlarged the sanctuary with papyriform and palmiform columns. During Dynasty XXII Bubastis became a major royal residence – in particular of Osorkon II who depicted the celebration of his jubilee in reliefs on the walls of the temple's great hall.

BUCKELURN A very ornate type of funerary ware introduced into England by the Anglo-Saxon invaders and settlers during the 5th and 6th centuries AD. *Buckelurnen* are cremation urns decorated with large oval or round bosses, stamped impressions and incised lines. Designs are usually geometric, though occasionally animals are drawn or stamped on the pot. Some vessels have simple bag-shaped bottoms, others small pedestal feet. There are very close stylistic links between the English examples, from cemeteries such as CAISTOR BY NORWICH and MUCKING, and *Buckelurnen* from the continental Elbe–Weser area, though the distinctive Anglian and Saxon styles are merged.

● **BUDDHA** Buddha was miraculously born at LUMBINI (India) in the 6th century BC. His father, king of KAPILAVASTU, brought him up surrounded by luxury in an attempt to foil the prophecy that he would become an ascetic. However, when out riding at the age of 29 he noticed a dying man, an invalid, a corpse and an ascetic whose sufferings moved him to renounce the world. He subjected himself to the rigours of severe asceticism but came to reject these as a road to enlightenment. After six years of meditation beneath the Bodhi tree at BODH GAYA,

▲

he achieved enlightenment. Thence he travelled to SARNATH where he preached his first sermon, proclaiming the middle way between asceticism and self-indulgence. He spent the rest of his life preaching. Among his converts were the kings of MAGADHA (*see* RAJAGRIHA), Kosala and Vatsa (*see* KAUSAMBI). He also ascended to heaven to preach to his mother, returning to earth at SANKISA. He died at the age of 80 at Kusinagara. His bodily remains were fought over by his followers and eventually deposited in eight STUPAS. *See also* AŚOKA; PATNA.

▲ **BUHEN, Egypt** A site, now under Lake Nasser, just north of the Second cataract. The fortress was subjected to detailed systematic excavation before its submergence; the garrison temple of Queen Hatshepsut was rescued and moved to Khartoum. Dynasty XII pharaohs constructed fort to protect southern frontier. A mudbrick wall (4.85m thick by 10m high) enclosed a rectangle 170m by 150m. The dry ditch and counterscarp, lower ramparts, and projecting towers with loopholes for archers give a strikingly medieval appearance to this structure. The entrance was via the main fortified gate facing the western desert and by two more gates facing an approach from the river Nile. The defences were reoccupied and altered during the New Kingdom. The garrison tower contained the Governor's Residence (a 2-storey building), barrack, and quarters for officers and officials. In a Middle Kingdom layer within a stratified deposit were found horse bones, proof that the horse was introduced into the Nile Vally at an earlier date than previously believed.

BURIED SOIL Where an earthwork has covered an ancient land surface to a sufficient depth, the buried soil may be well preserved. Identification of the soil type and of the associated land snails and/or pollen can provide information concerning the agricultural or other use of the land before the construction of the earthwork. Buried soils beneath BARROWS, banks and other monuments have provided information of major importance in the study of man's past environment. *See also* ENVIRONMENTAL ARCHAEOLOGY, POLLEN ANALYSIS, SOIL ANALYSIS.

BURIN Stone (usually flint) burins are especially characteristic of Upper PALAEOLITHIC industries. A tool for working and engraving antler (*see* GROOVE AND SPLINTER technique), bone, ivory and presumably wood, it possibly originated in the MOUSTERIAN. There are two categories. The 'faceted burin' has a working edge formed by the removal of one or more small slivers ('burin spalls') from a FLAKE or BLADE. The direction of the 'burin blow' that produces this edge is shown in drawings by an arrow. The 'beaked burin' has a point produced by fine RETOUCH and was probably used for detailed engraving work.

BURNISH A smooth shiny surface given to pottery. Besides giving the vessel an attractive appearance, burnishing also makes it watertight. A pot is burnished after it has been allowed to dry in the air, but before it is fired. While it is in this leather-hard state, a smooth, hard round-faced tool is rubbed over the pot so compacting the clay. A 'pattern-burnished' pot is one in which polished zones or lines contrast with the natural, untreated matt background.

■ **BUSH BARROW, Amesbury, Wiltshire** An Early BRONZE AGE Barrow, of the WESSEX CULTURE, excavated in the 19th ▶

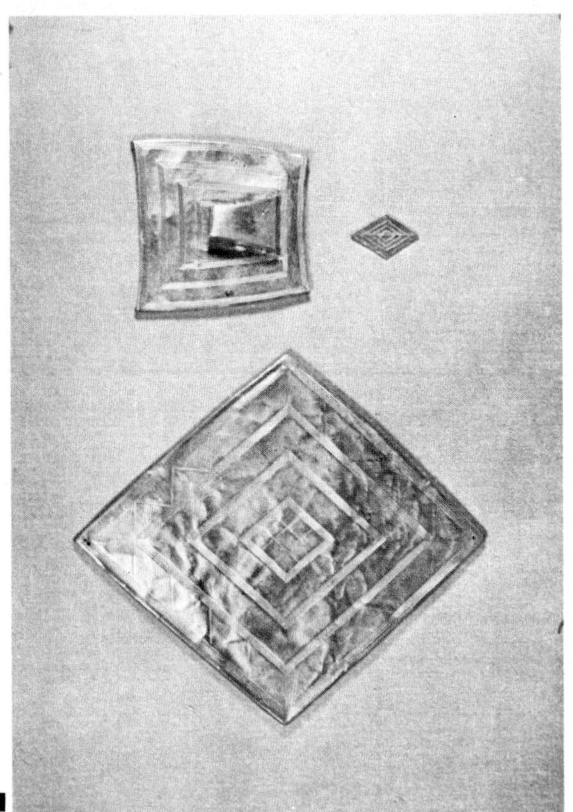

century. A rich burial, perhaps of a chieftain, contained a bone-mounted sceptre, gold plates and a limestone mace, as well as the bronze dagger and axe common in Wessex graves.

● **BUTSER HILL FARM PROJECT** A modern reconstruction on Butser Hill near Petersfield, Hants, of an IRON AGE farm of *c* 300 BC. Two iron age ROUND HOUSES have been built of wattle and daub with thatched roofs. Fields are ploughed with ARDS pulled by oxen and sown by hand with primitive emmer and spelt wheat. These are harvested with sickles and the grain has been stored successfully in experimental STORAGE PITS; germination after six months is close to modern storage values. Other crops include ancient vegetables and woad for blue dye. Experiments have also been tried on pot-firing and weaving. Primitive sheep are being raised here, and pigs from a cross between a Tamworth sow and a wild boar.

BYBLOS
see PHOENICIANS

BYLANY, Czechoslovakia The most extensively excavated of all LINEAR POTTERY settlements, near Prague in west Czechoslovakia. The many longhouses have been divided up into 21 occupation phases, each consisting of five to ten houses. It has been suggested that the site was reoccupied every 30 to 50 years as the SLASH-AND-BURN cycle brought the cultivators back to their original starting point. Thus there would have been a village at Bylany intermittently for at least 700 years. *See* KÖLN-LINDENTHAL.

BYZANTIUM, Turkey The original name of CONSTANTINOPLE, which occupied the site where the old city of Istanbul is now. Traditionally it was founded by a leader called Byzas *c* 658 BC. Its strategic importance was recognized by the Roman emperor CONSTANTINE THE GREAT who in AD 324 chose the city as his capital of the Eastern Roman Empire. Work was completed, and the new capital dedicated, in 330. The Byzantine period is the time when the eastern Mediterranean and south-east Europe were ruled from Constantinople. The Byzantine empire was reduced by SASSANIAN (Persian), OMAYYAD, ABBASID (Moslem) and SELJUK Turkish conquests, and ended when Constantinople fell to the Turks in 1453.

CADBURY CASTLE, Somerset A HILLFORT occupied from the Late BRONZE AGE to the post-Roman period. It was unfortified until the construction in the Early IRON AGE of a TIMBER-LACED rampart, filled with clay and rubble. This was rebuilt in the Late Iron Age, when oval guard houses were added. Typical ROUND HOUSES and STORAGE PITS were found on the site, together with 6- and 4-post rectangular buildings, usually interpreted as granaries. A shrine was built in the Late Iron Age. A series of burials associated with weapons took place at the south west gate *c* AD 70. The Roman occupation was sporadic and the defences were allowed to decay. In the sub-Roman period, a timber rampart with drystone facing was built; this and a timber hall of *c* 5th–6th centuries AD has been linked with the period of King Arthur.

CAERLEON (Isca Silurum), Gwent A Roman legionary fortress placed at the mouth of the river Usk in south

Wales. It was begun in AD 74 as a safeguard against the unruly local Silures tribe. Originally a timber construction, it was rebuilt in stone *c* 100, and reconstructed after *c* 209, perhaps following a tribal revolt. Some walls still stand; the AMPHITHEATRE is the best preserved in Britain; a large timber quay has been uncovered on the bank of the Usk.

CAESAREA, Israel An ancient city on the coast of Palestine founded in the 4th century BC. After 30 BC HEROD THE GREAT rebuilt and enlarged the city and harbour, giving it its present name. It was the seat of the Roman procurators of Judea; one of them, Pontius Pilate, the judge of Jesus Christ, is mentioned on an inscription found on a building in Caesarea. Most of the present ruins date from one of the CRUSADER occupations between AD 1101 and 1265.

CAIRN A heap of stones, usually placed over a burial. *See* BARROW.

CAISTOR BY NORWICH, Norfolk 500 urns have been excavated from this very large early CREMATION cemetery in EAST ANGLIA. It is the largest group of early Germanic pots found in England and promises to revise the dating of the first Anglo-Saxon settlement. Romano-Saxon pottery, late Roman military equipment and early Germanic burials have all been found in a small area. Comparison with the continental ceramics of the migration period indicates the possible arrival of FOEDERATI before AD 350.

CAJAMARCA A region of north highland Peru, on the upper Río Marañon, where a distinctive pottery style flourished from the Early Intermediate period (*see* PERU) following upon the Chavin Horizon style (*see* CHAVIN DE HUANTAR). Cajamarca ware is frequently called 'cursive' because of the small crowded motifs of wavy lines and spirals sometimes representing very stylized animal and bird figures. Colours are red, or red and black, on light orange or cream background and the commonest vessel form is the tripod bowl. The modern town of Cajamarca is also the site of the INCA town where Spanish soldiers under Francisco Pizarro first met the Inca emperor Atahuallpa stationed there with several thousand troops and retainers. There he was seized, held prisoner and finally executed by the Spaniards.

CALAH
see NIMRUD

CALENDAR (Levant and Mesopotamia) As is still the case in Judaism and Islam, the calendar in the LEVANT and MESOPOTAMIA was lunar; the month began at sunset on the evening upon which the new moon was first sighted. Twelve lunar months however amount to only 354 days, about 11¼ days short of the solar year. In order to make corrections, 7 months were added over a period of 19 years. The calendar was directly related to the seasons, as the main occupation was that of agriculture. The Hebrew text found at GEZER gives an outline of the year's activity in the fields, and reads:

Two months of ingathering: Two months of sowing
Two months of late sowing: Month of pulling flax
Month of barley harvest: Month when everything else is harvested
Two months of pruning: Month of summer fruit.

CALENDAR, Calendrics (Mesoamerican) In the New World, the use of a written calendrical system was restricted to MESOAMERICA and is especially important in Mexican and MAYA contexts. All Mesoamerican peoples used two basic calendars: the sacred one of 260 days (Aztec *tonalpohualli;* Maya *tzolkin*) for astrological purposes, and the 365-day solar calendar with 18 'months' of 20 days plus 5 remaining 'unlucky' days, Both were used synchronously. Any one day could therefore be expressed in terms of two different calendars, and the particular combination would not be repeated until 52 years had elapsed. This 52-year period is the 'calendar round'. The calendar round is first recorded about the beginning of the Christian era at MONTE ALBAN. The Maya possessed two further calendars: the 29-day lunar cycle and the 584-day Venus cycle which, like the sacred calendar, was also used in conjunction with the 365-day solar cycle. A correction formula was operated with the solar calendar to allow for the true length of the year which is a fraction over 365 days.

The Maya employed a system of bar-and-dot numerals, in which a bar equalled 5 and each dot represented a single digit. They also understood the concept of zero and place value, employing multiples of 20. A feature of Classic Maya civilization was the use of the Long Count or Initial series, in which dates were recorded by counting the number of days which had elapsed since a mythical starting point in the year 3113 BC. The Long Count was invented somewhere just outside the borders of Maya territory, and first appears on carved STELAE at Chiapa de Corzo (36 BC), Tres Zapotes (31 BC) and El Baul (AD 36). The oldest occurrence in the Maya lowlands is at TIKAL (AD 292). The following units of time were employed: the *baktun* (144,000 days), *katun* (7,200), *tun* (360), *uinal* (20) and *kin* (1 day).

CALENDAR ROUND
see CALENDAR (MESOAMERICAN)

CAMDEN, William (1551–1623) One of Britain's first antiquarians. Camden travelled all over the country to see and describe its monuments. In 1586 he published his *Britannia*, a guide to the island's antiquities written in a style surprisingly observant and scientific for his time. He published the first archaeological drawings in England, and was the first to describe and account for the phenomenon of crop-marks (*see* AIR PHOTOGRAPHY). He was also headmaster of Westminster School.

CAMEO
see INTAGLIO

CAMERTON–SNOWSHILL Two English CREMATION graves, containing daggers characteristic of period 2 of the WESSEX CULTURE. Dated *c* 1500–1350 BC.

CAMULODUNUM [Mod–Colchester, also **Colonia Claudia Victricersis), Essex** Camulodunum began as an OPPIDUM of the Belgic tribe the Trinovantes (*see* BELGAE); by the early 1st century AD it was the tribal capital of the king Cunobelin, the largest oppidum in Britain defended by miles of massive linear dykes, and including the mints of CUNOBELIN. A COLONIA was founded there in AD 49–50, intended to act as the capital of the new province, although this role was soon usurped by LONDON. Camulodunum was a centre of the Imperial cult, and had a temple dedicated to the deified CLAUDIUS. The colonia was destroyed in AD 60 by BOUDICCA and lavishly rebuilt soon afterwards; the substantial walls with the massive Balkerne gate were built

▲

■

late in the 2nd or in the 3rd century. Camulodunum was a centre of manufacture of pottery, including SAMIAN ware.

CANAANITES A branch of SEMITIC people who occupied Palestine during the 2nd millennium BC. Their ancestors were probably the people referred to in old BABYLONIAN texts as Amurru or AMORITES. The ISRAELITES and PHILISTINES displaced them from their cities (GEZER, HAZOR, LACHISH, MEGIDDO, for example) on the plains of Palestine. In the north they became the PHOENICIANS, a seafaring people.

CANOPIC JARS Pottery or stone jars, deriving their name from erroneous identification by early Egyptologists with god of Canopus (near Alexandria) who was OSIRIS worshipped as a fat-bellied vase surmounted by human head.

These jars were four containers for the viscera extracted from the corpse during mummification. Down to Dynasty XVIII the stoppers of these jars were shaped as human heads (e.g. the alabaster stoppers of TUTANKHAMUN, practically portraits of the king wearing NEMES-headcloth). Then they represent four minor deities (sons of HORUS), protective genii for the viscera – the jackal Duamutef guarded the stomach, the falcon Kebhsenuef the intestines, the ape Hapy the lungs, the anthropoid Imsety the liver. The jars themselves, put into a chest for the tomb, were placed under the protection of four goddesses: Neith, Selkis, Nephthys, Isis.

CANTERBURY, Kent Unlike most Roman towns Canterbury was not abandoned during the early SAXON period. Small GRUBENHÄUSER of *c* AD 500 have been found alongside derelict Roman buildings; when AUGUSTINE arrived in 597 he found the royal chaplain using an old Roman church. Canterbury quickly became an Anglo-Saxon town, the capital of Kent, and the seat of the premier archbishop in England. With London, HAMWIH and York it became one of the centres of international trade, dealing especially with Rhenish goods.

CAPE KRUSENSTERN, Alaska A site with over 10 successive cultural phases dating back to 8000 BC, located on a series of fossil beaches. One of the earliest occupations was of the DENBIGH FLINT COMPLEX, followed by the Old Whaling culture and then by a series of Eskimo cultures which included contacts with IPIUTAK and THULE. Occupation continued into the late prehistoric period.

■ **CAPITAL** The main distinguishing element of the orders of classical architecture, which occupied a position on top of the COLUMN and beneath the superstructure of the building. Originally plain (Doric), later more ornate with spirals and acanthus leaves (Ionic and Corinthian).

CAPITOL, Rome One of the seven hills of Rome and, like the PALATINE the heart of the ancient city. It was dominated by the temple of Jupiter, Best and Greatest, the oldest and most magnificent temple in the city, and was crowded with other important buildings such as the temple of Juno Moneta.

CAPSIAN Named after El Mekta, a site near Gafsa, Tunisia, a MESOLITHIC culture of north Africa which succeeded the ORANIAN. Capsian stone tools are commonly found in mounds beside the salt lakes in Algeria and Tunisia. The nature of the stone industry, which included

pieces made by the MICROBURIN technique, remained essentially the same (apart from the introduction of pressure FLAKING) after the arrival of pottery, domesticated animals and cultivated plants from *c* 5000 BC, resulting in the culture called 'Neolithic of Capsian tradition'. There is no relationship between the Capsian described here and the PALAEOLITHIC 'Kenya Capsian' of eastern Africa.

CAPSTONE A horizontal slab of stone used to roof a CHAMBER TOMB or a CIST.

CARAUSIUS, Marcus Aurelius Mauseus (AD ?–293) An able man who rose to become, in AD 286, the commander of the CLASSIS BRITANNICA, a fleet designed to protect Britain and Northern Gaul from Germanic raids. He was suspected of keeping the pirates' loot for himself and, fearing arrest, proclaimed himself emperor in Britain, also retaining for a while control of part of northern Gaul. He probably originated the SAXON SHORE defence system. His reign was a period of stability in Britain, and it is notable that the British silver coinage (of which he made great use as a propaganda medium) was considerably more fine than that of the rest of the empire. He was succeeded by his murderer and former colleague, Allectus, in 293; in 296 Constantius reconquered Britain and returned it to the empire.

CARBONIZED GRAIN Cereal grains that have been turned to charcoal by fire or intense heat. This frequently occurred accidentally during drying or parching, or when structures caught fire. Grain thus preserved has been very useful in the study of ancient cereal species.

CARCHEMISH, Syria A large TELL by the Euphrates river on the Turkish–Syrian border. It is strategically situated by one of the few fords. Although previously inhabited, it became an important city only under the HITTITE empire. It continued as an important city-state after the collapse of the Hittite empire until it was annexed by ASSYRIA in 716 BC. Excavations before 1914 investigated the town defences and also found buildings which were profusely decorated with RELIEFS.

CARIB AMERINDIAN group who settled the Lesser Antilles, West Indies, from South America at the expense of the ARAWAKS, whose language they later adopted. Spanish explorers called them 'Caribals' which became corrupted to 'cannibal' after their practice of eating prisoners of war.

CARMEL
see MOUNT CARMEL

● **CARNAC, Morbihan, France** Nearly 3000 MEGALITHS still remain in this remarkable area on the coast of north-west France. There are three groups of alignments, in which several parallel rows of stones stride across the countryside. The area is also rich in CHAMBER TOMBS. Among the various stones that do not form part of the main rows is the Grand Menhir Brisé, now lying in four pieces on the ground. If as some believe it once stood upright, it would have been the largest standing stone in Europe, nearly 20m high and weighing some 343 tonnes. It has been claimed that this served as a foresight for lunar observations, and that the whole complex was set out using a standard unit of measurement, the megalithic yard.

▲ 

■ 

CARNUNTUM, Romania One of the most important Roman fortresses on the Danube. There was a civil town near by which became a COLONIA after SEVERUS had been declared Emperor there. The fort was reconstructed in AD 375 but was burnt *c* 400. The civil town, after a boom in Severus's time, declined. Two AMPHITHEATRES have been excavated and one can be seen along with private houses.

CARNYX Large curved trumpet of the IRON AGE. Classical references suggest that they were used in war to frighten the enemy. These trumpets often had animal-head terminals in the CELTIC ART style, like those depicted on the ritual cauldron from GUNDESTRUP. An iron age trumpet came from the LLYN CERRIG BACH peat-bog deposit, and others are known from Irish bogs.

▲**CARTER, Howard (1874–1939)** British Egyptologist. In his early career he received training from PETRIE. He produced excellent drawings of archaeological work at Hatshepsut's temple, DEIR EL-BAHRI. He held high posts, responsible for monuments and supervising excavations.

In 1907 he excavated on behalf of Lord Carnarvon at THEBES, finding Hatshepsut's tomb and valley temple.

In 1922, in a last all-or-nothing season of excavation in the Valley of the Kings at Thebes, he discovered the virtually intact tomb of TUTANKHAMUN (Dynasty XVIII). The work of emptying the chambers, photographing, conserving and despatching the treasures to Cairo took Carter and colleagues a decade. He failed through poor health to produce a final detailed archaeological report on the dig and finds.

Main book (with A. C. Mace): *The Tomb of Tutankhamun* (3 vols. 1923–33).

CARTHAGE, Tunisia A PHOENICIAN trading colony founded in 814 BC on the north coast of Africa. Carthage led the former Phoenician colonies of north Africa in a period of great trading prosperity after the fall of Tyre to ASSYRIA, competing with first Greece and later Rome, to whom she lost Sicily and Sardinia in 241 BC after the first PUNIC WAR. The town was totally destroyed by the Romans in 146 BC, and her fields sown with salt, but Carthage was later rebuilt as a Roman colony. Considerable remains survive.

■**CARTOUCHE** Term used in Egyptology to describe the ovals (also called 'royal rings') which surround the last two names of the official titulary of the pharaoh and the names of the queen. The cartouche was called by the Ancient Egyptians 'shenu', deriving from the word 'to encircle'. Besides giving pre-eminence and magical protection to royal names, the notion behind the 'shenu' was that the pharaoh's dominion extended over all the lands encircled by the course of the sun. Some early examples show that the composition of the 'shenu' consisted of two juxtaposed lengths of rope with the ends tied to form a straight terminal to the oval.

CASA GRANDE, Salt River, Arizona, USA Late HOHOKAM town featuring massive ADOBE multi-storeyed houses, the largest of which is a rectangular four-storey structure with over 12 rooms and walls more than one metre thick.

CATACOMBS Underground Christian burial vaults found mainly around Rome and dating to the late 3rd and 4th century AD. They could accommodate many hundreds of bodies. They developed because of pressure on space in Rome's cemeteries but mainly because of persecution and

the need for secrecy. Many of the chambers have wall-paintings vital to the understanding of Early Christian art and iconography.

● **CATAL HÜYÜK [pronounced Chatal], Turkey** Tell on the Konya plain in central south ANATOLIA. It was excavated in the 1950s, 1960s and found to be one of the world's oldest towns. It was inhabited, according to RADIOCARBON dating, 6200–5400 BC. Wheat, barley, peas and vetches were cultivated, and sheep and cattle bred in the surrounding plains. The inhabitants' diet was supplemented with the proceeds of hunting. Materials such as obsidian and seashell were obtained by trading. The village consisted of rectangular mud-brick houses with no space between them, making access possible only by ladder through the roof. There were many shrines decorated with bulls and the mother goddess in statue, relief and fresco. The dead were buried under the houses after vultures had picked their bones clean.

CAUSEWAYED CAMP The name given to the ditched enclosures of the British Earlier Neolithic (WINDMILL HILL culture), found mainly on the chalk Downs of southern England. The characteristic feature of these 'camps' is a series of often shallow ditches enclosing a roughly circular area. There are sometimes several sets of such ditches, interrupted by frequent causeways; possibly they were not all open at any one time, but instead gradually accumulated over centuries of continuous activity. The function of the enclosures, like that of the succeeding HENGES, is unclear. One possibility is that they served as focal points for a number of separate farming communities, like a medieval fair.

CAVE ART The earliest art known to have been produced by man dates from the Upper PALAEOLITHIC and is found across Europe from Siberia to Spain. It is divided by archaeologists into two general categories: cave art (sometimes known as 'parietal art') and MOBILIARY art. Cave art consists of engravings and paintings on the walls, roofs and floors of caves, most of them in south-west France and north-east Spain (*see* ALTAMIRA; LASCAUX). The depictions are mostly of animals (e.g. bison, cattle, horse, mammoth), sometimes in groups but seldom, if ever, in scenes. Human figures are rare, and any natural features such as mountains are unrecognizable, if indeed present. Colours, deriving from naturally occurring mineral pigments, range from black to reds, browns and ochres.

The function of this art can only be guessed at, but it seems clear that most was not purely decorative. Much of it lies deep within dark caves well away from any habitable areas. Animal drawings and non-representational 'signs' are frequently superimposed, in some cases it is very difficult to discern what has actually been depicted.

CELLA The whole of a classical temple except its outer colonnade; or, the main room of a temple.

▲ **CELTIC ART** A particular art style originating among the Celtic peoples of central Europe. It was a combination of a number of artistic traditions. Many early motifs were copies and adaptations of Greek and ETRUSCAN designs, especially those on imported wine-drinking vessels. Celtic animal patterns were influenced by SCYTHIAN or Oriental designs: the forms tended to be very simplified, not naturalistic like those in classical art. Often the animals were used as part of the decoration. By the 4th century BC,

the art was almost completely abstract (the WALDAGESHEIM style), and it was used to decorate most flat surfaces from SWORDS to mirrors. The decoration is full of curves and tendrils, with very few straight lines. By the 3rd century BC, the Celtic art style was found on objects from France to Czechoslovakia. With ROMAN expansion, classical styles were used alongside the Celtic motifs, which were later swamped on the Continent by the more civilized art. In Britain however, the Celtic element continued throughout the occupation and Irish Celtic designs were introduced into England in the post-Roman period. Many early Christian gold ornaments and illuminated manuscripts, e.g. that from LINDISFARNE, were Celtic in style. The CELTS decorated everyday items with their art, and generally avoided sculpture in the round. The most beautifully decorated objects are those connected with warfare (e.g. swords); drinking; or personal ornamentation – all of which were important to the Celtic aristocracy, the artists' patrons. Figures of animals occur but are less common; representations of humans are rare. The exception to this were the SEVERED HEADS, which are numerous and widespread throughout the Celtic world.

CELTIC FIELDS Small square fields surrounded by LYNCHETS or stone walls may be preserved in areas of pasture (e.g. at PLUMPTON PLAIN), where they have not been ploughed out by later agriculture. Each field is $\frac{1}{5}-\frac{4}{5}$ hectares in area. This is probably the ground that could be ploughed in one day with an ARD drawn by two oxen. Thought at one time to be IRON AGE in date, they are in fact of any period from the BRONZE AGE to the Roman period. At GWITHIAN, square fields are dated to the Early Bronze Age, about the 16th century BC.

CELTS A group of barbarian tribes in Europe prior to the ROMAN conquests, united by a common CULTURE, CELTIC ART and INDO-EUROPEAN language. The various tribes were called by different names, e.g. BELGAE, Gauls (in France), or Galatians in Anatolia, but known collectively as the Celts. Even by the 7th-century BC HALLSTATT period, there were probably Celtic-speaking peoples from Jugoslavia to eastern France. The classical writers certainly knew of the Celts from 500 BC. Always known as a warlike people, the Celts came into violent contact with the civilized world when in 390 BC they sacked ROME, and later in 279 when they sacked DELPHI in Greece. Large-scale fortifications indicate unrest in Celtic society, with the growth of HILLFORTS like MAIDEN CASTLE and OPPIDA such as MANCHING. But despite their warlike natures, the tribes were disorganized, unable to unite, and were easily conquered by the superior Roman armies.

The Celtic aristocracy encouraged the growth of art, and also the Celtic religion. This was centred on a large number of local gods such as are depicted on the GUNDESTRUP cauldron, and certain cults, such as that of the SEVERED HEAD. Classical writers condemned the Celtic religion as barbaric. Prisoners and booty of war were often sacrificed, and like TOLLUND man thrown into bogs as votive deposits. Groves, bogs and wells were sacred to the Celts and to their priests the DRUIDS. There is some evidence of Celtic temples, e.g. at Maiden Castle. The Celts believed in an after-life: chieftains were buried with their CHARIOTS and their drinking utensils – wine was very important in Celtic life. Women were also important, as shown by the VIX burial and the fact that women (*see* BOUDICCA) were sometimes tribal rulers. The Celtic way of life survived only outside the Roman empire, in Scotland, Ireland and Wales.

CENOTE Large natural wells in limestone bedrock found in the lowland tropical regions of Mesoamerica, especially the Yucatan peninsula. The famous sacred well at CHICHÉN ITZÁ, which received the bodies of sacrificial victims together with rich offerings, was one of these. In many cases they were the sole supply of ground water and many CEREMONIAL CENTRES were located beside one.

CENTURIATION A system of dividing land into square plots in the Roman period. At first it was associated with land distribution around Greek colonies in Italy but it was mainly used at the beginning of the Empire to apportion land to retired soldiers after the civil wars of the 1st century BC. Large tracts of land in the Po valley were involved. Other large areas of centuriation are in Tunisia and the Rhône valley, especially around Orange where the apportionment plan, carved on marble and formerly displayed in the centre of the town, has survived. These areas were all found through AIR PHOTOGRAPHY, by the patterns of hedges or lanes which survive along the lines of the centuriation. The method of division, because it did not follow local topography and gave disputatious part-rights in rivers, for example, was abandoned by the end of the 1st century AD (and thus is unlikely to be found in Britain). The squares were laid out by *agrimensores* or land surveyors and were generally in multiples of the *actus* (120 Roman feet).

CEPHALIC INDEX A number used to describe the shape of a skull. This figure is obtained by dividing the maximum length of the skull (from front to back) by its maximum width. The resulting fraction is then expressed as a percentage. Skulls are often roughly categorized between dolichocephalic (long-headed) if the index is less than 75 or brachycephalic (round-headed) if it is greater than 80.

CEREMONIAL CENTRE A complex of temples, PYRAMIDS, palaces and PLAZAS representing the focus of religious and ceremonial interest for communities dispersed over a wide area. They are typically non-urban, and the best examples are from the MAYA civilization (*see also* COPAN, PALENQUE, TIKAL).

●**CERNE ABBAS, Dorset** A huge figure of a phallic, club-bearing man over 60m high is cut into a steep chalk slope at Cerne Abbas. It is possibly ROMAN in date, though definitely provincial in style.

▲**CERVETERI, Italy** This was anciently the ETRUSCAN city of Caere. It is situated in southern Etruria between the sea and lake Bracciano, a few kilometres from the coast. Excavated material shows that the settlement thrived from VILLANOVAN times through to the Roman period. The principal tombs are mainly in the Banditaccia cemetery which includes TUMULI up to 30m in diameter. Each tumulus usually contains two or three individual tombs, most of which date from the 7th and 6th centuries BC and are cut from the rock in replica of houses with doors, windows and ornamented or beamed ceilings.

CESS PIT Pit used for the disposal of kitchen and/or human waste. Such pits were extensively used in medieval and post-medieval times, when they were often built of stone or brick. Excavation of cess pits produces much evidence of diet, especially animal bones and the seeds of various fruits.

▲

CHAC MAYA rain gods represented with a long upward curling upper lip. They probably derive from the deity depicted on a stela at IZAPA of Preclassic date. *See also* MESOAMERICA.

CHACMOOL Stone sculpture of a human form resting on its back with flexed knees and hands clasping a bowl on the stomach for sacrificial offerings. The head is turned, and the face stares enigmatically to one side. They are characteristic of Postclassic Mexican TOLTEC tradition and appear at such sites as TULA and CHICHEN ITZA.

CHAITYA A building (generally Buddhist), designed to shelter a STUPA and worshippers. Rock-cut examples comprise a large vaulted hall with apsidal end, containing the stupa, and divided by two colonnades into a broad nave amd two aisles. *See also* ROCK-CUT ARCHITECTURE.

CHALCOLITHIC Meaning 'of the COPPER AGE', period at which copper-working was known but stone still used for most tools.

CHAMBER TOMB In 1876, MONTELIUS proposed a basic three-fold classification of the European MEGALITHIC tomb now known as single-chamber tomb, chamber-and-passage tomb (PASSAGE GRAVE; French *dolmen à galerie*), and long tomb (GALLERY GRAVE, French *allée couverte*). These three are collectively called chamber tombs. They are built of large stone slabs (or sometimes cut out of the living rock) and designed to take a number of burials over a period of time (hence they are 'collective tombs'). In Europe (where they are of NEOLITHIC, COPPER AGE or BRONZE AGE date) chamber tombs are found in Italy, Sicily, Malta, Corsica and the Balearic Islands; along the coast of Spain and Portugal and throughout France and southern Scandinavia; and in Ireland and along the west coast of Scotland, England and Wales. They are frequently free-standing, but probably most or all were originally covered by a stone or earth mound. *See* MEGALITH; WEST KENNET. The distribution of chamber tombs is world-wide and in many different cultural contexts, including India, the Far East and the MYCENAEAN and ETRUSCAN civilizations.

CHAMPLEVÉ A technique used in ENAMEL working. The metal object to be decorated is designed with a sunken area to receive the powdered enamel. The hollow field may either be cast in the original mould, or may be cut out after casting. Sufficient enamel is placed in each hollow to produce a coloured enamel surface flush with that of the surrounding metal. This method of decoration was used extensively in DARK-AGE Ireland in conjunction with MILLEFIORI glass and CLOISONNÉ jewellery.

CHAMPOLLION, Jean-François (1790–1832) French decipherer of Egyptian hieroglyphs, founder of Egyptology. By his twenties had exhaustively researched the Coptic language for ancient place-names. At the start he believed Hieroglyphic, Hieratic and Demotic scripts represented ideas not sounds, except for proper names. He obtained sound-values for the names Ptolemy and Cleopatra from cartouches on the Rosetta Stone and Philae obelisk. With inscriptions from Thebes he built a collection of phonetic hieroglyphs. His genius and knowledge of Coptic grammar led him to extend the phonetic system and to realize that hieroglyphs were basically signs for sounds, supplemented by unpro-

●

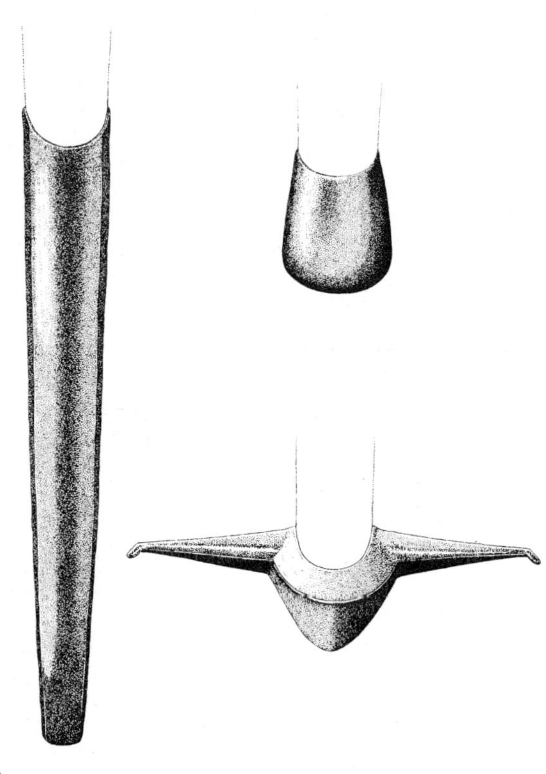
▲

● nounced signs to clarify sense. Full results were published in 1824 in *Précis du systéme hiéroglyphique*, and were accepted by the orientalist De Sacy as the key to ancient Egypt's language. A hard core of scholars continued to criticise Champollion's system until it was finally vindicated by LEPSIUS. Champollion visited Egypt and Nubia in 1828–30 making useful drawings and notes. On his return, he became professor at the Collège de France, dying only a few months afterwards.
Main books: *Lettre à M. Dacier relative à l'alphabet des hiéroglyphes phonetiques* (1822); *Monument de l'Egypte et de la Nubie* (2 vols, 1844–89).

CHANCHAN
see CHIMU

CHANSEN, Thailand A site in central Thailand with archaeological remains beginning in the Late Metal Age (dates *c* mid first millennium BC) and continuing to *c* AD 1200. From the earliest phase are found iron artefacts (such as knives and tools), bronze rings, bells and bracelets, pottery and evidence for woven textiles; during this period wild animals, especially deer, were hunted. Burial was by inhumation. Later such items as gold jewellery, glass beads, and an ivory comb appear, some imported from surrounding regions.

▲**CHAPE** A metal tip to the scabbard which contains the SWORD. During the HALLSTATT period of the European IRON AGE, winged chapes with side projections were used so that a mounted warrior could keep the scabbard steady with his foot while drawing the sword.

CHARCOAL IDENTIFICATION As charcoal does not decay, it is ubiquitous on archaeological sites. The charcoal may be debris from cooking fires or be associated with structures accidently destroyed by fire. Where the original use of the wood (e.g. post, floorboard, tool handle) is known, identifying the tree from which it came by microscopic examination of the preserved wood structure can yield considerable technological information otherwise unobtainable.

CHARIOT Vehicle with two wheels, used particularly in war, drawn by horses.

■ **CHARLEMAGNE** King of the FRANKS, born AD 742 and ruled 771–814, controlling an empire which stretched from the Danube to Brittany, from the Frisian Islands to the Mediterranean, including most of Germany and Holland, all Belgium and Switzerland, and almost all France. In art, learning, administration and warfare his reign recalled the achievements of the Roman empire; indeed, he was crowned emperor by the Pope in 800. Charlemagne was in diplomatic contact with the most important rulers of his time, among them the Eastern Roman Emperor; OFFA of MERCIA, and Harun al Rashid of Bagdad. In campaigns over the last thirty years of the 8th century the Franks conquered the FRISIANS and SAXONS, establishing a frontier with the Danes. The military system was reformed and laws codified. Although almost perpetually at war, Charlemagne assembled a number of great scholars at his court at Aachen, established a palace school under Alcuin and founded monasteries at Fulda and Tours. He was thus personally concerned with the mainsprings of the Carolingian renaissance.

■

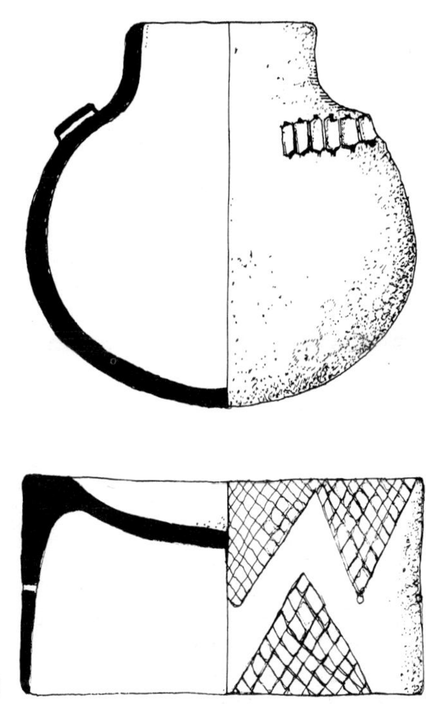

○

CHARSADA (Ancient Pushkalavati), Pakistan One of the two capitals of Gandhara (*see* TAXILA), Charsada is situated on the Peshawar plain. The dating of the Bala Hissar mound is uncertain, but it seems to have been occupied before Taxila, in the pre-Achaemenid period *c* 8th–5th century BC, and until *c* 1st century BC. There are ACHAEMENID and Persian pottery and terracotta 'mother goddess' figurines with *appliqué* features. These continued into the occupation of the later Shaikhan Dheri mound, which dates from the early 2nd century BC (on the basis of coin evidence). Like Sirkap at Taxila, this site was laid out in a regular grid of streets. It was occupied until *c* 4th century AD by Indo-Greeks and KUSHANS. As at Taxila, much of the native work here has a westernizing appearance, such as a terracotta of the Apollo Belvedere. An important house group, apparently looted and fired *c* AD 150, contained a Buddhist shrine with a variety of relics including a reliquary decorated with scenes from BUDDHA's life, and a number of pieces in the early GANDHARAN ART style. The house also contained a steel dagger and the remains of a PARTHIAN chain-mail helmet.

○ **CHASSEY** Originating in the early fourth millennium BC west of the Rhône in southern France (where it succeeded the IMPRESSED WARE culture), the Chassey culture (or Chasséen) quickly spread into central and northern France. One of the WESTERN NEOLITHIC cultures, its characteristic pottery was round-based, burnished to a brown glossy texture and decorated with incised geometric designs. 'Pan-pipe' lugs (consisting of parallel tubes of clay fixed to the neck of pots) are commonly found. The economy was typically NEOLITHIC, domestic animals (especially sheep or cattle) usually outnumbering wild animals in rubbish deposits; emmer wheat, barley and beans were cultivated, although wild plant foods (such as acorns) were still important. The type-site (Camp de Chassey, in the Massif Central) was a fortified hilltop.

CHÂTELPERRONIAN The earliest Upper PALAEOLITHIC industry in France, succeeding the MOUSTERIAN. A characteristic flint tool is the Châtelperron knife, a blade with a curved blunted back. The TYPE-SITE is the Châtelperron cave (Allier, central France).

CHAVÍN DE HUANTAR, Peru A site in the northern highlands giving its name to the art style and culture which predominated throughout the Early Horizon period, 900–200 BC (*see* PERU). The main buildings comprise several stone PLATFORM MOUNDS adorned with stone sculptures and reliefs depicting jaguars, eagles, caimans, snakes and anthropomorphic beings, all usually shown with such distinguishing features as snarling up-curled mouths with projecting fangs, eccentric eyes and serpentine hair. The origins of this style are obscure, but seem to lie in the coastal or Andean areas of north central Peru. There are several phases in its evolution, which can be traced in the successive building periods at Chavín de Huantar. The main temple complex, called the Castillo, typifies Chavín architecture, being honeycombed with chambers and galleries on three superimposed levels. At its heart, standing at the intersection of the two central passages, stands the 'Lanzon' or Great Image, a column over 4m high of carved white granite which, together with the Raimondi stela, incorporates the artistic symbols central to the style. Chavín is believed to have been a mainly religious phenomenon and its influence spread swiftly

through the northern highlands and as far down as the Central Coast of Peru. Farther south, the PARACAS culture shows marked Chavín influence in its pottery and textiles. By 200 BC, Chavín had died out altogether.

CHEDDAR, Somerset A royal site occupied in the middle and late SAXON periods. Excavation has revealed a large timber HALL of the 9th century AD which is 25m long, with slightly bowed sides and lateral entrances. An area of burnt clay indicates the central hearth. There are smaller ancillary buildings grouped around the hall in which the Witan (Royal Council) met in 941. In a second phase of construction was built another great hall 19m long, rectangular with entrances in the gable-end walls. This hall, with associated small buildings and chapel, continued in use, with modifications, until the 12th century. *See also:* YEAVERING.

CHEDWORTH, Gloucestershire A Roman VILLA. In the early 2nd century AD it consisted of three small and separate wings built in timber, and a stone bath-house. By about a century later all this had been incorporated into a single plan by linking the wings with corridors and connecting walls around a courtyard. A period of considerable opulence opened in the 4th century, when the bath-house was extended, a further one added, and a NYMPHAEUM built. The living-quarters were also greatly extended. The prosperity of the villa is further shown by its fine MOSAICS.

CHELLEAN A generally redundant term for the entire European Lower Palaeolithic HANDAXE tradition, named after Chelles-sur-Marne, near Paris, a site which has in fact only produced ACHEULEAN-type handaxes (hence the use of 'Pre-Chellean' as an alternative to ABBEVILLEAN). The term 'Chelles-Acheul culture' once used in Africa has now ceded place to 'Acheulean'. *See* PALAEOLITHIC.

CHENG CHOU, China This site in Honan is that of the first capital of the SHANG dynasty. Established *c* 1500 BC, the capital was later shifted to ANYANG *c* 1300 BC, 160km away. Cheng Chou is thought to be the city of Ao referred to in the ancient literature. Traces of a wall some 20m wide built of layers of rammed earth rose 8m high, enclosing an area 1700m by 2000m. Though the tombs and habitations found here are generally on a less grand scale than those around Anyang, skilled bronze casting was already evident.

CHEOPS' PYRAMID, Egypt Great Pyramid on the Giza plateau for Cheops – Egyptian Khufu – (Dynasty IV). Original measurements were 146m high by 232m base-length, sloping at 51° 56′. A permanent force of skilled masons, supplemented by the seasonal influx of labourers on the corvée (national service for the three months of the Nile inundation) constructed the pyramid from 2,521,000 blocks of limestone and granite. The blocks were hauled on sledges on rollers up ramps. A thick outer casing of dressed limestone covered the core.

A sloping passage diverted above ground level into a vaulted room wrongly called the Queen's Chamber. An ascending corridor forms the Grand Gallery to the King's Chamber with 406 tonnes of granite roofing. Relieving chambers prevent the weight of masonry crushing the room in which is a lidless sarcophogus. Beside the pyramid was a boat-grave for a large dismantled ship of

●

cedarwood for pharaoh's use in the afterlife.

● **CHEPHREN'S PYRAMID, Giza, Egypt** Chephren – Egyptian, Khafre – (Dynasty IV) built a smaller pyramid than his father Cheops. It was originally 143.5m high by 215.5m wide, at a slope of 53° 10′, the pinnacle still covered by casing of Tura limestone. The preliminary work in building this pyramid involved levelling a sharp slope on the plateau-surface. In 1818 BELZONI located one of the two entrances, both of which led into a long horizontal gallery cut in the rock. The burial chamber contained an empty highly polished granite sarcophagus.

CHEPHREN'S VALLEY TEMPLE Near the sphinx at Giza. MARIETTE's excavation produced the magnificent diorite statue of King Cephren (Dynasty IV) – his head protected by the wings of the hawk-god HORUS, the sides of his throne showing the papyrus of the north and the plant of the south combining around a central sign meaning 'unite'. This valley temple of Cephren's pyramid complex is one of the best surviving witnesses to the skill of Old Kingdom craftsmen with only copper tools. Constructed from massive blocks of limestone encased with polished red granite, it has a flooring of alabaster, a T-shaped hall of sixteen square granite pillars, and emplacements for over twenty statues of the pharaoh each of which would have been highlighted by rays passing through carefully-angled windows.

CHESTER, England The legionary fortress of the 20th 'Victorious Valerian' Legion whose main sphere of activities was north Wales. The main fortress, of 25 hectares, was started AD 76–8. It was rebuilt in stone in the 2nd century, destroyed in part at the end of the 3rd, and rebuilt in the 4th. It was probably abandoned *c* 380.

Because of its good position Chester has been occupied from Saxon times. Consequently, few Roman remains to be seen save for part of the AMPHITHEATRE, largest in Britain.

CHEVAUX DE FRISE Rows of stakes, or in upland areas upright stones, set around the defences of a HILLFORT to harrass the approach of mounted attackers. Sometimes used instead of a ditch.

▲ **CHICHÉN ITZÁ, North Yucatan peninsula, Mexico** A major MAYA CEREMONIAL CENTRE founded in the late Classic Period (*see* MESOAMERICA) becoming especially important in the early Postclassic period with the arrival of Putun Itzas from Tabasco and Campeche in AD 918, followed by a group of TOLTEC immigrants led by Kukulcan (Feathered Serpent) in 987. These latter initiated the building of a whole new quarter called 'New Chichén' with many of the buildings strongly reminiscent of TULA both in architectural style and decorative motif. Amongst these, the most important are the central Castillo or Temple of Kukulcan, the Temple of the Warriors with its Group of a Thousand Columns, the Great BALLCOURT measuring 150m × 35m, the Temple of the Jaguars with feathered serpent portals and interior reliefs of prowling jaguars and the *tzompantli* – a structure carved in relief with severed human heads. This last, together with the numerous CHACMOOLS, serpent heads, depictions of warriors with darts and shields, and human sacrifice, are all typical of strong Mexican Toltec influence in an otherwise

China

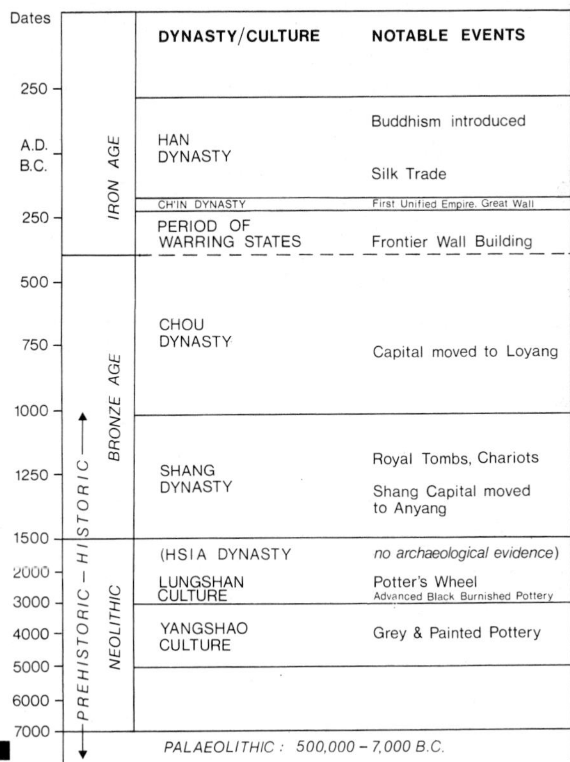

Maya medium. Chichén Itzá is famous for the sacred CENOTE, a deep natural well in the limestone bedrock where the remains of several hundred individuals have been discovered, along with many rich objects. At the end of the 13th century leadership passed to MAYAPAN.

CHICHIMEC Late prehistoric tribes of the DESERT TRADITION, speaking NAHUA dialects and living in the marginal farming regions on the northern and north-western borders of Mesoamerica. They periodically disrupted the civilized communities further south in Mexico with their nomadic incursions. *See also:* TOLTEC; AZTEC.

● **CHILDE, Vere Gordon (1892–1957)** Gordon Childe displayed an unmatched knowledge of Old World prehistoric material. Although he was professor of archaeology successively at Edinburgh and London Universities, he was born and died in Australia. He charted the development of Old World economies and societies by grouping material artefacts into 'CULTURES', a concept he described at great length. Where possible he equated 'cultures' with 'peoples', enabling him to entitle a book summarizing the major cultural advances from the PALAEOLITHIC onwards *What Happened in History*. In this and other works, Childe described what he considered to be two of the major events in prehistory, calling them the 'NEOLITHIC Revolution' and the 'Urban Revolution'. Recent work in Africa, Oceania and the New World has shown that the development of both agriculture and urbanism (occurring in different ways in several unconnected places) was more complicated than Childe could have known, but the idea of prehistoric economic 'revolutions' is still much discussed. His first-hand knowledge of European material was quite remarkable. Main books: *The Dawn of European Civilization* (1925); *What Happened in History* (1942); *Social Evolution* (1951).

▲ **CHIMU (or Chimor)** The northernmost, and archaeologically the best documented, of the four Late Intermediate (*see* PERU) coastal empires existing before the INCA conquest. The others were Cuismancu on the Central Coast, Chuquismancu in the South Central and Chincha to the south. At its maximum extent, the Chimu kingdom extended from Tumbes in the north down to Supe on the Central Coast, and the presence of the typical blackware pottery and Chimu art style suggest influences even further afield. Inca legends suggest a history going well back into the 14th century AD when the first emperor, Nancenpinco, started a programme of conquest which eventually made the Chimu empire second only in size and prestige to that of the Inca who conquered it. The capital city Chanchan was the largest ever built in the whole of Precolumbian Peru, covering a maximum area of 15 square km with 10 huge walled compounds built of ADOBE and averaging 8–18 hectares in area. These contained the royal apartments, store houses and mausoleums of successive rulers. Between these, and all around the city, were streets, houses, PLATFORM MOUNDS with ceremonial buildings, garden plots and fields. The Chimu built vast irrigation systems that linked several adjacent valleys and enabled them to cultivate crops on an intensive basis. They were masters of metalcraft, weaving, and of mass-produced pottery moulded into many shapes and styles. Their last emperor, Minchancamen, was still in the process of extending Chimu dominion when his empire was invaded from the

north by the Incas who subsequently carried him off as prisoner to Cuzco.

CHINAMPA Artificial islands built with vegetation and mud from lake bottoms, created for the intensive cultivation of crops such as maize and vegetables. The system was important in Mexico during AZTEC times, when it helped to sustain the large urban population of Tenochtitlan. Remnants of the system still function in Mexico today.

■ **CH'IN DYNASTY** The Ch'in, victorious at the end of the PERIOD OF WARRING STATES of the CHOU dynasty of China, unified the country in 221 BC under the emperor Shih Huang Ti, who set up an efficient, bureaucratic government. He joined together stretches of pre-existing walls into the GREAT WALL. This, and the use of long, narrow iron swords, were important factors in the military successes of the Ch'in. The Ch'in dynasty continued until 206 BC and the start of the HAN dynasty.

CHIPCARVING A technique originally used in the carving of hardwood and adapted by the Romans to metalwork. A running lozenge-pattern of conjoined Xs is marked out on the surface to be decorated. Chisel cuts are made along each line, the deepest part of the cut at the centre of the X. The result is a pyramid-shaped hole which, cast in metal, is light-catching and glittering. The Germanic metal-workers of southern Scandinavia adopted this mode of decoration and used it extensively on brooches and belt-plates in the 5th–6th centuries AD. Later it was adapted further and featured strongly in ANIMAL ORNAMENT.

CHIPPING FLOOR Also known as a 'working floor'. The area in which the chipping of stone was carried out, a process that produces great quantities of waste FLAKES. In favourable circumstances, stone age chipping floors may survive undisturbed. It is then sometimes possible to reconstruct CORES by fitting flakes together.

CHIUSI, Italy This site lies about 25km south-west of lake Trasimeno and was anciently known as Clusium. Chiusi was one of the major inland ETRUSCAN centres and has been in continuous occupation from late VILLANOVAN times until the present day. It was at its most prosperous during the 5th century BC. The city is surrounded by large cemeteries of cremation tombs with CANOPIC jars and funerary statues. A few CHAMBER TOMBS exist with wall paintings as at TARQUINIA.

CHOGA ZANBIL
see SUSA

CHOLULA, Mexico A large urban and CEREMONIAL CENTRE in the Puebla region, important for its influence in religion, politics and trade in the Classic and Postclassic Periods (*see* MESOAMERICA). Cholula was first occupied in Preclassic times, when a small PYRAMID only 17m high was constructed. This was enlarged four times until it came to be the largest man-made structure in the New World, 55m high and covering 16 hectares. Today it is surmounted by a Spanish Colonial church. In the early Postclassic the site was occupied by the Olmeca–Xicalanca 'Historic Olmecs' who dominated the region; Cholula was an active centre down to the Conquest. Many of the buildings date from the Classic period and show influences from the nearby great

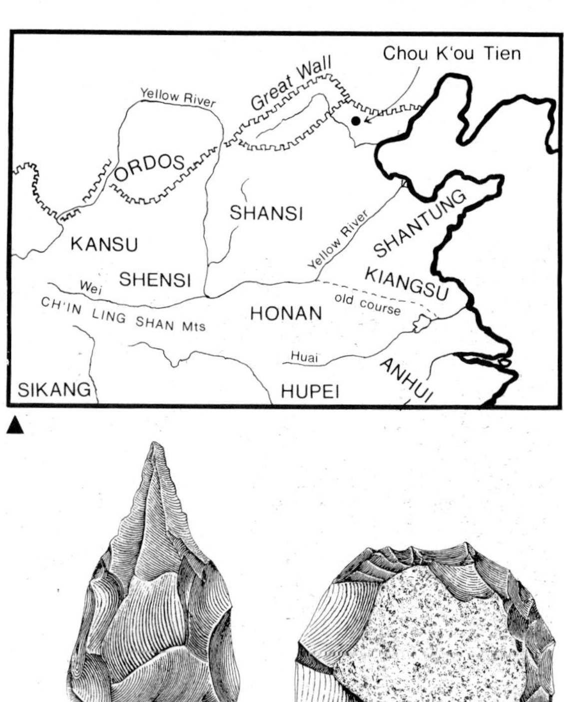

city of TEOTIHUACAN which controlled most of Mesoamerica until its fall. The typical TALUD-TABLERO architectural feature is present and there are fine polychrome frescoes of life-size figures drinking. Cholula is a centre for the manufacture of the bright polychrome Mixteca-Puebla pottery which spread widely during the Postclassic period.

CHOPPER A tool made out of a large pebble or lump of stone, with a working edge flaked from one side only. Like the CHOPPING TOOL, it was probably a crude all-purpose instrument, for use in cutting up game, plants, etc. Characteristic of OLDOWAN industries.

CHOPPING TOOL A pebble-tool with a cutting edge flaked from two directions (*see* CHOPPER). Especially characteristic of Middle PLEISTOCENE industries in Asia, e.g. CHOU-K'OU-TIEN.

● **CHOU DYNASTY** In 1027 BC SHANG rule was overthrown by the Chou dynasty, who invaded eastwards from their home in Shensi and Shansi, and pushed onwards to the sea, establishing feudal states. The early periods, known as the Western Chou, were based around Tsung Chou in Shensi until 771 BC when the capital was moved to LOYANG, Honan. The Chou dominated north China until the unification of the country in 221 BC, by a CH'IN emperor. Although settlement sites have been excavated, it is mainly tombs which have provided information to complement the written histories. The high-calibre bronze-work is a feature of the Chou, with new shapes and decorative styles, notably in ritual vessels, which at times seem regionally based. Inscriptions on the vessels tell of their presentation as gifts in ceremonies. Iron-casting in the Chou period is an early technological achievement in China, coming in about the 6th century BC, far earlier than such techniques in Europe. The late Chou period saw the wider use of iron for everyday implements. Bronze continued to be important for weaponry, though the single-edged sword of iron was known *c* 3rd century BC, and in the following centuries, especially during the HAN period, most weapons were made of iron. Use of the chariot continued in the Chou period, and buried examples accompanied by horses and charioteers are known, mainly from the Liu Li Ko burial pit, where 19 chariots were unearthed. At another site, Shang Ts'un Ling, earth casts have preserved the virtually intact shapes of 5 out of 11 chariots. By the last few centuries of Chou rule, central control had deteriorated, and in the resulting internal warfare of the PERIOD OF WARRING STATES, *c* 403–221 BC, the Ch'in dynasty was victorious, uniting the country under a single ruler.

▲ **CHOU-K'OU-TIEN, China** A major archaeological site with its first human occupation dating back to the Middle PLEISTOCENE. Located 42km south-west of Peking, it has been known archaeologically since 1918 for the many fossiliferous localities in the limestone caves and fissures of the area. Locality 1 is considered the most important, as it has yielded many human fossils and a great number of stone artefacts. The bones of early man found at this locality, often referred to as PEKING MAN, include those of more than 40 individuals, 15 of them children. Bones of numerous associated animal species have been found – mainly deer, though including remains of leopard, cavebear, sabre-tooth tiger, hyena, elephant, horse and boar. Besides hunting, early man also subsisted by collecting wild fruits, nuts, and other plants. The way some

of the human bones were broken may indicate cannibalism. The many pieces of charcoal found in the cave are evidence that Peking man knew the use of fires, and charred bones show that he cooked meat at times. His tools (some 100,000 stone implements) are mainly of quartz, fashioned by flaking and hammering into artefacts such as SCRAPERS, points and CHOPPERS.

Chou-k'ou-tien seems to have been occupied for some time; in the upper deposits, gradual progression in toolmaking skills can be seen. In the Upper Cave, specimens of HOMO SAPIENS were discovered. With his stone tools were found bone needles. Ornaments in the form of perforated teeth of deer, fox and polecat, along with shells and fishbones for stringing, were also unearthed. This Upper Cave seems to have been a burial place, as the earth had been strewn with haematite, perhaps as part of the funeral ritual.

CHRISTIANITY The influence of Christianity on archaeology is slight until the 4th century AD when CONSTANTINE accepted it as the official religion of the Roman empire. After this churches appeared and pagan temples were desecrated. The major period of conversion was in the 5th century after which Europe can be taken for the most part as a Christian area.

The earliest churches in Rome are houses simply converted by the addition of an altar. They are called *tituli* (there is one under St John in Lateran, Rome) and tend to be of 3rd century date. After the official acceptance of the religion these disappear and more conventional churches are built. The BASILICA is thought to be one of the origins of the early shape of a church, i.e. an apse and aisled nave. Some churches are round (e.g. Santo Stephano Rotundo, Rome), and probably derive from Roman MAUSOLEA. Other famous early churches are Sta Maria Maggiore, Rome (4th century), San Vitale, Ravenna (5th–6th century), and Hagia Sophia, Constantinople (6th century).

CHULLPA Stone or ADOBE burial towers of rectangular or cylindrical shape found in parts of South America, especially around lake Titicaca. The earliest crude examples are associated with TIAHUANACO pottery, but many date to the INCA horizon and are constructed of dressed stone.

CIMMERIANS A people who originally lived north of the Black Sea but were displaced south-westwards by the SCYTHIANS in the 8th century BC. Both Scythians and Cimmerians buried their dead in timber-framed TUMULI. A nomadic people, they were probably responsible for the spread of cart and horse burials in 8th-century BC Europe (the waggon or cart burials as far as France). The Cimmerians may have introduced horse riding into Europe, and the custom of using horse-bits with cheek pieces made of antler. *See* HOHMICHELE burial.

CIPPI Small STELAE found during later dynasties of Egyptian civilization. Their purpose was amuletic: to avoid by magical means toxic bites and stings. The design shows in raised relief a naked god HORUS the child (Harpokrates) wearing the curled side-lock that indicates his youth as the young son of ISIS. He stands on the backs of two crocodiles, holding in each hand dangerous or poisonous animals – lion, gazelle, scorpion, snake. Above his head is the semi-leonine face of the beneficial god Bes. This symbolism, together with prophylactic texts, made up

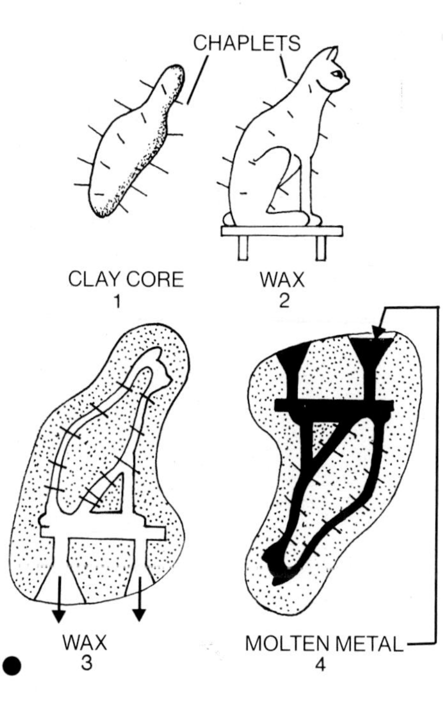

an ingenious amuletic device to counter superstitions and fears by presenting, as a *fait accompli*, the destruction of obnoxious forces by the young Horus.

CIRCUS An elongated race-track for horses, which developed from the Greek hippodrome. In Greece there were also stadia for foot-races (e.g. at OLYMPIA) usually rounded out at both ends. These died out in Roman times and only the circus survived. The track was open-ended at the starting point and had a barrier or *spina* down the middle to form a circuit. The most famous example, the Circus Maximus at Rome, was 600 × 200m and could hold 250,000 spectators. Few traces now exist. Good surviving examples are at Perge, MERIDA, and LEPTIS MAGNA. It is essentially a Mediterranean monument.

CIRENCESTER, England The largest town of Roman Britain after London. It was originally a fort built *c* AD 49 but the civil settlement continued after the fort was abandoned in the 70s and became the local tribal capital, Corinium Dobunnorum. The FORUM and BASILICA were exceptionally large and the wall circuit also big. Cirencester did not decline in the 3rd century as many British towns did (e.g. GLOUCESTER) and in the 4th century became the capital of Britannia Prima (probably the south-west part of the country) after the subdivision of the province. The site was occupied until its abandonment in the 5th century.

● **CIRE PERDUE** An ingenious technique, also known as the lost-wax method, for casting awkwardly-shaped objects in metal. The object is modelled in wax (2) over a core of clay (1) out of which protrude *chaplets* (supports). An outer layer of clay is applied to the wax model (3). Then the whole is baked in an oven to harden the clay. The wax melts and runs out of the mould, leaving an impression of its shape in the clay mould. The clay mould is then filled with the molten metal (4). After cooling, the mould is broken away from the casting, and leaves a metal object in the shape of the wax original. Objects made with this technique were found in the Royal Cemetery of UR indicating that it was known as early as 2800 BC in SUMER. The technique was employed in many parts of the world.

CIST A wooden or stone box for containing a human burial. Small cists of stone slabs are frequently covered by a BARROW.

▲ **CIVITAS (plural civitates)** The Roman name for the native tribal divisions of, e.g., Britain and Gaul. For administrative purposes the Romans incorporated the *civitates* into their own system, although their groupings do not necessarily correspond to the earlier native divisions: where for example no convenient civitas existed, an arbitrary grouping would be formed, e.g. the Regnenses of Sussex. There are some who deny the validity of the word in a Roman context, but it is generally employed and is supported by evidence from inscriptions. *See also:* PAGUS.

CLACTONIAN A crude Lower PALAEOLITHIC FLINT INDUSTRY of Mindel–Riss date (*see* GLACIATIONS), apparently restricted to Britain. It is characterized by thick, heavy FLAKES with prominent bulbs of percussion, and simple CHOPPING TOOLS. Related industries without HANDAXES extend across the north European plain through into east Asia. At the TYPE-SITE (Clacton-on-Sea, Essex) and at SWANSCOMBE, Kent, the Clactonian was succeeded

■

by a Middle ACHEULEAN industry, suggesting contemporaneity with the earliest Acheulean handaxe tradition.

The technological term 'Clactonian notch', describing a notch produced by the removal from a piece of flint of a single FLAKE, is not confined in its use to Clactonian industries.

CLASSIC [or Florescent] PERIOD
see MESOAMERICA

CLASSIS BRITANNICA The 'British Fleet' of the Roman navy, stationed at Boulogne and at several British ports, including DOVER, and responsible for patrolling the shores of Britain. Its main purpose was to supply the army in Britain and to move troops to and from the island, but it was used also in the Claudian offensive and in the early campaigns of Vespasian, AGRICOLA and FRONTINUS. In the late 2nd century AD its main duty was to patrol against the activities of Germanic and, later, Irish pirates; and it is likely that the fleet acted closely with the SAXON SHORE system. CARAUSIUS, an admiral of the Fleet, usurped the purple in Britain in the late 3rd century.

CLAUDIUS, Tiberius Claudius Nero Germanicus (10 BC–AD 54) The emperor responsible for the Roman conquest of Britain, Claudius came to the throne in AD 41 at a late age, having been chosen as emperor by the army after the murder of his nephew, Gaius Caligula. He was an eager historian and antiquarian, and is supposed to have been the last man to read the language of the ETRUSCANS. He suffered from severe physical disabilities and relied heavily upon his ministers, especially the freedman Narcissus; but proved himself an able ruler, modelling himself on AUGUSTUS. He himself played a small part in the invasion of Britain (AD 43), and celebrated a triumph. He was deified after death, and several temples dedicated to him have been identified, as at CAMULODUNUM.

CLIMATIC OPTIMUM A term now not widely used. It described the time during the POSTGLACIAL PERIOD when the climate was at its most temperate. The period roughly corresponds to that represented by the Atlantic period in modern terminology. *See* POSTGLACIAL PERIOD.

■ **CLOISONNÉ** Flat-cut precious or semi-precious stones, MILLEFIORI glass or ENAMEL may be set in a network of gold or silver cells built up from thin vertical bands of metal soldered or cast to a base plate of silver or gold. In the best-quality work a small piece of stamped foil is placed on the floor of each cell and gives a scintillating effect to the light reflected through the stone. This technique probably originated in the Black Sea area among the GOTHS and spread across Europe to the FRANKS and Anglo-Saxons, all of whom produced superbly colourful polychrome jewellery using many garnets and other stones imported from India.

CLOVIS A locality on the High Plains of eastern New Mexico, USA, Clovis is the TYPE-SITE for a distinctive form of north American fluted spear point, which is of lanceolate shape, between 70–120mm long and has a concave fluted base. Clovis points together with the FOLSOM type which developed from them (*see* BLACKWATER DRAW) are diagnostic of the BIG GAME HUNTING TRADITION of North America. The Clovis period is dated predominantly

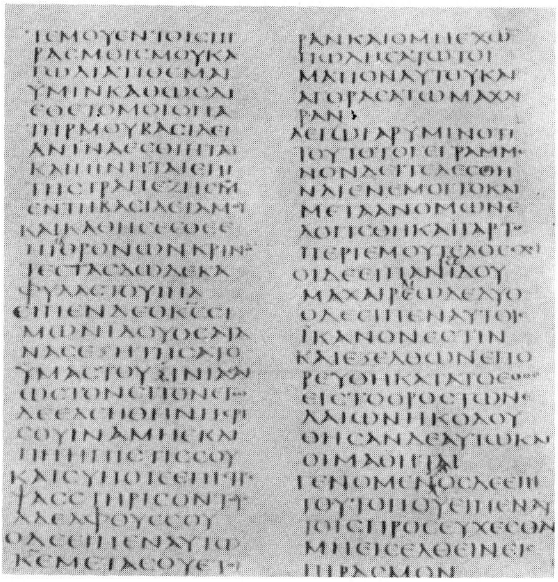

●

■

to the TWO CREEKS interstadial between 10,000 and 9000 BC. Other important Clovis finds occur at the Dent site in Colorado, dated *c* 9200 BC. They are widespread across the USA and their true region of origin is unknown, although earliest finds point to the south-western Great Plains.

COCHISE CULTURE Part of the DESERT tradition of southern Arizona, USA, which emerged *c* 7000 BC and lasted to the beginning of the Christian era. The earliest phase at Sulphur Springs has extinct fauna such as mammoth, horse and bison together with simple milling stones and big-game hunting equipment. The Chiricahua phase, 5–2000 BC and the succeeding and final San Pedro phase, have larger settlements and in the latter, intensive food gathering and incipient agriculture predominate. The archaeological record shows these changes through increasing refinements in the milling and plant-processing artefacts and in the introduction of basketry, textiles and finally pottery. (*See* BAT CAVE, and TEHUACAN for early agriculture.) By the close of the 1st millennium BC, the Cochise culture merged with the SOUTHWESTERN tradition.

CODEX [plural codices] A collection of sheets of writing folded and fastened together at one edge, sometimes between protective covers. During the 2nd and 3rd centuries AD the codex replaced the long scroll which was cumbersome to use. Both papyrus and parchment were used for this early kind of book. Religious writings, in ● particular those of the Christian Church, were the first to be kept in this way. Paul's request in II Timothy 4:13 may well be for codices.

In America the term is used for native Mexican or Maya manuscripts from before or immediately after the Spanish Conquest. Pictographic symbols were painted on sheets of bark-cloth or deer-skin which, when unfolded, stretched ▲ 10m or more in length. Four pre-Spanish MAYA manuscripts are known, the most famous is the Dresden Codex. Many more come from Mexico. Of these, the finest are MIXTEC and frequently contain historical and dynastic information. The Codex Mendoza is a copy of an AZTEC document and relates details of conquests, tribute and aspects of daily life. The Maya Chilam Balam books and the Mexican Tira de la Peregrinación were all produced soon after the Spanish Conquest.

CODY COMPLEX A north American flint industry of the late BIG GAME HUNTING TRADITION dated *c* 7500–5000 BC. Both Eden and Scottsbluff varieties of stemmed and PRESSURE-FLAKED projectile points were found here together with a distinctive asymmetrical stemmed knife called the Cody knife; scrapers, perforators, choppers, pounders and grinding stones also characterize the inventory which is usually associated with bison-butchering stations and camps.

■ **COFFIN TEXTS** In Middle Kingdom Egypt, large coffins of rectangular shape were most popular and standard for burials at all levels of society. Highly decorated with representations of food and objects for use in next life, they carried, in hundreds of columns of cursive hieroglyphs, spells to prevent hunger, thirst and obnoxious situations happening in the underworld. Much material was taken from Pyramid Texts and modified for suitable use by private individuals instead of only royalty – the collapse of central authority at the end of the Old Kingdom meant the usurpation of certain royal privileges and had widened the

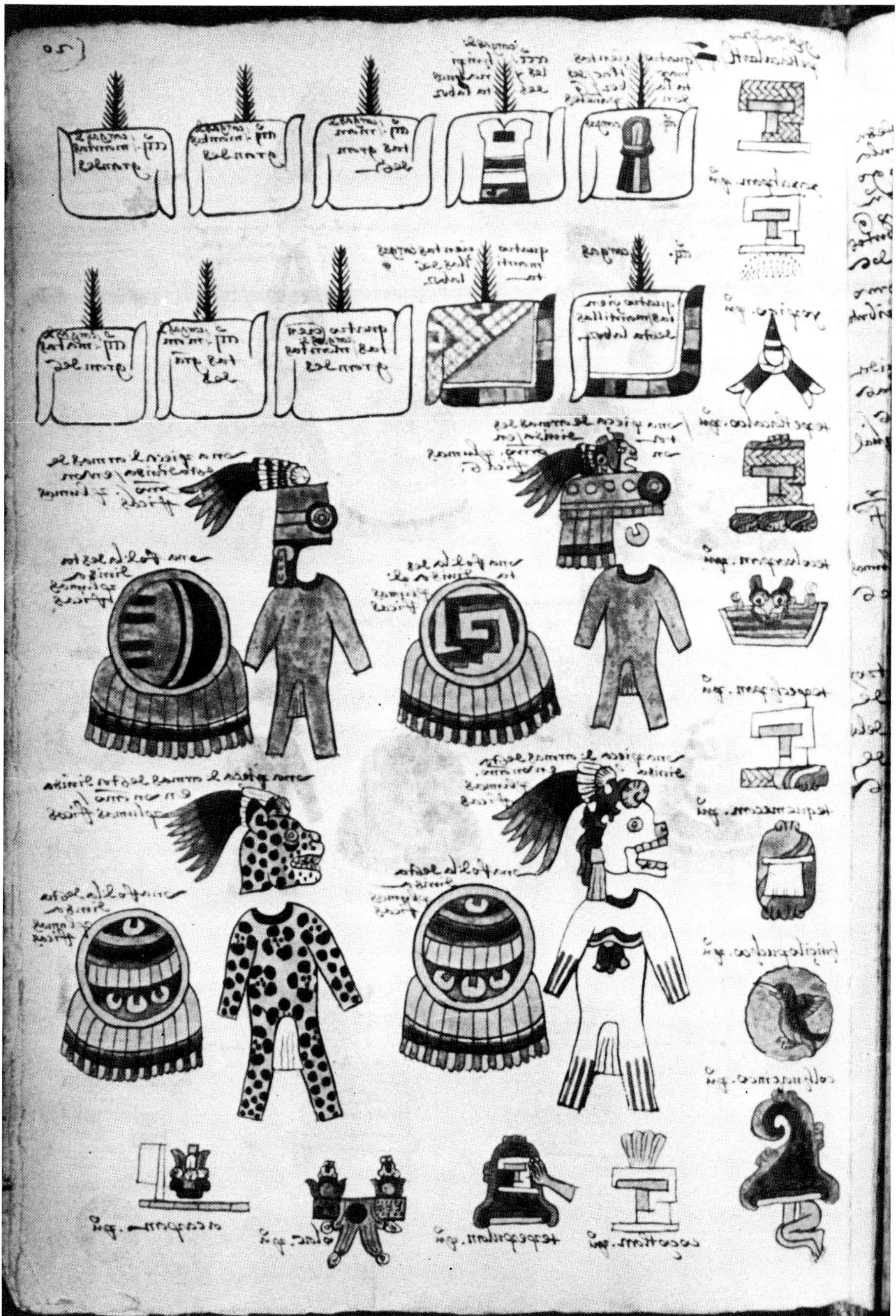

circle of participants in the underworld of OSIRIS. New spells reflecting contemporary religious tenets were added, and groups of spells clustered together to form longer passages – the prototype of the 'chapters' in the papyrus roll commonly known as BOOK OF THE DEAD.

Spells in coffins were introduced by rubrics giving synopsis and motive, usually in red ink, while the main text of the spell was in black ink. Coffin Texts were rarely put on walls of burial chambers, although a notable exception is the tomb of Queen Nefru (Dynasty XI) at DEIR EL-BAHRI.

COIMBATORE, India The district of Coimbatore lies on the overland route to ARIKAMEDU and the Madras coast. The coin hoards, mainly of 1st century AD, found throughout the district must represent not only the treasure of local mineral prospectors and the owners of pepper estates but also the loot of brigandage for which Coimbatore's situation at the convergence of three south Indian kingdoms suited admirably. *See also:* MONSOON.

COLOGNE, Germany The chief Roman town on the middle Rhine. It began as a civil settlement of the local tribe, the Ubii, but became a Roman colony in AD 50. The Roman town was used as a major centre in FRANKISH times and many aspects of its life, e.g. the glass industry, were preserved. Many mosaics and smaller finds are still to be seen, as well as part of the walls and the governor's palace.

COLONIA A town founded by the Romans, the populace of which had the status of Roman citizens: most, though not all, *coloniae* were founded to house discharged veterans of the army. The coloniae were self-administrating, with two pairs of annual magistrates responsible for justice and for the roads and buildings. There was also a local senate of about 100 members. The first colonia in Britain was Colonia Victricensis, at CAMULODUNUM, founded in AD 49 for veterans. The GREEKS founded many coloniae as trading stations: MARSEILLES is an example. *See also* MUNICIPIUM.

COLOSSEUM, Rome The largest Roman AMPHITHEATRE and the earliest one surviving apart from POMPEII. It was built by Vespasian as an arena for public entertainments and is oval in plan, 200m long and 50m high. He adopted the system of radial and annular passages used in THEATRES to facilitate entry and exit, so that some 50,000 people could be accommodated.

COLOSSI OF MEMNON, Egypt These two statues mark the entrance to an almost vanished funerary temple of Amenophis III (Dynasty XVIII). Height over 15.6m, not including bases (2.3m). They represent Amenophis III wearing NEMES headcloth on a throne with the emblem of united Egypt on the sides and small statues of the king's mother and wife beside each leg. Sandstone blocks making up the statues probably came from quarries at Memphis.

The northern Colossus was damaged in earthquake (27 BC) giving it a ringing noise at sudden changes in temperature (especially at sunrise) due to vibrating stones. Always a tourist attraction, its inscriptions in Greek and Latin on base and legs give names and dates of visitors (including HADRIAN) hearing statue apparently 'singing'. SEPTIMIUS SEVERUS repaired the damage, causing the phenomenon to stop.

Memnon, Trojan hero son of dawn goddess, is the evocative but wrong name applied by ancient tourists to these statues.

● **COLOUR COATED WARE** A type of Roman pottery, popular in north France, the Rhine and Britain in 2nd–4th centuries AD named for its black or brown slip. The decoration was usually in BARBOTINE, sometimes picked out with white paint. Centres of British production were WATER NEWTON, COLCHESTER, and the New Forest. On the continent, the Rhineland near TRIER and LEZOUX in central France produced this ware.

COLUMBA *c* AD 563 St Columba established himself on the barren island of IONA whence he led a successful mission to the northern PICTS. Under his leadership Iona was first among the Scottish monasteries, and consequently DALRIADA became a vital source of Irish Celtic Christian influence which was eventually transferred to the NORTHUMBRIAN church. After the failure of the Roman mission under PAULINUS in the north, a group of monks from Iona led by St Aidan founded the monastery on LINDISFARNE.

COLUMN Free-standing uprights were used throughout the pre-classical world to support superstructures. Egyptian technology had enabled the use of stone, but elsewhere, until the 7th century BC, columns had generally been of wood. The circular stone column of the Greek architect was developed from then on as the major element in the orders of architecture: Doric, Ionic and Corinthian. *See also* ARCHITECTURE, ROMAN.

COMBE-GRENAL, France A ROCK-SHELTER near Domme, Dordogne, containing Lower and Middle PALAEOLITHIC deposits. Late ACHEULEAN remains are buried by 55 successive layers attributable to the MOUSTERIAN. These layers contain material of all of the five main varieties of the Mousterian recognized in Europe.

CONSTANTINE THE GREAT, Flavius Valerius Constantinus (AD 288–337) Perhaps the most important of the later Roman Emperors, he came to the throne in 306. He was the son of Constantius Chlorus, who died at YORK, and a British woman Helena. He came to power after defeating, in the battle of the Milvian Bridge, his rival to the throne Maxentius; before the battle he believed that he saw a vision of the cross, and his consequent protection of Christianity was a turning-point in the history of that religion. He introduced religious toleration by the Edict of Milan in 313, and worked for Christian unity. He was responsible for massive reforms of the army and administration: he reformed the currency, and fixed prices. The capital of the Empire was moved to BYZANTIUM, renamed CONSTANTINOPLE. He died, after a death-bed conversion, in 337.

CONSTANTINOPLE, Turkey This city, on a prominent site commanding the route from the Black Sea to the Aegean, was founded as the capital of the Eastern Roman Empire in AD 330 by the Emperor CONSTANTINE THE GREAT. The city, sometimes known as New Rome, was built upon the site occupied by ancient BYZANTIUM. Although Constantinople was originally planned and built in the 4th century AD, the monuments that remain today date mainly from the 6th century rebuilding after large parts of the city

had been destroyed during the reign of JUSTINIAN. The new capital, unlike Rome, the capital of the Western Empire, remained the seat of Roman emperors throughout the Byzantine empire until its destruction in 1453 by the Ottoman Turks. A number of monuments still stand today, the most famous perhaps the church of Hagia Sophia, an enormous domed building constructed by order of Justinian and finished in AD 537. Other imperial Roman monuments are the defensive walls (built in the reign of Theodosius II), the aqueducts (which are still standing within the city), and the cisterns (vast vaulted underground water storage tanks), some of which are still in use. Remains of many other minor buildings of Roman and Byzantine Constantinople can still be seen, including theatres and the hippodrome.

COPAN, West Honduras, Central America A large Classic period MAYA CEREMONIAL CENTRE 600m up in forested hills, important for its wealth of stone carving in heavy ornate relief. The 'acropolis' comprises the main group of ceremonial buildings and includes the famous monumental staircase 27m high decorated with hieroglyphs, the Great PLAZA over 210m long with its carved stela and altars, and the famous BALL COURT.

COPPER AGE [Chalcolithic] A term for the period at which copper was used but BRONZE not yet introduced. Stone was still the most important material for tools; copper, which is softer than flint, was used mainly for ornaments. There were two centres of copper-working in Europe before 2000 BC, one in Iberia, and one in eastern Europe exploiting Transylvanian ores. *See also:* BEAKER PEOPLE.

COPROLITE Fossilized or otherwise preserved dung of human or animal origin. Analysis of the contents can give information on the diet or the internal parasites of prehistoric man and his animals.

COPTIC The name given to the ancient Egyptian language (and the basically Greek script used to write it) in its final manifestation. It was the medium by which Christian missionaries in Egypt aided the conversion of the country to the new religion by presenting the gospels in the vernacular. Coptic therefore is nearly always understood as referring to the Christian period before the Arab invasion (AD 641). The Coptic church still uses this ancient language in its ceremonies but it has not been a spoken idiom since the sixteenth century AD. The origins of Coptic are not, however, due to Christianity but to the simplification of the HIEROGLYPHS and DEMOTIC into an alphabetic script which would include writing in vowels omitted in all the other Ancient Egyptian scripts. This was felt necessary by native Egyptians following their traditional religion and superstitions, where in order for a word or a god's name to be magically or amuletically effective, correct pronounciation of it was essential. When the script became standardized in the fourth century AD it consisted of the Greek alphabet, already well-known in Egypt from officials and the trading community during the Ptolemaic period, with the addition of seven sound-signs from the Demotic script. There are five principal regional variations in Coptic, the most important dialects being Sahidic (the classical literary form) and Bohairic used in present-day church services. Although Coptic represents a much later stage of ancient Egyptian (with Greek influence), knowledge of it was invaluable to CHAMPOLLION

in his decipherment of hieroglyphs. Modern scholarship still draws on Coptic to understand grammatical subtleties of the pharaonic language.

● **CORBELLING** A technique, also called false-vaulting, used in the roof construction of MEGALITHIC chambers throughout western Europe from at least the middle 3rd millennium BC in PASSAGE and GALLERY GRAVES such as in the BOYNE area, or MAES HOWE. In the Aegean, corbelling does not appear before about 1600 BC, and in this region it is derived from earlier circular stone-vaulted tombs. Corbel or false arches were a distinguishing feature of MAYA architecture in Mesoamerica. Each successive stone course projected slightly above the one below until the walls either met or could be spanned by a CAPSTONE.

CORBRIDGE, Northumberland A Roman fort in the north of England. There was activity at Corbridge during the reign of SEPTIMIUS SEVERUS, including the building of great granaries (*see* HORREA). It has been suggested that a great unfinished store-building was the headquarters for a legionary fortress which was never built, but it is more likely that this and the granaries were intended to hold supplies for a Scottish expedition. There was a large civilian VICUS around the military installations.

CORDED-WARE/BATTLE-AXE CULTURE A NEOLITHIC CULTURE which spread, perhaps from Russia, into east and central Europe, the north European plain, Scandinavia and Holland; reaching the Rhineland by *c* 2500 BC. All over this area are found pots which had been decorated when wet with cord impressions. Stone shaft-hole axes were included in the male graves. These were under BARROWS, sometimes with a mortuary house like those of the KURGAN culture of the same period. *C* 2000 BC, BEAKER groups moved into the areas occupied by battle-axe cultures, and hybrid corded beakers became the dominant pottery.

CORE A piece of stone or 'nucleus' from which BLADES or FLAKES are removed. An essential requisite of a core is that it should have a flat surface, or 'striking platform', on which percussion or pressure can be applied to detach flakes (*see* FLAKING). During use, a core demands frequent trimming to enable flakes, and especially blades, to be successfully struck off. This trimming is sometimes erroneously described as 'SCRAPER RETOUCH', producing a spurious 'core scraper'. An implement, such as a HANDAXE, that is produced by working down a larger piece of stone is called a 'core-tool'.

CORINTH, Greece This town occupied a position of great importance in Classical times: it controlled the entry into the Peloponnese from the mainland and also trade from the Aegean into the gulf of Corinth. The 7th century BC was the ▲ town's greatest period when its trade, especially in pottery, covered much of the Mediterranean. By the 5th century it had been eclipsed by ATHENS but was still important enough to be razed by Mummius in 146 BC for resistance to the ROMANS. However, Corinth became a thriving Roman colony under JULIUS CAESAR and to this period most of the remains belong. Its exact dating makes it crucial to the cross-dating of other sites in the Roman east. It was the capital of Roman Greece (Achaia) and lasted into the 6th century AD.

▲

■

CORINTHIAN
see CAPITALS; COLUMNS

CORTAILLOD CULTURE The TYPE-SITE of this WESTERN NEOLITHIC culture is a village of pile dwellings on the edge of Lake Neuchâtel near Cortaillod in Switzerland. Contemporary with the more southerly LAGOZZA culture, the waterside location of settlements has resulted in the preservation of an unusually complete range of artefacts. Axes mounted in antler sleeves were used to fell trees, both for clearing forest for the cultivation of wheat, barley, peas, beans and lentils, and for shaping timbers for rectangular wooden houses. Wood, bark and basketry containers survive, as do fish nets and many linen textiles. It has been suggested that the wild apples collected were used for making a form of cider. Cattle, pigs and sheep were among the animals reared.

CRANNOG A settlement built on the edge of a lake, consisting of a brushwood and rubble island with an oak log surface, topped by a single ROUND HOUSE. In Ireland they date from the NEOLITHIC, in Scotland all are Roman Iron Age or later in date. Some were still in use in medieval times. *See also:* BISKUPIN; LAKE VILLAGE.

■ **CRAWFORD, O. G. S. (1886–1957)** A pioneer of field archaeology in Britain. He was among the first to realize the potential of AIR PHOTOGRAPHY and reconnaissance. His early work was published in *Wessex from the Air* (with A. Keiller, 1928), and *Air Photography for Archaeologists* (1929). He was the first archaeology officer to the Ordnance Survey (1920–51) and there developed the cartographic recording of archaeology, especially in period maps (e.g. *Map of Roman Britain*). In 1927 he founded and was the first editor of the journal *Antiquity* which fosters a closer understanding between the various branches of archaeology. Other main books: *Field Archaeology* (1921); *Archaeology in the Field* (1953).

CREMATION The practice of burning the corpse after death, as opposed to INHUMATION. In prehistory the ashes were often buried in an urn (*see* URNFIELD).

CRESWELLIAN The final Upper PALAEOLITHIC CULTURE of Britain, present at a number of sites including Kent's Cavern, Devon, and a series of caves at Creswell Crags, Derbyshire, from which the name derives. It dates mainly from the Older Dryas and the Allerød late glacial stages (*see* PLEISTOCENE). Comparisons have been made with the MAGDALENEAN and the HAMBURGIAN (Older Dryas) and especially the Tjongerian (Allerød) of Belgium and the Netherlands. It has sometimes been suggested that the latter descended from the Creswellian. The characteristic flint implement is a blade blunted down the whole of one edge to give an angular shape: the 'angle-backed blade'.

CRIS
see STARČEVO

CRO-MAGNON, France A ROCK SHELTER near Les Eyzies, Dordogne, discovered in 1868, with a burial of five adults, in deposits containing AURIGNACIAN stone tools. Although belonging to the HOMO SAPIENS group, 'Cro-Magnon man' is believed by some to represent a distinct race in the later Upper PLEISTOCENE, possibly displacing the partly contemporary NEANDERTHAL man.

CROMLECH
see MEGALITH

CROWNS (Egyptian) Most politically significant is the Double Crown – called Sekhemti (The Powerful Two) by Egyptians, Pschent by Greeks – symbolizing union of northern and southern Egypt into one state (*c* 3100 BC). It combines the crowns of the predynastic rulers of Lower and Upper Egypt: (1) Red Crown (Deshert) of the north, worn by war-goddess Neith and fire-spitting cobra Wadjet. Perhaps of wickerwork, it was flat-topped but with a tall thin back-piece and a curl projecting upwards. (2) White Crown (Hedjet) of the south, worn by vulture-goddess Nekhbet. Perhaps of animal-skin, it had a high conical shape with bulbous top.

The Blue Crown (Khepresh) becomes one of commonest worn from the end of Dynasty XVIII. It had a comfortable and convenient shape. Pharaoh wears it in war-chariot, officiating on state and religious occasions, or relaxing in his palace. Perhaps of leather with metal circlets or studs, from the front it had a half-acorn shape with streamline wings.

Many other complex elaborate crowns were worn by kings and gods e.g. the Atef crown – tall, plumed, sun's-disk ram-horns – associated with OSIRIS.

CRUSADERS Christians of western Europe who made a series of military expeditions aiming to take control of the Holy City of Jerusalem and other places associated with the earthly life of Jesus Christ. Between AD 1095 and 1291 there were eight such campaigns. The first crusade in 1095 established four principalities: Edessa, Antioch, Tripoli and Jerusalem. Subsequent crusades tried to maintain control of these areas. By 1189, however, Saladin, the caliph of Cairo, had regained control of the kingdom of Jerusalem and much of Tripoli. The Mamluk dynasty of Egypt ended Crusader influence. Antioch fell in 1268 and the great Hospitaler fortress, Krak des Chevaliers, surrendered three years later. Tripoli and Acre were last to fall in 1291. Many castles and churches were built by the crusaders and much of their work remains.

CRYOTURBATION STRUCTURES Folded and involuted structures in the ground which are thought to have been caused by freezing and thawing of the earth under PERIGLACIAL conditions during the PLEISTOCENE. These structures are particularly obvious when different deposits, such as clays and gravels, have become mixed during this action. They have sometimes been mistaken for archaeological features.

CUCUTENI
See TRIPOLYE

CULTIVATION Man's deliberate selection and propagation of plants for his own use. The practice of cultivation marked a change in economy away from the gathering of wild plants, and to some extent involved a more settled way of life. The earliest archaeological evidence of cultivation dated to *c* 9000 BC comes from south-west Asia, where primitive domesticated strains of wheat and barley have been found. Following the appearance of the earliest cultivars, other species were domesticated, either as sources of food (e.g. oats, beans), or as sources of raw materials (e.g. flax, cotton). The appearance of cultivated plants is one of the criteria by

▲

which the beginning of the NEOLITHIC PERIOD is recognized. *See also* DOMESTICATION.

CULTURE In archaeological parlance, 'culture' has two related meanings. The difference between these is subtle enough to cause great confusion if the distinction is not made explicit, but is at the same time fundamental.

The first meaning of 'culture' is as a general term for a pattern of behaviour which is learned (i.e. communicated by one person to another) rather than biologically inherited. Archaeologists have to form an impression of the culture of ancient societies from the very limited evidence of their material creations that happen to survive.

In the second sense, archaeologists speak of 'cultures' or 'a culture' rather than 'culture' in general. At the beginning of this century in Europe, attempts were made to distinguish social or ethnic groups in the material evidence of prehistory. CHILDE did a great deal to refine this concept and he identified a succession of 'cultures' throughout Europe, each with its own history. A culture in this sense is defined by an ASSEMBLAGE of artefacts (such as pots, flint axes, beads, etc) which repeatedly occurs, but over a limited area and time. It is gradually being realized that cultures thus defined need not indicate a tribe or similar human grouping, still less a race, but this does not invalidate the idea as a way of classifying and studying the patterning of material remains.

CUMAE, Italy A site on the west coast, 30km north of POMPEII. Its importance dates from 750 BC when the Greeks founded a trading colony here, although a settlement existed from the 10th century BC. From the 4th century BC, Cumae came under the domination of Rome.

CUNEIFORM The name of the form of writing developed and used in MESOPOTAMIA *c* 3500–500 BC. Because of the difficulty of drawing curved lines on clay, the normal medium for documents and letters on the plains of Mesopotamia, the pictograms (*see* WRITING) became stylized into groups of wedge-shaped incisions. An ▲example from an inscription of the ASSYRIAN king Sennacherib illustrates some of the shapes. The stylus used by the scribe was a square-ended reed. The script is written in horizontal lines from left to right and was used for a number of languages including SUMERIAN, AKKADIAN, Elamite (*see* SUSA), and HITTITE. At UGARIT it was used for an ALPHABET.

CUNOBELIN The greatest of the BELGIC leaders, immortalized by Shakespeare. He ruled over the Catuvellauni from *c* AD 7 for almost 40 years. By AD 9 he had seized control of the territory of the Trinovantes and the town of CAMULODUNUM, which became his capital. He was on friendly terms with ROME and his tribe prospered throughout his reign. The extent of Catuvellaunian trade is shown by the distribution of Cunobelin's coins and by exotic Roman imports found at CAMULODUNUM. Most of the rich Belgic graves of AYLESFORD type were found in his territory. On his death he was succeeded in 41–2 by his two sons CARACTACUS and Togodumnus.

CURRENCY BARS A name given to elongated iron bars found in IRON AGE contexts in Britain (e.g. at MAIDEN CASTLE, GLASTONBURY and LLYN CERRIG BACH), and to a lesser extent on the continent. About 1400 are known from Britain. The most common types are sword-shaped with a pinched end, and narrow spit-shaped. Both are often found

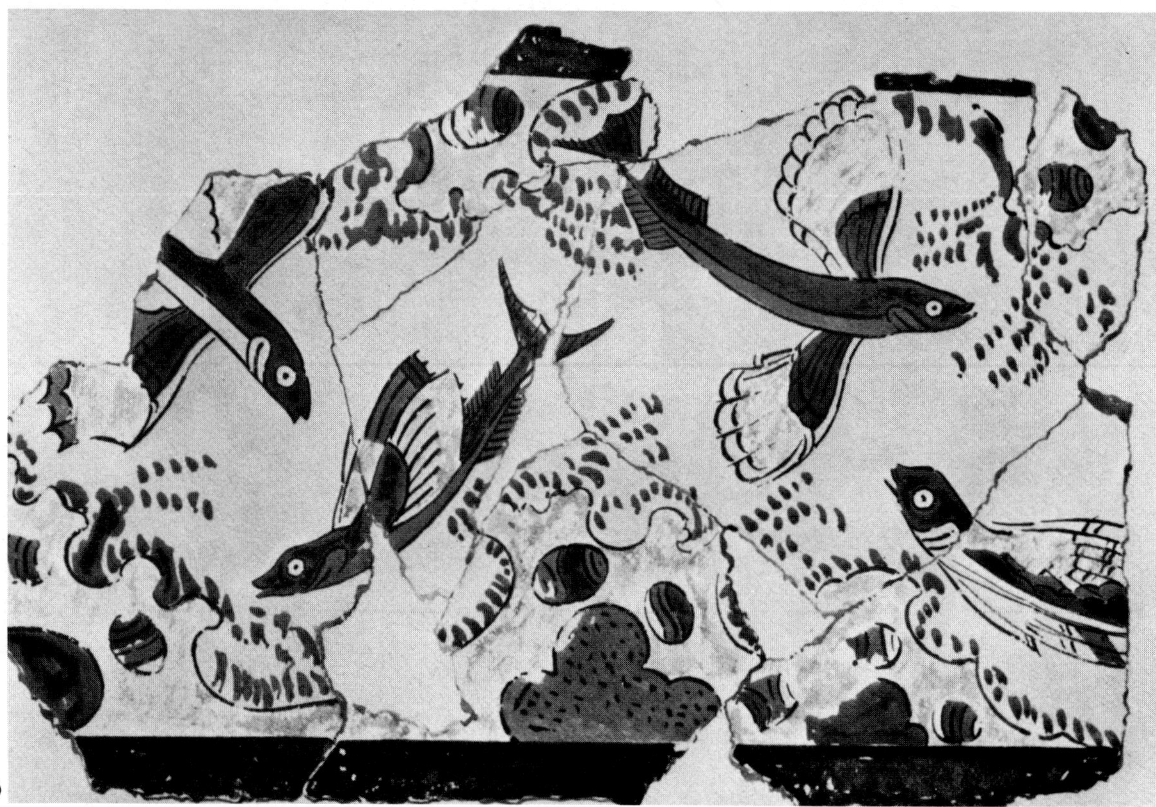

in hoards and it is assumed that these bars were used as a form of currency or barter which preceded the use of coins. On all sites where they can be dated (e.g. HOD HILL), their use had ceased before the introduction of the BELGIC coinage. Their existence suggests that iron production was a specialist industry by the 2nd century BC.

CURSUS The first cursus was discovered, and so named, by STUKELEY in the early 18th century, adjacent to STONEHENGE. It consists of two parallel banks, with their flanking quarry ditches, running for some distance across the landscape: the largest example, known as the Dorset Cursus, is some 10km long. The function of these earthworks, which are unique to the later Neolithic in Britain, can only be guessed, but an interpretation as some kind of ceremonial processional way seems acceptable.

CUTHBERT Born in AD 634, St Cuthbert first entered the monastery at Melrose where he preached for many years before being transferred to LINDISFARNE and consecrated bishop. He lived in the ascetic tradition of the Celtic church, and retired for most of his time to his isolated hermitage on the Farne Island. He died in 687 and was buried on Lindisfarne, but exhumed in 875 when the monks fled from the Danish attacks. His body was eventually reburied in Durham Cathedral in its original oak coffin, which still exists. Inside the coffin were his gold and garnet pectoral cross, a portable altar, chalice and liturgical comb, all of the 7th century. The grave was opened several times before the 19th century. Articles were not only removed from the coffin but also added to it; some of the few surviving SAXON embroideries were placed in it *c* 910.

CUZCO
See INCA

CUZOUL, France A cave containing SAUVETERRIAN and TARDENOISIAN deposits. The remains of sheep from the latter provide possible evidence for early domestication of animals in France.

● **CYCLADIC** The name for the Bronze Age in the Aegean or Cycladic islands. Early Cycladic starts *c* 3000 BC but not much is known until the Middle Cycladic, *c* 2000 BC, when the town of Phylakopi II developed on Melos. This site is a key to the chronology of the islands as it has a long occupation throughout the Bronze Age. Other sites are THERA and Paros. Phylakopi II was destroyed *c* 1750 BC but a third town succeeded it. This period, late Middle Cycladic – Late Cycladic II, is distinguished by the increasing influence of the MINOANS who placed colonies on several islands, e.g. THERA, DELOS and Kythera. Late Cycladic III sees the arrival of Late Helladic III elements which presumes Achaian (mainland) colonization, at much the same time as the decline of Minoan power.

▲ **CYPRUS** This Mediterranean island was first settled about 6000 BC by a people whose culture was found at KHIROKITIA. Nothing is known about their origin, or fate on the island. New settlers arrived at about 3500 BC and their underground dwellings found at Kalavassos are similar to those in southern Palestine at this time. Copper tools and pottery decorated with red paint on white background from Erimi of date *c* 3000 BC reveal a new cultural stage. The rich copper deposits were mined by the growing population which increased further about 2300 BC

●

▲

with an influx of people from ANATOLIA. A little of the Anatolian style as well as the exuberance of the Cypriot potter can be seen in such vessels as composite vases. Trade with the eastern Mediterranean became important after about 1900 BC and ports like ENKOMI flourished. Large amounts of MYCENAEAN pottery at sites show that after about 1400 BC trade also went westward. In the unrest of about 1200 BC much of Cyprus was destroyed. With recolonization, cities such as SALAMIS grew in size, developing their own variety of Greek culture mingled with eastern influences and local originality. Earthquake has been a constant threat to the island and few of the magnificent buildings of the Greek and Roman period remain.

DALRIADA A DARK AGE kingdom occupying roughly the area of modern Argyll. It was founded in the 5th century AD by Fergus who led the migration of SCOTS from Ireland to western Scotland. Its most famous king, Kenneth MacAlpin, conquered the PICTS *c* 843, assimilated their kingdom and so created the kernel of the kingdom of Scotland. Dalriada was an early Christian area with close links with the Celtic church in Ireland. St COLUMBA settled in IONA, a Dalriadan island, from which the conversion of northern Pictland and the reconversion of NORTHUMBRIA were spearheaded.

DAMASCUS, Syria The modern capital. The site was inhabited in prehistoric times and is mentioned in Egyptian texts and the BIBLE, but it is not until it becomes an ARAMAEAN city-state that it is well known. ISRAELITE kings after King Saul *c* 1000 BC and ASSYRIANS from Ashurnasirpal *c* 883 BC fought regularly against the Aramaeans of Damascus. It was captured by the Assyrians in 732 BC and not until 111 BC did it re-emerge as a capital city under the Seleucid king Antiochus IX. After short periods of Nabataean (*see* PETRA) and Armenian control, Damascus became a Roman city in 64 BC. The lay-out of the inner city today dates from this period.

DANELAW After the great Danish armies of AD 865–80 had gained control of most of NORTHUMBRIA, MERCIA and EAST ANGLIA, a political boundary was drawn between the occupied areas where Danish customary law prevailed (the Danelaw) and the areas which followed West Saxon or Mercian custom. In a treaty between ALFRED and Guthrum made *c* 890 the frontier was drawn up along Watling Street, i.e., roughly along a line from Chester through Shrewsbury, Lichfield, Bedford and Hertford on to London which remained in English hands. Within the Danelaw lay the confederation of the Five Boroughs: Stamford, Leicester, Derby, Nottingham and Lincoln, which remained independent until the mid 10th century when they were conquered by Edmund.

DANUBIAN The central European 'Danubian civilization' was defined by CHILDE, who split it into seven periods: Danubian I to VII. The Danubian I culture is now generally called the LINEAR POTTERY culture group, since it has been recognized outside the area drained by the Danube river. Danubian period VII was equated with the Early IRON AGE.

DARIUS I
see BEHISTUN; PERSEPOLIS

DASHUR, Egypt South of MEMPHIS, a pyramid site investigated since the early 19th century where Sneferu, founder of Dynasty IV, built two stone pyramids. Although the northern pyramid is on a large base (220m square), its height of 99m at an angle of about 43° makes it look flattened. Sneferu's southern pyramid is known as the Bent Pyramid – it slopes at 54°31′ until about 49m from the ground when the angle changes to 43°21′. Suggested reasons for this change include avoiding the masonry crushing the interior, or a hasty and careless completion. Large cedarwood beams in the burial chamber may have come from Sneferu's expedition to the Lebanon.

From the valley temple, with its reliefs of the royal estates personified, a causeway 700m long leads to the pyramid courtyard.

Other badly-ruined pyramids of this site mark the revival of pyramid-building under rulers of the Middle Kingdom; tombs of princesses revealed spectacular examples of the goldsmith's craft.

DEAD SEA SCROLLS
see QUMRAN

DEEP SEA CORES At depths of 1500–4000m considerable areas of the ocean floor are covered with an ooze named Globigerina after a type of shell which it contains. The ooze consists largely of calcium carbonate derived from the shells included in the deposit. The ratio of oxygen-16 to oxygen-18 dissolved in water depends on temperature, and is reflected in the ratio in the calcium carbonate. Analysis of oxygen-16 to oxygen-18 ratio at different points in a core sample of the ooze reflects changes in the average temperature of the ocean. These temperature fluctuations have been used in attempts to date the glacial stages of the PLEISTOCENE. So far, only the last glaciation has been successfully dated with this method.

● **DEIR el-BAHRI, Western Thebes, Egypt** (1) Pharaohs (Dynasty XI) chose this area, against a dominating mountain, for their necropolis. Nebhepetre Mentuhotep built a funerary complex of temple, rock-and-pyramid tomb combined.
(2) Senenmut, architect for queen Hatshepsut (Dynasty XVIII), built a powerful tiered temple against the mountain. An avenue of sphinxes leads to ramps rising to three terraces. Reliefs show Hatshepsut's divine birth and expedition to Punt (Somaliland?) for myrrh and exotic produce. There is a chapel to the cow-goddess Hathor, who is shown suckling the queen. Tuthmosis III, on gaining rulership, ordered mutilation of step-mother's monuments.

First excavated by MARIETTE, and still being investigated.

DEIR el-MEDINA, Western Thebes, Egypt Near the Valley of the Kings. A valuable site for village life in ancient Egypt during late New Kingdom. Masons, sculptors and artists working on royal tombs lived fairly isolated in this privileged community. Houses were of mudbrick with living rooms, terraces and cellars. The French Institute of Archaeology has extensively excavated in this area. Papyri and limestone fragments (OSTRACA) give information on stores and equipment used by workers, as well as lively sketches. Their tombs can show skill as professionals, e.g. Sennedjem 'servant in the Place of Truth' (Deir el-Medina) with vividly coloured scenes from the underworld.

A fine Ptolemaic temple near this village is dedicated to goddesses Hathor and Maat (Truth).

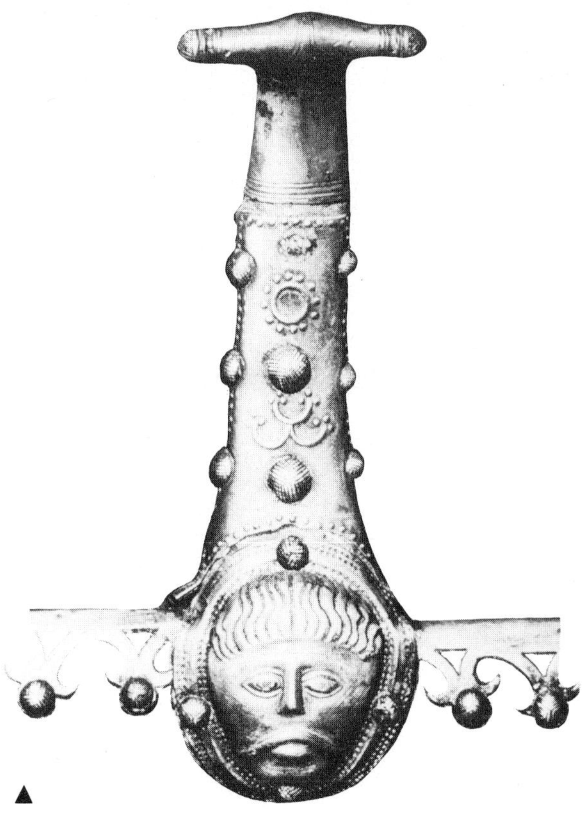

▲

■

▲ **DEJEBJERG, Denmark** A bog in Jutland where two votive waggons of the LA TÈNE period of the IRON AGE were discovered. The construction, particularly of the wheels, was highly sophisticated. They were decorated with bronze fittings like the earlier HALLSTATT waggon from VIX. *See also* GUNDESTRUP.

DELOS, Greece Aegean island, birthplace of the Greek gods Apollo and Artemis and subsequently one of the leading religious centres of the GREEKS. Earliest traces date from *c* 2000 BC and there was extensive MYCENAEAN occupation, but the first religious use of the island was in the 10th century BC when Ionian colonists set up the cult of Leto. The DORIANS brought Artemis and from the 7th century Apollo became the major object of devotion. ATHENS took care of the island in the classical period. It became a major trading centre in Roman times but was sacked in 88 and 69 BC and never really recovered.

■ **DELPHI, Greece** A religious centre of classical and HELLENISTIC Greece famous for its oracle. Dedicated to Apollo, this oracle delighted in giving evasive and ambiguous replies to its royal and imperial clientele. Its influence was greatest during the Hellenistic and Roman periods when many important decisions were made after consulting it. The clients often gave shrines or offerings as a sign of goodwill. Many such shrines survive. Also here was the *omphalos*, or the navel stone of the world.

DEMOTIC Term (meaning 'popular') used by Egyptologists to describe the latest and ultimate cursive abbreviated form of HIEROGLYPHS. In Demotic the original hieroglyphs are summarily represented and experts often have to look closely at styles of handwriting to recognize the sign from which the Demotic character is derived. It developed out of business HIERATIC as a faster script, written right to left with many signs joined together, about the time of the Saite Dynasty (XXVI).

Demotic occurs mainly in ink on papyrus or limestone flakes, although the centre section of the ROSETTA STONE shows that it was occasionally sculptured. Its uses are primarily bureaucratic: tax returns, legal documents on marriage and property. It was in fact the normal business medium for the Egyptian language during the Ptolemaic and Roman periods. Nevertheless, important literary works are found in Demotic, e.g. the code of moral behaviour known as the Instructions of Onkhsheshonquy. Demotic died out in the fifth century AD, its complicated structure of signs having been losing ground for a couple of centuries to the simpler alphabetical system of writing the Egyptian language, known as COPTIC.

DENARIUS The principal silver coin of the Romans, introduced *c* 169 BC. The silver was at first very fine, and the coin soon settled at a fairly high value. Under Nero the coin was debased by some 10 per cent: this was the beginning of a long decline, debasement increasing and the value of the coin dropping rapidly, By *c* AD 301 the coin had declined into the copper *denarius communis* of little worth.

DENBIGH FLINT COMPLEX A flint industry present in Alaska by 3000 BC which spread across the Arctic to Greenland. It is characterized by flint MICROLITHS, BURINS, bifacially pressure-flaked points and knives. It emphasized blades, bladelets and crescents which would have been set in spears and harpoons for the hunting of caribou and

walrus. The type-site for the industry is Iyatayet, Cape Denbigh, and other main sites include a camp at CAPE KRUSENSTERN and ONION PORTAGE. The culture merged with the earliest ESKIMO tradition to which it contributed some elements, around 1000 BC.

● **DENDERA, Egypt** Downstream from Luxor, site of temple of ancient cow-goddess Hathor, paramour of HORUS. Two mammisi (birth-houses) of Dynasty XXX and the reign of Augustus are dedicated to child of this union.

Excavations by PETRIE revealed the tomb of an Old Kingdom priest of Hathor. Also uncovered were mummified animal burials (remarkably no cows) from New Kingdom down to Ptolemaic times.

Late Ptolemies and Roman emperors constructed the present sandstone temple. Reliefs show Cleopatra VII and her son by Julius Caesar burning incense. There are also depictions of constellations and the sun emerging from the vulva of the sky-goddess to illuminate Dendera temple personified as Hathor herself.

The most fascinating architectural elements are the 12 narrow crypts in temple wall and underground – probably storerooms for precious ritual objects and treasure.

DENDROCHRONOLOGY Most trees form distinct annual growth rings throughout their lives. The width of each ring depends on the climate of the particular year in which the ring was formed. For example, a year of drought will result in an unusually narrow ring. Thus a definite pattern of ring size is formed, reflecting fluctuations in annual climate. The dating of archaeological material by dendrochronology requires the construction of a master plan of variations in ring width for the relevant climatic region. This is done by sampling living trees and plotting the variations in ring width for each year of their lives. The patterns shown in the early life of these trees are then matched with the later rings of older timbers (such as medieval roof timbers) and so on, thus extending the chronology backwards. Once the master plan has been constructed, archaeological samples of WATERLOGGED or carbonized wood can be dated by comparison with the plan.

This technique was first used in south-western North America, but tree ring chronologies are now being constructed for a number of regions, including southern England and central Turkey. A master plan based on the BRISTLECONE PINE has been used to correct RADIOCARBON dates. It is likely that this method will play an increasingly important part in archaeological dating as more suitable timber samples are found and existing master plans can be improved and extended.

DESERT TRADITION Cultures located in the arid regions of western North America, especially the Great Basin, whose economic activities depended on the seasonal routine of gathering wild plants and trapping game. The tradition had emerged by 3000 BC (and may be older still). In areas such as the Great Basin it remained until the early historic period. In other regions such as highland Mesoamerica and the southwest, collecting and trapping activities of 'Desert' types gradually gave way to agricultural practices and the development of settled village life and in Mesoamerica, to civilization (*see* MESOAMERICA; TEHUACAN). Characteristic tools are simple pestles and mortars for the crushing and grinding of wild seeds and plants, various chopping tools for the processing

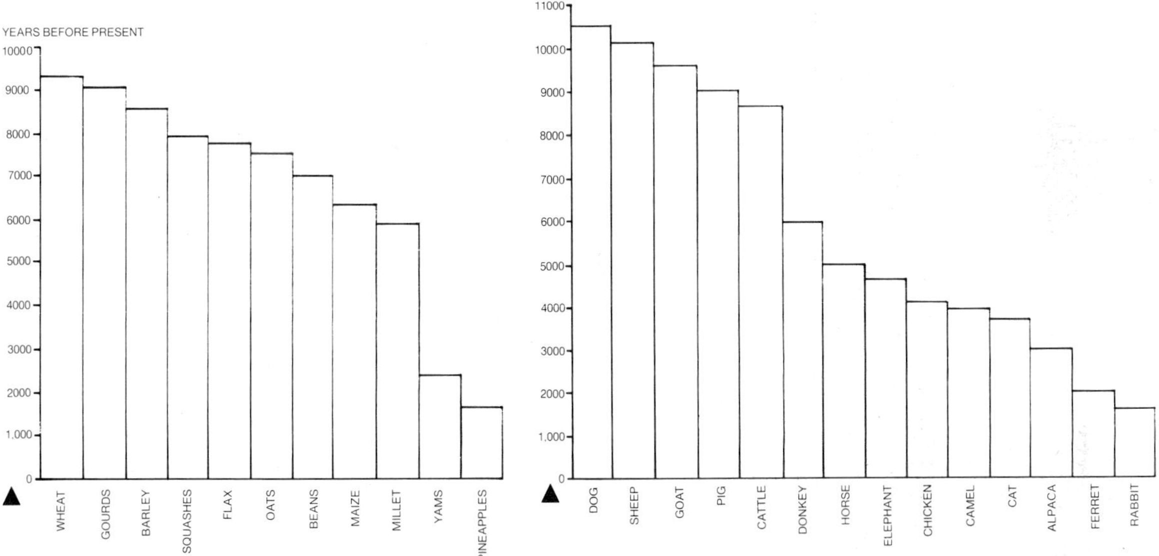

of wild plants, baskets, nets, sandals, simple cotton textiles and chipped stemmed dart points for hunting small game. *See also* COCHISE CULTURE.

DEVEREL–RIMBURY CULTURE The Deverel BARROW and Rimbury CREMATION cemetery in Dorset, excavated in the 19th century, were thought to be Late BRONZE AGE in date, *c* 800 BC. All settlements with similar pottery types were said to be of the Deverel–Rimbury CULTURE and dated Late Bronze Age. However, radiocarbon dates, from ITFORD HILL (Sussex) for example, have redated the culture to the Middle Bronze Age, 1300–1000 BC.

DEVON DOWNS, Australia A limestone ROCK SHELTER in south Australia, excavated in 1929. Six metres of stratified deposits included faunal remains, trimmed stone artefacts (including TULA-ADZES) and bone tools. The earliest cultural levels have been radiocarbon-dated to *c* 2300 BC.

DJED Extremely frequent and powerful Egyptian amulet, both as an object in a variety of materials (e.g. FAIENCE or in the gold counterpoise with inlaid glass of TUTANKHAMUN's triple scarab necklace where the Djed supports an arm of the god of Millions of Years), or as a depiction (e.g. on an anthropoid coffin or one of the four magical bricks protecting the burial chamber). Probably it originated as a regional emblem, variously suggested to be a tree-trunk, stake or bundle of stalks. It conveys the idea of 'stability', the unchanging, favourable status quo. It is closely associated with MEMPHIS and with rituals surrounding the god Ptah. A splendid gilded wooden figure of Ptah clasping the Djed was among Tutankhamun's funerary equipment. It is also a symbol of OSIRIS, god of the underworld. For example a vignette in the BOOK OF THE DEAD belonging to the scribe Ani shows a Djed, animated with arms holding the royal sceptres and wearing the crown of Osiris, flanked by the goddesses Isis and Nephthys.

DOLICHOCEPHALIC
see CEPHALIC INDEX

DOLMEN
see MEGALITH

DOLNI VESTONICE, Czechoslovakia An eastern GRAVETTIAN camping site, occupied by mammoth hunters, in Moravia. Some of the many mammoth bones from the site were used in the construction of tent-like huts, in which were found quantities of carved bone and ivory and modelled clay, including a terracotta female figurine.

▲ **DOMESTICATION** The domestication of wild species of plants and animals marks a major development in prehistoric economy. Domestication and the change from hunting and gathering to a more sedentary way of life were extremely slow, as can be seen from the fact that the domestication of the major food plants and animals occupied several thousands of years.

Clear evidence for domestication appears only when new strains have developed from the wild varieties. The date given in the charts for the earliest known domestication of any one species is the date of the earliest deposit containing recognizably domestic forms. It has been held that because the earliest evidence for domestication is found in the Middle East (notably at the sites of ZAWI CHEMI SHANIDAR and BEIDHA), domestication must have started in that area and spread from there to all other parts of the world. This theory of diffusion from one centre is no longer considered possible. It is now thought that domestication started independently in several different areas of the world, and this is upheld by the discovery of the early domestication in central America of maize, a plant not found in the old world (*see* TEHUACAN VALLEY). Domestication is a continuous process; throughout antiquity new species were domesticated and new forms of previously domesticated species developed. Archaeological evidence for the domestication of animals comes from bones recovered from habitation sites. Evidence for plants usually comes from deposits of accidentally burnt seeds or grains (*see* CARBONIZED GRAIN) or from the GRAIN IMPRESSIONS found in pottery. *See also* CULTIVATION.

● **DONG-S'ON, Vietnam** Excavated in the 1930s, this site is thought to date from the centuries just before the Christian era. Early opinion heralded it as the TYPE-SITE for early metal-working industries in south-east Asia, though more recent excavations in the region have proven this inaccurate. Bronze artefacts at Dong-S'on include kettle-drums, axes, bucket-shaped vases, arrowheads, daggers, halberds, tools, and ornaments. Objects such as mirrors and coins of HAN dynasty origin demonstrate relations with China. In particular the drums have been the objects of much investigation; their decorative motifs generally consist of low-relief patterns either of a geometric or representational nature; the drum tops typically feature a central, multi-pointed star. As drums have also been recovered from the necropolis at SHIH-CHAI-SHAN, 700km away in Yunnan province, the relationship between these areas has been much debated, though the exact connection has not been resolved. In addition, similar drums are well known in the islands of south-east Asia.

DONNERUPLUND ARD A primitive ARD discovered in a Danish bog in 1944 and dated to the Late Bronze Age, *c* 500 BC. The ard consisted of a draught beam (probably for a pair of oxen), a handle, and two shares, one above the other. These were of oak, with no reinforced tip.

DORESTAD (modern Duurstede), Holland Sited under the modern town of Wijk-bij-Duurstede, the ancient settlement was the centre of FRANKISH commerce on the Rhine. It controlled traffic northbound from Cologne, the flow of precious goods from the east, trade in wine and Rhenish glass, as well as having a productive hinterland specializing in wool and woven goods. Dorestad covered about 12 hectares, comparable in size with BIRKA. Houses extended along the Rhine bank. There was a defensive pallisade and an artificial dock. Originally a FRISIAN town, it passed into Frankish hands and trade declined. VIKING raiders hit hard in 863, destroying the mart completely.

DORIANS The people responsible for the invasion of Greece in the 12th century BC and the destruction of MYCENAEAN culture. They were the first iron-users in Greece and seem to have originated in north Greece or the south Balkans. Their invasion precipitated the Greek 'Dark Ages' out of which came Archaic Classical Greece from the 9th–8th centuries BC onwards.

DORIC
see CAPITALS; COLUMNS

DORSET An ESKIMO culture which emerged between 800 and 600 BC in the eastern Canadian Arctic and Greenland from preceding Arctic Small-Tool traditions and lasted into the 13th century when it was replaced in many areas by the eastward-expanding THULE culture.

DOVER [Dubrae], Kent A major port on the south-east coast of Britain. Dover was one of the bases for the CLASSIS BRITANNICA, with store-rooms and naval yards, and a harbour protected in Roman times by lighthouses. There is also fresh evidence for the existence of a fort at Dover. It appears to have taken precedence from RICHBOROUGH as the major British port after the 1st century AD.

DRUIDS A priesthood of the CELTS, almost as powerful as the aristocracy, and able to excommunicate and sentence offenders to death. They taught belief in an after-life, and held groves and bogs sacred; particularly important were oak woods and the mistletoe from oak trees. Druidic lore was retained by memory, not written down. Also associated with the Druids were bards (singers and poets) and seers (interpreters of sacrifice). The Romans destroyed the sanctuaries of the Druids in Gaul because of their political influence and their alleged sacrifices of human captives. The centre of Druidic power was transferred to Anglesey, but broken by Suetonius Paulinus in AD 60 (*see* LLYN CERRIG BACH).

DUN Small fortified Scottish drystone tower, with walls up to 3m high. Duns had solid walls, unlike the BROCHS. They were occupied from the Late IRON AGE (2nd century BC) to medieval times.

▲ **DURRINGTON WALLS, Amesbury, Wiltshire** One of four large HENGE monuments recognized in Wessex, the others being AVEBURY (12 hectares) and Marden (14 hectares), Wiltshire, and Mount Pleasant, Dorset (5 hectares). Durrington Walls (12 hectares) had two entrance causeways through the encircling ditch and outer bank. Recent excavation has shown that it contained at least two circular timber structures, very large by any standards. Nearly 40m in diameter, it has been estimated that its roof (assumed to be what the five concentric circles of posts whose sockets remained once supported) would have been 10m from the ground at its highest point. It has been further estimated that 3.5ha of woodland would have had to be felled to provide the necessary timber. Marden and Mount Pleasant have enclosed structures of a similar nature, and a further two were excavated in the 1920s on Overton Down (*see* AVEBURY) and at WOODHENGE (adjacent to Durrington Walls). They are all of late Neolithic date and associated with GROOVED WARE.

DUWEIR, Tell ed-
see LACHISH

DVARAVARTI An early south-east Asian kingdom which existed from 6th to 11th centuries AD north of Bangkok. Thailand. It is believed to have covered a fairly large portion of central Thailand; aerial surveys have revealed numerous sites which included oval settlements with moats and earthen ramparts thought to be of the period. Included among the antiquities attributed to Dvaravarti are statuary, Buddha images, and votive tablets.

EAST ANGLIA The kingdom of East Anglia comprised Norfolk and Suffolk and was one of the first areas settled by Anglo-Saxon FOEDERATI before AD 500. Its great wealth and importance during the period of the HEPTARCHY is illustrated by the finds from SUTTON HOO, the cenotaph of King Raedwald. There is little documentary evidence concerning the early history of the kingdom, unlike WESSEX. Few monasteries were founded in East Anglia, and they were devastated by the Danish raids. East Anglia maintained its independence until late in the 8th century when it was absorbed by MERCIA. In *c* AD 830 Egbert of Wessex annexed the kingdom to his own, but by 890 the area lay within the DANELAW, having endured the rampages of the Great Army and the death of King Edmund.

EGTVED, Denmark A bronze age BARROW burial. As in other similar Danish burials, special conditions made preservation excellent. The oak coffin still contained an ox-hide, wrapped around the body of a young woman aged 18–20. The bones had disappeared, but her skin, teeth, hair and dress were well preserved. She wore a bronze disk on her belt and bronze bracelets. In the coffin were a bark bucket and container and beneath the body were a child's CREMATED bones.

● **EGYPT** The Nile valley, north of the natural Egyptian frontier at ASWAN on the First Cataract, reaching the apex of the Delta downstream for the ancient capital of MEMPHIS. The Delta is made up of the alluvium deposited over thousands of years by the Nile. Its terrain is marshy, the network of canals and pools making it difficult to cross in an east-west direction. The climate of the Delta contrasts strongly with the dry valley. The dampness of the soil has made the archaeologist's work more difficult in the search for well-preserved material, and the deeper strata of a site are often below the water table. The practically rainless climate of the Nile valley proper is the major reason for the fine condition of monuments and artefacts. The diverse nature of these two regions is at the root of the Ancient Egyptian's concept of his country. Historically the north and the south were separate federations until the final war of unification in 3100 BC. Even after Egypt had been formed into one political entity we find the notion of duality vigorously represented in state protocol: the pharaoh is 'He who belongs to the sedge [southern emblem] and the bee [northern emblem]', i.e. Upper and Lower Egypt. For political administration the country was divided into 'nomes' (whose governors, called nomarchs, could almost become so powerful as to be small pharaohs – *see* BENI HASAN). Memphis and the Delta region consisted of twenty nomes while Upper Egypt had twenty-two, including the extremely fertile FAIYUM.

The year revolved around the regime of the river Nile which until modern times annually flooded the narrow strip of arable land. This caused the violently sharp divide between the cultivated zone and the desert. By late September Egypt was under maximum inundation. By the following May the waters had receded to their lowest level. The Egyptian farming calendar began its year with the season of Inundation (Akhet – summer and autumn) followed by the season for crop-sowing (Peret – winter and spring) and lastly harvest-time (Shemu – spring and summer). This calendar was based on the observation that the Nile began to rise in mid-July at the same time approximately as the dog-star Sirius (Sothis) could be seen with the sun at dawn. The Egyptian civil calendar, which made no provision for leap year, gained gradually more on the astronomical farming calendar so that the New Year only coincided exactly once every 1,460 years.

At the top of Egyptian society was the pharaoh whose decrees became instant law, unalterable except by another pharaoh. The first pharaoh of a united Egypt was most likely Narmer (called Menes by the Greeks) who in 3100 BC conquered the northern kingdom and established a new administrative centre for the whole country at MEMPHIS. The succession usually passed to the son of the pharaoh's Great Royal Wife if possible, or to any eligible son who legitimized his claim to the throne by marrying the most senior princess. To the ancient Egyptians the pharaoh was the manifestation of the falcon-god HORUS who was given the right to rule Egypt by a tribunal of other gods. The king was also the son of Re, the sun-god of HELIOPOLIS whom he joined in the sky after death (*see* PYRAMID TEXTS and CHEOPS' PYRAMID). On his accession the pharaoh assumed five 'Great Names' that formed the royal protocol describing his political and religious strength – the Horus name equating him with the hawk-god, the name indicating that the vulture-goddess of the south (*see* ▲ NEKHBET) and the cobra-goddess of the north (*see* URAEUS) protect the King, the 'Golden Horus' name, the title king of Upper and Lower Egypt and the name 'son of Re'. Of this titulary the last two names were each put into a CARTOUCHE. One important royal ceremony which the king celebrated during his lifetime (and would expect to do so after death as the ritual buildings in the STEP PYRAMID complex indicate) was called the Heb Sed. This festival was the thirtieth anniversary of the king's coronation during which the king renewed his power and strength to control the country and ensure that the rich harvests continued. The ceremony involved dramatic enactments of myths and ritual dances performed by the pharaoh. It reflected a more primitive society (not attested in dynastic Egypt) where a ruler was ritually put to death when his faculties began to fail.

The aristocracy and high officials could either be relatives of the royal family or men who had achieved their eminent position by proven capabilities in the civil administration or the army. Their tomb-reliefs and paintings (*see* TOMB OF TI and SHEIKH ABD EL QURNA) show the leisured life that they hoped would continue after death ■ – supervision of large estates (cattle-count, harvest-time), recreation (hunting ducks or hippopotami in the papyrus swamps), and socializing (musicians and curvaceous dancing girls entertaining guests at parties).

One way for an Egyptian to reach the highest posts in the land such as vizier or governor in charge of the gold-supply was to become a scribe. This involved years of education in a 'House of Life', an academy attached to a temple complex or to the royal residence. Accounting and bureaucratic procedures had to be learnt as well as mastery of the complicated scripts (*see* HIEROGLYPHS, HIERATIC and DEMOTIC). The hard work that was necessary to become a trained scribe can be understood from the many exhortations to students to keep to their studies and not be attracted into seemingly easier jobs. The rewards however were extremely high, and privileges and exemptions ensured that the civil administration had the necessary quantity of executives.

The craftsmen of Ancient Egypt have left many

Egypt

Dates			DYNASTIES	NOTABLE PHARAOHS
A.D. / B.C.		ROMAN DOMINATION		
250	IRON AGE		Ptolemaic Dynasty	Cleopatra VII Ptolemy III Euergetes Ptolemy I Soter
		RULE OF ALEXANDER THE GREAT		
		LAST NATIVE EGYPTIAN KINGS	DYNASTY XXX	Nectanebos, Nectanebes
500		PERSIAN DOMINATION	XXVII	Darius Cambyses
		SAITE PERIOD	XXVI	Psammetichus
750		DOMINATION OF ETHIOPIAN PHARAOHS	XXV	Shabaka Taharqa
		LATE NEW KINGDOM	XXII (Libyan Dynasty)	Osorkon II Sheshonq
1000			XXI	Psussenes I
	COPPER/BRONZE WORKING	NEW KINGDOM	XX	Ramesses III
1250			XIX	Ramesses II Sethos I
1500			XVIII	Tutankhamun Amenophis IV Akhenaten Amenophis III Tuthmosis III Queen Hatshepsut
1750		SECOND INTERMEDIATE PERIOD	BREAKDOWN OF CENTRALISED GOVERNMENT	
		MIDDLE KINGDOM	XII	Ammenemes III Sesostris III Sesostris I
2000			XI	Nebheptre Mentuhotep II
		FIRST INTERMEDIATE PERIOD	DECENTRALISATION OF PHARAOHS' AUTHORITY	
2250		OLD KINGDOM	VI	Phiops II (Pepi)
			V	Sahure Nyuserre Unas
2500			IV	Sneferu Cheops Chephren Mycerinus
			III	Zoser Sekhemkhet
2750		ARCHAIC (EARLY DYNASTIC)	II	
3000			I	Narmer (Menes) Aha Den
4000	NEOLITHIC	PREDYNASTIC	Nagada II Civilisation Nagada I Civilisation Badarian Civilisation	
5000				

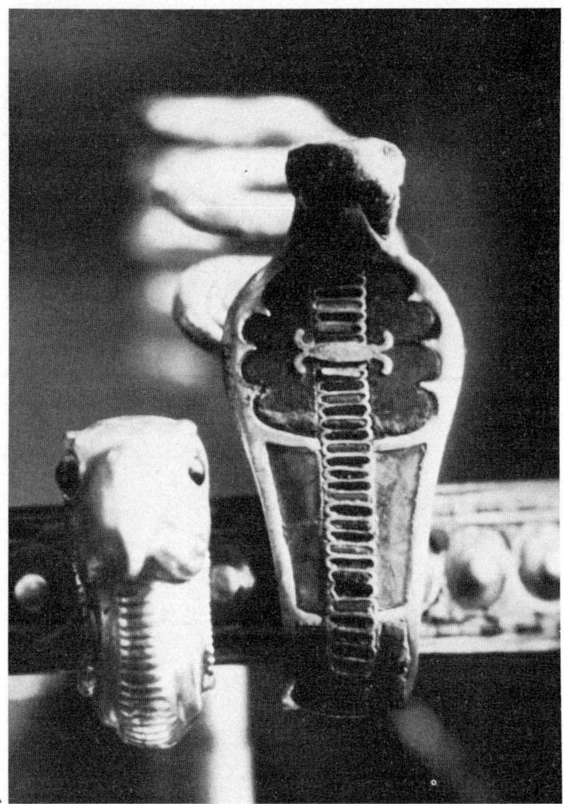

outstanding examples of their ability. Early in Egyptian civilization stone-masons developed techniques for carving both soft limestone and hard granite with only the simplest of copper tools and diorite pounders. Painters and draughtsmen produced the scenes decorating mastabas and rock tombs, using rough outline sketches and a conventionalized representation of the human figure sufficiently accurate to enable it to act magically at the request of the dead person's soul. The jewellery recovered from burials shows advanced techniques (especially in the Middle Kingdom) including the inlaying of shapes outlined in gold strips (cloisonné) and GRANULATION.

Finally, the section of the population who had the hardest life of all were the workers on the estates, especially those responsible for digging irrigation channels according to a state programme for sowing the crops (barley, emmer wheat) and harvesting them. Pulling flax for the linen industry was also exhausting work. Wooden models placed in tombs, in particular in the Middle Kingdom, in order to spring to life to serve the tomb owner show a variety of tasks: bread- and beer-making, spinning, butchering, ploughing. Together with the lively and often subtly humorous tomb paintings, we get an unparalleled insight into ancient daily life such as in the tomb of Menna where two young girls squabble, instead of working, and two workers take a break under the shade of a tree; or in the tomb of Khnumhotep at Beni Hasan where three artful baboons sitting perkily among the branches of a fig tree enjoy the fruit while two workers try to rescue as much of it as possible for the dinner table. During the period of the Nile inundation, a great deal of the population with little work to do because of the submerged land was taken into compulsory state service (the corvée system) for three or four months. During this time they were required to help build the pharaoh's funerary monuments (e.g. the pyramids at Saqqara or Giza) or additions to the great temple complexes. Certainly during the Old Kingdom the contribution of foreign slave labour was negligible and we can witness in the pyramids the impressive achievement of the Egyptian working population.

ELAM
see SUSA

EL KAB, Egypt Upstream from Thebes; a town of predynastic origins, cult centre of southern mother-goddess Nekhbet (White Vulture). Large walled fortified enclosure (possibly Dynasty XXX), 6m high by 12m thick, contains vestiges of ancient town. Excavations were impeded by destruction caused by *sebakhim* (diggers for mud bricks). Remains of buildings from Dynasties XVIII–XXX, e.g. temples to Nekhbet and Thoth. Mountainside necropolis of extreme interest. The tomb of Ahmosis, son of Abana, head of the navy, has inscription on military campaign of founder of New Kingdom against HYKSOS invaders.

ELM DECLINE A characteristic of the NEOLITHIC forest clearances in western Europe is the decline in the proportion of elm relative to other trees in POLLEN ANALYSES of the period. The elm decline is so widespread that it has been used to mark the Atlantic–Sub-boreal transition (*see* POSTGLACIAL PERIOD). The decline was originally attributed to the drop in temperature associated with the onset of the Sub-boreal period. This theory is not now generally accepted, as there is no decline of other similarly cold-sensitive species. Today the most widely accepted theory is that the decline is due to extensive use of elm foliage as fodder at a period when there were few grasslands. Such treatment would lead to a decline in the pollen production of the tree. The use of elm in this way can still be found in primitive pastoral communities.

ELOUERA This Australian stone implement is a flake or BLADE, triangular in section, with retouch or step-flaking on the thick back; it resembles a large, crescent-shaped geometric MICROLITH. Use-polish is often extensive. Confusion at times arises in differentiating it from smaller, backed-blade tool types and scrapers. Examples are known from several regions of Australia, with a concentration around OENPELLI.

EL TAJÍN, Veracruz, Mexico A large Classic Period (*see* MESOAMERICA) CEREMONIAL CENTRE on the Gulf Coast dating AD 600–1200. El Tajín was partly contemporary with such sites as TEOTIHUACAN in the Mexico Basin and MONTE ALBAN in Oaxaca. Artefacts and ideas were exchanged between the three sites, and the distinctive Tajín contribution was an art style based on interlaced scroll and volute motifs. This is found on intricately carved stone objects, decorated with human, bird and animal designs, which were widely traded through Mexico. Art and architectural styles also influenced the near-by MAYA. The Pyramid of the Niches is one of the main buildings at El Tajín. Besides this, there are seven BALL COURTS and many palace-like structures with CORBEL-vaulted ceilings and great colonnaded doorways.

● **EMERY, Walter Bryan (1903–71)** British archaeologist. His passion for Egypt overcame early obstacles and by 1923 he was digging at AMARNA. He later carried out preservation work at SHEIKH ABD el-QURNA (notably the tomb of Ramose), and he discovered the Bucheum at ARMANT. While working on an archaeological survey of Nubian monuments threatened by the heightening of the Aswan barrage, he discovered rich royal burials (4th–5th century AD) in tumuli at BALLANA and Qustul.

His 1935 excavations at SAQQARA on mastaba superstructures unearthed advanced copper-work of the early Archaic period, and a possible mini prototype of the Step Pyramid in a burial chamber. His archaeological career was interrupted by war and by years in the diplomatic service. In 1951 Emery became professor of Egyptology at University College London, and resumed fieldwork at Saqqara where he excavated MASTABAS of the First Dynasty. He also excavated the fort of BUHEN in the Sudan revealing its advanced military architecture. Back at Saqqara he uncovered catacombs of countless mummified ibises and baboons (sacred to THOTH) and hawks (sacred to HORUS). His career came full circle with the discovery of burial of cow-mothers of the Apis bulls.

Main books: *Hor-Aha* (1940); *Archaic Egypt* (1961); *Egypt in Nubia* (1965).

ENAMEL A true enamel is a vitreous substance fused to a metallic surface. Highly fusible potash or soda glasses are ground down, coloured, and applied to the metal which is then heated until the glass melts and fuses with the base plate. When cold the enamel surface is polished down with an abrasive until it is flush with the surface of the CLOISONNÉ or has filled the decorative field of the design in CHAMPLEVÉ.

ENEOLITHIC Another name for the COPPER AGE.

ENKOMI, Cyprus A large settlement in the east coast of CYPRUS frequently excavated since 1896. It began as a small village in about 2000 BC; 500 years later it became an important copper-smelting site and many ingots of bronze have been found. The wide variety of foreign pottery found at the site testifies to the prosperity of the trade during the 15th and 14th centuries BC. In the 13th century, however, Enkomi was destroyed by the MYCENAEANS who lived there until they were defeated by the sea people *c* 1200 BC. Enkomi then declined and was abandoned about 1050 BC.

ENNEAD The Great Ennead of HELIOPOLIS represented nine gods forming the transition from primeval watery chaos to cosmic order. As a religious explanation of cosmogony it goes back at least to Dynasty V.

The priests who formulated the Ennead have accounted for the creation of the world and worked out a logical structure to the universe.

Out of Nun (watery chaos) a mound emerged with the self-created god Atum. His name means 'totality' or 'completion'. This sun-god merged with Re to form Re-Atum, standing at the head of solar worship in Egypt. Being without a feminine counterpart his act of creation was by masturbation – resulting in the first couple, Shu (air-god) and Tefnut (moisture). They produced Geb (earth-god) and Nut (sky-godess). Having explained their known environment, the Egyptians linked these cosmic deities with the human, political world through interpolating into the Heliopolitan theology four deities whom they made the offspring of Geb and Nut: Osiris (the sun-god's serious rival for the 'hearts and minds' of the Egyptians), Isis, Seth and Nephthys, the major participants (with Horus) in the myth concerning the struggles for the throne of Egypt.

ENTREMONT, France An important OPPIDUM in the Midi, dating from the 4th century BC to its destruction by the Romans in 123 BC. It was defended by massive stone ramparts, with small crowded houses and streets within. Many Roman BALLISTA bolts found in the latest occupation levels are evidence of the actual defeat. Imports during the occupation included AMPHORAE and other classical pottery types. Most important was the sanctuary of the SEVERED HEAD cult, like that at ROQUEPERTUSE nearby. There were friezes of carved heads, stone figures associated with detached heads, and human skulls hung on iron nails in niches.

ENVIRONMENTAL ARCHAEOLOGY This covers all the physical and biological components of man's environment. It includes research into the geological and geographical factors affecting man, as well as the study of the environment as a source of raw materials. The changes that take place in the environment, whether natural or man-induced, are examined using the evidence provided by such organic remains as seeds, pollen, animal bones, snail shells and insects. *See also* BURIED SOIL, CHARCOAL IDENTIFICATION, LANDNAM, POLLEN ANALYSIS, SOIL ANALYSIS, THIN SECTION.

EOLITH Once the idea that man had a long prehistory was accepted (*see* BOUCHER DE PERTHES), many collectors claimed pieces of stone as works of ancient man. Among these were 'eoliths' (Greek 'dawn stones'), now recognized

to be flakes produced by natural agencies such as frost or river action. There was much dispute about the true nature of eoliths in the 19th and early 20th centuries (*see* EVANS, Sir John.

EPHESUS [Modern Selçuk], Turkey One of the 12 Ionian cities of Asia Minor, situated on the west coast of Anatolia. Because the silting of the near-by river Cayster blocked the port of the Ionian city, the later Hellenistic city, built about 300 BC, was erected 1½km to the west on the changing coastline. However, silting continued and *c* AD 700 the idea of a port was abandoned and the city returned to its original site. The sea is now 5km distant. Ephesus is famous for the Temple of Artemis (Diana), one of the Seven Wonders of the ancient world, and as a place where the apostle Paul resided (Acts 19). Continuing excavation of Hellenistic Ephesus is revealing a city of fine buildings, some of which are being restored.

● **EPIDAUROS, Greece** A religious centre dedicated to Asclepius, the god of healing, dating from the 6th century BC, famous for its theatre which survives virtually intact. The setting is magnificent. The theatre uses the surrounding plain as a backcloth and the hillside as the foundation for the seats. It is perfectly proportioned along classical lines, using the Pheidonian cubit of 490mm as a unit, and was designed by Polycleitos in the 4th century BC.

ERBENHEIM
see SWORD

ERECHTHEUM
see ACROPOLIS

ERIDU (Tell Abu Shahrain), Iran A site 19km south-west of UR in southern Mesopotamia excavated in 1918–19 and 1946–9. A series of deep pits showed that the site was occupied from the UBAID period in about 5000 BC. The later excavations discovered a series of temples beginning in the Ubaid period and continuing into the URUK period. The earliest temple was a rectangular room of simple house type. Each successive temple incorporated the remains of the walls of its predecessor in a large platform, and was correspondingly larger and more complex. This procedure led to the construction of ZIGGURATS.

ERMINE STREET, England The Roman road from LONDON to the north, running through LINCOLN and YORK. The name is Anglo-Saxon.

ERTEBØLLE The final MESOLITHIC culture of the west Baltic coast. Following contact with early farmers to the south, aspects of a NEOLITHIC farming economy were adopted (including pottery and polished flint axes) although the people continued to rely substantially on hunting, fishing and the gathering of shell-fish (the latter activity leaving behind the characteristic shell heaps or KITCHEN MIDDENS). Chisel-ended flint arrowheads are common in Ertebølle settlements, and were probably used in the hunting of water fowl.

ESHNUNNA (Tell Asmar), Iraq TELL in the Diyala Valley 35km north-east of Bagdad. Excavations completed 1930–36 uncovered a number of temples, a palace and some private houses of the early 3rd millennium. A hoard of statuettes found in the Abu temple portrayed men in a pose of worship with their hands clasped in front of them.

▲

Eshnunna later became an important city state opposed to the old ASSYRIAN empire and disappears from history after its capture in about 1761 BC by HAMMURAPI of BABYLON.

ESKIMO Peoples living within the Arctic circle from east Siberia to Greenland of Eskimo-Aleut physical type and racially distinct from the AMERINDIAN groups occupying the remainder of the Americas. Origins are obscure, but the Eskimo almost certainly came after 10,000 BC from Siberia. Their economy and cultural tradition was based on the hunting of Arctic sea-mammals and caribou with bone and antler harpoons and points from skin kayak boats or sleds. Huts were constructed from skin and whale bone, drift wood, earth and rubble or ice-blocks. Carved ivory figurines are amongst the finest Eskimo works of art. *See also* CAPE KRUSENSTERN, DORSET, IPIUTAK, OLD BERING SEA, ONION PORTAGE, THULE.

ESTE, Italy A site in the Po valley which gave its name to the URNFIELD culture of the Veneti, from 900 to 182 BC. The burials in the cemetery at Este consist of CREMATIONS in urns. In the early period the only grave goods were FIBULAE and perhaps a razor. From the 4th century BC, CELTS settled in the Po valley. Under their influence, richer grave goods such as bronze jugs appear in the burials, and trade with central Italy and the Orient increased. From 182 BC, the Veneti came under Roman political control and influence.

▲ **ETRUSCANS** The people today known as Etruscans occupied the part of central Italy which is defined by the rivers Arno and Tiber, the Apennine mountains and the west coast. The territory roughly corresponds to that of modern Tuscany. At the height of their power the Etruscans controlled an area stretching from Salerno to the Po valley and from Sardinia to the Apennines. The characteristics of the Etruscan culture first began to emerge from the indigenous Iron Age cultures (*see* VILLANOVAN) towards the end of the 8th century BC and the civilization attained its peak during the 6th and 5th centuries. However, by the 4th century Etruria had started to decline as a result of the growing influence of Rome, and by the 1st century BC the culture had been absorbed by that of Rome.

The 'Etruscan problem' has long concerned archaeologists and philologists. It arose partly from the ancient controversy about the origins of the Etruscans and their language, and partly as a result of the affinity of much of their art with that of pre-Etruscan Italy and of the Aegean. This affinity and the absence of any Italian parallel for the Etruscan language led to the explanation, originally suggested by Herodotus, that the Etruscan nation resulted from a massive migration from the coast of Asia Minor and the substitution of this eastern Mediterranean culture for that of the indigenous community. An opposite theory was proposed by Dionysius of Halicarnassus – that Etruscan culture was the ultimate development of an ancient Italic people without external stimuli. It is now generally accepted that the Etruscan emergence results from a colonization of Etruria by seafarers ultimately derived from some area of the eastern Mediterranean. It is supposed that the ensuing reaction between the indigenous and the invading cultures resulted in the Etruscan civilization.

The language of the Etruscans is still largely undeciphered and will remain so until a substantial bilingual text is discovered. The origin of the language remains equally obscure; however, discoveries of inscriptions in an etruscoid language from Lemnos in the Aegean have shed

▲

▲

some light on the subject. Similarly, the discovery of three inscribed gold tablets (two in Etruscan and one in PUNIC, the language of CARTHAGE) in the sanctuary at Pyrgi have aided the work of decipherment.

The Etruscans had three principal deities: Tinia, Uni and Menrva (corresponding to the Roman Jupiter, Juno and Minerva). These were accompanied by a number of secondary gods, most of which had Graeco-Roman or Asiatic counterparts. Etruscan use of temples with external altars is also similar to the practice of many archaic eastern religions. The most common temple plan consisted of a cella which opened on to a columned pronaos (porch), and was related to the temples of Archaic Greece.

The Etruscans are best known for the richly-furnished stone-built tombs which are their major surviving monuments. These tombs reflect not only their art but also their considerable skill in building, which can also be seen in the surviving fragments of city walls surrounding such sites as Signia. Most Etruscan art has been found in funerary deposits and is not therefore representative of their art as a whole. The surviving material shows that the ▲ Etruscans worked in a number of media, including bronze, terracotta, stone and wall-painting. The themes most often illustrated concern religion and the funerary rite.

Etruscan bronze-working is mainly represented either by incised sheet metal decorated with mythological groups or representations of deities, or by moulded statuettes of warriors or deities. Ornamented sheet bronze was often used to decorate wooden furniture and vessels.

Terracotta was principally used for architectural ornament (especially on temples), sarcophagi and statuary. The ornament usually took the form of friezes in low-relief, though some figures were occasionally modelled in high-relief. The sarcophagi are often surmounted by reclining male and female figures, usually considered to be portraits of the dead. Most of the surviving statues in both stone and terracotta seem to have been votive offerings. Funeral feasting and ceremonial are the most common themes in Etruscan tomb-paintings; other frequently occurring subjects are from everyday life, such as hunting.

It is clear that the main stylistic links are with Archaic Greece and the Aegean. Although trade with the Greek world continues throughout the Etruscan period (including the importation of much fine Greek pottery), Etruscan art does not develop in the same manner as that of the Greeks, but keeps much of the Archaic style.

● **EVANS, Sir Arthur J. (1851–1941)** Son of Sir John EVANS. After a spell in the Ashmolean Museum (Oxford) and a brief interest in British archaeology, Evans turned his eye abroad, first to the Balkans (until he became *persona non grata* because of the political situation) and later to Crete. It is for his work on Crete that he is most famous. Until his excavations began at KNOSSOS in 1899 no one had an inkling of the MINOAN civilization. Evans in describing the site laid the firm foundations of Minoan archaeology. His careful cross-dating with EGYPT also made many prehistoric dates in Europe more certain. Main books: *The Palace of Minos* (4 vols, 1921–35).

■ **EVANS, Sir John (1823–1908)** One of the greatest British antiquaries. His lifetime saw the setting of the foundations of modern European archaeology. He actively involved himself in antiquarian disputes of the day, including those surrounding worked flints from the Somme, which he accepted as genuine (*see* BOUCHER DE PERTHES), and the

EOLITHS from Kent (which he rejected); modern archaeology sides with him. He was present at the excavations at the site of HALLSTATT, an experience recorded in his letters to England. He published three catalogues of finds from Britain, in their own way still unique. Sir John was the father of Sir Arthur EVANS. Main books: *Coins of the Ancient Britons* (1864); *The Ancient Stone Implements, Weapons, and Ornaments of Great Britain* (1872); *Ancient Bronze Implements, G.B. and Ireland* (1881).

● **EYE OF HORUS** Prosperity-bringing amuletic emblem in the form of a human eye with a hawk's cheek markings below it. The eyes of HORUS, the sky-falcon, represent the sun and moon. In their vicious struggle for the right to rule Egypt, the desert-god Seth, murderer of Horus' father OSIRIS, tore out the lunar eye of Horus, smashing it to pieces. The god THOTH reassembled and restored it to Horus in pristine condition – hence often called the Wedjat (sound) eye. The possession of this powerful amulet brought success and personal benefits. It can be seen painted on the sides of sailing-boats to give protection and a safe voyage. A gold cloisonné pectoral of TUTANKHAMUN shows the sun (as a chalcedony scarab) with the wings of a falcon pushing the lunar boat carrying the Eye of Horus around the sky. In funerary contexts a pair of amuletic eyes decorates coffins from the Middle Kingdom – fulfilling the double role of talismans protecting the corpse and of 'windows' for the dead to look through onto the world of the living.

FABRICATOR A term coined by Sir John EVANS to describe a type of flint implement found in Britain, probably of NEOLITHIC and BRONZE AGE date, which he believed had been used for working flint. Their true function is not known.

▲ **FAIENCE** 'Egyptian faience' is used to describe manufactured glazed material in no way related to true faience or enamelled earthenware (e.g. Maiolica). Powdered quartz is fused (perhaps with solution of natron or salt) into a core, then coated under heat with vitreous alkaline glaze. A copper compound gave typical colour blue or green – therefore useful in jewellery to imitate highly-prized stones like lapis lazuli, turquoise or feldspar. From simple beginnings in predynastic beads, faience was skilfully employed in the Step Pyramid complex (Dynasty III) blue tiles imitating palace rush matting. Its adaptability resulted in mass production: necklaces rings, amulets, SHABTIS, bowls and vases. Amarna excavations produced fine examples (Dynasty XVIII) of polychrome faience (e.g. floral collars) and thousands of red pottery moulds for producing faience objects. Faience beads made by this technique and found in the Aegean and at European bronze age sites may have been made in Europe.

FAIYUM, Egypt Fertile depression west of the Nile, connected to the valley geologically and by the river, Bahr Yusef. The lake (Birket Karun or Moeris) is much desiccated since antiquity. Middle Kingdom pharaohs devised large-scale irrigation projects to reclaim land, and for a while it became the capital of Egypt.

Under the Ptolemies came a period of expansion with cities of Greek settlers. For example:

(1) Crocodilopolis (on site of earlier Shedet) – a centre for the worship of Sobek crocodile god. Temple ruins

▲

show constructions of Middle and New Kingdom (Ramesses II). Mounds containing Demotic Greek and Roman Papyri give information on social life. Looters and diggers for decomposed brick for fertilizer hampered archaeologists, but a large quantity of clay lamps and figurines was found.

(2) Tebtynis – where papyri were found in wrappings of mummified crocodiles.

(3) Dionysias (Kasr Karun) – ruins include large, towered, mainly mud brick fortress (94m × 81m) from the time of Diocletian. *See also* HAWARA; LAHUN.

FALSE DOOR A vital link in Ancient Egypt between the soul of the deceased and the rituals and food-offerings of the outside world. Its usual position in Old Kingdom mastabas was on the south face, fitting into a panelled and recessed wall simulating domestic architecture. In the centre a narrow panel represented the doorway through which the dead person's spirit could pass as if through a true entrance or exit to the tomb. Sometimes on door panels the dead man is represented with his staff of office. Around the door are smaller figures of his family and servants bringing drink, legs of beef, and entertaining with music and dancing. Above a stone imitation of a roll of matting is a tabloid STELA showing the deceased and his wife in front of a table of food. Some doorways contain carving in very high relief of the tomb-owner looking as if about to step down from the niche to collect his food and drink. False-door designs in miniature were painted on large rectangular wooden coffins of Middle Kingdom date, exquisitely representing colourful matwork hangings, e.g. a splendidly decorated coffin of Djehuty-nakht in the Boston Museum of Fine Arts.

FARAH, Tell el-, Israel A TELL in central Palestine excavated by De Vaux 1946–60. Occupation of the site began in the 4th millennium BC. It grew into a fortified city which was destroyed *c* 2600. It was reoccupied from about 1900 to 600 BC. Excavation of domestic quarters has shown social divisions between rich and poor when this was the ISRAELITE capital under King Omri, a division against which Old Testament prophets spoke.

FAURESMITH Sometimes called late ACHEULEAN, a PALAEOLITHIC INDUSTRY of south and east Africa. It occurs in a more open and steppe-like environment than does the contemporary forest SANGOAN. At Saldanha, Cape Province, it is probably associated with a NEANDERTHAL-like skull.

FAVERSHAM, Kent The richest of all Anglo-Saxon cemeteries, it was unfortunately not scientifically excavated. The 6th century AD pagan inhumations were all furnished with the possessions of the dead person, which in many cases included much fine jewellery. Kentish jewellery was particularly splendid, whether the ordinary CHIPCARVED gilded bronze brooches or the more flamboyant polychrome gold and garnet CLOISONNÉ disk brooches and pendants. An astounding quantity of glassware was also found in the graves, perhaps suggesting local manufacture.

FELL'S CAVE, Patagonia The deep accumulation of human refuse at this site has yielded pressure-flaked fish-tail points, flake SCRAPERS, bone fabricators and awls and lava disks together with the bones of horse, ground sloth and guanaco. Radiocarbon dates of *c* 8800 and *c* 6700 BC at a nearby cave, Palli Aike, with a similar occupation, show

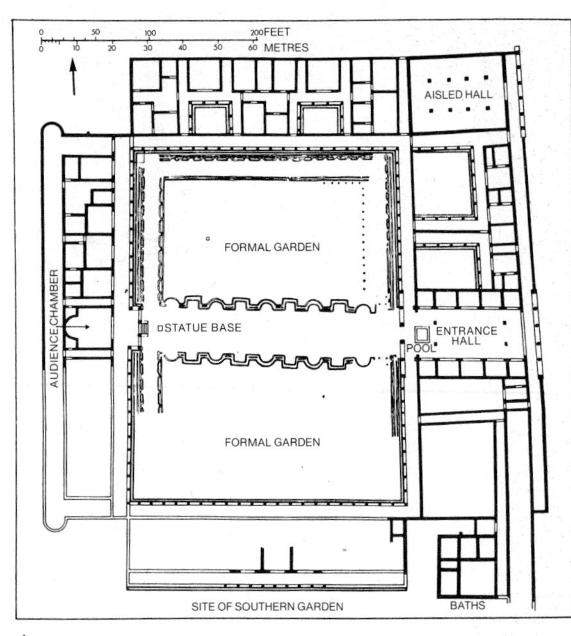

▲

that men had reached the tip of South America by the 9th millennium BC at latest. Similar tool types have been found elsewhere in South America.

FERRULE A socketed metal end to the shaft of a spear, in use from the BRONZE AGE onwards; they are either pointed or tubular.

FERTILE CRESCENT An area of a rough crescent shape which includes MESOPOTAMIA, LEVANT and EGYPT. This area contains relatively fertile land and has a Mediterranean climate. Its fertility largely depends on using the major rivers for irrigation. It is in this area that sedentary life is thought to have begun *c* 10,000–8000 BC. The fertile crescent is the area of the Bible story and contains the countries from which Greece and Rome derived much of their culture.

FIBULA A decorated safety pin used as a brooch or fastening. Fibulae are usually of BRONZE though later ones may be of IRON. The earliest type known in Europe is the simple PESCHIERA or violin bow fibula; later examples were more elaborate. Fibulae took over from the buttons used earlier, e.g. by BEAKER and UNETICE peoples.

● **FIGURINE** A statuette of a human or an animal. Figurines can be made of stone, wood, clay, metal or ivory. They are sometimes naturalistic, often stylized. They are generally considered to have a religious purpose, although some may be nothing more than toys.

FILIGREE A technique used in the decoration of glass, gold or silver objects. In the case of glass, a number of differently coloured rods are fused together and then reheated and drawn out. The thread of glass produced by this means is then applied to the surface of a glass vessel so as to create a pattern. With jewellery, pieces of gold or silver wire are soldered either to each other or onto a base plate to form the desired decoration. A similar goldsmith's technique is GRANULATION.

FIREDOGS Iron objects found in LA TÈNE graves in Europe. Probably firedogs, though some may be parts of stands for AMPHORAE. Over 12 complete examples come from Britain, all animal-headed.

▲ **FISHBOURNE, Sussex** A recently-discovered Roman palace. The site, on a river inlet near Chichester, was first occupied by the military, probably as a depot for the invasion forces of AD 43. A timber building followed in the 50s, to be replaced a decade later by a substantial masonry building with a colonnade, baths, and servants' quarters. This sumptuous structure was probably one of only half-a-dozen of this period in Britain, all along the south coast, However, it was replaced *c* 75 by an enormous courtyard building, the whole of which covered about 4 hectares. The west side held the audience-chamber and reception rooms, the north side the guest rooms, the east side the entrance, servants' and bath quarters, and the south side the main living rooms. The owner of this palace may have been Cogidubnus, a philo-Roman king of the conquest period, but a high-ranking Roman official is as likely. In the 2nd century the buildings were altered, especially to the north wing. In the 3rd century a fire caused the abandonment of the building.

▲

FISSION TRACK DATING When the radioactive isotope uranium-238, a common impurity in many minerals, disintegrates, it causes minute damage trails in the surrounding mineral. These trails (or fission tracks) are preserved in crystalline or glassy materials, as long as the crystal structure is not destroyed by excess heating. A count of number of the fission tracks present in a sample can be used to estimate its age, when both the HALF LIFE and the concentration of uranium-238 in the sample are taken into account. This technique can be used to date deposits (containing suitable material such as quartz, hornblende, olivine, etc.) of ages up to 1000 million years.

FLAKE A fragment detached from a larger piece of stone or CORE (*see* FLAKING). There are a number of signs that indicate a flake to have been intentionally removed by man, although general shape sometimes has to serve as a criterion: flakes produced by 'natural' processes, such as the action of frost or the passage of wheeled vehicles are not always distinguishable from the deliberate products of a stone 'knapper'.

FLAKING The process of producing FLAKES, by percussion or pressure. There are two main types of percussion. The CORE can be struck with a hammer ('direct percussion'), which may be a rounded stone (a hard hammer) or a rod of antler, bone or even of hard wood (a soft hammer). In 'indirect percussion' an antler, bone or wooden punch is placed between the hammer and the core, giving the operator greater control over his work.

Pressure-flaking was probably normally carried out by forcing off flakes with a tool similar to the punch used in indirect percussion. This can be done in the hands, but there are records of AZTECS removing BLADES from cores by placing the weight of the body on a wooden shaft against the chest, with the other, spiked, end of the shaft resting on a core between the feet (a technique known as 'impulsive pressure-flaking'). A few of the many flakes produced in flaking or 'knapping' can be transformed into 'flake-tools', often with further RETOUCH. The hollow left in a piece of raw material by the removal of a flake is known as a 'flake-scar'. An implement with flake-scars all over both faces is called 'bifacial' (hence 'biface', an alternative term for bifacial HANDAXES). A unifacial implement is worked on one surface only.

FLANDRIAN
see POSTGLACIAL PERIOD

FLINT, tools and techniques
see FLAKE

FLOTATION A method used to retrieve environmental and economic evidence from archaeological sites. Suitable excavated soil is poured into a water tank which contains a frothing mechanism. Light matter is carried to the surface and the scum formed on the water contains small objects such as charcoal fragments, carbonized seeds, small mammal bones, etc. The scum is removed, washed on a fine sieve and the objects retrieved. Material recovered by the method is less subject to damage than is normally the case, and a higher percentage of small seeds and bones are retrieved. The system was first developed for the recovery of CARBONIZED GRAIN from Near Eastern sites, but has since been used throughout the world with considerable success.

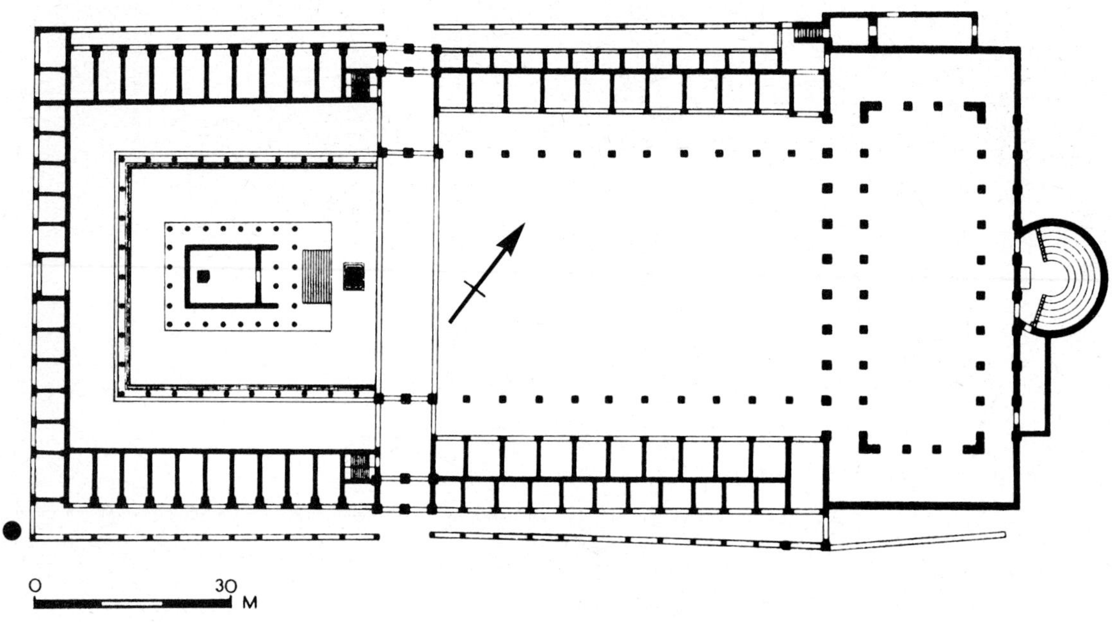

FLUORINE TEST This test is used to establish the relative dates of bone material from a single site. After burial, bone acquires fluorine at a steady rate, and by comparing the proportions of fluorine present in a number of bones from the same deposit, it can be shown whether or not the collection is all of the same age. This method was used to date relatively the Galley Hill skeleton (found in 1888), and the skull from SWANSCOMBE (found in 1935). Both finds were said to have come from the same deposit of river gravels. Fluorine analysis showed the Galley Hill Skeleton to be of considerably later (though unknown) date than the skull. Fluorine tests were also used in the examination of the PILTDOWN man, and helped show that some fragments of the skull were modern.

FOEDERATI [Laeti] Towards the end of Roman rule in Britain in the 4th century AD Germanic mercenary soldiers were introduced to help defend the country against attacks from Ireland, Scotland and the continent. *Foederati* or *Laeti* had settled in England some time before the final abandonment of the province as is shown by the distinctive early metalwork and continental style of pottery from sites such as MUCKING and CAISTOR BY NORWICH. Most of the mercenaries came from the Elbe–Weser region, the continental homeland of the ANGLO-SAXONS, and were the invited forerunners of the great migrations of AD 450.

FOLSOM, New Mexico, USA Type-site for a distinctive form of north American fluted spear point found mainly in east New Mexico, east Colorado and east Wyoming, and dating to the final phase of the Two Creeks interval and the Valders advance (*c* 8800 BC). Finds at the CLOVIS site of BLACKWATER DRAW, Colorado, indicate that the Folsom point was developed from the earlier Clovis form. The use of Folsom points reached its climax by 8000 BC. Another major site is Lindenmeier in north-eastern Colorado, a kill- and camp-site where the bones of an extinct species of bison have been found with Folsom points and other chipped stone artefacts, including unfluted projectiles, knives, choppers and scrapers, and some bone implements.

FOOT PLOUGH [or taclla]
see INCA

FORUM The forum of a Roman town was a development from the Greek AGORA as the central element in TOWN-PLANNING. It was usually given strong axial emphasis with a TEMPLE facing a BASILICA across a rectangular colonnaded courtyard. With new foundations such as AUGST and many towns in the Western Empire, the forum could be composed from several rectangular town blocks. In older towns such as GLANUM and many towns in the east, the forum was imposed on an irregular plan.

FORUM JULII (Modern Frejus), France A town in Provence founded by AUGUSTUS as a COLONIA for veterans of the Eighth Legion, and as a naval base. It had an artificial harbour, protected by a lighthouse and flanked by two forts, and a naval yard. The town itself boasts an AMPHITHEATRE of *c* AD 70 and a theatre dating from the time of Augustus. Some arches of the town's AQUEDUCT still stand. The town is unusual in having been planned to combine military and civil functions.

FOSSE WAY, England A Roman road stretching from Exeter to LINCOLN. This remarkably accurate piece of

surveying (it strays overall no more than 10km from its alignments) acted as a frontier in the early stages of the Roman conquest in the 40s AD. It divides highland from lowland Britain, except the Cheshire plain, and may have been intended as the final frontier in the first years of occupation. However, resistance from the highlands forced the Romans to advance beyond the Fosse Way.

FRANKS Originally settled by the Romans east of the Rhine, the Franks rapidly extended their territory in the 5th century AD, and under the Merovingian kings Childeric and Clovis became one of the supreme powers of post-Roman Europe in the 6th. They were a heavily romanized people, speaking a Latin dialect, Christian, and with a Roman type of legal system. Pottery and glassware are also fundamentally Roman, but their Germanic roots are revealed in decorative metalwork. Gold and garnet ▲ CLOISONNÉ jewellery was predominant, as was CHIPCARVED ANIMAL ORNAMENT on typical radiate brooches with straight or lozenge-shaped feet. Bird forms with curved beaks are also diagnostically Frankish. In the 8th century the Merovingian dynasty failed and was succeeded by the Carolingians, who achieved greatness under CHARLEMAGNE.

■ **FRERE, John (1740–1807)** British antiquarian. In 1797 he announced the discovery of flint implements from a brick pit at Hoxne, Suffolk (now recognized as ACHEULEAN HANDAXES), which he described as 'weapons of war, fabricated and used by peoples who had not the use of metals'. His observations went largely unnoticed, and it was not until the publicizing of BOUCHER DE PERTHES' finds by Sir John EVANS and Prestwich in the 1850s and 1860s that Frere's discovery attracted any wide attention.

FRISIANS A maritime trading people living in central coastal Holland who practically controlled the international commerce of northern Europe in the 7th–9th centuries AD. They established colonies in London and York, and traded especially with the Baltic ports of BIRKA and HEDEBY. Their principal town was DORESTAD. Goods carried were Rhenish wine, English and Frankish weapons and woollen products, hunting dogs and Oriental silks which were exchanged for amber, furs and slaves. *See also*: TERP; SCEATTA.

FRONTINUS, Sextus Julius (*c* AD 30–104) A distinguished Roman administrator who held consulships in *c* 74, 98 and 100. Under Nerva he was in charge of Rome's water supply, writing the intelligent and well-informed *de aquis* on the subject of AQUEDUCTS. 74–8 he was governor of Britain, his greatest feat being the subjugation of the Silures of south Wales.

FUKUI CAVE, Japan Site in Kyushu where, in 1960, was unearthed what is at present the oldest known pottery in the world, dated by radiocarbon as earlier than 10,000 BC. This 'Ryutaimon' (raised-band pattern) pottery is so named after the narrow strips of clay attached below the rim. As pottery appears suddenly in this rather sophisticated form, it is assumed to have been preceded by more basic attempts, either locally or in neighbouring countries, at a still older date.

FUNAN This early south-east Asian kingdom, centred in the lower Mekong area around the southern coast of present-day south Vietnam and southern Cambodia, is thought to date back to the 1st century AD, and continued until incoporation into the neighbouring Chenla kingdom in the 6th century. The Funanese city of OC EO was an important port of the mercantile kingdom. Chinese written records described Funan by the mid third century AD as having walled cities, elegant palaces, archives, and a taxation system.

FUNNEL BEAKER CULTURES [German Trichterbecker or TRB] The earliest NEOLITHIC groups of the north European plain and south Scandinavia, from *c* 3000 BC. An economy based on stock-raising and cereals was probably adopted by local MESOLITHIC peoples from later LINEAR POTTERY cultures. The first TRB groups were contemporary with the MICHELSBERG and the WESTERN NEOLITHIC cultures to the south. Communities of about 50 families lived in rectangular houses. At Barkaer (Jutland) two parallel buildings, 80m long, were divided into 26 rooms each provided with a hearth; the structures were separated by a cobbled trackway. A variety of CHAMBER TOMBS is associated with the TRB group, including the *dyss* (Denmark), *hunebed* (Netherlands) and the Kujavish grave (Poland) the mounds of which are sometimes over 100m long, but still cover only a single burial. There are many regional variants in the TRB group, and these are sometimes seen as representing tribal or social divisions (but *see* CULTURE). They are generally succeeded by CORDED WARE groups.

GADES [Modern Cadiz], Spain A town on the southern coast of Spain, traditionally said to have been founded by PHOENICIAN colonists in 1100 BC, but now believed not to have existed until the 6th century BC. During the PUNIC WARS the town voluntarily went over to the Roman side. The *populae* was granted the great honour of Roman citizenship by JULIUS CAESAR in 49 BC, and the town flourished under Roman administration as a centre of the fishing industry and of pickled fish and GARUM.

GALLERY GRAVE [French allée couverte] A type of CHAMBER TOMB in which the burial chamber is a long stone passage (hence the alternative term 'long tomb'). The tomb is sometimes divided into sections by 'transverse slabs', and these may be pierced by 'portholes' (*see* SEINE–OISE–MARNE culture). In Europe it is found in north-east Spain, France, Sardinia, southern Italy, and further north in Britain and Sweden.

GALLO-BELGIC COINS Certain gold coins introduced from Gaul into southern Britain by Belgic invaders. This archaeological evidence confirms the record by Caesar of invasions of BELGAE prior to 55 BC. There are two types of coins: those minted on the continent (Gallo-Belgic A–F), and British imitations. The Gallic coins themselves were imitations of Greek coins. The earliest probably date from *c* 130 BC, with British derivatives from 100, 70 and 45 BC. British coins were not inscribed with leaders' names until the coins of Commius *c* 10 BC. It is not until this date, therefore, that coins can be associated with particular tribal areas. *See also* IRON AGE; POTIN COINS.

GALLUS SITE
See KOONALDA CAVE

● **GANDHARAN ART** From the time of ALEXANDER THE GREAT, Gandhara (the former NW Frontier Province of India) was open to influences from the West, at first Greek via the ACHAEMENID empire, then Roman and Alexandrian via their PARTHIAN successors. The art of Gandhara clearly reflects these influences: many pieces are direct copies of western sculptures or motifs, although others have a more Indian character. From *c* AD 75 representations of the Buddha in human form appear in sculptures and reliefs, and these also reflect western styles. Western elements include classical naturalism and the depiction of all the figures in a scene equal in size. The free representation of deities in classical art may have provided the incentive to overcome the ideological prohibition on the representation of the Buddha in human form. *See also* MATHURA ART.

GANGES CIVILIZATION Following the period of PAINTED GREY WARE in the Ganges–Jamuna Doab, and of BLACK-AND-RED WARE in the central Ganges valley of India, these areas saw the development of true city states characterized by NORTHERN BLACK POLISHED WARE pottery. What is known of the history of the area suggests the growth of states in the time of Buddha (7th–6th century BC) through the conquest of weaker neighbours by stronger cities, leading to the sixteen MAHAJANAPADAS (major states) mentioned in the literature relating to the period. The central states, especially Kosala and MAGADHA, were involved in a great power struggle which ended by the 4th century BC with the supremacy of Magadha, whose territory was enlarged under Chandragupta Maurya to form an empire extending from the boundary of the ACHAEMENID empire in the north to Andhra Pradesh in the south. By the early 2nd century BC the power of the MAURYAS had waned and the empire was disintegrating.

Much information about the Ganges civilization comes from literary sources. These are of various types and include Buddhist, Jain and Sanskrit texts and other works written in the main long after the events they record. There are also contemporary writings such as the *Arthasatru*, attributed to Chandragupta's minister Kautilya, and inscriptions, notably those of AŚOKA. The works of contemporary foreigners like Megasthenes, Achaemenid envoy at the Mauryan court, also contribute to our knowledge of the period.

The literary information from the earlier part of the period is scanty, of limited reliability, and tends to give an idealized picture of the cities: these are required to have a moat, a rampart with towers and gates near which dwell the poor, streets set aside for particular crafts, organized town-planning in square sectors, and a citadel comprising the ruler's palace, courts and offices. Outside the city walls lie craftsmen's villages and city suburbs, and beyond, the villages of the agrarian population.

The archaeology of the Ganges civilization suffers greatly from the limited nature of the vertical soundings made and the almost total lack of horizontal excavation. Most of the city sites excavated have revealed fortifications, generally of mud and often massive, some seemingly pre-dating the appearance of Northern Black Polished Ware. However, at many of these sites the fortifications date only from the period following the breakdown of the Mauryan empire. Little monumental architecture is actually known. It is probable that many of the large buildings were constructed in brick or perishable materials; the exceptional preservation of a wooden wall at PATNA seems to support this.

The evidence of less spectacular aspects of life is more satisfactory. RINGWELLS are a common feature of all Northern Black Polished Ware sites. The material culture contains abundant fine and domestic pottery, terracotta figurines, tools of iron and copper, inscribed seals in the Brahmi script, known to be in use by the Mauryan period but probably developed earlier, bone arrowheads and punchmarked silver and cast copper coinage (*see* INDIAN COINS). The abundance of silver, a mineral not found in this area, demonstrates the existence of foreign trade.

The Ganges civilization remains a shadowy period due to inadequate excavation, which prevents the proper comparison of the archaeological and literary evidence.

See also ATRANJIKHERA, HASTINAPURA, KAUSAMBI, RAJGHAT, RAJAGRIHA, RUPAR, UJJAIN, VAISALI.

GANGES COPPER HOARDS These are found in the Ganges–Jamuna Doab region of India and link with OCHRE-COLOURED POTTERY. The artefacts in these hoards include antennae-hilted swords, anthropomorphic axes, flat axes of a type common in post-Harappan contexts and a variety of objects with Iranian or Caucasian affinities. They seem to represent the indigenous inhabitants contemporary with the INDUS CIVILIZATION and later.

GARUM [liquamen] A sauce made from rotted tunny-fish, an important feature both in Roman cuisine and in the economy of the province of Spain: few Roman recipes do not include this ingredient. The product was exported all over the empire in AMPHORAE, and the scale of the industry is represented by the Monte Testaccio in Rome, a hill composed entirely of broken oil, wine and garum jars. The industry was the mainstay of former PHOENICIAN trading-colonies on the southern coast of Spain, such as Baesippo, Malaca and GADES. The recipe has fortunately been lost.

GEOCHRONOLOGY A general term for all dating methods dependent on the analysis of natural processes, such as RADIOCARBON dating and DENDROCHRONOLOGY. *See also* ARCHAEOMAGNETISM, FLUORINE TEST, OBSIDIAN DATING, POTASSIUM–ARGON DATING, THERMOLUMINESCENT DATING, VARVE DATING.

GEOMETRIC
see GREEK POTTERY

GEZER, Israel A large TELL which commands the western approaches of Jerusalem. Egyptian texts and the BIBLE testify to its importance. Extensive excavations reveal that after its initial occupation in the 4th millennium BC the site was strongly fortified. The foundation of a gate is similar to ones at HAZOR and MEGIDDO and is probably part of the city built by Solomon in about 950 BC (I Kings 9:15ff). A water tunnel 66m long may also have been built by Solomon. An OSTRACON with the CANAANITE ALPHABET and a CALENDAR in Hebrew were important finds. The city declined after about 37 BC, although it was the Moslem headquarters for their war against Richard the Lionheart in AD 1191.

GHASSUL (Teleilat), Jordan A few small TELLS 2km north-east of the Dead Sea, excavated by a number of expeditions since 1930. The occupation of the site 3500–3000 BC is of special interest. Many shapes of pottery were represented with decoration in black, white, red and brown paint. Houses were built of *pisé* (*see* MUD-BRICK) and originally the walls were decorated with frescoes.

GILGAMESH, epic of An ancient SUMERIAN poem that has been found in a number of places after the initial discovery on TABLETS from the 7th century BC at NINEVEH written in CUNEIFORM script. The hero Gilgamesh is possibly the 5th king after the flood mentioned in the Sumerian king list; he later became a folk hero. In the poem he was a king of URUK who because of his improper behaviour was attacked by the beast-man Enkidu. The two became friends and went on a conquest together, but when Gilgamesh spurned the love of the goddess, ISHTAR, she retaliated by killing Enkidu. Gilgamesh then set out to seek the key of immortality which, although he found it, was stolen from him. The inclusion of a story about a flood with some similarities to the BIBLE's story of Noah has evoked much interest.

GIRDLE-HANGER During the pagan Anglo-Saxon period (AD 400–600) women were often buried with their personal possessions which included a girdle or *chatelaine* from which hung T-shaped pieces of flat bronze usually found in pairs. These apparently functionless objects have been interpreted as imitation keys, perhaps symbolizing the woman's authority within the household. Sometimes small toilet implements such as tweezers, ear-scoops and combs also hung from the girdle-hanger on bronze rings.

GIRDLE OF ISIS Powerful Egyptian AMULET, frequently found among mummy-wrappings, signifying the protection given by the goddess ISIS with whom a red jasper or glass version is connected in a spell from the BOOK OF THE DEAD. Called the 'tyet', it occurs in amuletic decorations at the beginning of the Old Kingdom. Its association with Isis gave added security to funerary equipment – for example its use on the foot-board of the magical bed of the divine cow on which TUTANKHAMUN was to journey into the realms of the sun-god. Its precise nature is still problematic: it is usually regarded as the tie or strap of the girdle worn by Isis, although it could also be taken as a stylized representation of the goddess's sexual organs.

GIZA, Egypt On the west bank of Nile, just south of Cairo. The name given to a site in Libyan desert chosen by pharaohs of Dynasty IV for their pyramids. *See also* CHEPHREN'S PYRAMID, CHEPHREN'S VALLEY TEMPLE, CHEOPS PYRAMID (Great Pyramid), MYCERINUS PYRAMID, SPHINX.

GLACIATIONS These occur when the earth's ice caps extend beyond their normal limits in the form of ice sheets or valley glaciers. They are associated with a drop in sea level which exposes large areas of continental shelf. During the PLEISTOCENE there were at least four separate glaciations in the northern hemisphere. Glaciations cause much of the original land surface to be eroded and reshaped, the material thus removed is deposited as BOULDER CLAY or sands and gravels after withdrawal of the ice sheets.

GLACIS A dump rampart combining both ditch and earthwork. Used in defence of late IRON AGE HILLFORTS in the 1st century BC. At MAIDEN CASTLE invaders had to climb a slope of 40°, which rose 26m sheer from the bottom of the ditch.

GLANS PLUMBEA A lead bullet made to be hurled from a sling; a common find of the Roman period. It is oval in shape, and often inscribed either with the name of the leader of the army (Pompey's name is frequent), or with some such exhortation as 'take that'.

● **GLANUM, France** A town near the mouth of the river Rhône, founded by the Greeks in the 3rd century BC on the site of a native shrine. Buildings of the Greek period include council chambers as well as private houses. At the end of the 2nd century BC the town was occupied by the Germanic Cimbri, until 101 BC, when the ROMANS drove them out and reconstructed the town: this is one of the few examples of Roman settlement in Gaul before JULIUS CAESAR. Roman monuments include the mausoleum of the Gallo-Roman family the Julii, and an elaborate arch of the end of the 1st century BC, reminiscent of the Augustan Ara Pacis in ROME.

GLASTONBURY, Somerset An IRON AGE 'LAKE VILLAGE', established on marshy peat in the SOMERSET LEVELS, by the side of the river Brue. It was excavated 1892–1907. There were about 90 houses, 20–30 of which were occupied at any one time. The earliest types were rectangular timber buildings, later replaced by timber and wattle ROUND HOUSES, built on clay mounds with gravel or clay HEARTHS. Gravel paths joined the mounds, and a wooden palisade surrounded the settlement. Preservation was extremely good, due to WATERLOGGING. Many specialist tasks were carried out: lead net sinkers, a wooden boat and fishbones indicate fishing; bone weaving combs, triangular loom-weights and spindle whorls, weaving. There were metal-working crucibles and very fine wooden objects such as bowls, ladles, buckets and wheels. Trading connections were extensive: commercially-made pottery came from Cornwall and shale objects from KIMMERIDGE. Stone for QUERNS and also metalwork were imported, even some FIBULAE from the continent. The village dates from *c* 250 BC until AD 60, when it was abandoned due to a rise in the water level. *See also* MEARE.

GLOUCESTER, England A Roman COLONIA for retired troops. The town was a converted legionary fortress of the 60s AD, which, having been abandoned by the advance to south Wales in the 80s, was made into a colonia in the period 96–8. The troops appear to have retired into virtually unaltered barrack blocks. The town was successful in the 2nd century but could not compete with CIRENCESTER in the 3rd and 4th. Very little now remains.

GOBI MICROLITH Tiny stone tools (*see* MICROLITH) from the steppe and desert of the Mongolian region, often found in the sand dunes of ancient oases, and extending south into Tibet and north China. Usually considered Upper PALAEOLITHIC in origin, at times their context is MESOLITHIC or NEOLITHIC. These geometic implements were made mainly from quartz pebbles, using secondary trimming technique to produce a triangular point with bifacial chipping. These microliths could have been attached to long shafts, or used as arrowheads.

GOKSTAD, Norway In 1880 a Norwegian VIKING ship of *c* AD 900 was excavated from this mound near OSEBERG on the Oslo Fjord. The ship was 25m long, 6m wide, with a mast and sail as well as 16 pairs of oars. Organic preservation was excellent, and timber burial chamber in the stern contained the skeleton of a chieftain lying dressed and armed on a bed. The ship was equipped with all the necessities of life: beds, kitchen utensils, small rowing boats, a gaming board, carved sledge, clothes, tools and weapons. 12 horses had been slaughtered at the time of this SHIP BURIAL.

GONEIM, Zakaria (1911–59) Egyptian Egyptologist. His short but fruitful career saw him responsible for the Theban necropolis and later SAQQARA. Among his useful excavations and clearances were the causeway to the Unas pyramid, the sphinxes in front of the temple at LUXOR and the tomb of the powerful Theban governor Mentuemhat. He is most remembered for his discovery, in 1954, of an unfinished step pyramid with some fine gold jewellery in its underground galleries, but with an empty sarcophagus. It was planned by its builders to almost the dimensions of the Step Pyramid of Zoser and belonged to one of his successors in Dynasty III called Sekhem-khet.
Main book: *The Buried Pyramid* (1956).

GORDION
See PHRYGIANS

GOTHS A group of Germanic tribes which adopted a nomadic horse-riding way of life through contact with peoples of the Russian steppes. In the 3rd century AD the Goths reached the Black Sea area, where they established the OSTROGOTHIC and VISIGOTHIC confederacies which became very important powers in post-Roman barbarian Europe.

GRAIN IMPRESSION Cereal grains or other seeds often became incorporated in the clay of unfired pots or other artefacts such as tiles. On firing, the grain was burned away leaving a negative impression preserved. The plants which made such impressions can often be identified and have provided useful information where other evidence of prehistoric crops is not available.

GRAND PRESSIGNY, Indre-et-Loire, France A COPPER AGE flint-mining and workshop site, whose products achieved a wide distribution. There was some controversy in the 19th century about the nature of the Grand Pressigny *'livres-de-beurre'* (pieces of worked flint about 300mm by 100mm). Sir John EVANS, in characteristic fashion, visited the area and reported back to fellow antiquarians in Britain that, correctly, these were cores for the production of long flint knives. The cores themselves were traded.

GRANULATION A gold-working technique comparable with FILIGREE work. Small spherical drops of gold were soldered on to a gold backing or base plate. The granules were probably produced by melting the metal and pouring it slowly into cold water.

GRAVETTIAN An Upper PALAEOLITHIC industry (named after the French site of La Gravette, Dordogne) which succeeds the AURIGNACIAN. It is distinguished by 'Gravette points', which are small pointed BLADES with blunted backs. It has been suggested that much of the CAVE ART of France and Spain is of Gravettian age; representations of human figures are common on MOBILIARY ART. Under the name Eastern Gravettian, the industries extend across the loess lands of central Europe and Russia (*see* DOLNÍ VĚSTONICE).

GREAT SHANG
see SHANG

● **GREAT WALL OF CHINA** From the 4th century BC in north China, stretches of wall were built to separate the settled peasants from the nomadic tribes to the north. Consolidated into a continuous frontier by the first emperor of CH'IN *c* 221 BC, the wall was further elaborated as a line of defence under the HAN Dynasty, with 25,000 towers, a length of 2500km, and a width sufficient for horse and cart to pass along the top.

GREECE Palaeolithic deposits at Franchthi cave mark the earliest occupation in Greece. However the Neolithic is the first coherent culture and sites such as Dhimini, SESKLO and NEA NIKOMEDIA have provided the best evidence of it. The Bronze Age, called HELLADIC, is marked by an increase in the number of sites, especially in south Greece. Late Helladic is known as MYCENAEAN and this culture was very powerful throughout the Mediterranean and beyond. It had succeeded the MINOAN culture of Crete. The Mycenaeans faded away in the late 13th century BC, probably due to DORIAN invasions. Little remains from the following period, which seems to have suffered more invasions.

Out of this came Archaic Greece and the beginnings of classical civilization. GREEK POTTERY styles developed and the city states established themselves from the 8th century BC onwards (e.g. ATHENS, SPARTA, CORINTH). 750–500 BC was the greatest period of the city states when many colonies were established (e.g. MASSILIA, AMPURIAS, CUMAE, AGRIGENTO) and religious centres set up (e.g. DELPHI, DELOS, EPIDAUROS). The wars with Persia occurred in the 5th century BC and after beating her off, the city states, by now either oligarchic or democratic, started warring amongst themselves. This happened in the Peloponnesian War, in which Athens and the mainland fought against Sparta and the Peloponnese. The colonies came under attack at this time, especially by the CARTHAGINIANS against the colonies of south Italy (or Magna Graecia) and by the Lydians against those of Asia Minor. The Macedonians played a major part in Greek history when Philip of Macedon conquered Greece in 338 BC and put an end to the strife between the city states. ALEXANDER succeeded Philip and the period known as HELLENISTIC ensued. New cities were set up (e.g. RHODES, ALEXANDRIA) in this relatively peaceful period. Greece passed under the control of Rome, from *c* 200 BC, and Greece became the Roman provinces of Achaia and Macedonia. The Greeks continued to be highly influential, especially in their culture, and their language became the standard eastern tongue in BYZANTINE times.

GREEK POTTERY Classical Greek pottery had its origins in sub-MYCENAEAN styles of the 12th century BC where Attic styles developed into Attic proto-geometric. The period 900–700 BC is the era of geometric styles, with painted decoration marked by the predominance of squares, rhomboids, parallel lines, Greek keys, etc. The 8th century saw the relaxing of this style and the addition of plant and animal motifs in a period known as 'Orientalizing'. After this, distinct schools of pottery grew up in several areas, the first being CORINTH because of its good trading position and exposure to Orientalizing influences. However, the later and probably more artistic centre was ATHENS and Attica, which produced a type of pottery,

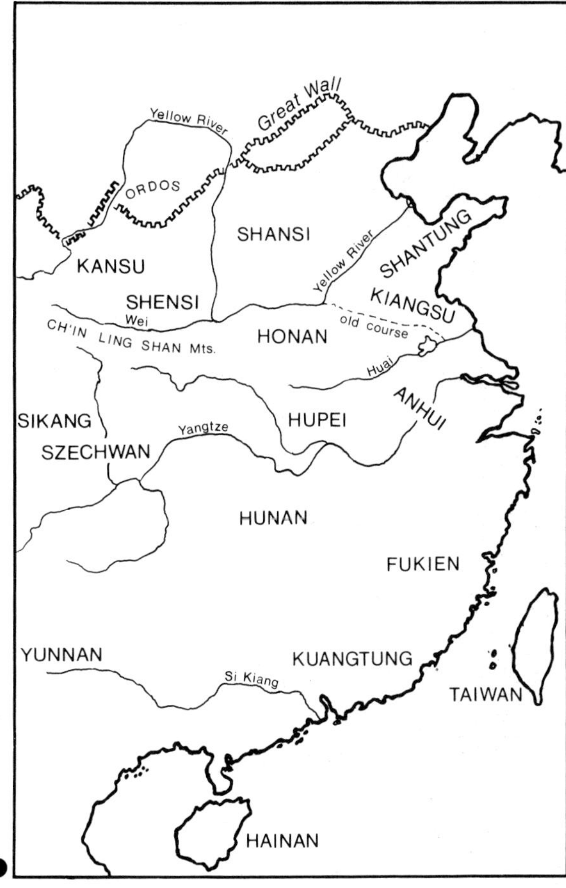
Great Wall
Yellow River
ORDOS
SHANSI
KANSU
Yellow River
SHANTUNG
SHENSI
KIANGSU
Wei
old course
CH'IN LING SHAN Mts.
HONAN
Huai
ANHUI
SIKANG
HUPEI
Yangtze
SZECHWAN
HUNAN
FUKIEN
YUNNAN
KUANGTUNG
Si Kiang
TAIWAN
HAINAN

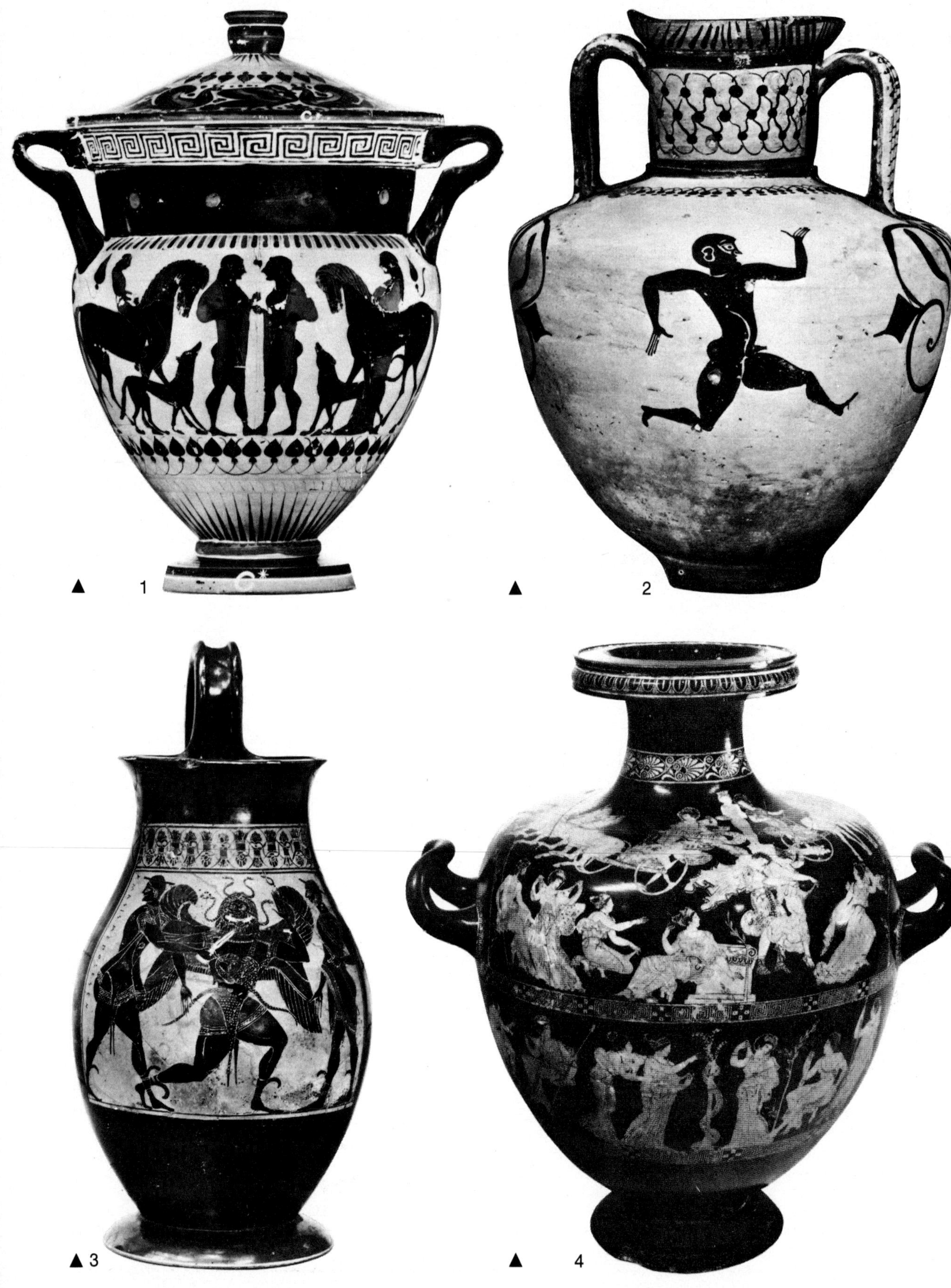

▲ 1

▲ 2

▲ 3

▲ 4

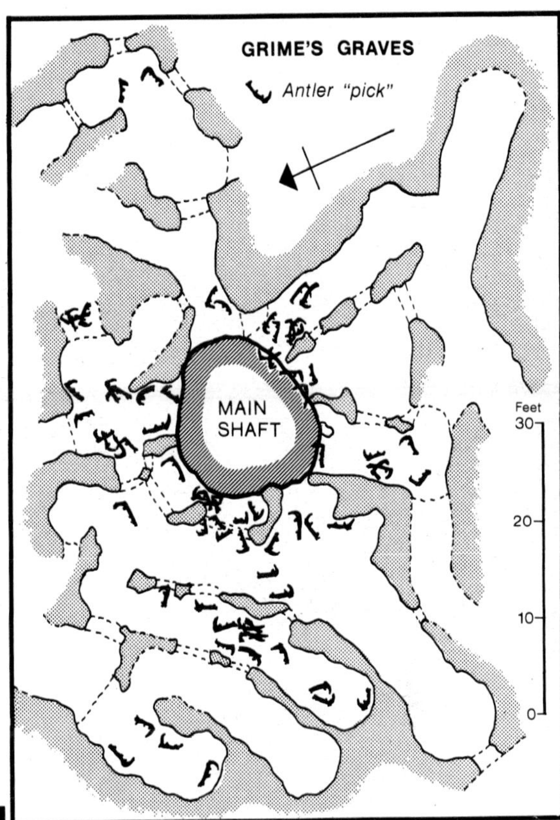

called 'black-figure', in which the pot is painted with a slip or gloss which fires black in the shape of the figure. The details are incised or highlighted in white. The scenes are mainly mythological (1–3).

By the end of the 6th century Attica dominated the market with the products of artists such as Kleitas, Nearchos and Exekias. However, at about this time (530–525 BC) potters in the Kerameikos district of Athens made a great change in potting techniques. 'Red-figure' developed, with figures in red against a black background. The black is a surface slip and its colour differed from the main fabric (both were virtually the same clay) due to carefully controlled firing conditions. Figures were formed by painting the background and highlights to leave a red outline. Scenes of a more secular character are common (4). This technique continued until the 4th century BC when it declined.

▲ Greek pots have many names, not all of which can be related to particular vessels. Some common ones are *krater* (wine mixer) (1), *skythos*, *cantharos* (cups), *oinochoe* (pitcher), *hydria* (water-jug) (4), *amphora* (wine or olive oil jar) (2), *lekythos* (funerary oil jar), *alabastron* and *aryballos* (ointment jar).

GREEN GULLY, Australia Site (at Keilor, Victoria) of a flake industry, including large side-scrapers, which spans the period 15,000–4500 BC. Early examples of Australian FABRICATORS were also part of the stone industry. Human skeletal remains, which seem to represent bones of segments of two individuals, were found buried together in 1965, and have been dated to 4500 BC. 4km away, the Keilor cranium was discovered in 1940. Its exact age is not clear, but thought to be several thousand years older than the Green Gully remains. Both skulls have been described as of 'modern' structure.

GRIMALDI, Italy The locality of a group of caves near Monaco, containing Middle and Upper PALAEOLITHIC deposits, ranging from MOUSTERIAN to AURIGNACIAN and Grimaldian (an industry comparable to the GRAVETTIAN). The caves are especially noted for FIGURINE finds and a number of human burials. The latter include two children buried side by side in the Grotte des Enfants of typical CRO-MAGNON type; in the same cave were found two skeletons with negroid features. In the Cavillon cave were the remains of a body smeared with red ochre and crowned with an arrangement of perforated stag teeth.

■ **GRIME'S GRAVES, Norfolk** The site of a large group of Neolithic flint-mines near Brandon on the Norfolk–Suffolk border. The mines cover between 15 and 37 hectares; some hundreds of shafts down through the chalk exist. It has been estimated that several million axes must have been exported from this centre. Its major associations seem to be Late Neolithic (GROOVED WARE). Several smaller mine centres were operating perhaps more than a millennium earlier on the Sussex Downland. ANTLER PICKS are found in some quantities in archaeological excavations of such mines.

GROOVE AND SPLINTER TECHNIQUE The process of removing slivers from antlers for making into objects such as pins or harpoon heads. The antler may be softened by prolonged soaking in water. Then two parallel grooves are cut along the length of the antler shaft with a flint tool such as a BURIN. The splinter is then lévered out, and ground

smooth or carved into the required shape. Specimens illustrating the various stages were found at STAR CARR.

GROOVED WARE A distinctive type of pottery, partly contemporary with PETERBOROUGH WARE of the British Later NEOLITHIC. It has been found from Scotland to Devon and was once called Rinyo-Clacton pottery (after sites in the Orkneys and Essex) but not in Ireland. Its characteristic features are a flat base, and heavy decoration formed by adding and taking away clay from the surface. It is commonly found at HENGES, such as DURRINGTON WALLS. Grooved Ware, unlike other types of British Neolithic pottery, is often associated with chisel-ended arrowheads (used for hunting birds).

GRUBENHAUS Sunken-floored huts *(Grubenhäuser)* are the most common type of dwelling in the Elbe–Weser area of the continental homelands of the Anglo-Saxons. They are found in England from the 5th century on sites such as MUCKING where there is evidence of LAETI or FOEDERATI occupation. There are many different types of *Grubenhäus*, but the average length is about 6m, with the floor dug about 1m deep. The superstructures were of wood or wattle and daub and had varying post construction: some have no main posts, others 2, 4 or 6. All types have been excavated at WEST STOW and CANTERBURY. *Grubenhäuser* were probably the normal houses of the poorer classes of Anglo-Saxon society, and are often found grouped around the larger HALLS of richer people.

GUA CHA, Malaya A ROCK SHELTER excavated in 1954. Material of both HOABINHIAN and Neolithic stages was found, though the fine, bifacial pebble tools are of a greater relative sophistication than many typical Hoabinhian assemblages. A gap was seen between the Hoabinhian and Neolithic material, which was interpreted as representing migration of new populations. Subsequently, other views were proposed, and analysis of the fragmented human remains did not indicate appreciable evidence of change in physical type. Elements described as Neolithic innovations are extended (rather than flexed) burials, flake tools (interpreted as remains of workshop debris), cord-impressed pottery, and quadrangular axes. In the later Neolithic, more advanced and varied stone and ceramic technology, and richly furnished burials appeared. Faunal remains from Gua Cha comprised more than 90 per cent young pig bones.

GUA KECHIL, Malaya An inland ROCK SHELTER, excavated in 1962 in Pahang, contained a HOABINHIAN tool assemblage, including cord-marked pottery, animal bone and shells. Subsequently the Hoabinhian was seen to have been replaced, with the introduction of polished stone and bone tools, a great increase in pottery, and the appearance of a new, distinctive red-slipped and burnished ware. As these changes were accompanied by a marked decrease in animal and shell remains, this progression may represent a shift from a hunting and gathering mode of subsistence to some sort of agricultural activity *c* 2500 BC.

GUA LAWA, Indonesia ['Bat Cave'] A site excavated in Sampung, east Java, in the 1920s. Much of its 3–4m deep cultural deposit comprised a MESOLITHIC bone tool assemblage known as the SAMPUNG BONE INDUSTRY, of which Gua Lawa is the TYPE-SITE. The bone and antler implements are exemplified by fishhooks, spatulas and awls.

▲

Stone implements were represented at Gua Lawa by winged arrowheads, unretouched flakes and blades, and numerous mortars and pestles (some still bearing traces of haematite). In addition, shell scrapers and ornaments and cord-marked potsherds were unearthed. The animal bones included those of four species today extinct in Java. Several poorly preserved human skeletons were found, buried in a flexed position, some covered by large slabs of rock. From the uppermost layers of the cave came pieces of bronze and iron, intermingled with a few rectangular polished stone adzes.

▲ **GUNDESTRUP, Denmark** A bog where panels of a magnificent silver cauldron were found. The cauldron was dismantled and probably intended as a votive offering to the gods (*see also* LLYN CERRIG BACH). There were originally 8 outer and 5 inner plates and a base plate, decorated in relief in the CELTIC ART style. Each plate has a central Celtic deity, some of whom wear TORCS. One of the gods may be Cernunnos (the horned god); few are identifiable. The gods and goddesses are surrounded with scenes from Celtic mythology, sacrificial scenes, mythical animals and warriors carrying LURS. The cauldron was probably made in Romania, Bulgaria or France in the 2nd century BC.

GUNDLINGEN
see SWORD

GWITHIAN, Cornwall A site where remains of CELTIC FIELDS have been excavated. Surrounding three huts was a complex of small square fields, which were crossploughed using an ARD. The fields were under intense cultivation, and probably manured with seaweed. Prehistoric spade marks were recognizable at the edges of the fields, some of which were marked by LYNCHETS. The settlement is dated to the end of the Early Bronze Age, *c* 1300 BC.

GYPSUM BURIAL A Roman method of burial where the body, usually in a coffin, was covered with gypsum to preserve it for an afterlife. It originates apparently in Algeria, occurs in France and, by the 3rd and 4th centuries AD, was quite common in the wealthier areas of Britain, especially at Dorchester (Dorset), YORK, and around the Thames estuary.

HACILAR [pronounced Hajilar], Turkey A small site in south-west Anatolia excavated in the 1950s. It is comparable to ÇATAL HÜYÜK although RADIOCARBON dating gives a longer occupation, from *c* 6750 to *c* 5000 BC. No pottery was found in the earliest levels. Wheat, barley and lentils were cultivated, and the bones of sheep and cattle were found (though their DOMESTICATION was not proved). Houses were constructed of mud-brick, wood and stone, with upper storeys of wood.

HADDA, Pakistan This Buddhist site in the Peshawar plain of Pakistan has revealed material reflecting the art of the west, including the stucco figure of an effeminate youth. *See also* BEGRAM, CHARSADA, TAXILA.

HADRIAN, Publius Aelius Hadrianus (AD 76–138) A Roman emperor of a practical and military nature, Hadrian came from a distinguished family in Spain to succeed, in AD 117, the Emperor Trajan who had adopted him. His military policy, for which he is chiefly remembered, concentrated on strengthening the frontiers of

●

the empire by linear defences, along the Rhine and Danube as well as in Britain (*see* HADRIAN'S WALL). He had an intense homosexual relationship with the youth Antinous, later drowned in the Nile. Hadrian carried out economic reforms at Rome and was a patron of the arts, founding the Athenaeum. He was succeeded in 138 by Antoninus Pius, and was buried in a mausoleum of his own design, the Castel Sant'Angelo in Rome.

● **HADRIAN'S VILLA, Italy** Built AD 118–38 as a country residence for the Emperor Hadrian. He seems to have used several of the buildings that he had seen on his many travels as ideas for his rambling villa. The 'Poikele' has part of the Painted Stoa at Athens in it, and 'Canopus' resembled the temple to Isis at Canopus in Egypt. The period of its building was one of Rome's greatest architectural phases and there are several interesting features including the daring 'Island Villa', a set of rooms composed of segments of circles within a round moat.

▲ **HADRIAN'S WALL** The greatest surviving monument of Roman Britain, Hadrian's Wall was constructed between *c* AD 122 and *c* AD 128, a wall of stone running 120km from the Tyne to the Solway. It was constructed in two phases. Small forts, fitted with a sally-port, are situated at intervals of one Roman mile, with two turrets between each pair of these; sixteen larger forts also garrisoned this northern frontier of the empire. Behind the wall ran the VALLUM. The wall was abandoned due to a change of frontier policy *c* 138, and the defences breached; by 160 it had been re-garrisoned and repaired. It was destroyed in 196, rebuilt by SEVERUS, but destroyed again in 296 and 367. It was included in Count Honorius' system of defences, but *c* 400 had been finally abandoned. The precise military function of the wall is a matter of debate.

HAJI POTTERY The traditional red-ware of Japan during the TOMB PERIOD used as domestic ware and by the masses as funerary vessels. Often simple, undecorated, and generally of round-bottomed form, these pots show similarities with some of their YAYOI predecessors. *See also:* SUE POTTERY.

HALAF, Syria A TELL by the Khabur river near the Turkish–Syrian border. Excavations in 1911–14 uncovered a culture to which the name of the tell has been given. The Halaf culture belongs to the 5th millennium BC and follows the HASSUNA–SAMARRA period. It has been found at many sites in northern Iraq and Syria. Mud-brick appears as a building material for the first time in MESOPOTAMIA and cobbled streets indicate community ■ organization. Some structures known as 'tholoi' were found from this period at Arpachiya. These were constructed of *pisé* (*see* MUD-BRICK) and are vaulted to form a shape similar to the 'beehive' house still used in northern Syria. Craftsmen were skilled at making small stamp SEALS, AMULETS and FIGURINES. The finest pottery from Mesopotamia belongs to this period. Many different shapes were produced – some with very thin walls and decoration minutely executed in many colours. The Halaf culture ends abruptly and is replaced by the UBAID culture.

HALBERD A weapon about 70cm long, riveted at right angles to the handle, which was in widespread use during the European Bronze Age, from Ireland to Poland and Portugal (200 examples come from Britain) and elsewhere.

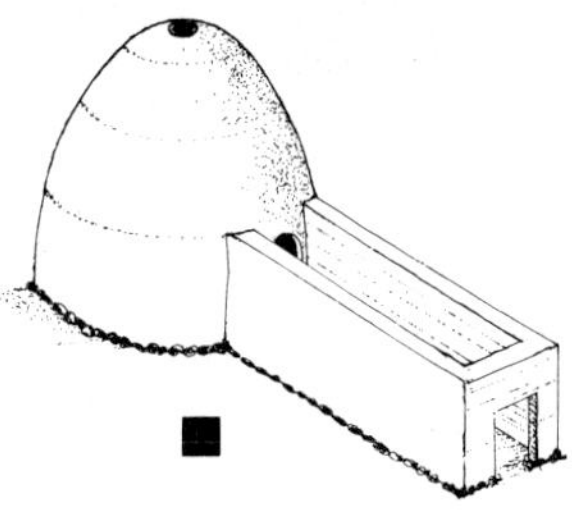

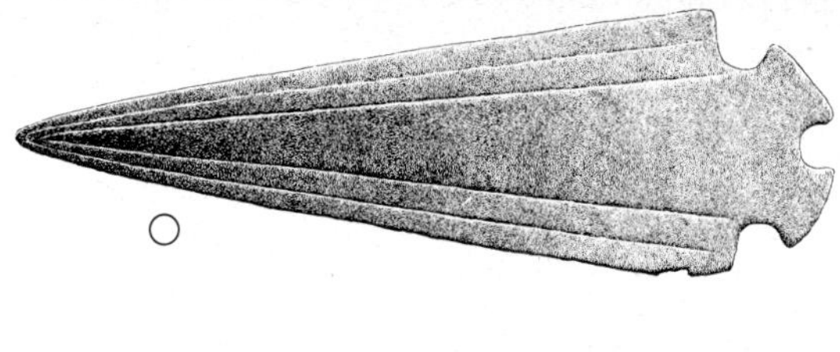

HALF-LIFE A measurement of the radioactivity of a substance. The half-life of a radioactive isotope is the time required for the intensity of radiation to fall to half its original value. It also represents the time required for half of the atoms in a sample to disintegrate.

HALL (Anglo-Saxon) All the main business of life in Anglo-Saxon England – eating, drinking, sleeping and entertaining – was carried out in the lord's hall. In contrast to the GRUBENHÄUSER of the common people, halls were large and spacious, 25m or more long at the royal sites of CHEDDAR and YEAVERING. Like most secular buildings of the period they were built of timber posts and/or planks. The high roofs were supported by the outside walls, sometimes buttressed, and often two longitudinal lines of internal posts which divided the hall into three aisles. Doors were normally on opposed walls. Rarely, a small private room was built at one end.

HALLSTATT, Austria A site in the Salzkammergut which has given its name to the first part of the European IRON AGE period; Hallstatt itself dates from 750 to 500 BC. Most of the finds are from the cemetery and the salt mines, as the settlement site in the valley is now beneath the modern village. The cemetery is on the mountain slope above the village; in the 19th century over 3000 graves, both male and female, were excavated. A few graves date from the Late BRONZE AGE, but most are Hallstatt or early LA TÈNE in date. The grave goods are very wealthy, as a result of the salt trade from the mines: salt was an essential commodity and even more valuable than metal ores. Imports from Greece and ETRUSCAN Italy, especially of wine, were perhaps exchanged for salt. Like the cemetery, the mining galleries at Hallstatt start in the Late Bronze Age and are more numerous in the Iron Age; in them the salt has preserved actual clothing and mining implements of the Iron Age miners. In the early La Tène period, the centre of salt production moved to Durrmberg near Hallein, and Hallstatt declined in importance. The Hallstatt period is distinguished from the preceding URNFIELD phase by the use of iron. Some iron objects appeared in 8th-century BC Urnfield Europe, but not until the Hallstatt period was it used on a large scale, e.g. for the iron SWORDS in Hallstatt graves. By the 6th century BC, iron-using communities extended from Jugoslavia to France. A new burial practice is associated with the Hallstatt Iron Age, replacing the Urnfield CREMATION cemeteries: waggon graves with wooden mortuary houses. This may be due to influence from the CIMMERIANS who certainly introduced the new forms of horse harness found in the graves (*see* VIX and HOHMICHELE burials). In the 7th century BC similar burials were to be found in Bohemia and Austria, and by the 6th century BC, they had reached Germany and France. Cultural continuity from the Urnfield into the Hallstatt period is clear in other respects, with the continued building of HILLFORTS like the HEUNEBERG, though TIMBER-LACED ramparts were further developed. Likewise, division between the Hallstatt and later La Tène period is more apparent than real.

HAMA [Biblical Hamath], Syria A TELL by the river Orontes. Excavations in 1931–8 revealed that the site had been occupied from *c* 6000 BC. During the 2nd millennium BC Hama was a large city, although it is not mentioned in ancient records until *c* 1000 BC when it becomes an ARAMAEAN city-state. King Toi of Hama sent gifts to the

ISRAELITE king, David (2 Samuel 8:9–12). The city was destroyed in 720 BC by the ASSYRIANS. A previous attack by Shalmaneser III is recorded in bronze RELIEFS. The city was rebuilt *c* 200 BC by the Greeks and later belonged to the Romans and Moslems.

HAMBURGIAN A late GLACIAL group of reindeer hunters in north Germany and Holland, named after a series of sites near Hamburg. The Hamburgian was contemporary with the later stages of the MAGDALENEAN, from which it is thought to have derived, with roots also in the late eastern GRAVETTIAN. The flint industry is characterized by shouldered or tanged points and the absence of axes, the latter compatible with the relatively treeless late glacial environment. *See* AHRENSBURGIAN.

HAMMURAPI [Hammurabi] The 6th king of the First Dynasty of BABYLON 1792–1750 BC. Much knowledge of him comes from the archives found at MARI, which cease when he captured the city toward the end of his reign. He appears as a strategist and an organizer very capably handling international affairs. However, he is best known as a legislator. A STELE removed from BABYLON by the Elamites was found in excavations at SUSA. The stele is 2.3m high and contains a series of judicial pronouncements – about 280 in all. At the top of the stele is a RELIEF of Hammurapi receiving the symbols of kingship from the god SHAMASH.

HAMWIH, Hampshire The Middle SAXON port and town of Southampton had a special relationship with WINCHESTER and WESSEX, to which it acted as outport and industrial centre. From *c* AD 700 there was much trade with the FRISIANS and a SCEATTA mint was early established. Contact with northern France, probably with QUENTOVIC, with the Rhineland, and with DORESTAD is proved by finds of coins, glass and pottery. Hamwih was attacked several times by the Danes in the 9th century, and the site of the town was moved to the more defensible position of modern Southampton.

HANDAXE A CORE-TOOL worked on both faces characteristic of certain Lower PALAEOLITHIC flint industries (*see* ABBEVILLEAN; ACHEULEAN). The function of these implements is not known, but it is probable that most of them were general-purpose tools rather than axes; or if axes, were hafted rather than held in the hand.

● **HAN DYNASTY** The Han dynasty of China began in 206 BC, following the short-lived CH'IN dynasty. The new dynasty copied the example of its predecessors and set up a bureaucratic state with its emperors ruling from capitals at Sian in Shensi, and LOYANG, Honan. Its programme of territorial expansion was aided by a highly organized military programme, complete with well constructed roads and troops equipped with iron swords and the cross-bow. This latter was especially important in campaigns at the GREAT WALL.

Most archaeological knowledge of the Han period derives from excavations of tombs, some of which display sophisticated construction, including true arches and vaulted and domed roofs. Grave goods, including house models, clay figurines, and lacquer-ware witness a rise of realism, as opposed to the earlier more stylized motifs. At times the finds are extraordinarily spectacular, as at Ma-wang-tui, near Ch'ang-sha, Hunan, in the Yangtze valley.

▲

In Tomb 1 was found the well-preserved body of a noblewoman, Lady Li, who died in the mid 2nd century BC at about 50 years of age, and was buried in a pit 20m deep with steps leading down into it. Layers of charcoal and white clay kept out moisture and oxygen, thus preserving her body well enough for an autopsy to be undertaken on the soft tissues. Lady Li was found to have suffered from gallstones and arterio-sclerosis, among other ailments. Thousands of funerary objects were placed with her, including silks, food, figurines and lacquer-ware, all displaying fine workmanship. Tomb 3 was that of a young man, thought to be Lady Li's son. Excavations there revealed early Chinese maps, treatises on medical matters, and the texts of several classic books, written on silk. Man-ch'eng, Hopei, was the site, too, of unique finds. Here were the tombs of Liu Sheng, the brother of an emperor, and his wife, the Princess Tou Wan. Their rock-cut tombs contained bronze and pottery vessels, figurines, horse skeletons and chariots, as well as fragments of wood and lacquer. But the most outstanding objects of all were the burial suits made of jade tablets. Each contained more than 2000 tablets, held to each other by gold wires and completely encasing the bodies. It is thought that the suits were manufactured either for spiritual significance, or in the hope of preservative qualities; the bodies themselves, however, had disintegrated.

The Han dynasty fell in AD 206, and the country divided into small, hostile states.

HANGING BOWL Hemispherical bronze bowls, fitted at the rim with loops for suspension and ornamented with circular panels of CHAMPLEVÉ ENAMEL AND MILLEFIORI glass inlay, have been found in Dark Age graves in England and Ireland, and in Viking Age graves in Scandinavia. The decorative mounts are CELTIC rather than Anglo-Saxon, consisting mainly of developed spiral motifs. Whether Irish or NORTHUMBRIAN in manufacture, their presumed use as ecclesiastical fingerbowls or sanctuary lamps is entirely Mediterranean in origin.

▲ **HANIWA** Ceremonial miniature Japanese clay sculptures or models used during the TOMB PERIOD. They were placed on the slopes of the burial mound, or at times in the tomb itself. The subjects portrayed included houses, animals, warriors and shields.

HARAPPA, Pakistan One of the twin 'capitals' of the INDUS CIVILIZATION, Harappa was situated on the Ravi, a tributary of the Indus in the Punjab. It was excavated by the Archaeological Survey 1920–34, and by WHEELER in 1946. The mature phase is preceded by a brick-walled settlement whose pottery defines the northern culture province of the pre-Harappan culture. The lower town is somewhat larger than at MOHENJO-DARO and includes a series of granaries, tiny single-roomed houses and working-floors between the river and the citadel.

HARPOON A throwing spear with a barbed point, usually made of bone or antler. The point is loosely attached to the shaft so that when it hits its quarry, the entire head becomes lodged in the animal, which is prevented from escaping by a line tied to the point. Two barbed points hafted with the barbs facing each other form a LEISTER.

HASSUNA, Iraq A site 35km south of Mosul where excavations in 1943–4 found a prehistoric culture with distinctive pottery. The architecture is similar to that found at JARMO, but the presence of bowls and jars with glossy surfaces and decorated with geometrical shapes in red indicated that this was a higher culture. Similar pottery has been found as far away as JERICHO, implying a common culture throughout the FERTILE CRESCENT in about 6000 BC. The houses were similar in plan, size and building material to modern ones in the area. In the upper levels of Hassuna a very advanced form of pottery was found, of a type first seen at Samarra, about 120km north of Baghdad. It is known as Samarran. Samarran pottery consists of large plates, bowls and round-bellied pots decorated not only with geometric patterns but also with representations of birds, fish, scorpions, antelopes and human beings.

HASTINAPURA, India One of the main villages of the *Mahabharata* epic (the story of feuding village states on the Ganges, *c* 8th–6th century BC) which ties in with the Painted Grey Ware (PGW) period at many Ganges sites. The evidence of a flood at Hastinapura is confirmed by the archaeological evidence that a considerable portion of the PGW occupation has been swept away. Iron slag and ore appear in the upper levels of the PGW period but iron artefacts are not found until the succeeding, NORTHERN BLACK POLISHED WARE period, from *c* 600 BC, when coinage ● also appears. RINGWELLS lined with rings or jars are now common. In about 250 BC the site was destroyed by fire. *See also* ARYANS; GANGES CIVILIZATION.

HAUA FTEAH, Libya A cave in Cyrenaica, overlooking the Mediterranean, with a long archaeological sequence beginning *c* 80,000 BC. The earliest deposit is a variant of the AMUDIAN of the Levant, and is followed by MOUSTERIAN, Dabban, ORANIAN and CAPSIAN industries. Finally a NEOLITHIC level provides early evidence for the domestication of sheep or goats in Africa, *c* 6000 BC. Sea shells and sediments from the cave testify to fluctuations in temperature and humidity contemporary with the temperature changes of the last glacial stage in Europe.

HAWARA, Egypt In the Libyan desert towards FAIYUM, the site has the mud-brick pyramid (once cased in limestone) of Ammenemes III, of Dynasty XII. In spite of anti-theft devices (blind corridors, false-shafts, and systematic blocking of the circuitous true passage), the 100 tonne quartzite sarcophagus was robbed.

Nearby is the Labyrinth – a name given by the Greeks to the huge intricate funerary complex of Ammenemes, allegedly two levels each with twelve courts and 1500 chambers, enclosed by colonnade wall. PETRIE excavated at the site, producing a partial plan from surviving limestone and granite fragments.

The elaborate architectural system and sheer size cause discussion of its funerary purpose: was it that of royal residence, or administrative centre? These questions can be resolved only by archaeological investigations.

Petrie's discovery of lifelike portraits attached to mummies of Roman period illustrate the beginnings of BYZANTINE iconography.

HAZOR, Israel A large TELL in northern Palestine excavated 1955–8 and 1968. The ancient city is mentioned in Egyptian texts from the 19th century BC and in the MARI documents. The city began in about 2700 BC, and by 1700 BC an area of 80 hectares was within the walls. One of the gates of this time has been reconstructed. Five temples from the period have also been found; one was dedicated to the moon god SIN and another to the weather god ADAD. After destruction by Joshua (Joshua 11:10ff), Solomon rebuilt the city (I Kings 9:15) and a contemporary gate, palace, storehouse (similar to BEER-SHEBA) and water system have been found. Sporadic occupation of the site is known after its destruction by the ASSYRIANS in 743 BC.

HEATHERY BURN, Durham A cave near Stanhope containing Middle BRONZE AGE objects buried due to a flooding of the burn. The deposit is important because, unlike most Bronze Age groups, it represents domestic equipment, rather than a votive hoard (like LLYN FAWR) or grave goods. The objects include bronze weapons and implements; gold, bronze and stone ornaments; and bone cheek pieces and CHARIOT fittings. Similar objects in the Heathery Burn tradition are found throughout the north of England at this period, and many of them are paralleled in Ireland. Domestic debris, such as human and animal bones, and marine shells, was also found in the cave.

HEDEBY, Germany From *c* 800 to 1050 AD Hedeby was the largest town in north Europe. It was situated on a narrow fjord whence it controlled the trading route between the Baltic and North Sea. A massive defensive rampart encircles the 25 hectares of town on the landward side. The boggy ground has preserved organic material remarkably well; foundations of HALLS and GRUBENHÄUSER with plank or wattle and daub walls still stand quite high. There were three cemeteries, one containing very richly furnished graves. There is much evidence of industrial activity as well as many imported luxury goods. Hedeby is famed as the scene of the first Christian mission to Denmark by St Ansgar. *See also* BIRKA, DORESTAD.

▲ **HELIOPOLIS, Egypt** The oldest and most influential cult-centre of sun-worship in Egypt, north-east of the capital Memphis. Its temple contained the 'ben-ben' stone, resembling a short obelisk, which emerged out of chaos in primeval times as the focal point for the act of creation. Two gods Re (sun-god) and Atum (a more abstract concept – perhaps 'totality') coalesced to become the chief god in the genealogy which the priests of Heliopolis gave to their nine special gods (ENNEAD). Heliopolis also had a living incarnation of the sungod in the Mnevis bull. Heliopolis' prestige lasted even when THEBES became the wealthier religious centre. It is basically lost to archaeology, having been a source of stone in Ptolemaic and Roman times for Alexandria and Italy. One of the two obelisks survives, set up by Sesostris I (Dynasty XII) in front of the temple to celebrate a jubilee.

HELLADIC This name is used for the Bronze Age of mainland Greece (*c* 3000–1200 BC). It is divided into three periods, Early, Middle and Late; the last is better known as the MYCENAEAN period.

HELLENISTIC The period in Greece and Asia Minor from Philip of Macedon (mid 4th century BC) until the firm establishment of Roman rule in the 1st century BC is usually deemed Hellenistic. It is a period when Greece was dominated by outside powers, and when the country itself was therefore stable but relatively uninspired. Greek science established itself during this time, and writers such

●

▲

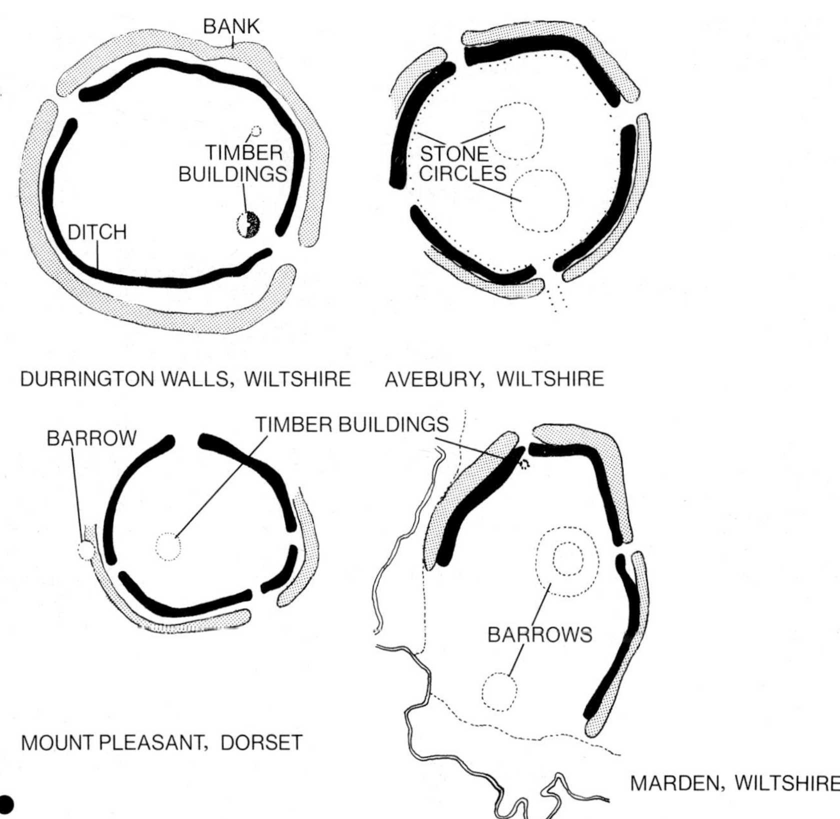

as Menander, Demosthenes and Apollonius of Rhodes, were active. Chief events were the invasions of the CELTS *c* 300 and the war with the Romans in the 3rd century BC, in which Rome eventually conquered Greece and turned it into the provinces of Achaia and Macedonia. CORINTH was destroyed 147–146 and the Mithridatic War affected Greece 86–85. After this the Romans used Greece more and more as a cultural centre; during the Empire ATHENS, especially, was favoured as a university town.

HELWAN, Egypt On the east bank of Nile opposite Memphis, its cemeteries of Archaic period show earliest use of limestone blocks in constructing underground burial chambers in thousands of graves. The funerary equipment of these officials includes vases which exemplify the ability of craftsmen to work in a variety of stone – limestone, alabaster, schist, diorite. Jewellery of ivory and semi-precious stones was also found. Unfortunately this important early necropolis has never been fully published in archaeological reports.

● **HENGE** A general term for circular earthwork enclosures of the Late Neolithic in Britain, distinguished particularly by the bank normally being *outside* the ditch. The class includes a great variety of sites, some of them ritual and enclosing stone circles (e.g. AVEBURY), others apparently more domestic in character and enclosing large timber buildings (e.g. DURRINGTON WALLS). Henges have been divided into two classes. Class I have a single entrance through the perimeter bank and ditch, and Class II two entrances. This division has become less useful now that so wide a range in size and shape, and probably function, has been recognized. They are usually associated with pottery of PETERBOROUGH and GROOVED WARE type. The word 'henge' comes from STONEHENGE, which literally means 'hanging stone'.

HEPTARCHY The period from the late 6th century to the end of the 7th century AD in England is known as the period of the heptarchy (government by seven rulers), though there were more than seven kingdoms. These were NORTHUMBRIA, Lindsey, MERCIA, Essex, Middlesex, Kent, WESSEX and Sussex. The title *Bretwalda* was given to the high king or overlord of all the kingdom.

▲ **HERCULANEUM, Italy** A small Campanian city on the slopes of the volcano Vesuvius, on a coastal promontory. It was traditionally founded by Hercules, and was originally a Greek city: the first mention of it is in 314 BC. During the 5th century BC it fell to the Samnites, and by 89 BC had become a Roman city. It was destroyed, together with POMPEII, in a volcanic eruption of AD 79. Despite difficult conditions, excavations have continued sporadically since the 18th century, uncovering the theatre (begun in the reign of AUGUSTUS) the baths, and several large and luxurious private houses; many buildings survive up to the roof height.

HERMOPOLIS, Egypt The religious capital in Middle Egypt, chief sanctuary of the moon-god THOTH and for the OGDOAD. Excavations revealed the temenos of the temple and monuments from the Middle and New Kingdoms. It was clear that there had been a landscaped enclosure of tamarisk trees. Ramesside pharaohs, in their destruction of Akhenaten's city just to the south, brought back reliefs from AMARNA and reused them in the foundations of their

own buildings at Hermopolis. These reliefs are now an important source for archaeologists in interpreting the Amarna period. Greek influence can be found in the ruins of a large AGORA and in the demolished Temple of Thoth built by the priest Petosiris. *See also* TUNA EL-GEBEL.

HEROD THE GREAT (73–4 BC) The Romans gave him the title 'King of the Jews' in 40 BC, as well as military aid so that he could oust the PARTHIAN-appointed king of Judea. After three years of fighting, Herod secured his kingdom in Palestine and ruled it for 33 years as an ally of Rome in spite of his precarious position on the frontier of the Roman and Parthian empires. By his charm and diplomacy he was friends with Cassius, Antony and Octavian (later Augustus) in succession. He undertook lavish building projects in his own kingdom and elsewhere (in Athens for example). He rebuilt SAMARIA and CAESAREA. He fortified Masada, a flat-topped mountain to the south of the Dead Sea, and built a spectacular palace hanging on the northern cliff face. As a descendant of the Edomites, Herod was hated by the Jews even though he built them a magnificent temple in JERUSALEM. They remembered him as the murderer of their High Priest's family. The world remembers him for the slaughter of the infants at Bethlehem. Near Bethlehem is a high artificial hill on which Herod built a fortress (the Herodium) and it was here that he was buried.

HEUNEBERG, Germany A large HILLFORT of the HALLSTATT period of the Iron Age (6th century BC). It was a well-defended site following the contours of the hill with TIMBER-LACED walls. In the second phase, unbaked bricks were used for part of the wall – a Mediterranean technique soon abandoned. There are many imports here, from Greek pottery to Italian wine, showing the wealth of the inhabitants. These objects were perhaps imported via the hillfort at Mont Lassois, associated with the rich burial of VIX. The Heuneberg too is connected with a rich burial: the HOHMICHELE, which lies near by.

HIERAKONPOLIS, Egypt Upstream from Thebes, an extremely fertile site of the capital of the south in Predynastic times (with ruins of fortress of this period). Local gods were Horus (the falcon), and deified predynastic rulers (Souls of Nekhen). Wall-painting (now destroyed) in a tomb showed predynastic battle and hunting scenes. A slate palette found during Quibell's excavations depicted Narmer (Menes) conquering the northern ruler to become the first pharaoh of United Egypt. Old Kingdom monuments excavated include a spectacular copper hawk-head covered with gold sheets and with eyes in obsidian, and largest bronze statue found (of Pepy I).

HIERATIC Term used by the Greeks to describe a modified form of the ancient Egyptian hieroglyphic script. By the time the Greeks came into contact with it, Hieratic was restricted to a formal usage on religious papyri (hence the word 'hieratikos': priestly). However, Hieratic had almost as ancient a history as HIEROGLYPHS. It evolved as a more cursive script eminently suited to writing done by a rush brush on papyrus. In its early stages many signs are recognizably contracted Hieroglyphs, e.g. in the first real corpus of hieratic signs found in the temple-revenue accounts on papyri from ABUSIR (Dynasty V). By the Middle Kingdom vertical columns of writing gave way to the script written from right to left, thereby giving the scribe more scope for developing a distinctly cursive script written quickly. Separate signs became joined (ligatures) so that the brush need not be lifted so frequently from the papyrus. Hieratic was extensively employed for administration and business documents, mathematical papyri, literature and private and exhortative correspondence. Variation in style, care and formality can differ greatly between a literary text and a bureaucratic record. Hieratic was superseded in commercial and secular usage by DEMOTIC in the seventh century BC.

● **HIEROGLYPHS** Name given by the Greeks to the picture-writing of ancient Egypt which appeared as an already-advanced script as early as Dynasty I (3100 BC). Although for practical and bureaucratic purposes the cursive abbreviated scripts, HIERATIC and DEMOTIC became the far more extensively used on PAPYRUS, hieroglyphs continued to be sculptured on temple walls, columns and pylons, and for official decrees or funerary texts until the fourth century AD. The stimulus to develop phonetic and communicative signs from straight-forward pictures is considered by some to have reached Egypt from Mesopotamia (where CUNEIFORM began as a pictorial script before becoming totally stylized). Even if this is the case, the signs used by the Egyptians derived entirely from observation of their own environment. This included such things as the papyrus-plant and the ibis (sacred to the god Thoth), both given their own hieroglyphs. The total number of signs exceeds 700. Although it would have been within the Egyptian competence to simplify their script into an alphabet (since there were 24 hieroglyphs each with a single sound value), this step was not taken.

The direction of hieroglyphic writing is found right to left, left to right and in vertical columns. The signs face into the direction from which one should start reading, e.g. the birds' beaks will point to the beginning of the line.

A hieroglyph can stand in some cases for the object it depicts, such as a house, or by extension it can represent a sound value in words of unrelated meaning, e.g. the house sign forming the sound 'pr' in the verb 'to go'. Sound signs can represent one, two or three letters under one hieroglyph, although the unilateral signs were often used quite unnecessarily to supplement the sound elements conveyed by the biliterals and triliterals. In addition a word phonetically written normally had a determinative, i.e. a hieroglyph attached to the end of the word to clarify its sense and avoid ambiguity with other words of a similar sound value. No vowels were represented in the hieroglyphic script, the basis being the invariable consonant structure of the words. Reconstructions (some hotly debated) of original vowel sounds have been suggested by using the pharaonic names occurring in Cuneiform diplomatic correspondence (which gives approximate vocalizations of how Egyptian words sounded to Middle Eastern scribes), by comparing versions of names in ancient Greek accounts, and by studying COPTIC.

HILANI, Bit- A suite of reception rooms found in many palaces of MESOPOTAMIA and the LEVANT. It consists of a portico with one to three columns, such as has been reconstructed for a palace of about 1400 BC at ALALAKH, and a throne room. There are usually additional subsidiary rooms for security, storage and conveniences. The Bit-Hilani only forms part of the entire palace complex which also has living quarters and administrative offices.

HILLFORT A fortified settlement on a hill, plateau top or promontory (e.g. BISKUPIN). Hillforts in Britain developed from the Late BRONZE AGE palisaded farming settlements like RAMS HILL. An early hillfort is IVINGHOE BEACON, dated to *c* 8th century BC. By 400 BC marketing centres were defended by ramparts and ditches. With the increase in centralized authority prior to the Roman conquest, many small hillforts were abandoned and power was concentrated in a few very large hillforts like MAIDEN CASTLE. Hillforts in Britain are small, usually 4–8 hectares in area, though Maiden Castle enclosed 18 hectares. On the Continent far larger hillforts like the HEUNEBERG developed into OPPIDA in the later IRON AGE. These were well organized, planned settlements, acting as religious centres and markets. Though British hillforts sometimes had shrines, and rows of houses along streets, they are not nucleated settlements on the scale of the European oppida. The early Iron Age ramparts which developed from Bronze Age palisades were often TIMBER-LACED for strength, though the MURUS GALLICUS did not appear in Britain. The earliest defences were UNIVALLATE. In stony areas walls were built of stone rather than earth and laced with timber. Many hillforts in the highland zone also had CHEVAUX DE FRISE. In Scotland, VITRIFIED FORTS are common. From 100 BC defences became MULTIVALLATE, and entrances were extremely elaborate. All these methods of fortification were effective against CELTIC cavalry, but not against the Roman armies, and many British hillforts were sacked during the Conquest.

HISSAR, Tepe A TELL near Damghan in north-east Iran excavated by Schmidt in 1931–2. Settlement of the site began in the 4th millennium by a people with copper articles and hand-made decorated pottery. These people were indigenous to Iran and were replaced in the 3rd millennium by people from the north who made dark grey pottery and had many weapons. This is thought to be the first movement of INDO-EUROPEAN people from central Asia to Iran. The site was destroyed in the 2nd millennium BC and except for some occupation in the SASSANIAN period, 3rd century AD, has remained unoccupied.

HITTITES An INDO-EUROPEAN-speaking people of unknown origin who appear in ANATOLIA (Turkey) early in the 2nd millennium BC. After making Boghazkoy their capital, they expanded their kingdom in Anatolia under King Labarnash *c* 1680 BC. Their territory extended into Syria with King Murshilish I capturing Aleppo in about 1610 BC and raiding as far as BABYLON. The Hittites vied with Egypt and MITANI for control of the LEVANT, reaching a peak of power under King Shuppiluliumash I *c* 1350 BC. The Hittite empire ended abruptly *c* 1230 BC when marauding bands from the north captured Boghazkoy. The Hittite language was written in CUNEIFORM script for administrative records such as those found at Boghazkoy, and in HIEROGLYPHS for public monuments. Hittite wealth came largely from metals: copper, lead, silver, and in particular iron (they were among the first iron-workers). Boghazkoy (ancient Hattusas) is situated in central Anatolia and has been excavated often since 1906. Although the city was previously occupied, most remains are from the Hittite period when it grew to a size of 300 hectares. The city was strongly fortified. Some of the gates were decorated with reliefs of either sphinxes, warriors or lions. Four very large temple complexes have been

A Vulture = mwt
B Mouth = r
C Seated lady = *determinative for woman*
D Sandlestrap =ʿnḫ (ANKH)
E Horned viper = f
F Heart and windpipe = nfr
G Heart =ỉb
H Quailchick = w
I Water = n
J Owl = m

excavated as well as many houses. Some of the administrative records of the Hittite empire were found on a large number of inscribed clay tablets discovered in storerooms. Nearby is the rock sanctuary of Yazilikaya. Although the buildings there are now destroyed, the rock faces still contain reliefs and HIEROGLYPHIC inscriptions which represent the gods of the HURRIANS.

HOABINHIAN This south-east Asian tool industry was first defined after excavations during the early decades of this century in the Hoa Binh province of Northern Vietnam. Found throughout mainland south-east Asia from south China, down through Malaya and into northern Sumatra, remains are usually found in upland karst riverine, or in coastal marine environments. The main characteristics are stone tools manufactured from river pebbles, with FLAKING either unifacial or bifacial. Also present are grinding stones and, in the upper levels, the introduction of cord-marked pottery and edge-grinding on the flaked pebbles; shells and animal bones are, in addition, frequent components. Though in the past this industry was generally considered MESOLITHIC, mainly because it contained no extinct species, it is now thought to be of Late PLEISTOCENE and Recent dates. This revision was made necessary by excavations in south-east Asia which have shown that faunal assemblages which appear essentially modern may date back to 30–40,000 BC. The Hoabinhian is thought to have grown out of the earlier CHOPPER–CHOPPING TOOL complex of the region.

HOD HILL, Dorset The only British native hillfort to include the remains of a subsequent Roman fort, Hod Hill has a considerable importance in the archaeology of the time of the Roman conquest of Britain. The occupation of the hillfort dates back to the earliest Iron Age, and the site became a fairly important tribal centre of the Durotriges. Catapult-bolts and the burning of huts inside the hillfort mark the assault by Roman troops under Vespasian; the Roman fort was constructed soon afterwards in a corner of the hillfort. Its importance appears to have been restricted to the initial period of conquest.

HOHMICHELE, Germany A burial mound of the HALLSTATT period *c* 6th century BC, associated with the nearby HEUNEBERG hillfort. It contained a central wooden mortuary chamber, and seven secondary burials. The grave goods of the rich central grave included the remains of a waggon, a bow with iron arrowheads, and male and female burials. Several wooden coffins were preserved in other graves. The Hohmichele also contained the earliest piece of silk cloth known from Europe, imported from the Mediterranean or the Far East.

HOHOKAM A culture of the SOUTHWESTERN tradition which developed from COCHISE antecendents in the desert regions of southern Arizona, USA, starting around 100 BC and continuing through four main phases until historic times. SNAKETOWN in the lower Gila valley is one of the main Hohokam sites. Large irrigations systems indicate an emphasis on maize agriculture, although plant-collecting and game-trapping were supplementary. Early architecture consisted of wattle and daub houses developing from rectangular to predominantly oval shapes, but in the Classic period AD 1200–1400, huge multi-storied apartment-like dwellings were built, typified by the ruins at CASA GRANDE. Artefacts included painted pottery, milling stones, chipped and ground stone tools, basketry, cotton textiles and metal trinkets such as copper bells. The elaborate shellwork, mosaic plaques and pyrite mirrors display craft proficiency. Links with MESOAMERICAN civilization are demonstrated through the building of BALL COURTS and temple PLATFORM MOUNDS. Contacts were maintained with contemporary MOGOLLON and ANASAZI cultures.

HOLOCENE
see POSTGLACIAL PERIOD

HOMO The word *homo* (Latin for 'man') gives its name to the genus to which man belongs.

In the first stages of human evolution fossils are so rare that the new discovery of a single skull can sometimes change people's ideas about the details of the evolutionary tree. Thus there exists no single agreed picture. The general outline, however, is clear enough. There seem to have been three or four major stages. The first has been called the pre-● human phase, and is represented by the AUSTRALOPITHECUS genus. This is regarded by some as inseparable from the second phase, the early human (*see* HOMO HABILIS). The late human phase (*see* HOMO ERECTUS) is followed by the final sapient phase (*see* HOMO SAPIENS) which includes modern man. All representatives of the first three phases, and some of the last, are known only from fossil bone remains.

Habilis and *sapiens* are translated as 'clever, able' and 'wise' respectively – referring to the development of the human mind – and *erectus* refers to the upright walking position. Individual fossils assigned to the group *Homo habilis* are said to belong to the genus *Homo* and the species *habilis*; and similarly, *erectus* and *sapiens* are other specific forms of the same genus. All are hominids.

▲ **HOMO ERECTUS** *Homo erectus* (or *Pithecanthropus* – 'ape-man' – hence 'pithecanthropines') represents the third phase in the development from ape to modern man (*see* HOMO). The pithecanthropines, dating from around a half million years ago, are widely distributed in the Old World. Finds include JAVA man, LAN-T'IEN man, PEKING man from CHOU-K'OU-TIEN, China, and a number from Africa: Ternifine, Algeria, and OLDUVAI GORGE (Bed II) are two examples. The Heidelberg jaw, from near Mauer in Germany, is a possible European representative (although some anthropologists consider it intermediate between ■ *Homo erectus* and NEANDERTHAL man). The skeletal evidence indicates that the pithecanthropines were little more than 1.6m tall.

HOMO HABILIS *Homo habilis* represents the second phase in human evolutionary development (*see* HOMO; AUSTRALOPITHECUS). Like the earlier australopithecines, *Homo habilis* has not yet been found outside Africa; some anthropologists would class the *habilis* remains themselves with the *Australopithecus* genus. Whichever the case, the evidence points to man having originated in the African continent. *Habilis* bones have been found at OLDUVAI GORGE, along with *Australopithecus* remains, and *Homo habilis* is generally held responsible for the manufacture of the crude stone tools in the same Bed I.

○ **HOMO SAPIENS** *Homo sapiens*, which includes all living forms of man, belong to the final phase of human

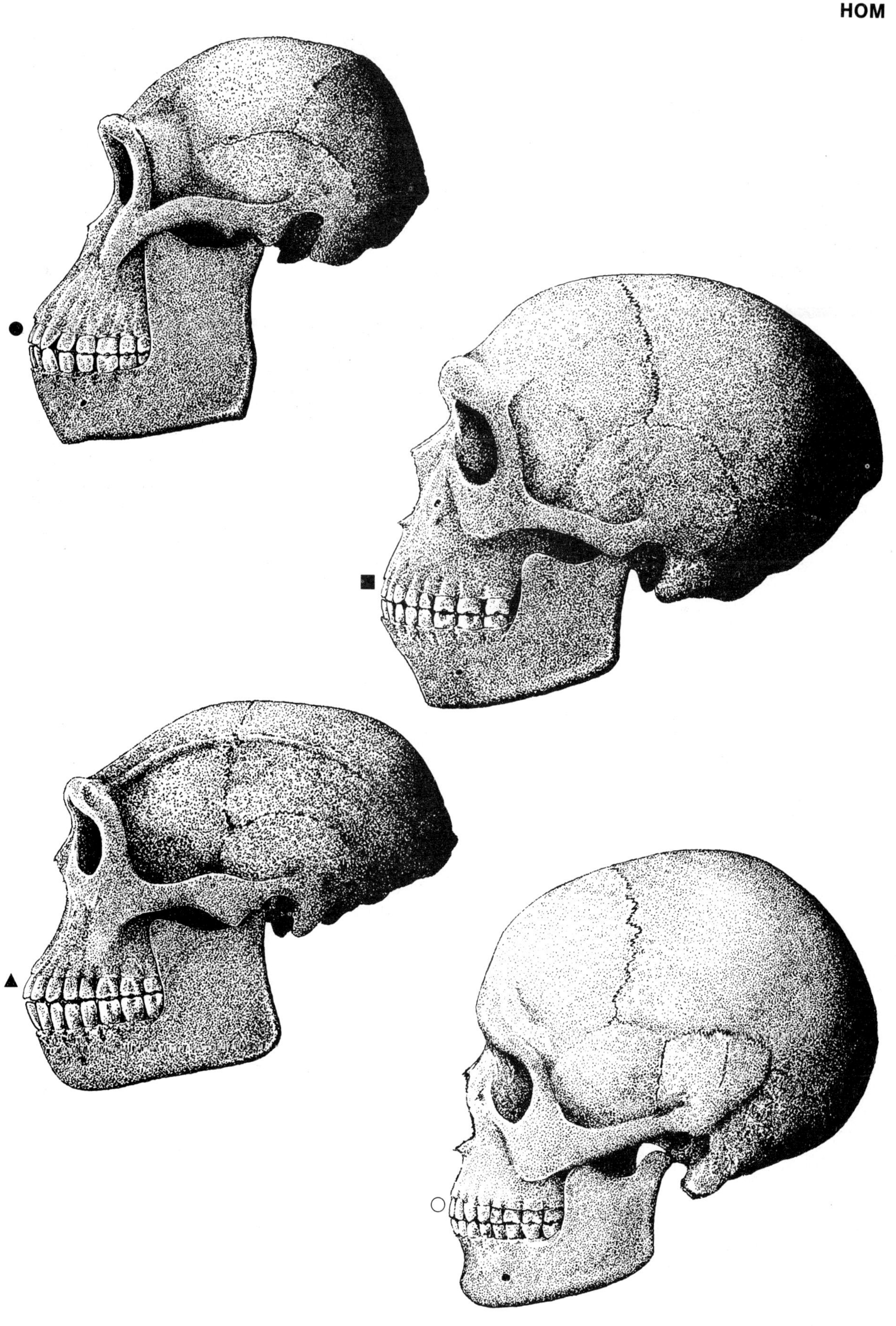

development to date (*see also* HOMO). In the Upper PLEISTOCENE, NEANDERTHAL man and CRO-MAGNON man stand out as being noticeably different from modern man. Sites where Pleistocene remains of *Homo sapiens* have been found include Broken Hill, Zambia, VÉRTESSZÖLLÖS, Hungary, STEINHEIM, Germany, SWANSCOMBE, England, and MOUNT CARMEL, Palestine.

HOPEWELL Southern Ohio and Illinois, USA. A culture of WOODLANDS tradition, evolving from the earlier ADENA complex towards the end of the 1st millennium BC, and reaching its climax 100 BC–200 AD. It is characterized by large oval or elongated mortuary mounds, often set in huge enclosures with rich grave goods accompanying the dead. Craft works include large sheet copper and mica cut-outs, carved and polished stone pipes, fragments of painted textiles, quantities of fine flint and obsidian blades, and cord marked, stamped or incised pottery. The height of Hopewell saw the maintenance of long-distance trading networks which provided the craftsmen with the necessary exotic raw materials. Settlements were small semi-permanent villages with a partially agricultural economy, supplemented by hunting, fishing and gathering. Hopewell had declined by AD 400.

HORGEN Succeeds the Swiss CORTAILLOD culture. This Middle Neolithic culture, like the SEINE–OISE–MARNE culture of which the Horgen is really a non-megalithic variant, continued to emphasize hunting as a significant part of the economy, although in a full NEOLITHIC context. Horgen itself is the site of a settlement on the edge of Lake Neuchâtel, Switzerland.

HORIZON CULTURES
See PERU

HORN CORES Bony extensions from the skulls of horn-bearing animals, in life covered by horn. As the bony tissue survives in most archaeological contexts, unlike the horn itself, cores are frequently the only available evidence for any industry based on horn-working.

HORREA A Roman granary or warehouse. They are frequently distinctive in having a large number of supports for the floor, presumably to lift it out of the reach of vermin; they also usually have special provision for ventilation. They are a common feature in Roman forts, and there are good examples from TRIER and CORBRIDGE.

HORUS Ancient Egyptian god who in his form as a hawk represents a sky deity. As the royal god with whom the living pharaoh (*see* EGYPT) was equated, he represents the son of OSIRIS and ISIS. His struggle to regain the throne of Egypt, usurped from the murdered Osiris by Seth, involved protracted close-quarter fighting with his opponent, in the course of which one of his eyes was torn out and had to be magically restored (*see* EYE OF HORUS). Depiction of Tutankhamun on a papyrus boat armed with harpoon and lasso indicates one episode in this contest where Seth turned himself into a hippopotamus to destroy Horus, who however speared him. Eventually the contention was ended by a tribunal of gods declaring Horus to be the legitimate ruler of Egypt: the pharaoh as a manifestation of Horus therefore had a mandate from the gods to govern the country.

In a funerary context Horus can be seen in vignettes from

▲

the BOOK OF THE DEAD leading the deceased into the presence of Osiris. The four sons of Horus shown as stoppers on CANOPIC JARS are the gods responsible for the safekeeping of the internal organs removed during MUMMIFICATION.

▲ **HOUSESTEADS, Northumberland** This is one of the best preserved forts of HADRIAN'S WALL. It was completely excavated in the 19th century and is in the process of being uncovered again for the public. The fort, built *c* AD 124, is later than Hadrian's Wall itself, a stretch of which was demolished to make way for the fort. Its layout is for 500 auxiliary infantry with six barracks, a headquarters, chief officer's house, hospital and the well-known latrines, the best preserved in Britain. The garrison was changed several times, but was always made up of foreign auxiliaries, e.g. Tungrians from Belgium. From the 3rd century civilians were allowed in the wall area and a settlement grew up below the fort with fields terraced into the hillside. The fort was altered in the 4th century and the whole complex abandoned at the end of the century.

HSIA DYNASTY An early Chinese dynasty which, according to the histories, existed prior to the SHANG dynasty. No archaeological traces have yet borne this out.

HSIAO-T'UN, China An important SHANG site in the region of ANYANG, Honan, the last capital of the Shang dynasty. Excavations at Hsiao-T'un began in 1928, and revealed storage pits and graves containing thousands of ORACLE BONES, pottery, bronze vessels and weapons. The spectacular tombs of the nobility contained the sacrificial burials of humans and animals, including charioteers and their chariots. Rectangular building foundations up to 30m in length were unearthed as well.

HUACA Derives from the Quechua word for a place of sanctity, now applied generally throughout South America to describe any archaeological ruin, hence the term *huaquero* meaning tomb-robber. *See* HUACA PRIETA.

HUACA PRIETA, Peru Located at the mouth of the Chicama Valley on the north coast, this is an early sedentary village dated to the Preceramic Period (*see* PERU) 2500–1800 BC. The site consists of a deep MIDDEN of domestic refuse containing the bones of fish, sea-mammals, birds and shells along with plant remains that show the inhabitants cultivated cotton, gourds, squashes, peppers, lima and jack beans to supplement their predominantly fishing economy. These inhabitants, numbering no more than a few hundred persons, lived in pit-like dwellings built of cobble-stones set in mud and roofed with beams and whale bones. They fished with cotton nets held in place with stone sinkers and gourd floats, and above all, were renowned for their production ■ of twined, looped, knotted and woven textiles and in the intricate excised decoration of gourds, with designs that variously show human faces, condor birds, crabs and snakes with a head at each end. ▶

HUARI, Mantaro Basin, south-central highlands, Peru The capital of one of the two great empires of the Middle Horizon period (*see* PERU; TIAHUANACO) controlling a region which stretched in the highlands from the Middle Marañon down to the Urubamba basin and on the coast from Chicama in the north to Ocoña. Around AD 60, Huari

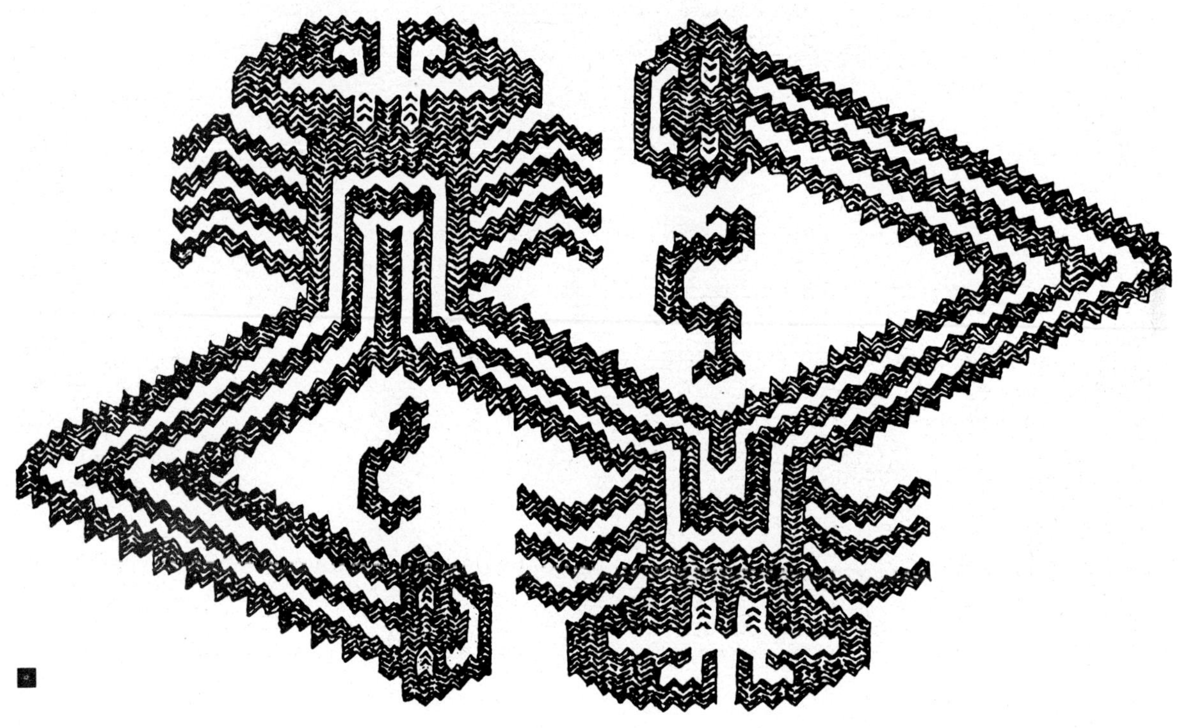

absorbed strong influences from Tiahuanaco, and transformed these into a similar, but nevertheless distinctly local style especially remarkable for its large ceremonial painted urns depicting such themes as the Tiahuanaco 'Gateway God' with running winged figures carrying serpentine-headed staffs. Within the following century, these elements appear in profusion all along the coast, but especially on the south in the Nasca region, where some direct exchange of embassy is implied through the appearance of south coast pottery back in Huari. Similarly on the central coast, close communication between the two areas is demonstrated by the rise of the city PACHACAMAC and the development of its own distinctive variant of the Huari style. By AD 800, Huari was abandoned and its empire fell with it. For the next two hundred years the Huari style remains, until its eventual breakdown into the 'Epigonal' groups with the upsurgence of old regional traditions along the coast.

HUNS A group of non-Germanic horse-riding peoples whose homelands lay east of the Danube. *C* AD 376 they began to sweep south towards the Imperial frontiers of the eastern provinces, and were established in central Europe by the early 5th century. Employed by the FRANKISH Merovingians against the VISIGOTHIC threat from Spain, the Huns, led by Attila, invaded Gaul in 451. Defeated, they turned to Italy, but made peace in 452 and returned to central Europe.

HURRIANS A people who inhabited eastern ANATOLIA. *C* 1500 BC they expanded to the south, establishing the kingdom of MITANI. In Anatolia itself they became vassals (servants) of the HITTITES, who recorded the Hurrians' pantheon of gods at Yazilikaya. In the 13th century BC the ASSYRIANS, who called eastern Anatolia Urartu, made attacks on the Hurrians whose capital was at Lake Van.

HUT CIRCLE A circular depression, ring of stones or post-holes marking the site of a former structure.

HYPERCEPHALI Disks of linen (occasionally bronze) which have been stiffened with plaster, found for protective purposes below the heads of corpses during the Saite period of Egyptian history. Amuletic representations of deities and magical efficacy were aided by a spell from the BOOK OF THE DEAD to restore body temperature of a living person to the mummy.

● **HYPOCAUST** A specialized type of Roman structure in which underfloor vaults and wall flues were incorporated. These acted as a vent for a furnace, which was usually external and wood-burning, so that hot air was drawn up to heat the floor and walls. This heating system was used in wealthier domestic buildings and BATHS.

ICELAND Detailed evidence of the colonization of Iceland by Scandinavians is in the *Landnámabók (The Book of the Taking of Land)*, written *c* AD 1200 but referring to the VIKING period. Settlement by migrating Norwegians mainly from the west coast began in the late 9th century and ended *c* 930 when the desolate and remote island had been fully populated. Expeditions to Greenland and VINLAND continued the colonizing impulse.

ICE WEDGES In PERIGLACIAL regions, where the ground is subject to intense cold (–20°C to –40°C), areas of soil contract, leaving a network of cracks in the surface. During the summer the cracks fill with water which freezes and expands, forming a wedge which forces the earth apart. Later, this contracts as the temperature drops again. The cracks are thus enlarged each year and eventually, on thawing, become filled with fine surface material. The study of these wedges and other periglacial features has contributed to our knowledge of the climatic succession and man's environment during PLEISTOCENE times.

ICKNIELD WAY A pre-Roman road running south-west from East Anglia to Essex along the chalk ridges of the Chilterns. It continues further west as the Berkshire Ridgeway. These ridgeways are presumed to have been the major communication routes in prehistory.

IDEOGRAM
see WRITING

IMPRESSED WARE Along the Mediterranean coasts of France, Corsica and southern Italy in the 6th millennium BC and in eastern Spain in the 5th millennium, communities began to practise a NEOLITHIC economy. The details of this economy varied in different areas. Sheep were widely herded, although wild animals and plants often continued to play a significant role. Cereals were being grown in Spain and southern France by the mid 5th millennium. A unifying economic feature is the strong representation of sea food. At the Cap Ragnon cave near Marseille the animal bones included those of sheep, as well as deer and rabbit, but predominant were remains of fish (eight kinds, including tunny and sea-bream) and shellfish (among six kinds were mussels and spider-crabs). The dependence on the sea is reflected in the round-based pottery, which is frequently decorated with impressions of the cockle shell (*Cardium* genus – hence Cardial Impressed Ware).

With time, shell impressions on the pottery become less common; as with the LINEAR POTTERY cultures of central Europe, regional diversification occurs. The origin of the Impressed Ware culture is uncertain: one suggestion is the STARČEVO culture. It ended in the mid 4th millennium.

INCA A small tribe from the Urubamba basin in the southern highlands of Peru who spoke the Quechua language and founded their dynasty under their first ruler Manco Capac at Cuzco, the capital. Their history is recorded by 16th century Spanish and Indian chroniclers, supplemented by archaeology, which together suggest that the Incas emerged *c* AD 1200 and embarked on an extensive programme of conquest under their ninth ruler Pachacuti in 1438. Two successive rulers, Topa Inca (1471–93) and Huayna Capac (1493–1525), expanded and consolidated the empire until it stretched for over 3000km from the northern borders of Ecuador down to central Chile, including parts of highland Bolivia and Argentina. The Incas took their name from the title given to their head of state, who represented not only an earthly but also a divine autocrat, worshipped as a god who traced his ancestry back to the sun. The Incas are renowned for their superb organizational abilities; their state was strongly centralized and governed by a nobility drawn from the royal household and from the dynasties of conquered tribes. To enforce its supremacy, the state kept a standing army which could move through the empire over two great

▲

highways stretching its entire length, one in the highlands and the other on the coast. State transactions and news passed swiftly along these, carried by relays of runners based on the wayside inns.

The death of Huayna Capac in 1525 precipitated a bloody civil war between two of his sons who contested the realm. The armies of Atahuallpa, governor of Quito, finally routed those of his half-brother Huascar at Cuzco in 1534, but before he could consolidate his victory, Atahuallpa was seized and later executed by the Spanish soldiers of Francisco Pizarro (*see* CAJAMARCA). The empire, weakened by the five-year war and epidemics of European diseases like smallpox, easily capitulated to foreign rule once the head of state was gone. Rebellions continued into the 18th century and for a while an exile kingdom existed in the montaña; but these had little significance.

Archaeology traces the Inca culture through its ▲ distinctive stone masonry and its pottery which included such types as the ARYBALLUS and the KERO, spread widely as hall-marks of Inca dominion. Comparatively little precious metalwork survived the Conquest, although the Incas worked quantities of gold, silver and bronze and owed their mastery of metallurgy to the North Coast CHIMU craftsmen whose state they had conquered. Alphabetical writing was unknown, but numerous economic and political records were kept using the QUIPU. Agricultural terraces built in the highlands facilitated intensive cultivation of crops that included maize, beans, oca and cotton at lower altitudes and quinoa and potato higher up. Llama and alpaca were domesticated well before the Inca empire and provided wool, meat, and to a limited extent transport. Other domesticated animals were the guinea pig, dog and duck. Cultivation of the fields was achieved through the use of the foot-plough or *taclla* – a more complex version of the digging stick. The Incas carried the arts to their finest through the state institutions where specially-trained women produced large quantities of fine cloth.

INCHTUTHIL, Perthshire A Roman legionary fortress situated on the river Tay in Scotland, founded to accommodate the Twentieth Legion. It guarded the movements of tribes in the Highlands, and was a spearhead of the occupation of Scotland under AGRICOLA. Its importance was short-lived: the fort was abandoned *c* AD 87 and the legion moved to CHESTER or WROXETER. This may have been due to the depletion of the army in Britain following the withdrawal of the Second Legion Adiutrix. The fort, which includes the earliest stone defensive wall in Britain, was systematically demolished on abandonment, the extracted nails being carefully buried.

INDIAN COINS The first Indian silver coins were issued by the MAHAJAMAPADAS. They were either cut from a metal sheet or poured as molten metal on to a flat surface and stamped while soft. The weight standards and symbols varied greatly between states. Copper was not used until the MAURYAN period; copper coins were generally made by casting from moulds. Mauryan silver coinage was of a baser alloy than that of the preceding dynasties. The reverse often bore a series of marks which were probably *bona fide* marks made by bankers or checking authorities; these were not found on earlier coins. On the obverse were five punched symbols representing the king and the issuing authority. *See also* SILVER BAR COINS.

INDO-EUROPEAN The languages spoken over most of Europe and much of Asia have a common root, and are collectively called Indo-European languages. From a homeland in the Caucasus and the Carpathians, north of the Black Sea, migrations of peoples spread the Indo-European languages into Europe, the Near East and India. The environment of the 'homeland' is indicated by shared words such as those for bear, wolf, beech, mountain, river, fish. Gold, copper and bronze, the wheel, grain agriculture, and domestic animals including the horse were also known. It is possible that the peoples of the KURGAN culture in Russia, *c* 2500 BC were the original Indo-Europeans. Indo-European languages are divided into those that use 'k' (e.g. Latin: *centum* – a hundred), and those that use 's' instead (e.g. Avestic: *satem*). Celtic is further subdivided.

■ **INDUS CIVILIZATION** One of the four 'primary' Old World civilizations, the Indus Valley (or Harappan) civilization of Pakistan and north-west India was largely concentrated in the alluvial plain of the Indus and its tributaries, and the southward-flowing Ghaggar to the east. Outposts, probably concerned mainly with trade, were situated on the Makran coast to the north, and to the south as far as the Narbada river. Related sites are known as far afield as Alamgirpur near Delhi.

Sites in Baluchistan dating from the 4th millennium BC show strong affinities with contemporary sites in Iran but later phases at these sites already foreshadow elements of the Indus Valley culture. In the Indus plain itself, closely related sites of a pre-Harappan culture exist from the early 3rd millennium; they seem to represent an expansion into this fertile area. Evidence suggesting a native contribution to this culture is slight. Pre-Harappan sites occur over a wide area similar in extent to the nucleus of the full Harappan culture. The pottery from these sites is related to later, Harappan ceramics, and the material culture contains many other elements, including terracotta figurines, copper objects and stone blades. Monumental architecture, in the shape of massive mud-brick walls, probably built as a flood defence, heralds a famous feature of the Indus civilization, while the use of bricks of a standard size at KALIBANGAN anticipates the remarkable uniformity that characterizes that culture.

Both at AMRI and at KOT DIJI, the Indus civilization is immediately preceded by fire damage; however, at all sites of the Pre-Harappan culture there seems to be continuity in the cultural sequence and material culture, showing that the Indus civilization is largely derived from the Pre-Harappan culture.

Trade with Mesopotamia flourished throughout the Harappan period. Although the archaeological evidence on the Indian site is confined to the presence of three Mesopotamian SEALS at Mohenjo-Daro and a few metal objects of probable Mesopotamian origin, Mesopotamia provides much literary information on the subject of trade with Meluhha, believed to be the Indus region. This is borne out by the finds of Harappan seals and distinctive carnelian beads in Mesopotamian cities. Both countries also have a few objects of Persian Gulf origin, supporting the theory that the Gulf acted as an *entrepôt* and intermediary in this trade network, These links, along with radiocarbon dates from Indus valley sites, suggest a time range of *c* 2300–1700 BC for the mature phase of the Indus culture.

Indus valley trade was not confined to the civilized world. Many of the raw materials used by the Harappans were probably imports from less civilized neighbouring

areas: gold from Mysore, silver from Afghanistan and Iran, copper from Rajputana, South India and Arabia, and precious stones from areas to the east and west.

Finally must be mentioned the very efficient commercial network throughout the Indus civilization itself. Many of the objects in common use were of purely local origin, such as the fine flint from the hills at Rohri and Sukkur, and were spread abroad by an effective system of redistribution. Craft specialization within the cities was highly developed and the products of this craft were probably similarly distributed.

The use of inscribed SEALS seems to have been important in this context. Although the Indus script remains undeciphered, the uniformity of seal design, showing an animal accompanied by a number of ideograms, and the evidence, from cloth or cord marks on the reverse of many seals, that they were used for sealing merchandise, suggests their importance in the regulation of internal exchange. Use of standard weights and measures is shown by the numerous stone weights found at Mohenjo-Daro. Vast granaries at Harappa and Mohenjo-Daro emphasize still further the highly organized nature of this culture, whose economy was based on the fertile alluvial plains which produced the staple foods, wheat and barley. Leguminous plants, too, were grown for food, also dates, sessamum and mustard for oil, and cotton for cloth. Sheep, goats and fowl were kept as domestic animals; pig, cattle and buffalo may also have been domesticated, while hunted deer and tortoise were also eaten. Occasional elephant bones, coupled with the popularity of the elephant as a seal design, suggest that these creatures may already have been domesticated.

Without written information it is impossible to be sure of the precise social organization but the evidence suggests the rule of an oligarchy, whether of a priestly or a secular nature, controlling the highly organized systems of production and redistribution, and imposing strict uniformity upon urban development. The twin 'capitals' MOHENJO-DARO and HARAPPA each consist of a citadel area and a lower town of private houses carefully laid out in a grid pattern. The houses present a blank façade to the main street and open on to smaller side streets; they vary in size from single-roomed abodes to vast complexes opening on to courtyards. Bathrooms are found in the vast majority of houses, and from them run drainage channels linking with main drains down the centre of the street. These in turn connect to frequent sumps. The architecture is mainly of dried or fired mud-brick, although timber was used for roofing, and stone very occasionally.

The smaller provincial centres (*see* KALIBANGAN) repeat this urban design on a smaller scale. Little is known about the smallest units of settlement.

Craft production seems often to have been governed by the standardization apparent in other aspects of life. Bronze, copper and stone tools, pottery, seals and beads display remarkable uniformity of design, showing technical competence without much creative spirit. However, the rare figurines of cast bronze or stone and the ubiquitous terracotta models show that creativity was not lacking when scope was offered. Some of the seal designs seem to portray supernatural beings, giving a shadowy insight into Indus Valley religion which may share some elements with Hinduism. The treatment of the dead throws no light upon religion: cemeteries are rarely found and contain a variety of rites of which extended inhumation with a few pots is by far the most common.

In the latest phases of the civilization houses were built from the decaying rubble of previous structures and a lower standard of living seems general. The reasons for the end of the Indus civilization are far from clear. Various theories argue for a natural disaster: a change in the course of the river leading to wide flooding or the loss of the essential water supply; over-exploitation of the environment causing deforestation and loss of fertility. Unburied bodies in the streets of Mohenjo-Daro offer further explanations. Pestilence is one; more likely is early incursions of the ARYANS whose literature mentions the destruction of indigenous strongholds and whose first appearance in India was probably *c* 1800 BC. The evidence to test these hypotheses unfortunately is lacking.

See also LOTHAL.

INDUSTRY A repeatedly occurring ASSEMBLAGE of artefacts of one class, especially flint tools. If more than one class of artefact is present (e.g. pottery, bone and metal tools), the assemblage may represent a CULTURE.

● **INGALADDI ROCK SHELTER, Australia** Deposits in this sandstone ROCK SHELTER on Willeroo Station, Northern Territory, have yielded thousands of trimmed stone implements. It contained the largest stratified assemblage of TULA-ADZE flakes in Australia along with stone points and edge-ground axes. These are dated *c* 1000 BC. Earlier levels, dated to *c* 3000 BC, revealed CORE and FLAKE assemblages. A 2000–year gap between the earlier and later levels has been noted. Of special interest is the site's engraved and painted art, including motifs of human feet and linear markings. The linear marks date back 3–5000 years BC.

INHUMATION Practice of burying the dead body, instead of burning it (CREMATION).

INTAGLIO A name for a common type of Roman gem where a design is cut into the surface of (usually) a semi-precious stone, giving a hollow image for use as a seal stone or in a signet ring. The other form of Roman gem is a cameo, formed of two differently coloured layers of glass cut so that the design appears in the top layer against a background of the bottom layer. Plain Roman gems are very rare. AQUILEIA was a major gem cutting centre.

INTERLACE In Britain elaborate ribbon interlace first appears in manuscript art *c* AD 675 in the Book of Durrow, produced in NORTHUMBRIA. The intricate interweaving of abstract ribbon patterns and ANIMAL ORNAMENT of the carpet pages of the LINDISFARNE Gospels shows the blending of CELTIC and Germanic art styles in the 7th century which is also illustrated in monumental stone crosses of Ireland, NORTHUMBRIA and the PICTS.

INTERSTADIAL
see PLEISTOCENE

IONA, Scotland A small, barren island in the Inner Hebrides on which St COLUMBA founded a monastery in AD 563. It was the mother house of monasticism in Scotland and through its activity the northern PICTS were converted to Christianity. Aidan, a monk from Iona, became the founder of the monastery at LINDISFARNE, NORTHUMBRIA.

IONIC
see CAPITALS; COLUMNS

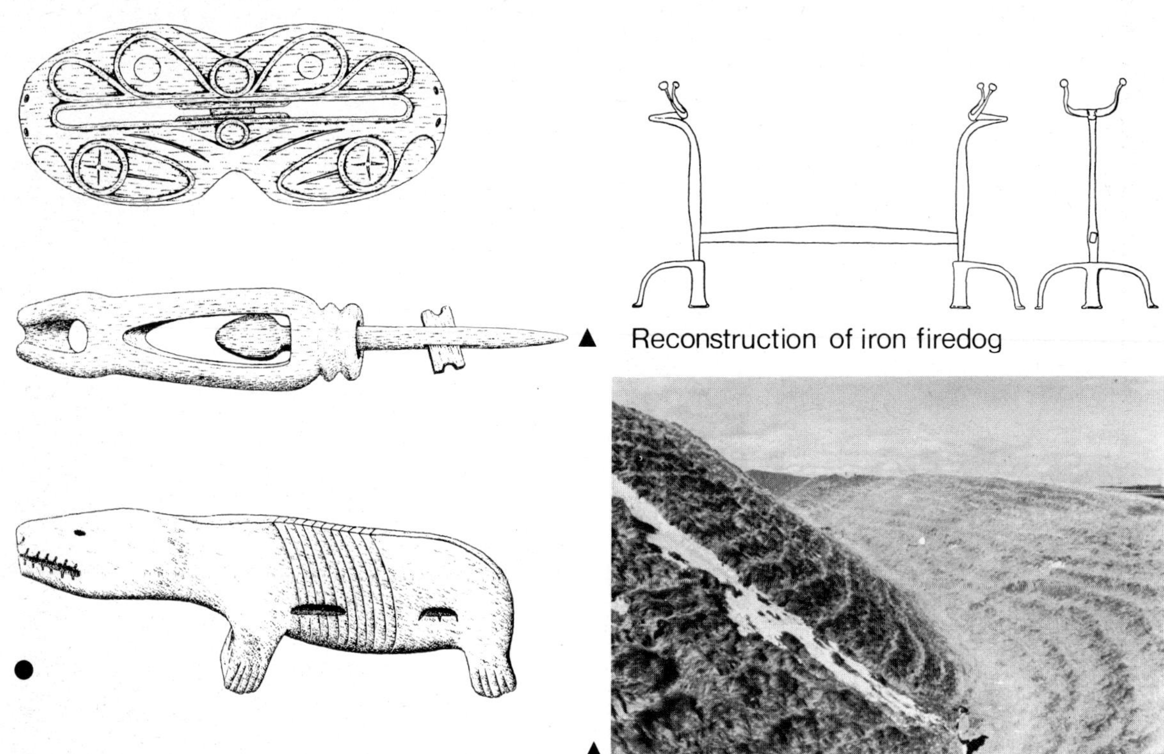

▲ Reconstruction of iron firedog

●**IPIUTAK, Point Hope, Alaska** One of the largest known ESKIMO villages, with over 600 semi-subterranean sub-rectangular houses, located on the coast and associated with an extensive cemetery. The site dates to *c* AD 300 and the elaborate ivory carvings show Scytho-Siberian contact.

IRON AGE Iron was first used by the HITTITES before the 15th century BC and the secret of iron-working spread into Europe only with their downfall. It was in use in Greece by the 11th century BC, and in central Europe by the late URNFIELD period *c* 8th century BC. Iron-using communities, probably already Celtic-speaking, covered Europe by the 7th century BC, the HALLSTATT period. The earliest evidence of iron in Britain is the sickle from LLYN FAWR, in the 6th century BC. The Hallstatt iron age period (*c* 700–600 BC) was followed in Europe by the LA TÈNE period (500 BC to ROMAN conquest). In Britain the Iron Age was divided by Hawkes on similarities with continental material into A (corresponding to Hallstatt), B (La Tène) and C (Belgic) phases. Not all scholars accept this classification.

Archaeology in Iron Age Europe is supplemented, particularly after 100 BC, by classical accounts of the barbarian areas. It was the classical writers who used the name CELTS for the people of Europe in an area from Gaul to Czechoslovakia. One feature of the Celtic world during this period was the intensification of trade. In the Hallstatt, imports came into Europe via MASSILIA and the Rhône Valley, so that HILLFORTS like ENTREMONT flourished; in the La Tène period, trade tended to come through the Alps, and the rich graves, e.g. WALDALGESHEIM, are found in Germany. Wine in particular was imported from southern Europe, as AMPHORAE in the graves show. Other wine-drinking vessels included ETRUSCAN flagons, which have been found in *c* 60 Celtic graves. Greek pottery was also widespread, being found in the Hallstatt grave of VIX and the La Tène grave at KLEIN ASPERGLE. Major trading centres coordinating imports and exports existed in the hillforts and later OPPIDA. Traded objects included those produced in the hinterland of the oppida themselves. Wheel-made pottery and salt, for example, found their way across Europe and south of the Alps as well. An important innovation of the period was gold coinage. At first coins were based on the Greek coinage of Philip of Macedon and were close copies, but gradually they became more Celtic in style until by the 2nd century BC local coins were produced in most areas. As a result of the trading network, Iron Age culture became uniform over much of Europe. Not only was there a similarity in language, religion and art styles, but also in such fundamentals as hillfort defences.

Against the European continent, Britain seems a provincial backwater. At first the appearance of iron in Britain made little difference to the Bronze Age type of culture. The settlements were small, weakly-defended farms. After *c* 400 BC power increasingly became ▲concentrated in major hillforts, e.g. MAIDEN CASTLE, which acted as markets, religious and political centres, and refuges in times of war. Smaller settlements as at GLASTONBURY continued to be occupied into the later Iron Age, and indeed into the Roman period. The farms of the Iron Age have very uniform constituents. ROUND HOUSES were widespread (although rectangular structures are not unknown). STORAGE PITS were used for grain and for rubbish disposal. On most sites cattle were the most

important food animal, and sheep were kept for their wool. Most sites have bone-weaving combs and loom weights, perhaps for making the cloaks which were exported to Europe. According to Roman authors, tin, corn and slaves were also exported from Britain, and slave chains like those from LLYN CERRIG BACH confirm this. Trade with the continent, especially Italy and Greece, intensified from 200 BC. Throughout the period continental styles influenced British workmanship, though direct immigrations seem to have been few. An exception is in Yorkshire, where the ARRAS chariot graves markedly resemble important French burials. From 100 BC (Iron Age C phase), invasions of BELGIC tribes brought new ideas into southern Britain, particularly the use of coinage (*see* GALLO-BELGIC). The boundaries of the Belgic chiefdoms have been established by the distribution of their coins on the assumption that this represents the extent of tribal influence. Wheel-made pottery was introduced in the Late Iron Age, much of it decorated in the CELTIC ART style (e.g. from Glastonbury). Coarse pottery was still made in the home, but some fine wares with a widespread distribution were apparently made by professional potters. Also introduced into the Belgic areas were CREMATION cemeteries, e.g. at AYLESFORD and Swarling, which include some very rich graves. The end of the Iron Age in Britain came not with JULIUS CAESAR's expeditions in 55–54 BC but with the conquest of CLAUDIUS in AD 43. By this time much of Europe was under Roman control. In Scandinavia however, which was never conquered, the Iron Age continued into the migration period, *c* 4th–6th centuries AD.

IRON PAN A hard, compact layer in the soil cemented together principally by iron oxides, though other oxides and hydroxides are involved. Iron pan has been used for the small-scale production of iron but usually deposits are not thick enough to be economically viable.

ISHTAR [Sumerian – **Innin**; West Semitic – **Astarte**; Biblical – **Ashtorath**] A female god of the Near East. She is considered to be the planet Venus and was extensively worshipped for a variety of attributes. War and fertility were her two major characteristics. In the former she is depicted leading the ASSYRIAN army to battle. She was originally represented by a bundle of reeds, but later an eight-pointed star became her most common symbol. As goddess of fertility her sexual aspect was emphasized and she was therefore worshipped by the performing of immoral acts. These practices were particularly common in the LEVANT 2000–500 BC where she was known as Astarte. A temple dedicated to her was found at BETH SHAN. She was worshipped by the PHOENICIANS and so was widely known throughout the Mediterranean where she became identified with other goddesses: with Isis and Hathor in Egypt, and in the Greek and Roman worlds with Aphrodite and Artemis, Diana and Juno.

■ **ISIS** Ancient Egyptian goddess whose origins are obscure. The symbol of a seat or throne often shown on her head (though she frequently wears cow-horns and a sun's disk like the goddess Hathor) has led to the suggestion that she personifies the pharaoh's power. In mythology she is the sister and wife of OSIRIS and the mother of HORUS. Bronze statuettes show Isis with the young Horus on her lap being suckled and protected against Seth, the murderer of his father Osiris. Her role as a universal mother goddess increased over the centuries until in the HELLENISTIC world

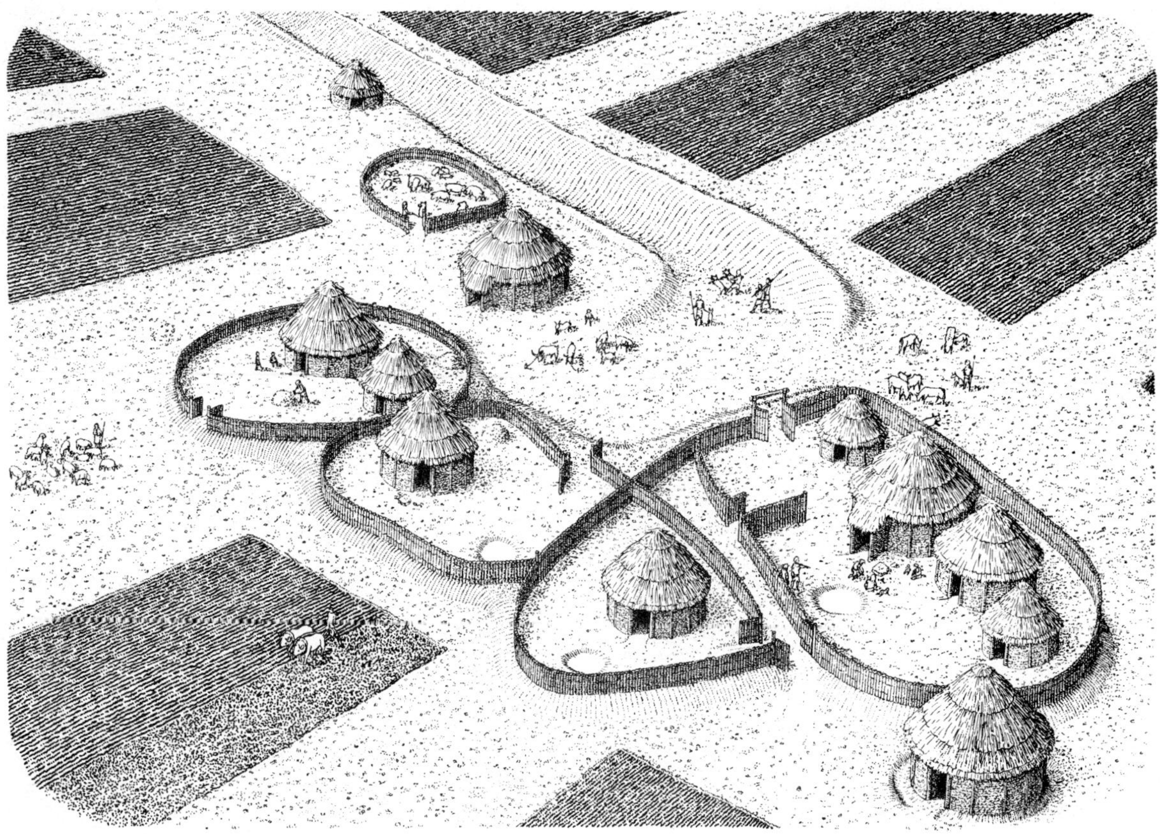

her mystery-cult spread not only through Mediterranean countries but far out in the Roman empire. In Egypt itself her main sanctuary was on the island of PHILAE. Her skill in magic enabled her, according to one legend, to cure the sun-god Re of an ailment (which she herself had inflicted) in return for him telling her his secret name. This gave her increased power and the knowledge was passed to her son Horus, so that in his manifestations as pharaoh of Egypt his privileged relationships with the all-powerful sun-god would be unquestioned. In funerary rituals Isis is one of the four goddesses guarding the container holding the CANOPIC JARS.

ISRAELITES A group of SEMITIC people who in the BIBLE are traced back to a nomadic ancestor, Abraham. However, in Biblical history many other peoples who accept the Israelite way of life are absorbed into the nation. They displaced the CANAANITES in Palestine although Canaanite religious practices remained attractive to them. After the rule of Solomon, Israel became two kingdoms, Israel and Judah; the Israelites were deported by ASSYRIA in 722 BC and the Judeans by the BABYLONIANS in 586 BC.

●**ITFORD HILL, Sussex** A Middle Bronze Age farming settlement in Sussex dated to *c* 1100 BC. There were about 13 round huts, built of timber posts, daub and thatch, each set on a raised platform; some were surrounded with palisades to form a farmyard. Small cattle were the most important animal kept in the hamlet, with only a few sheep. One of the STORAGE PITS was filled with 4½kg of carbonized barley, presumably grown on the fields adjoining the site. 100m north of the settlement was the cemetery, a BARROW containing between 14 and 19 CREMATIONS. A sherd from one of the urns fitted onto another found in the settlement, which proves them to be of the same date. Itford Hill is estimated to have been occupied for 25–50 years. *See also* DEVEREL–RIMBURY.

IVINGHOE BEACON, Buckinghamshire A prominent HILLFORT with TIMBER-LACED defences, occupied from the Late Bronze Age, *c* 8th century BC: this is one of the earliest dates for a hillfort in Britain, which were at one time thought to be an IRON AGE phenomenon. All the pottery from Ivinghoe is coarse and undistinguished and could as easily be Iron Age as Late Bronze Age. The hillfort continued in occupation into the Iron Age.

IWAJUKU, Japan The site in Honshu of the first archaeological demonstration (1949) of human occupation in Japan during the PLEISTOCENE. This, the first-known pre-ceramic site, yielded oval bifacial HANDAXES, as well as an early blade industry, including blades and scrapers, and is considered of probably Upper Pleistocene date. *See also* FUKUI CAVE; JOMON.

IZAPA Pacific coast, Chiapas, Mexico Izapa was a thriving CEREMONIAL CENTRE with a long history, although it is especially important for its late Preclassic occupation (*see* MESOAMERICA), when many temple-PYRAMIDS built around PLAZAS were erected and a fine art style flourished in stone carving on altars and STELAE. This style links interestingly with the preceding OLMEC and the later MAYA through the depiction of a peculiar long-lipped deity (*see* CHAC; QUETZALCOATL; TLALOC). There are many more links with important contemporary sites, such as KAMINAL-

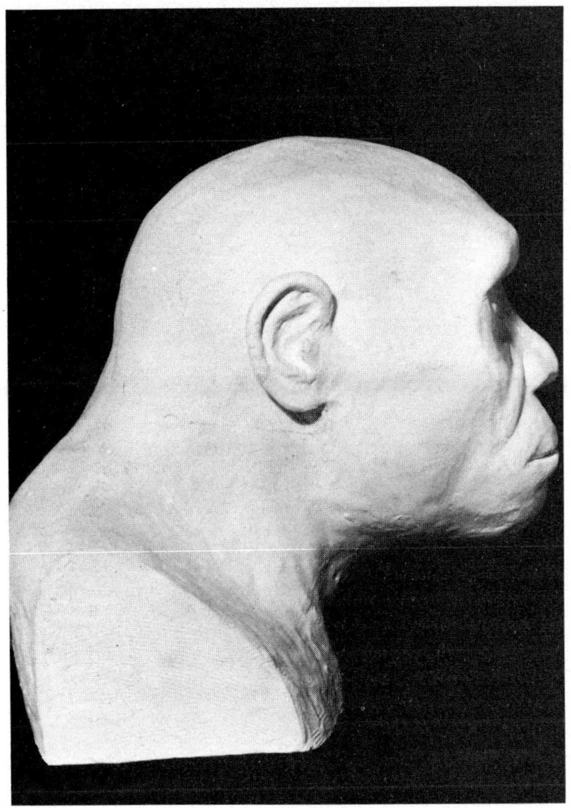

JUYU and others on the Pacific coast and eastwards in the Maya lowlands. Nearby, at El Baul, an Izapan stela carries an early Long Count date of AD 36 (*see* CALENDAR).

JABRUDIAN At the Tabun cave, MOUNT CARMEL, the Jabrudian industry of south-west Asia lies stratified between an earlier ACHEULEAN-type culture and a later MOUSTERIAN deposit. Characterized by thick stone SCRAPERS, and occasional HANDAXES and Amudian-type BLADES, the INDUSTRY is comparable to a certain stage of the European MOUSTERIAN. The Jabrudian is broadly contemporary with the AMUDIAN and the later Acheulean.

JARMO, Iraq A site in the Zagros mountains. Excavations in 1948–55 revealed it to be a very early farming community. Impressions in clay of wheat grains have been found, together with CARBONIZED wheat, barley, peas, lentils and vetchling. Wheat grew wild in this region and it is logical that the population should have encouraged its growth artificially. Houses in the village were square and built of pisé (*see* MUDBRICK). The village began 7000–6500 BC.

JARROW, Tyne and Wear The sister monastic house to Monkwearmouth, founded in AD 685 and 674 respectively, both by Benedict Biscop. Biscop intended to establish great centres of learning of the Roman Church which had recently triumphed over the Celtic church of NORTHUMBRIA. He collected religious works of art, introduced stained glass to England, improved church music and built up a great library. The most famous scholar from Jarrow is the Venerable BEDE. Both monasteries were sacked by the Danes in 794.

JATAKA STORIES Tales of the miraculous activities of the BUDDHA in previous incarnations. The background detail of the stories provides a valuable insight into life in 7th–6th century BC India. Jataka scenes were often used as decoration on STUPAS. *See also* AMARAVATI, BHARHUT, SANCHI.

▲**JAVA MAN** The first brain case of HOMO ERECTUS (formerly called *Pithecanthropus*) was found near Trinil in Java in 1891, and probably dates back to at least 500,000 BC. The remains of several other fossil hominids have since been found in Java.

JAWA
see JORDAN

JEMDAT NASR, Iraq An ancient city 80km south of Bagdad. Excavated in the 1920s it is known for a particular type of pottery found only in small quantities elsewhere and representative of the period *c* 3100–3000 BC. The distinctive pottery consists of large buff-coloured jars ■ decorated with geometrical and naturalistic designs in red and black paint. WRITING was beginning at this time and numerous examples were found at Jemdat Nasr.

JERASH
see JORDAN

JERICHO, Israel The name refers to a number of TELLS in an oasis area north of the Dead Sea. The most ancient tell, Tell es-Sultan has been excavated by Kathleen Kenyon and others. The earliest permanent settlers (in maybe 8500 BC) built a 2m-thick town wall which was found in a deep

●

▲

trench. They lived in circular houses of mud-brick but had no pottery. Their custom was also to plaster the skulls of their dead in life-like fashion. There are few archaeological remains until *c* 3200 BC, when a strongly fortified city was built. Frequent earthquake and war caused 17 repairs and rebuildings of the city wall before its final destruction *c* 2100 BC. Another city was built *c* 1900 BC. Little remains of the later period, which was associated with the ISRAELITE attack. Nearby tombs have yielded many artefacts. King HEROD rebuilt Jericho on a different tell.

JERUSALEM, Israel There has been constant archaeological investigation of this city for more than a century. Later occupation has destroyed many ancient remains, and much of its material history is uncertain. Almost nothing has been found of the 2nd and 3rd millennia BC settlements which were on the Hill of Ophel, south of the present city. The ISRAELITES under King David captured the city *c* 1000 BC by climbing the water tunnel. A further water tunnel was built by King Hezekiah *c* 729–690 BC (2 Kings 20:20), enabling him to withstand siege (*see* CUNEIFORM). To the north of the City of David, Solomon built a temple which was completely destroyed with the capture of city by the Babylonians in 587 BC. The city was rebuilt and came to include a second ridge, west of Ophel. After a second revolt by the Jews in AD 132, Emperor Hadrian destroyed most of the city and rebuilt it as a smaller pagan city. During the reign of Emperor Constantine (324–337) it became a place of pilgrimage and many churches and monasteries (such as the Church of the Holy Sepulchre) were built. In 637 the city became Moslem and in 691 OMAYYAD Caliph Abd al-Malik built the ● magnificent 'Dome of the Rock'. The CRUSADERS captured it in 1099 and after its recapture by Saladin in 1187, Jerusalem was controlled from Egypt until taken by the Turks about 1535.

▲**JOMON** This long-lasting Japanese culture began approximately 7000 BC, at e.g. NATSUSHIMA shell-midden, and continued through several stages until approximately 300 BC, when it was replaced by the YAYOI culture, which was then to see the introduction of intensive agriculture and the advent of metal-working in Japan. The Jomon period is named from its characteristic pottery, often decorated with impressions of twisted cords, though diverse local variations existed. These populations were hunter–fisher–gatherers, with early steps towards agriculture not undertaken until probably the latest Jomon period. Typical prey included deer and wild boar. Bone fish-hooks and clay or stone net-sinkers were used for fishing. These people made wooden utensils such as cups and bowls, and objects of wicker and matting. A few bows of cedar have been discovered at one site, with one bow still bearing traces of red lacquer. Shells, animal teeth, clay and stone were fashioned into necklaces, bracelets and earrings. Clay was also used for human and animal figurines which perhaps had ritual significance, such as to promote fertility. The dead were buried in flexed or extended positions, at times covered with haematite, and sometimes deposited in jars. The practice of building stone circles, sometimes with burials, occurs in the Jomon, and carried on into later periods, perhaps representing an early worship of the Sun Goddess, which was recorded in writings much later. Jomon traits include shell middens, of which thousands have been found, and semi-subterranean dwellings, (at times equipped with fireplaces and paving

▲

■

stones). Stone implements included CHOPPING TOOLS, chipped and partially polished axes, hunting points and scrapers.

JORDAN The area east of the Jordan river. Mountains rise abruptly from the rift valley which contain the Dead Sea, and then fall away further east to form a desert plateau. At Beidha near PETRA a settlement of *c* 7000 BC was found. Initially the dwellings were circular but by *c* 6500 BC rectangular with plaster floors and very thick walls. There were probably upper stories to the houses. During the 4th millennium GHASSUL and a site in the desert called Jawa were occupied. Jawa was a large, heavily fortified town which had a cleverly-devised water system for domestic and agricultural purposes. During the 3rd millennium Bab edh-Dhra near the Dead Sea indicates a rich agricultural community in that area. There are numerous cemeteries immediately south of the Dead Sea which would have belonged to the cities of that time.

Little is known about the three groups, Ammonites, Moabites and Edomites, that inhabited Jordan *c* 1000 BC. It seems that the Edomites had considerable mineral wealth in their territory south of the Dead Sea, and it may be from there that King Solomon obtained copper. For a short period (200–0 BC) PETRA dominated the area politically. In the north Greek cities were built and in 63 BC became part of the Roman empire and formed into a league of 10 cities called the Decapolis. Excellent remains are found at a number of these. The forum and the colonnaded ■ street at Jerash are examples of unusual Roman planning. Under the OMAYYADS, Jordan was assisted because of its place between Mecca and Damascus; but when Baghdad became the ABBASID capital, it was soon a backwater.

JULIUS CAESAR, Gaius (*c* 100–44 BC) The man who more than anyone else decided the fate of the old Roman Republic. He became sole dictator in Rome after the civil wars and the defeat of his main rival, Pompey. He was a man of considerable military genius and gained for Rome huge areas of GAUL and Germany, even launching two expeditions to Britain, although neither was consolidated. He had many enemies, both would-be despots and angry democrats, but his murder in 44 BC at the hands of Brutus and others led to the transfer of his power to the young Octavian, who after crushing the ambitious Mark Anthony established firmly the Imperial system. Caesar was beloved by the army and was several times offered the crown, which he refused.

JUSTINIAN, (AD 483–565) During his reign as Eastern Roman Emperor, which began in AD 527, his greatest accomplishment was the complete codification of the law. At a time when the empire was under extreme barbarian pressure he was successful in holding the frontiers against invaders from the Balkans and Persia, while his general, Count Belisarius, was able to recover much of the lost empire in Europe and Africa. His greatest memorial is the church of Hagia Sophia, CONSTANTINOPLE.

JUTES A Germanic people from northern Jutland who, according to BEDE, settled in Kent, the Isle of Wight, and the Southampton area during the 5th century AD. Although they are classed with the other invaders like the ANGLES, SAXONS and FRISIANS as 'Anglo-Saxon', the Jutes maintained more individuality than the others, shown by the exclusively Kentish distribution of small cruciform brooches of early date, only paralleled in Danish material.

KADESH (Tell Nebi Mend), Syria Large TELL on the river Orontes south-west of Homs. The site has been occupied from before 2000 BC. In the 2nd millennium BC it was a large city state on the border of the Egyptian and HITTITE empire. It achieved fame as the site of the inconclusive battle between Ramesses II of Egypt and Muwatallis of the Hittites 1286 BC.

KAFIAVANA, New Guinea In the eastern highlands. Excavation has revealed a stone industry with PEBBLE TOOLS, CORE-SCRAPERS and flake tools. Ground-stone axes from this site date to 7500 BC, while broken specimens go back to 8700 BC; these therefore precede by several thousand years any evidence for horticultural activity in New Guinea.

KALABSHA, Egypt Site name of the Temple of Mandulis. It stood originally 40km south of Aswan but was dismantled and removed just above the High Dam to avoid flooding by Lake Nasser. This Nubian temple is second only to ABU SIMBEL in size. The Roman emperor Augustus rebuilt it on the site of an earlier temple of Amenophis II (Dynasty XVIII). In addition to the local god Mandulis (apparently a version of HORUS with similar 'older' and 'younger' forms) there are dedications to the ithyphallic fertility-god Min, the ram-headed creator god Khnum and the sky god Harmachis. A jetty formed the entrance from the Nile. Screen walls imitate ornamental matwork of secular buildings. An important Greek inscription of the 5th century AD records the victory of Silko (king of the Christian Nobadae–Nubian tribe) over the Blemmyes, who had earlier caused the Roman emperors trouble on Egypt's southern frontier.

KALAMBO FALLS, Zambia A site at the south-east end of lake Tanganyika in the basin of the Kalambo river. The river sediments contain a long archaeological sequence as well as pollen which reflects changing humidity and temperature contemporary with the last glaciation. The earliest tools are late ACHEULEAN, from which the waterlogged conditions have preserved wooden digging sticks and a club; there is also evidence for the use of fire. Following this are tools of SANGOAN, LUPEMBAN and MAGOSIAN types, and a MICROLITH INDUSTRY of WILTON type. The sequence ends with remains of early farming communities.

KALIBANGAN, India This site is a typical smaller urban centre of the INDUS CIVILIZATION, in all ways a smaller version of the 'capitals' MOHENJO-DARO and HARAPPA. A pre-Harappan settlement with massive mud-brick ramparts predates the main settlement; its material culture shares many elements with AMRI and KOT DIJI, but includes also purely local features. The mature Harappan period is dated from 2100 to 2000 BC by radiocarbon.

KAMINALJUYU, Guatemala An important highland MAYA ceremonial centre founded in the early Preclassic period (*see* MESOAMERICA) with a large central quarter of huge ADOBE and stone temple PLATFORM MOUNDS, PYRAMIDS and PLAZAS. An especially rich burial of the late Preclassic period contained offerings of jade, marble and pottery vessels. During the early Classic period, AD 400–600, influences from highland Mexican TEOTIHUACAN were so strong as to suggest actual conquest. Typical features such as the TALUD-TABLERO method of building, Teotihuacan pottery and religious motifs are numerous.

These influences disappear in the Postclassic with the waning of Teotihuacan power and its eventual collapse. The most significant feature of this phase are the huge basin-shaped BALL COURTS.

KAPILAVASTU, Nepal Home of the BUDDHA. Massive ramparts at Tilaura Kot in Nepal, 15km from LUMBINI, of 1st century BC date or earlier, can probably be identified with Kapilavastu; Piprawa, Uttar Pradesh, is an alternative possibility.

KARANOVO
see STARČEVO

KARATEPE, Turkey A site in Cilicia excavated since 1947. Its position on the route from central Turkey to Syria made it an important town. At one of the gateways an inscription in PHOENICIAN and HITTITE was found, together with a large number of reliefs. This inscription enabled the Hittite script to be deciphered.

KARLE
see ROCK-CUT ARCHITECTURE

●**KARNAK, Egypt** Eastern Thebes. Major cult centre for the state-god Amun, his wife Mut (vulture-goddess) and their son Khons. Monuments from Middle Kingdom down to Roman period:
(1) Great Temple of Amun
From the Nile canal, an avenue of ram-headed sphinxes led to the first of ten pylons within enclosure-wall of 2,400m. Off the Great Court lies a temple of Ramesses III (Dynasty XX) with chapels for and reliefs of sacred boats of Amun and family in processions. The Great Hypostyle Hall (102m wide, 53m long, with 134 colossal columns) is essentially work of Sethos I and Ramesses II (Dynasty XIX). Reliefs of battle of Kadesh (1286 BC) show Ramesses' chariot-charge into the HITTITES. Near the centre of the sanctuary, Tuthmosis III (Dynasty XVIII) put up records of the campaigns extending the Egyptian empire to the river Euphrates.
(2) Temple of Mut
The work of Amenophis III (Dynasty XVIII), with numerous diorite and granite statues of lioness goddess Sekhmet (wife of Ptah of Memphis).

KASSITES
see BABYLON

KAUPANG, Norway A VIKING period town once thought lost and now being excavated at Kaupang in south Vestfold. Originally called Skiringssal, it seems to have been an undefended trading centre similar to BIRKA and HEDEBY, with which it was probably in contact. In graves of the 9th century AD are Irish and Anglo-Saxon metalwork, finely-woven cloth, Rhenish glassware, imported pottery and foreign coins.

KAUSAMBI, India Located on the river Jamuna, near its confluence with the Ganges. The earliest defences, a rampart with brick revetting, occur in a period characterized by a red ware possibly related to OCHRE-COLOURED POTTERY, and by the use of iron. In the later NORTHERN BLACK POLISHED WARE period guard-rooms and bastions were added. A palace is located in the SW corner of the site; the dating of this is uncertain. The inscription on a temple identifies it as the Ghositarama monastery where the BUDDHA spent some time: a large courtyard with a STUPA and interior rooms. *See also:* GANGES CIVILIZATION.

KENNIFF CAVE, Australia Site in Queensland with levels dating from 14,000 to 500 BC. The collection of stone tools covers most Australian prehistoric types. Scrapers of flakes or large cores were present from the early levels, while the introduction of more specialized stone tools did not begin until approximately 2000 BC. These included backed BLADES, with crescent-shaped and trapezoidal geometric MICROLITHS, ELOUERA points, TULA-ADZE FLAKES, and ground stone.

▲**KERO** A wooden beaker with either straight or flaring sides common during the INCA period. It derives from an earlier pottery form of the TIAHUANACO era, and continued into Post-Conquest times. ▶

KHAFAJAH [ancient Tutub], Iraq A group of mounds in the Diyala valley north-east of Baghdad. The site is best known for its temples and statues excavated 1930–38. A temple with 10 building phases dedicated to the moon god, SIN, enables the development of the culture during the 3rd millennium to be traced. A second temple built on a rectangular platform and surrounded by a massive oval wall has been reconstructed. Included within its wall were store-houses and priests' quarters.

KHIRBET KEREK [ancient Beth Yerah], Israel A large site on the southern shore of the lake of Galilee, occupied from *c* 3200 BC. It is particularly known for distinctive pottery, highly burnished with red or black slip and often decorated in RELIEF. It may have been introduced by immigrating people *c* 2500 BC.

KHIROKITIA, Cyprus A neolithic settlement of *c* 6000–5500 BC in southern CYPRUS. Part of the site containing about fifty dwellings has been excavated. Each house, of the 'tholos' type, consists of a circular room up to 10m in diameter. Inside were hearths and benches, and underneath the floor the dead were buried with grave goods. Common gifts to the dead were stone bowls which were made from andesite gathered from a near-by river bed. Tools were made from andesite, flint, bone, and obsidian imported from Turkey or Syria.

KHMER EMPIRE
see ANGKOR

KHORSABAD [ancient Dur Sharrukin], Iraq An ASSYRIAN city near Mosul built by Sargon II in 717 BC as his new capital. It was laid out $1\frac{1}{2}$km square. Its magnificent palace has been excavated and a rich collection of sculptures, RELIEFS, CUNEIFORM inscriptions and TABLETS was found. A temple and gateway were among the other buildings excavated. Khorsabad ceased to be the capital of Assyria when Sargon died in 705 BC.

KIDDER, Alfred Vincent (1885–1963) Much of his research was based on the archaeological study of the north American SOUTHWEST where he was responsible for some of the earliest scientifically excavated and recorded PUEBLOS. He became involved in Mesoamerican, especially

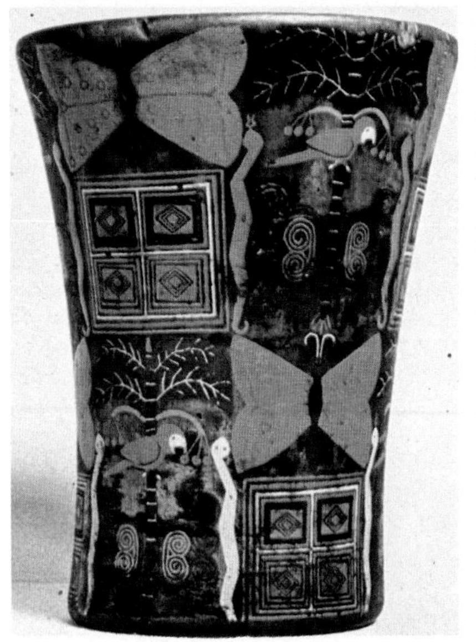

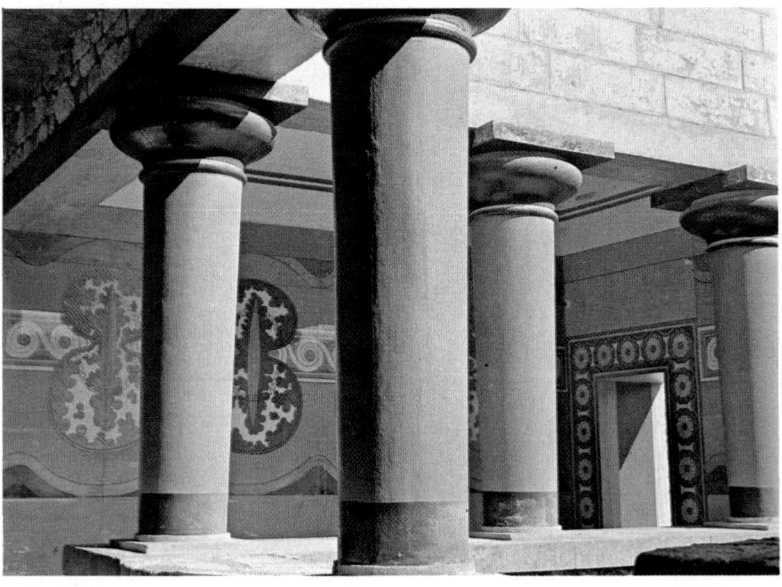

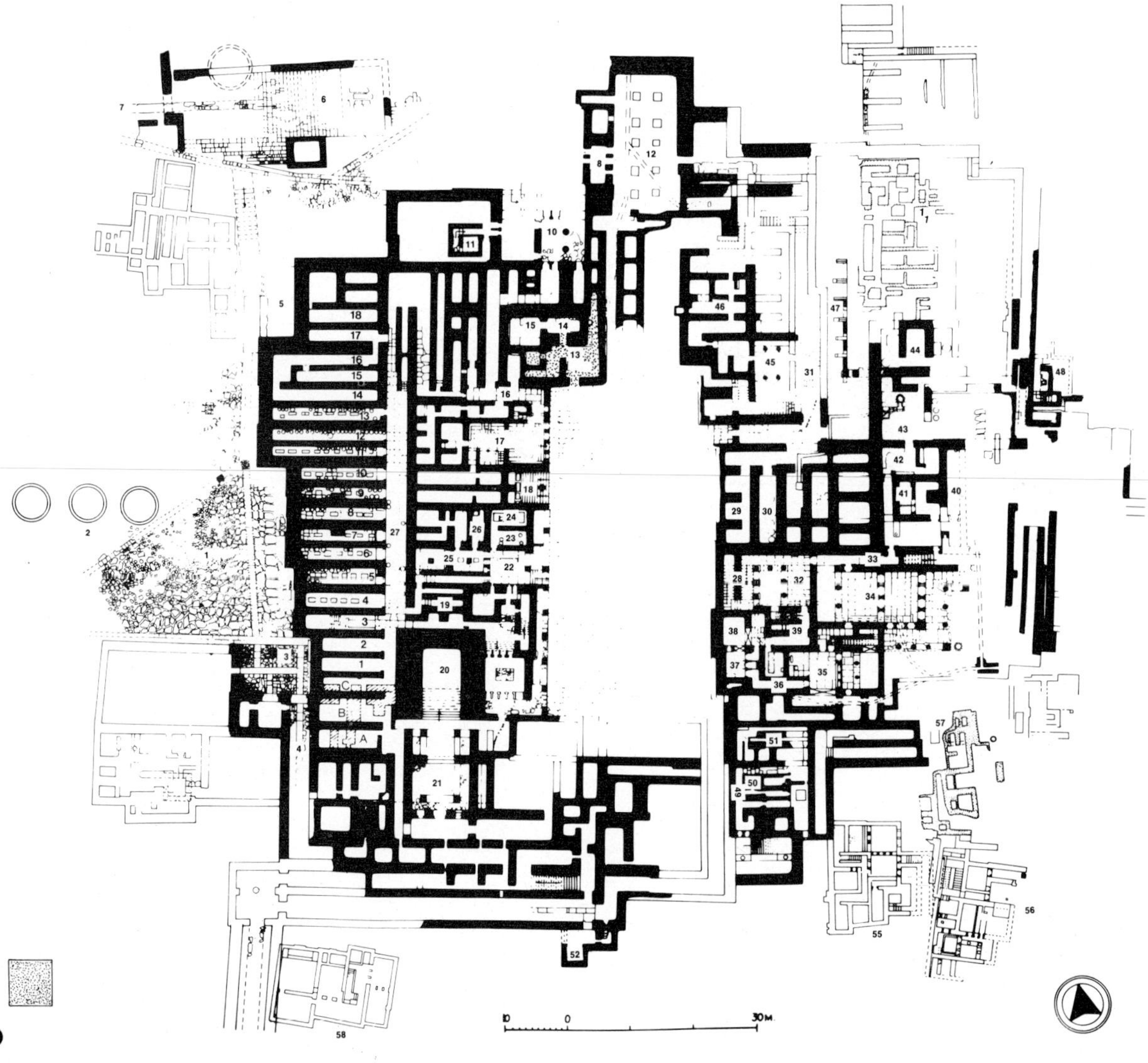
1
2
3
4
5
6
7
8
10
11
12
13
14
15
16
17
18
19
20
21
22
23
24
25
26
27
28
29
30
31
32
33
34
35
36
37
38
39
40
41
42
43
44
45
46
47
48
49
50
51
52
55
56
57
58
A
B
C
10 0 30M.

MAYA, archaeology after he was appointed director in 1929 of the Maya programme for the Carnegie Institution in Washington. Under these auspices, his most important works were his excavations at the ceremonial site of KAMINALJUYU and his studies of Maya architecture at UAXACTUN.
Main book: *An Introduction to the Study of Southwestern Archaeology* (1924).

KIMMERIDGE, Dorset Shale from here was in the IRON AGE and ROMAN period made into bracelets, cups and even table legs. Blanks from the centres of the bracelets, e.g. from GLASTONBURY, were once wrongly thought to be money.

KITCHEN MIDDEN A once popular term used to describe any deposit thought to represent the domestic activities of prehistoric man. Although it literally means any dump of domestic or food rubbish, it has come to be associated with the large mounds of shells left by certain hunter–gatherer–fisher groups (the ERTEBØLLE – originally called the 'Kitchen midden culture' – or the JOMON culture).

KIVA Generally circular, occasionally rectangular, subterranean chambers built within PUEBLO settlements and used for ceremonial functions. *See* ANASAZI.

KLEIN ASPERGLE, Germany A BARROW of the early LA TÈNE period, *c* 450 BC. The CREMATION grave contained imports from Italy and Greece, such as a bucket and an Attic red-figure cup (*see* GREEK POTTERY). This was decorated with open goldwork in the very earliest CELTIC ART style – the motifs are copies of classical designs. Also in this style were a pair of gold drinking horns with ram's head terminals. The grave also contained an accurate copy of an ETRUSCAN flagon.

● **KNOSSOS, Crete** The chief town and palace of the MINOAN culture. The site was heavily occupied in the NEOLITHIC but the palace was not built until the Middle Minoan period (*c* 2000 BC). It consists of a large courtyard with royal apartments on one side and state-rooms on the other. The apartments were well appointed, with running water and flushing toilets as well as a basic layout on the MEGARON or open, porched, hall plan. Many of the rooms are frescoed. Underneath the palace are large storerooms, many with massive pottery jars (PITHOS) to store grain and oil.

The site survived the eruption of THERA (*c* 1450 BC) only to be dominated thereafter by the MYCENAEANS. By the Iron Age the town was deserted.

KNOWTH, Eire A NEOLITHIC PASSAGE GRAVE cemetery in the BOYNE VALLEY, Co. Meath (near New Grange and Dowth). There is a large central mound containing two passage tombs, one of which has a CORBELLED roof. Like New Grange, the stones of both passage and chamber have large numbers of carvings. Surrounding the main TUMULUS is a series of about 15 smaller satellite cairns, some perhaps IRON AGE or VIKING in date. During the early Christian period, from the beginning of the 9th century AD, Knowth was the residence of the kings of Brega, who were under the high kingship of Tara.

KO The Chinese halberd; an important weapon during the SHANG and CHOU dynasties. Though usually of bronze, ritual specimens of jade have been found as well. The ko consisted of a blade generally 150–250mm long, up to 50mm wide with a slight curvature and a flat tang going through a metre-long shaft, to which the blade lay at a right angle. The tang often bore a monster-mask decoration.

KOFUN CULTURE
see TOMB PERIOD

KÖLN-LINDENTHAL, Germany Site of a LINEAR POTTERY settlement on the outskirts of Cologne. The excavation of the site in the early 1930s was a pioneer application of the stripping of large areas to uncover evidence for buildings and other features (a technique later followed at the Iron Age site of LITTLE WOODBURY in southern England, again by a German archaeologist). What were at the time described as 'pit-dwellings' are now interpreted as pits from which was quarried the material used for daubing the walls of the timber-built long-houses (which were originally regarded as barns). Like the settlement at BYLANY, Köln-Lindenthal appears to have been intermittently occupied, in this case over a period of about 400 years, during which 20 houses were rebuilt on seven separate occasions.

KONDANE
see ROCK-CUT ARCHITECTURE

KOONALDA CAVE, Australia The Gallus site in the limestone Koonalda Cave, Nullarbor plain, south Australia has revealed evidence of early human occupation, dated to *c* 20,000 BC. The few tools found were trimmed flakes and waste material. Animal bones were well preserved, though no giant marsupials have been identified. Deep inside, a dark, inaccessible area of the cave bears wall-engravings consisting of finger markings and grooves covering hundreds of square metres. This interior area has also yielded evidence that flint nodules imbedded in the walls were quarried.

KÖRÖS
see STARČEVO

● **KOT DIJI, Pakistan** This pre-Harappan site is located about 50km east of Mohenjo-Daro. A massive defensive wall of limestone rubble and mud-brick with bastions surrounds the site. House floors are known from the middle of the occupation. The pottery is distinctive and includes a decorative motif which developed into the popular Harappan fish-scale design. Later levels include an increased amount of Harappan material followed by a full INDUS CIVILIZATION occupation.

KOW SWAMP, Australia This site, located near the Murray River in northern Victoria, contained the skeletal remains of at least 15 individuals, dated to approximately 8000 BC. Shell, quartz, and ochre were found in several graves. Of special interest is the fact that the skulls display morphologically archaic features, in contrast to the hominid material recovered from LAKE MUNGO, which (though it dates to some 25–30,000 BC) reveals gracile, modern features. The skeletal material from these two sites may, therefore, represent the two extremes of variation within a single hominid line, rather than two distinct hominid forms. *See also* HOMO.

KREMIKOVCI
see STARČEVO

▲ **KROEBER, Alfred Louis (1876–1960)** A founder of modern archaeological research in the Americas who extended his interests into the fields of anthropology, ethnology of the north American Indians, folklore and linguistics. He was responsible for two major seriations – for pottery styles of the American SOUTHWEST and for Peruvian cultural development – both basic to modern study of either region, and only recently superseded. Much of his work involved surveys of different parts of the Peru coast and excavations in the Nasca valley.

KULTEPE [ancient Kanesh], Turkey A TELL in central ANATOLIA. Excavations in 1925 and since 1948 have illuminated ancient trading practices. A small subsidiary tell was inhabited by a colony of ASSYRIAN merchants who organized trade from Assur to various cities in Anatolia during the 19th century BC. Their records in CUNEIFORM script on clay TABLETS give a detailed account of trading procedures and commodities. Treaties were made with local Anatolian princes to whom the merchants paid taxes in return for safe passage through the princes' territory. Trade was by barter or exchange of currency. Gold, silver and precious stones were exported from Anatolia in exchange for tin and textiles.

KURGAN CULTURE A collective name for a group of CULTURES in eastern Europe and southern Russia, *c* 2500 BC, whose burials were under kurgans or BARROWS. At Maikop in the south Caucasus, wooden mortuary houses with exceptionally rich grave goods were built beneath the barrow. Cattle or sheep and wheeled carts were also buried, a practice which continued into the Iron Age (*see* ARRAS, HOHMICHELE, VIX). The kurgan people of this period may have been the earliest INDO-EUROPEAN speakers. The kurgan burial first appeared with the use of copper, but rich timber graves in the Caucasus still included cattle, sheep and horses in the graves *c* 15th century BC. Even later, but in the same area, the 8th-century BC SCYTHIANS and CIMMERIANS buried their dead in timber-framed TUMULI with carts and horses. *See also* PAZYRYK.

KUSHANS A nomadic tribe from the borders of China who settled in Bactria in the early 2nd century BC. Thence they invaded PARTHIA and AFGHANISTAN and penetrated as far south as the borders of the Indian Deccan. They established a strong empire in north India which lasted into the 3rd century AD. *See also* BAGLAN, BARBARICUM; BEGRAM, CHARSADA, GANDHARAN ART, TAXILA.

LACHISH, Israel A TELL in central Palestine identified with Tell ed-Duweir. The city was strongly fortified from 1900 BC, but in spite of its defences fell a number of times. The Egyptians captured it *c* 1580 BC, and when the ISRAELITES took it *c* 1220 BC they rebuilt it as part of their national defence. The capture of the city by the Assyrians in ■ about 701 BC is recorded in RELIEFS from Nineveh which show siege engines in use. After the city's final destruction by the BABYLONIANS *c* 588 BC there is little evidence of occupation. Three groups of inscriptions have been found: a dagger of *c* 1700 BC with ALPHABETIC writing on it, four inscribed vessels from a temple of about 1400 BC and a group of OSTRACA under the Babylonian destruction layer.

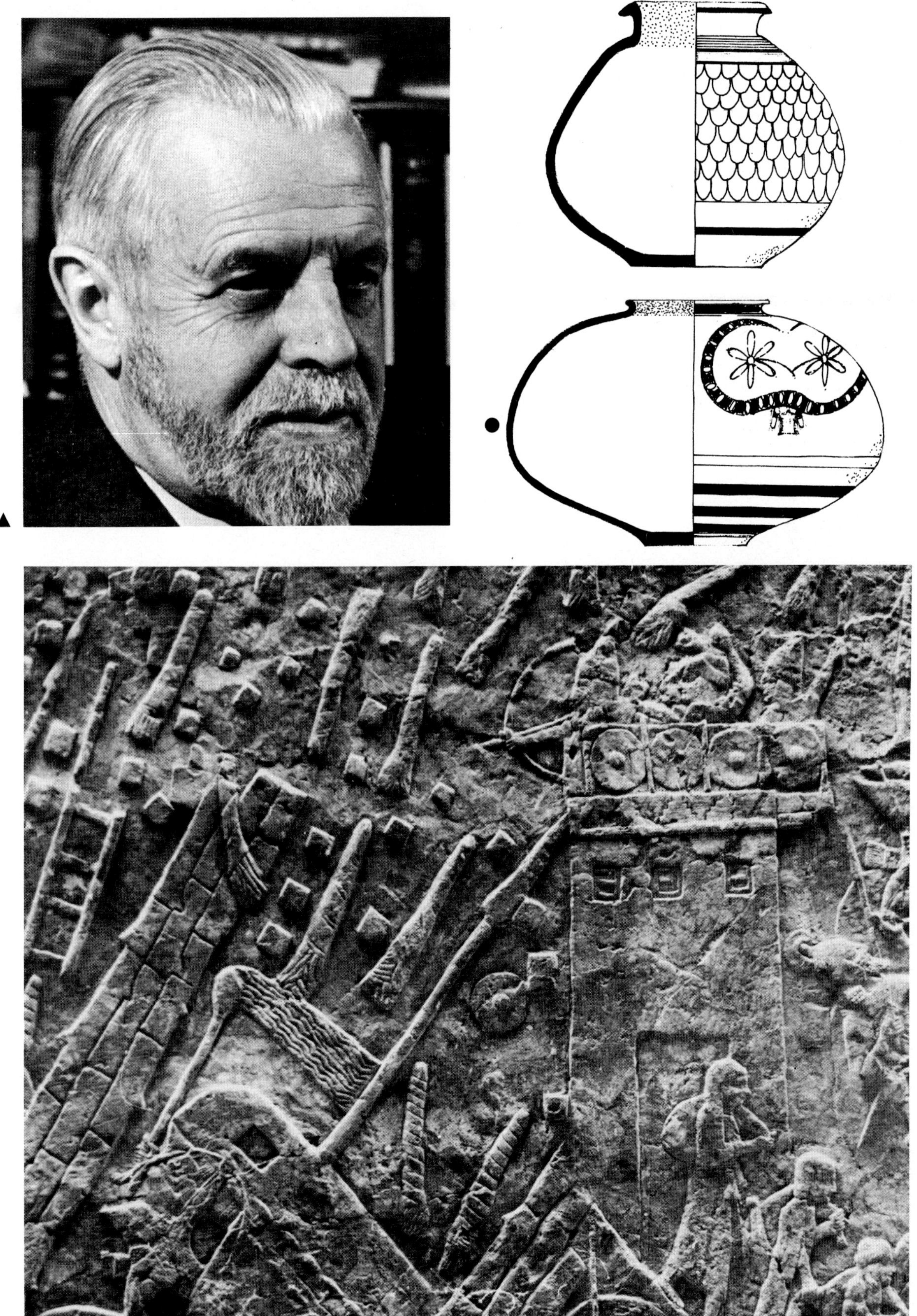

▲

●

■

LAETI
see FOEDERATI

LAGASH [modern Telloh], Iran City-state of SUMER north of UR. Under the kingships of Eannatum (2500 BC) and Gudea (*c* 2100 BC), Lagash became a leading city of Sumer but later was defeated by a rival city. Excavations at the TELL have brought to light many CUNEIFORM TABLETS which are concerned with social and economic affairs. Also found ● were a number of statues of Gudea; one carved in diorite gives a clear indication of the appearance of Sumerian rulers.

LAGOZZA (Po valley late neolithic culture) A WESTERN NEOLITHIC culture in north Italy, related less to the preceding Middle Neolithic in the area than to the French CHASSEY culture, with which it shares highly burnished round-based pottery. The TYPE-SITE (Lagozza di Besnate near Milan) was a lakeside settlement of *c* 3000 BC. Preserved in the waterlogged conditions were wheat, barley, lentils and flax as well as pears, apples, cherries, nuts and acorns (the fruit and nuts probably all picked from wild trees).

LA GRAUFESENQUE, France The major centre of production of south Gaulish SAMIAN ware, exporting all through the empire throughout the 1st century AD until it lost the domination of the market to LEZOUX.

LAHUN, Egypt This site in the Libyan desert towards the FAIYUM has a pyramid of Sesostris II (Dynasty XII) with a superstructure of mud and with walls of natural rock and limestone. From the southern entrance depart shafts and corridors to foil thieves. Splendid inlaid jewellery was recovered from the nearby tomb of a royal princess.

Most interest, however, comes from the excavation of the town site – a rare occurrence in Egyptian archaeology. Excavations by PETRIE uncovered houses for the workmen who built the pyramid-complex and for the supervisory officials. The workmen and officials were socially segregated by town planning. The eastern section of the town occupied two-thirds of the site and had spacious multi-room penthouses, in the smaller western quarter were several hundred crammed houses. Finds of hieratic PAPYRI (including scientific and literary texts) show Egyptian bureaucracy in action, with census-records, letters and financial and legal documents.

LAKE MENINDEE, Australia An area of ancient sand dunes and lake shores in western New South Wales. Artefacts, consisting of a few stone FLAKES were found in an excavated deposit which also yielded a varied collection of bones of giant, now extinct, marsupials. Remains at Menindee are dated *c* 24–18,000 BC. *See also* LAKE MUNGO.

LAKE MUNGO, Australia A PLEISTOCENE lake (now dry) in western New South Wales, where in 1968 the cremated remains of a young adult female were found. Fragments of the cranium show that the conformation lies within the range of recent Australian skeletal form. In the regions of the burial were found numerous hearths, charcoal, stone tools (consisting of CORE TOOLS and scrapers) and burnt animal bone fragments. Only one bone belonged to a now-extinct form, in contrast to material from LAKE MENINDEE, 160km away. On stratigraphic and radiocarbon evidence, the Lake Mungo material dates to the period

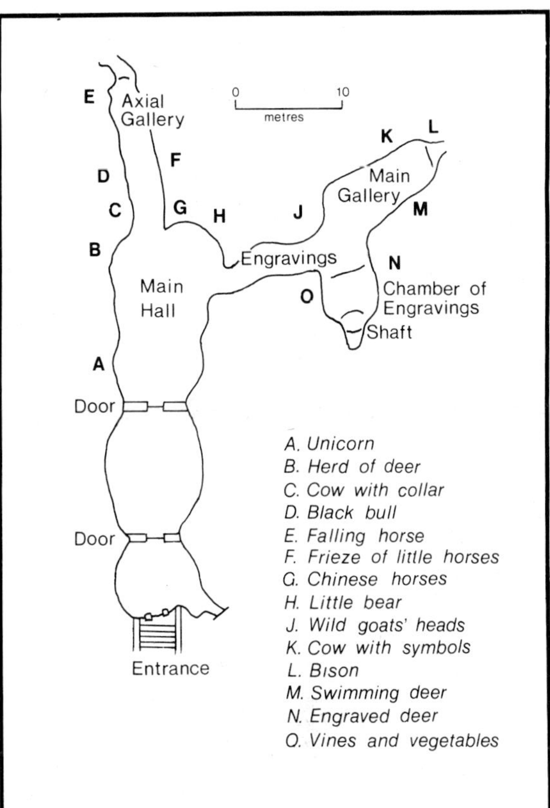

▲

23,000–30,000 BC making it the oldest human remains yet recorded in Australia. The 'modern' appearance of the cranial features when compared with the 'archaic' appearance of those at KOW SWAMP (which is of more recent date) raises problems regarding the relationship and development of hominids in Australia. *See* HOMO.

LAKE VILLAGE [lake dwelling, pile dwelling] Names given to a variety of settlement types found in Europe where timber structures have been preserved in conditions of WATERLOGGING. Many were discovered in the last century when areas of marsh were drained. Others came to light when lake levels fell, including those of Lake Neuchâtel (*see* LA TÈNE and Lake Zurich, Switzerland. At the latter location, wooden posts were interpreted as the piles supporting buildings above open water, but it is now known that the settlement was on wet ground near the lake edge. Such sites of the WESTERN NEOLITHIC cultures (*see* CHASSEY, CORTAILLOD, LAGOZZA) have provided much evidence for aspects of material culture normally vanished. MEARE and GLASTONBURY are two well-known Iron Age lake villages in south-west England. *See also* BISKUPIN; CRANNOG.

LAMBAESIS, Algeria A fortress for the Third Augustan Legion. This legion was the only garrison of the Saharan border in the Roman empire and was stationed here from AD 81. Excavations of the deserted site have revealed the total plan of a legionary fortress with several unusual points such as the 'Praetorian Hall' and the gateways of non-standard shape.

LANDNAM A Scandinavian term, indicating clearance of forest with the help of fire, followed by the cultivation of the cleared area, and its subsequent desertion and recolonization by the forest. This succession was first observed by Johs Iversen, the Danish pollen analyst, whilst studying the vegetation change in Ordrup Bog, Jutland. It has since been recognized in many other areas and is accepted as a standard pattern in the early agriculture of prehistoric Europe.

LAN-T'IEN MAN Specimens found in Shensi province dated to the Middle PLEISTOCENE, *c* 500,000 BC, and representing the oldest certain examples of HOMO ERECTUS in China. The Lan-t'ien skull exhibits an extraordinarily thick cranial wall, approximately half as thick again as that of PEKING MAN. His brain capacity is slightly less than that of Peking man, however, suggesting that Lan-t'ien man was somewhat more primitive.

LARNIAN A MESOLITHIC hunter-fisher culture, found in coastal areas of northern Ireland and adjacent south-west Scotland, contemporary with the OBANIAN. From *c* 3500 BC domestic animals and polished stone axes are found associated with typically Larnian flint implements. The TYPE-SITE is Larne (north-east Ireland).

▲ **LASCAUX, France** A famous cave system near Montignac, Dordogne, discovered as recently as 1940 and containing some of the most spectacular known Upper PALAEOLITHIC CAVE ART. Among the animals represented in the paintings, the cow and the horse are common. A number of 'scenes' have been identified. These include a row of deer heads, interpreted by some as representing a herd of deer swimming, and a complicated 'composition' consisting of a disembowelled bison, a man, a rhinoceros

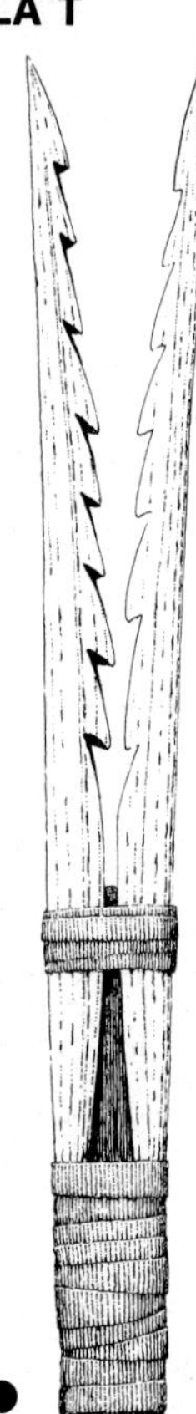

●

▲

and a number of indecipherable signs. Excavation within the cave has produced many clay lamps, probably used both in creating and in viewing the paintings.

LA TÈNE, Switzerland A site on the edge of Lake Neuchâtel. La Tène gave its name to the second phase of the European IRON AGE, from 500 BC to the Roman conquest. The excavations from 1907–17 revealed a mass of wooden piles on the bed of the river adjoining the lake. These were originally thought to be the piles of the settlement, but are more likely to have been a bridge or jetty. Another suggestion is that La Tène is the site of a great votive deposit, similar to the La Tène deposits at GUNDESTRUP and LLYN CERRIG BACH. From the excavations came a mass of finds including 116 SWORDS, 270 spears, wooden wheels, bowls and shields, and domestic tools and AXES. The metalwork has widespread parallels from all over the CELTIC world.

Important changes took place in Europe during the La Tène period. The Celts increased in importance as a European power, until in 390 BC they sacked Rome. With the rise of OPPIDA in this period, there was a more centralized administration, and many goods, such as the pottery from MANCHING, were professionally made. At the same time there was a widespread similarity in the decoration of objects; CELTIC ART was a phenomenon of the La Tène period. Imports from southern Europe increased, perhaps because the Celts found a market for their exports south of the Alps. Another innovation was coinage. One minor change that distinguishes the HALLSTATT phase from that of La Tène was the introduction of CHARIOTS, which are found in rich graves in the Rhineland and the Marne area.

▲**LA VENTA, Mexico** Located on a small swampy island in the Tabasco lowlands near the gulf of Mexico, La Venta is one of the earliest CEREMONIAL CENTRES in Mesoamerica, constructed by peoples of OLMEC culture *c* 1000 BC. The total area of the site is 5 square km with the central group of buildings stretching for 2km on a north-south axis. Of this group, two of the most important structures are the great rectangular PLATFORM MOUND, 120 × 70m and 32m high, together with the large earthen, fluted, cone-shaped mound standing 110m high. A large ADOBE wall topped by basalt columns encloses the central PLAZA and ceremonial buildings. Some of the more important finds include three 'pavements' constructed of green serpentine blocks and coloured clays in the likeness of a stylized jaguar face, which were buried presumably for ceremonial purposes. A rich cache of jade celts, figurines, beads and earplugs was found hidden in a pit just above one of these, together with concave mirrors of highly polished magnetite and ilmenite. Monumental stone sculptures including carved altars, STELAE and giant stone heads also characterize the site, as they do similar Olmec sites in this area (*see* SAN LORENZO; TENOCHTITLAN). The largest of these stelae weighs around 50 tonnes. La Venta was probably destroyed around 600 BC; the site was deserted by 400 BC.

LAYARD, Austen Henry (1817–94) After travelling in Iraq and Persia, Layard became interested in the remains of ASSYRIA. In 1845–7, with the assistance of Hormuzd Rassam, he excavated at NIMRUD which he wrongly thought to be Nineveh. Later he did excavate at Nineveh, where he found the palace of Ashurbanipal containing the royal library. He excavated for the British Museum 1849–51 and returned with many antiquities including the

large winged bulls (*see* ASSYRIA) which inspired much public interest. His best-known book is *Nineveh and its Remains* (1848), which is actually about Nimrud.

●**LEISTER** A fish-spear, with two barbed points hafted opposite each other. As usually the barbs only, not the haft, survive in the archaeological record; the leister is difficult to recognize archaeologically.

LEON, Spain A Roman town whose name derives from the Latin *legio*, the name of the army unit stationed there. This was the only garrison in the whole of Roman Spain after the campaigns of conquest had ceased. Still visible are its late Roman walls with unusually closely spaced bastions.

LEPENSKI VIR, Jugoslavia A recently excavated site in the Iron Gates gorge. The rich food potential of the river Danube supported a series of MESOLITHIC settlements, from which survived the stone foundations of many trapezoidal houses. These contained a number of unique stone carvings with fish-like faces. The Mesolithic settlements were covered by a STARČEVO deposit. The site has now been raised up the side of the gorge, to save it from the rising waters of the river.

■**LEPSIUS, Karl Richard** (1810–84) One of the most outstanding Egyptologists to follow CHAMPOLLION whose hieroglyphic system he adopted and added to. He also effectively removed doubts as to its validity by his discovery of the bilingual Decree of Canopus at TANIS which corroborated Champollion's findings from the ROSETTA Stone.

In 1842–5 he led a team of draughtsmen to survey the monuments of Egypt and Nubia. His excavations using stratified sections across a site were far in advance of his time. In 1859 his pictorial record of this expedition was published in twelve huge volumes known as *Denkmäler aus Aegypten und Aethiopien*. The accuracy and beauty of its plates are due to Lepsius, early training in copper engraving and lithography.

○**LEPTIS MAGNA, Libya** This town was a CARTHAGINIAN foundation of the 6th century BC. Continually expanding and becoming richer 1st century BC–1st century AD, it achieved its ultimate development under the Emperor Septimius Severus, who was born there and started an enormous redevelopment scheme to transform the city centre and create a new artificial harbour. Much is still to be seen, especially the Severan work, the market hall with its stone counters, an almost perfect set of baths (the Hunting Baths), the THEATRE and the CIRCUS.

LERNA, Greece This myth-ridden site was excavated in the 1950s and revealed traces of occupation going back to the NEOLITHIC and ending in MYCENAEAN times. The most important building is the 'House of Tiles' (*c* 2200–2100 BC), one of the best buildings of pre-Mycenaean Greece. This is now on view and under cover. Two later shaft graves were found and suggest connections with early Mycenaean peoples.

LEVALLOISIAN Literally a flint ASSEMBLAGE of unretouched flakes made by the LEVALLOIS TECHNIQUE, but more generally used to refer to the widespread INDUSTRIES using the Levallois technique. These range from Africa, through Europe and into Asia.

LEVALLOIS TECHNIQUE Used in the PALAEOLITHIC (especially common in some MOUSTERIAN industries) for producing well-shaped FLAKES with very sharp edges. The essence of the process was to prepare a CORE so that the shape of the flake removed from it (frequently only one) was predetermined, thus making any secondary work or RETOUCH unnecessary. A Levallois core is domed on one face but flat on the other, resembling a tortoise. Similarly, a Levallois flake carries the scars of flakes removed from the parent core on its upper or 'dorsal' surface, while its lower 'ventral', surface is plain. The technique is named after the site of 19th-century discoveries in Levallois-Perret, Paris.

LE VALLONET, France A cave in Provence which has produced the only certain evidence for the existence of the earliest forms of man outside Asia or Africa. A few FLAKES and pebble-tools are dated by the associated animal remains to the Upper Villafranchian (*see* PLEISTOCENE), although no actual human remains have been found.

LEVANT The modern name for the area of the eastern Mediterranean comprising Syria, Lebanon, Jordan, Israel and Cyprus. The Levant is situated between two great areas of Near Eastern civilization – Egypt and MESOPOTAMIA. Although the area was largely inhabited by SEMITIC people, Egyptian and INDO-EUROPEAN influences are apparent at many sites. The flint tools scattered over the desert regions and in the caves of MOUNT CARMEL signify that Palaeolithic man was present in the area. JERICHO, situated in a fertile oasis, is the earliest Near Eastern village with fortifications and an agricultural basis. It seems there was a constant movement of people out of the desert and down from the Anatolian plateau. The geographical diversity of the area has meant that, rather than large kingdoms, smaller city-states have been the most frequent political organization. As an area that depends on rain for its fertility, the Levant has often incurred drought, disrupting people and causing them to move out, as happened to the Hyksos. The main contribution made to the world by people of this area has been the diffusion of Near Eastern culture and religion. The PHOENICIANS and the Jews are two prominent examples of this process.

LEZOUX, France One of the main centres of the manufacture of SAMIAN ware after *c* AD 85. Among the earliest Lezoux potters was Libertus, whose stamp is also found at LA GRAUFESENQUE; it is possible that he brought the trade with him. One Samian workshop at Lezoux covered an area of 900 sq.m and had the highly specialized kilns needed for firing this ware – the output of such kilns was tremendous. Lezoux is also the find-spot of a beautiful bronze figure of a CELTIC god, wearing the winged cap of Mercury but identified by an inscription as Esus. It is probably of the 1st century AD.

LIGHTHOUSES, Roman Navigational aids such as beacons and lighthouses are probably as old as sailing the sea. However, there are several famous ancient lighthouses, especially the gigantic *pharos* over Alexandria harbour, one of the Seven Wonders. This no longer exists, but a more prosaic beacon on the harbour at LEPTIS MAGNA has been found. In the northern provinces the most famous example is at Dover where the tower survives for some 15m. It was originally 24m high, and built in diminishing octagonal stages. It had a twin, now demolished, on a hill opposite, and a partner at Boulogne

across the Channel, whose *tour d'ordre* once stood 35m high but was demolished in the 16th century. These two were similar in design to the surviving example.

LIMES The Latin word for frontier. Early Rome had no real frontiers until all Italy was hers and the Alps acted as a frontier. Later expansion used the great rivers of the Rhine and Danube as frontiers. Other *limes* were the sea, the Sahara desert, the Syrian desert and the Anatolian highlands. All these natural barriers seemed the best frontiers for the Roman empire, which guarded them closely once they were in operation. Many of them were supplemented by lines of forts (e.g. along the Rhine) or roads with forts along them (e.g. the Sahara desert and the FOSSE WAY) or a continuous barrier (e.g. in the Black Forest, part of the Sahara, the mouth of the Danube, HADRIAN'S and the ANTONINE Walls). These last two are the most sophisticated and best preserved. The army's efforts (especially those of the auxiliary forces) concentrated on defending the *limes* after the early 2nd century AD.

LINCOLN, England A legionary fortress founded AD 60–61 for the Ninth Spanish Legion. It was later replaced by the Second 'Helper' Legion and in AD 77 they, too, left and the fortress was turned over for use as a COLONIA. In the middle 2nd century the town was so large that an extension or lower colonia was incorporated into the wall circuit. The modern town obscures much, but the Newport Arch, the north gate of the upper colonia, survives, the only Roman gateway in Britain still in use.

LINDISFARNE, Northumberland A small island off the NORTHUMBRIAN coast which is connected to the mainland at low tide. Also known as Holy Island, it was the site of a monastery founded in AD 635 by St Aidan from IONA. After the eventual failure of St PAULINUS'S mission to Northumbria, Lindisfarne became the centre of Celtic Christianity in northern England. It is principally famous for the superb ▲illuminated MANUSCRIPTS especially the Lindisfarne Gospels produced there during the cultural renaissance of *c* 700. St CUTHBERT was the most venerated member of the community. The monastery was destroyed in the first Danish raid on England in 793.

LINEAR A, LINEAR B The scripts used by the MINOANS and MYCENAEANS. Linear A, the earlier form and not yet translated, is a syllabic script in which each symbol stands for a syllable (unlike the phonetic ALPHABET in which each letter represents a single sound). The language of the Linear B TABLETS is an early form of Greek. *See also* VENTRIS.

LINEAR EARTHWORK A stretch of bank and ditch, or multiple banks and ditches, built more or less straight across country for boundary or defensive purposes rather than as an enclosure. They vary in length from a few hundred metres to 90km or more, and were built during many different periods. Bronze Age examples from south-west Britain appear to have marked minor property boundaries, while others, especially those from the Iron Age and Anglo-Saxon period such as Grim's Ditch (Berks.) and the Devil's Dyke (Cambs.) are strategically placed to bar the Icknield Way and other important routes.

LINEAR POTTERY CULTURES One of the three main cultural groups that brought a farming (*see* NEOLITHIC)

economy into Europe, the other two being the STARČEVO group and the IMPRESSED WARE culture.

The Linear Pottery cultures (sometimes referred to as the DANUBIAN I culture) spread rapidly through central Europe in the 5th millennium BC, covering an area stretching between Jugoslavia and eastern France and Belgium. The speed of colonization is attributed to the nature of the farming cycle practised. Settlements are found exclusively on loess soils, which quickly lose their fertility when cultivated. Thus it was necessary to periodically clear fresh forest, using the SLASH-AND-BURN method, the settlements following the plots under cultivation. Wheat and barley were grown in these plots, as well as peas, beans and flax.

The cultures are especially linked with each other by their pottery (*see* BANDKERAMIK) and the construction of their buildings. The main dwellings were 'longhouses', large timber structures, about 6m wide and anything up to 50m long. Each house may well have been inhabited by a group of related people. Sometimes small fenced enclosures are attached to the longhouses, probably for penning up stock. (*See* BYLANY; KÖLN-LINDENTHAL.)

In the later periods, the remarkable uniformity of the material culture of the Linear Pottery group broke up, and a number of regional variations (Danubian II) developed. These included the Tisza culture of the middle Danube region, and the related Lengyel culture in Hungary, Czechoslovakia and Poland; the makers of Stroke-ornamented Ware (German *Stichbandkeramik*) in Bohemia and central Germany and the Rössen culture further west into eastern France. These developments had all occurred by *c* 3500 BC, when the earliest copper objects were beginning to appear.

● **LISHT, Egypt** The necropolis, south of MEMPHIS opposite the FAIYUM, for the new capital of Ammenemes I (Dynasty XII) who moved from Thebes for closer supervision of Lower Egypt. Northern pyramid of Ammenemes I used blocks from the Old Kingdom necropolis opposite Memphis. The burial chamber is permanently flooded, being below the level of the subsoil. The Southern pyramid was built for Sesostris I (Dynasty XII). French and American archaeologists have dug here extensively. The King's Horus name was found on a massive surrounding wall, between which and the pyramid were smaller pyramids for the royal family.

LITTLE WOODBURY, Wiltshire A classic IRON AGE site, excavated in 1938 by Bersu. Many of the features common to Iron Age sites were found here, such as an early surrounding palisade and a later ring ditch. Structures included 4-post granaries, ovens, large numbers of STORAGE PITS and ROUND HOUSES. The numerous postholes made it difficult to sort out the houses, especially as postholes were frequently re-cut on the same spot. There have been many different reconstructions. As at GLASTONBURY and MAIDEN CASTLE, finds included clay loom weights, weaving combs and spindle whorls, and slingstones for defence. Animal bones show that cattle and sheep were important, pig, horse and dog less so: this is a similar pattern to hundreds of Iron Age sites in southern England. At one time Little Woodbury was thought to be a typical Iron Age site, representing the indigenous culture rather than foreign influences. But Woodbury-type sites are found only in southern England, and even then with many variations. Little Woodbury is not so much a TYPE-SITE as an exception.

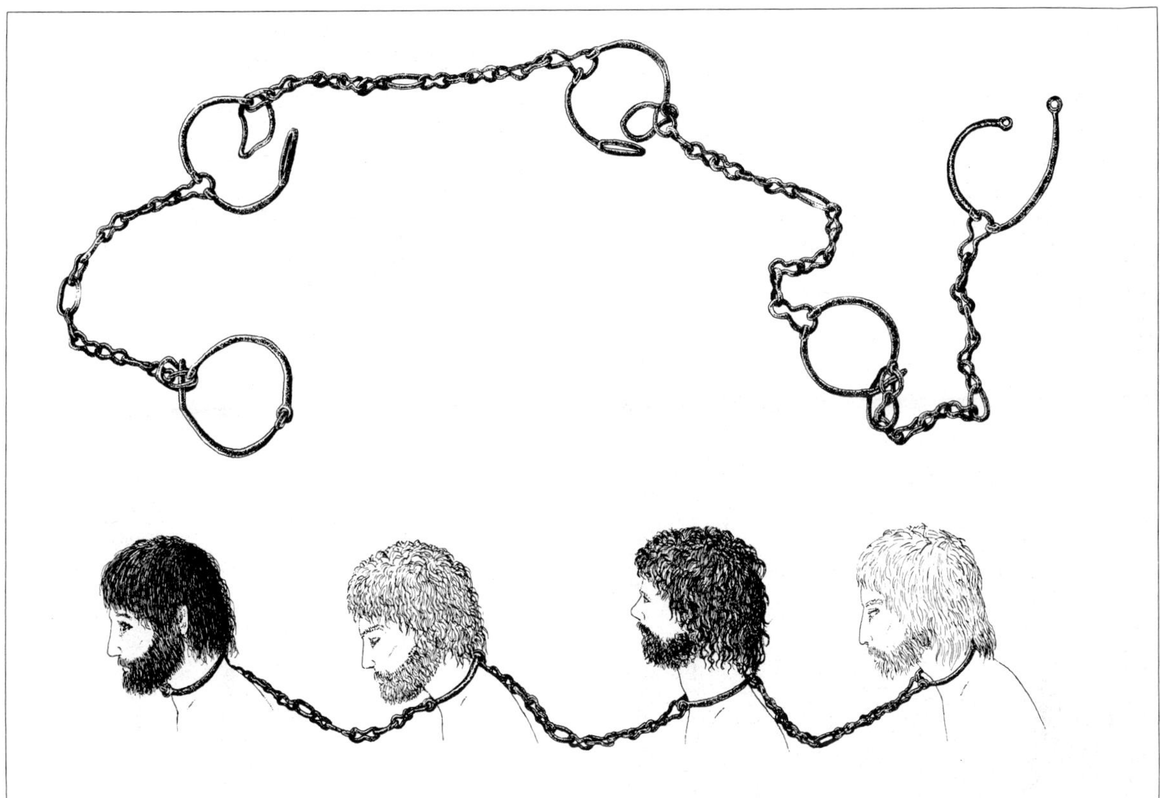

▲

LIU SHENG
see HAN DYNASTY

▲**LLYN CERRIG BACH, Anglesey** A site where 138 metal objects of the pre-Roman IRON AGE were deposited in peat at the side of a lake. The finds range in date over 200 years from the 2nd century BC to AD 50, and come from Ireland, south-west, east and south-east England. They include CHARIOT fittings, horse harness, weapons, cauldrons, LURS, CURRENCY BARS and slave chains. The Llyn Cerrig Bach material was probably either a votive deposit like the GUNDESTRUP cauldron, or a cache of objects hurriedly hidden by the DRUIDS prior to their defeat by Suetonius Paulinus in AD 60.

LLYN FAWR, Glamorgan A tarn where a hoard of 21 metal objects was discovered in 1911. The hoard is of Late Bronze Age date (*c* 7th–6th century BC). Most of the objects, including two cauldrons, are of bronze, but a sword, spearhead and locally made socketed sickle are of iron. This is the earliest example of iron-working in Britain. The hoard may be a ritual deposit like the Iron Age one from LLYN CERRIG BACH where cauldrons were also found.

■**LONDON [Londinium]** Although it began as a fairly small trading centre at an important river crossing, it was not long before London superseded CAMULODUNUM as the administrative centre of the Roman province of Britain. The town was certainly well-established when it was destroyed in AD 60 by BOUDICCA; it was burned down again during the time of HADRIAN. Before the end of the 1st century AD the town had a permanent garrison, although the walls were not built until the 3rd century. By the 4th century, London contained the provincial treasury and the palace of the provincial governor, and finds of writing-tablets, etc, stamped with the seal of the procurator show that the civil service was centred there. Recent excavations have demonstrated the existence of a river-front wall and substantial timber waterfronts. A fort existed at Cripplegate in the north-west corner of the town from an early date.

LONG COUNT
see CALENDAR

LORICA The cuirass which made up the main body-protection of a Roman soldier's armour. Early types include the *lorica hamata* of mail and the rather impractical *lorica squamata* of overlapping metal scales. By the 1st century AD, however, had been perfected the far more successful *lorica segmentata*. This consisted of broad, overlapping bands of iron, arranged horizontally around the trunk and vertically across the shoulders: it was hinged at the side and fastened with buckles. It afforded excellent protection, but was sufficiently light and flexible to allow men wearing it to march and even throw up MARCHING CAMPS, as is shown in scenes on TRAJAN'S COLUMN.

○**LOS MILLARES, Almería, Spain** The site of a COPPER AGE walled township in south-east Spain, outside which stands a 'cemetery' of about 80 CHAMBER TOMBS. The Millaran culture, which takes its name from these monuments and their associated finds, is distinguished particularly by the decoration (found engraved on stone slabs or pillars in the tombs, on small plaques or on pots) which frequently takes the form of two eyes (or *'oculi'*) implying a face. These ▶

designs have suggested to some that a Mother Goddess was worshipped, although any such interpretation can only be a matter of guessing. Some of these patterns have been compared to art of the BOYNE PASSAGE GRAVES. One theory is that Millaran settlements were 'colonies' of people from the Aegean, who brought new ways and ideas (such as copper-working) with them. Another is that the Millaran culture was a local development of the ALMERIAN culture. It was succeeded by BEAKER people.

LOST-WAX CASTING
see CIRE PERDUE

LOTHAL, India Situated on the Gulf of Cambay, this is the only known port of the INDUS CIVILIZATION. Beside the settlement stretches a long dock with a massive brick wharf, which is connected by channels to an ancient tributary of the Sabarmati river. On its edge were found heavy pierced stones which resemble modern anchor stones. The settlement differs from other Indus cities in having the citadel as a raised corner of the walled area. It also includes workshops of gold- and silver-smiths.

LOTIFORM COLUMN Ancient Egyptian imitation in stone of the bundles of unopened lotus flowers used as supports to construct ephemeral shelters and buildings. Painted leaves at the base of the stone columns indicate six bundles – the stalks tied by rope just below the buds of the capital. Above the binding-rope are small representations of single lotus flowers, budding or open.

LOYANG, China The CHOU dynasty city in Honan which in 771 BC became the second capital of that dynasty, having succeeded the earlier capital at Tsung Chou, Shensi. Several sites in this area have yielded the material remains of the Chou.

LUG Small handle projecting from the body of a pot, sometimes perforated so that a cord could be passed through and used as a sling.

LUGDUNUM [modern Lyons], France Lying at the confluence of the Rhône and the Saône, Lugdunum was founded in 43 BC as the capital of all of the three Gauls: it had great importance as the administrative centre, and a mint was sited there. The FORUM adjoins the palace in which visiting emperors lived. Public buildings were on a grand scale – the theatre was partly faced with marble, and even what survives of the AMPHITHEATRE is very impressive; both of these structures were enlarged by HADRIAN. Fine villas lie in the suburbs, and four AQUEDUCTS supplied the city with water. A Capitoline temple faced the forum, and close to the amphitheatre were the shrine and altar of the Three Gauls. Lugdunum finally fell to the barbarians *c* AD 360.

LULLINGSTONE, Kent A small Romano-British villa, known chiefly for its evidence of Christianity. Early buildings are known, but the main building phase was in the 2nd century AD when pagan cult rooms and baths were added. After desertion in the 3rd century the villa was reoccupied in the 4th century and in *c* 360 a couple of rooms were made over into a house chapel. Evidence of this is chiefly in the wall-plaster, where chi-rhos and praying figures are depicted, and also a mosaic of Bellerophon, often associated with the Early Christian iconography.

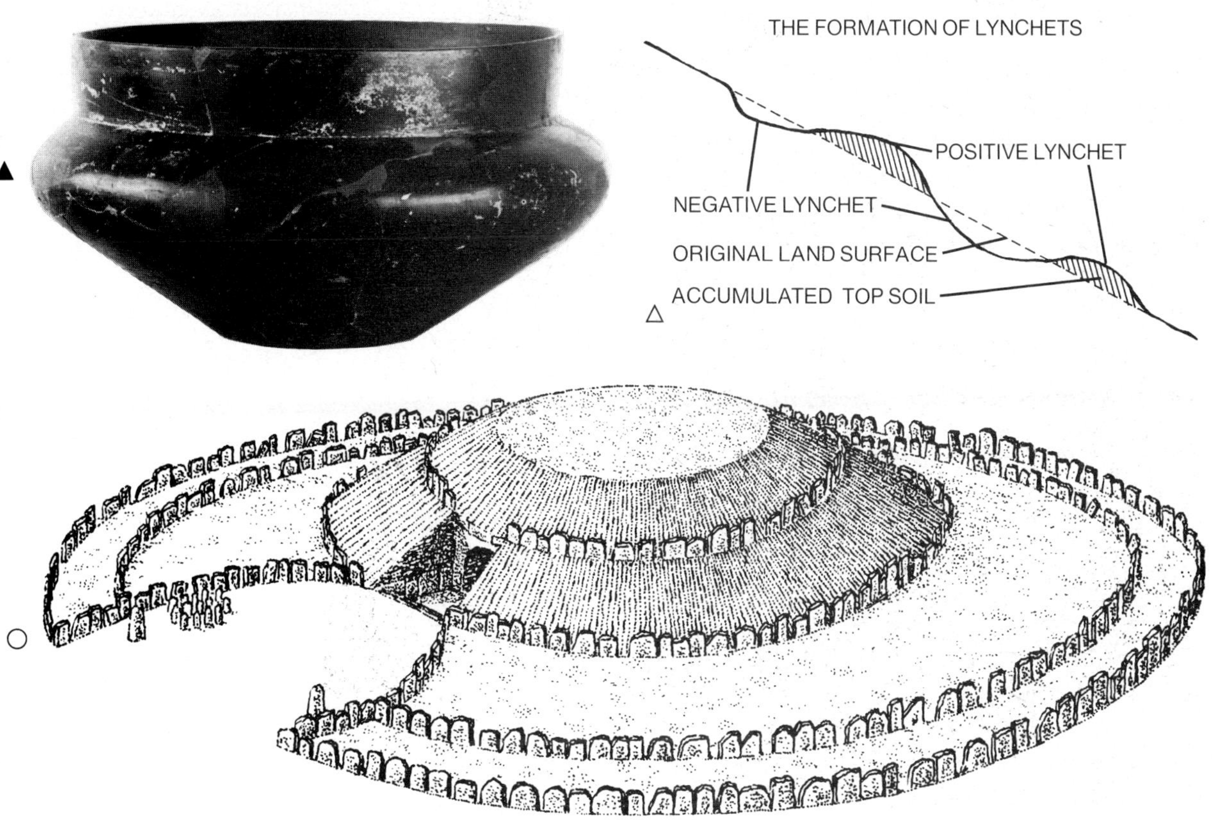

The villa can still be seen as excavated. There is also a rare inscribed mosaic of Europa and the Bull with a couplet based on a line from Vergil's *Aeneid.*

LUMBINI, India Traditional birthplace of the BUDDHA. NORTHERN BLACK POLISHED WARE gives evidence of occupation in the Buddhist period. An AŚOKAN PILLAR records the emperor's pilgrimage visit here.

LUNG-SHAN An important Chinese late NEOLITHIC culture, beginning *c* 3000 BC, situated mainly on the lower reaches of the Yellow River and towards the coast in the east; it often is found to supersede the previous YANG-SHAO culture. The main hallmark of the Lung-shan is its fine, ▲ black-burnished and generally wheel-made pottery, with angular profiles. Frequent forms are tripod vessels, and carinated or footed bowls. In addition, a coarser ware of black, grey or red was made. Their experimentation with white kaolin clay would, in later times, eventually lead to the white porcelain known as 'china'. Rice, millet and possibly wheat were cultivated by these agricultural communities. Domesticated animals seem to have been the same as those of the YANG-SHAO culture. Dwellings appear to resemble those found at PAN-P'O, though Lung-shan houses sometimes had floors and walls covered with white plaster. Burial practices too were not much altered from the Yang-shao period. Changes in the stone tool-kit from the preceding phase are the more frequent use of polished axes, and the occurrence of flat, rectangular axes, as well as a shift from oblong sickles to a more crescent-like form. Bone was commonly used for arrowheads and spearheads. Un-inscribed ORACLE BONES lead on to the practice of scapulimancy well known in the following SHANG period. Another Lung-shan custom which continues into Shang is the building of defensive walls of rammed earth.

LURISTAN An area in the Zagros mountains of western Iran where tombs with distinctive bronze and iron objects have been found. They date from the early 1st millennium BC and are thought to be the graves of a nomadic people. The objects are made in a composite style which gives little indication of the origin of the craftsmen.

LURS Enormous curved bronze trumpets first used in Denmark in the Late BRONZE AGE (after 1000 BC). 31 have been discovered in Danish peat bogs, perhaps as ritual deposits. Bronze Age lurs had double S-curves; later trumpets are straighter.

■ **LUXOR, Egypt,** Eastern Thebes. Temple of the state god Amun, and focal point for festival procession from KARNAK at New Year. Work of Amenophis III (Dynasty XVIII) and Ramesses II (Dynasty XIX). Egyptian archaeologists have uncovered an avenue of ram-headed sphinxes leading to Karnak. From the pylon-entrance came the finely-carved obelisk of Ramesses II now in the Place de la Concorde, Paris. The columns of the colonnade, courts and hypostyle hall imitate papyrus plants with umbels open or closed. In a chamber off the sanctuary (rebuilt by ALEXANDER THE GREAT) is depicted the birth of Amenophis III attributed to union of his mother with the god Amun. The site was used as a fortified camp during the Roman occupation.

LYDIANS
see SARDIS

● 

▲ 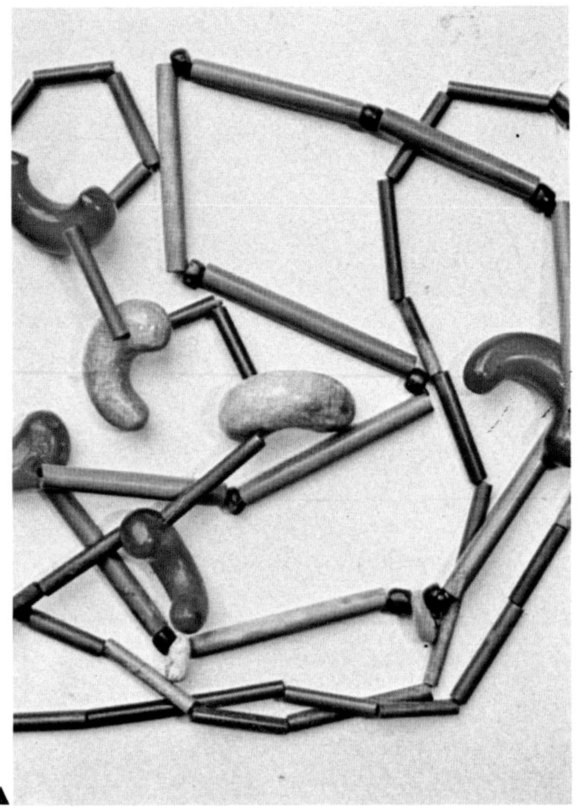

◄ △**LYNCHETS** These were formed during the cultivation of prehistoric and medieval hill fields. Topsoil, loosened by ploughing, gradually moves downhill under the influence of gravity. The resulting accumulation of topsoil at the bottom of a sloping field is a positive lynchet, whilst a depression at the top of such a field caused by the loss of topsoil, is a negative lynchet.

LYNGBY CULTURE Recently redefined as the Lyngby–Bromme–Segebo culture, a late GLACIAL hunter–fisher group of the north European plain. It is especially known for its tools made of reindeer antler; the type-site (Nørre–Lyngby, Jutland) was the location of such a find in 1889. Like the AHRENSBURGIAN and the SWIDERIAN culture, its flint industry is characterized by the presence of tanged points, the Lyngby points being larger. It dates from the Allerød and Younger Dryas late glacial stages. *See also* PLEISTOCENE.

●**MACHU PICCHU, Peru** A fortified INCA citadel located in a saddle of the Andes 500m above the Urubamba valley. It was first discovered in 1911 by Hiram Bingham and is a complex of stone built temples, PLAZAS and gabled houses surrounded by steep agricultural terraces.

MAES HOWE, Orkney An impressive PASSAGE GRAVE covered by a cairn 35m across and surrounded by a wide ditch. The chamber and passage were built out of evenly-splitting flagstone, so that fine architectural features were possible. A passage over 10m long leads to a 5m square central chamber, covered with a good example of CORBELLING. Recent radiocarbon dates indicate that it was built *c* 2800 BC. The tomb was looted in the 12th century AD by Vikings who left a record of their visit by carving RUNES and animal designs in the chamber.

MAGADHA, India One of the sixteen MAHAJANAPADAS (major states) of the GANGES CIVILIZATION Magadha rose to supremacy under Chandragupta Maurya and declined after the death of his grandson, AŚOKA. *See also* MAURYAS.

▲**MAGATAMA** Japanese adornments of curved jewels or beads unearthed in great numbers from tombs of the TOMB PERIOD. They served as symbols of imperial power and charms of protection. At times hundreds were placed in each tomb. Made of various stones or of glass, the largest are many centimetres long. Origins of the magatama seem to lie in the latest JOMON period, when they were occasionally made of stone.

MAGDALENEAN The final PLEISTOCENE culture in western Europe, succeeding the SOLUTREAN. The main hunting quarry comprised the large herds of reindeer, bison, woolly rhinoceros and mammoth suited to the cold conditions of the last (Würm) GLACIATION. The Magdalenean is well known for its CAVE ART (e.g. at ALTAMIRA in Spain) and fine decoration of bone and antler equipment. Much decorated bone was found at the TYPE-SITE itself (a cave at La Madeleine, Dordogne, France).

MAGICAL KNIVES Gently-curved Egyptian amuletic weapons made of hippopotamus ivory, found in Middle Kingdom times, but deriving their shape from traditional flint knives or throwsticks. Also called wands, these knives were used by Egyptians to trace the outline of a magical barrier against snakes and dangerous desert animals – real and mythical. Represented on the ivory surface were the tutelary deities of the household: Bes the dwarf god of good luck and the childbirth-goddess Thoueris shown as an expectant hippopotamus. Other defence-mechanisms depicted symbolic defeats for deadly animals – lion or cat (manifestation of the sun-god) destroying or devouring a snake (chthonic hostile force). Also represented were bizarre creatures of the Egyptian imagination going back at least into late Predynastic times: griffins with pair of wings or winged human head on back, beasts with fantastically long necks and leopard heads.

MAGLEMOSEAN The MESOLITHIC culture centred on an area that includes the north German plain and what is now the North Sea (a marshy landscape until *c* 6000 BC, when the Straits of Dover were finally breached by a rising sea). The flint industry, comprising both MICROLITHS and TRANCHET AXES, reflects a hunting and fishing economy in a forest environment, and Maglemosean camp sites would have been found along river banks and lake shores on the woodland edge. One such location is STAR CARR. Another is the TYPE-SITE, the *magle mose* (great bog) at Mullerup, Denmark. The water-side location of many sites has resulted in the survival of an unusual number of artefacts in perishable materials. These include a dug-out canoe from Pesse, Holland, wooden bows and arrows, and fish nets. Fish were also caught with lines, using barbless hooks. The Maglemosean was succeeded by the ERTEBØLLE culture.

MAGNA GRAECIA
see GREECE

MAGNETIC SURVEYING An archaeological prospecting technique which works by measuring the different magnetic susceptibilities of buried features or structures; the variation in the earth's magnetic field caused by a buried feature is called an anomaly, and may be measured by a magnetometer. The simplest form is the proton magnetometer, which measures the different oscillations of protons, small particles of hydrogen atoms the movements of which are influenced by changes in local magnetism. A more sophisticated device is the gradiometer, employing two detectors and measuring the magnetic difference between the two.

MAGOSIAN A series of stone industries in central and southern east Africa, in which BLADES and MICROLITHS make their first African appearance. It lies chronologically between the STILL BAY culture and the WILTON CULTURE, *c* 13–8000 BC.

MAHAJANAPADAS The sixteen mahajanapadas or major states of north India came into being in the 7th–6th centuries BC, when military activity led to the fusion of the earlier village states. They included MAGADHA and GANDHARA. BUDDHA was linked with those of the Ganges area. *See also* GANGES CIVILIZATION; INDIAN COINS.

MAIDEN CASTLE, Dorset An important and impressive HILLFORT, excavated by Wheeler in 1934–7. The defences were begun in the Early IRON AGE with a TIMBER-LACED rampart; later this was enlarged and a complicated gateway constructed. In the BELGIC period, *c* 50 BC, MULTIVALLATE ramparts were built, the main rampart reaching 26m in height. This was in the GLACIS style. Sling

stones were used in defence; 20,000 were found ready at the east entrance. Maiden Castle was stormed by the Romans in *c* AD 43, and the 38 dead men from this attack were buried in a war cemetery. One soldier still had an iron BALLISTA bolt in his spine. Settlement within the hillfort was close packed, with round and square buildings laid alongside metalled streets. Cooking ovens and evidence for metal-working were found. Typical iron age objects like those from GLASTONBURY were discovered: loom weights, spindle whorls and bone weaving combs; stone QUERNS, and objects of KIMMERIDGE shale. In the Roman period a Romano-Celtic shrine was constructed, but the hillfort was for the most part abandoned.

MAINZ, Germany The chief Roman town of the upper Rhine. It started life in 15 BC as a fort for campaigns in free Germany but by the 3rd–4th century AD the civil settlement was more important.

MALLIA, Crete Palace and town of the MINOANS. The palace plan follows the familiar courtyard pattern of KNOSSOS and PHAISTOS. The town was founded by Early Minoan times but the palace is later (*c* 1900–1450 BC). It did not survive the explosion of THERA.

MANCHING, Germany A very large Bavarian OPPIDUM in the Danube valley, dating from the middle of the LA TÈNE period, 1st century BC. The defences are 7km long, enclosing an area of 400 hectares with a MURUS GALLICUS construction. Extensive excavations have shown that the centre of the enclosed area was built up with houses, workshops, barns and shops, arranged along streets. A wide strip was left between the buildings and the fortifications, probably as a pasture for stock. Manching was a manufacturing centre producing various types of metal objects, glass ornaments and coins among other items. Pottery was wheel-made; one particular type, containing a large proportion of graphite and with distinctive potters' marks on the base, was exported to Austria and Czechoslovakia. Because of good communications along the Danube, Manching was well situated for coordination of widespread trade.

MANO The hand-held grinding stone used to grind maize on a METATE in the Americas. *See also* QUERN.

MANSIO Rapid communication was essential to the Roman empire, and officials of the civil service or the post were afforded special facilities along the roads. Changes of horses were available at establishments known as *mutationes*, stationed at intervals from 10 to 20km, depending on conditions. A more elaborate posting-station, a *mansio*, was positioned at the end of a day's ride, and provided food, baths and lodgings. Excavations at Alfoldean in Sussex and near Chelmsford in Essex have revealed rectangular enclosures, sometimes protected by a bank, with the road running through.

MANUSCRIPTS (Illuminated) The art of writing and illuminating books was brought to Anglo-Saxon England by Roman and Celtic missionaries. The Mediterranean influence is seen especially in the naturalistic representation of the human figure. The Irish monks contributed elaborately decorated initials. Native Anglo-Saxon art added ANIMAL ORNAMENT and INTERLACE. The earliest Gospel book surviving is the Book of Durrow, NORTHUMBRIA *c* AD 675. The LINDISFARNE Gospels, from AD 700, are the finest example of English manuscript art.

MARCHING CAMP A defensive earthwork, rectangular in shape, thrown up by a Roman army at the end of a day's march. Troops carried wooden stakes with them to construct the rampart, but the main defences consisted of a single bank and ditch. They could be of considerable size: some Agricolan camps in Scotland cover 50 hectares, enough for three legions and an equal number of auxiliaries. The form tends to be very standard, and an army could construct a camp very rapidly at the end of a day. Owing to their essentially temporary nature, excavation of these camps is not generally rewarding.

MARI [modern Tell Hariri], Syria A TELL by the Euphrates river near the Syrian-Iraq border. Excavations begun in 1933 have cleared the large palace of Zimri Lim (1779–1761 BC), the last king of Mari. The palace covers 3 hectares and had walls finely decorated with paintings. Among statues found was one of an offering-bearer. About 25,000 TABLETS were found in the palace. These are mainly diplomatic correspondence and show treaty details and decisions relating to other cities and peoples. Details of trade with other cities as well as gifts exchanged between rulers are also given. The constant incursion of nomads from the desert meant that troops had to be deployed. Mari was finally destroyed by HAMMURAPI *c* 1759 BC.

MARIB
see YEMEN

▲ **MARIETTE, (Pasha) François (1821–81)** French Egyptologist. Inspired by a relation's travels in Egypt, he learnt hieroglyphs and Coptic. The Louvre Museum gave him experience in copying and deciphering inscriptions. Commissioned to find biblical manuscripts in Egypt, which proved unrewarding, he devoted his energies to excavation. Difficulties from officialdom and sand-clogged terrain slowed progress but in 1851 he found the entry to the underground catacomb containing tombs of APIS bulls (New Kingdom – Ptolemaic period) and thousands of objects such as STELAE. In many ways the first modern excavator, his records were not written up into scientific reports. He supervised (often inadequately, incurring PETRIE's indignation) excavations at more sites than anyone else.

He was largely responsible for more enlightened attitudes to preservation of monuments and for the establishment of the Egyptian Antiquities Service.

Main books: *Voyage de la Haut-Égypte* (2 vols, 1878–80); *Le Sérapéum de Memphis* (1882).

MARZABOTTO, Italy ETRUSCAN settlement, whose ancient name is unknown, not far from the modern village of Marzabotto in the Reno valley near Bologna. The ancient city lay on the main road from Etruria to Felsina, the capital of northern Etruria (i.e. the region surrounding the Po valley). Archaeological evidence suggests that the settlement flourished between the 6th and 4th centuries BC. It is most noted for its rectangular grid plan. The city, which was focused on a sanctuary containing the major religious buildings, was laid out in the last decades of the 6th century, and resembles Greek cities such as Naples.

MASSILIA, France A colony of the Phocaean Greeks in southern France, founded *c* 600 BC. It was the first colony in France and proved very influential in introducing Mediterranean tastes to HALLSTATT and LA TÈNE peoples in northern France and Bavaria. Many rich finds of silver flagons, Attic pottery and glass have been found at, e.g. VIX and HOHMICHELE. These indicate the long trade routes in luxury goods operating at the time. Massilia's trading peak was in the 6th century BC; in the following century trade routes across the Alps circumventing the Rhine route came into operation. The town continued as a colony during the Roman period.

MASTABA Ancient Egyptian rectangular flat-topped tomb, the name comes from the Arabic for 'brick bench'. Early kings built mud-brick mastabas (with exterior surfaces of deeply recessed panelling designed to recreate the front of the royal palace) until Zoser (Dynasty III) had the Step Pyramid constructed. Nobles and officials continued the custom of mastaba-burial near their pharaoh's pyramid. From reliefs in them we learn much about life and recreation in the Old Kingdom. The mastaba had two basic elements:

(1) A rectangular superstructure consisting of a mass of masonry with a series of cells for storerooms and for the funerary chapel containing a STELA or FALSE-DOOR to which living relatives and contract-priests had access. Adjoining this chapel, but sealed off except for a peep-hole at eye level, was the Serdab – a connecting link between the dead person's spirit (residing in his portrait-statue) and outside offerings and incense.

(2) An underground burial chamber reached by a or deep shaft. *See also* ARCHAIC MASTABAS; TOMB OF TI.

● **MATHURA ART** The art of Mathura (Ganges valley) and central India was based on a subtle blend of ancient Indian popular art (known from Yaksha figures representing protective deities), ACHAEMENID and Persian influences absorbed during the MAURYAN period, and other western influences transmitted through contact with GANDHARAN ART; but the essential character remained Indian. The earliest statues of BUDDHA in Mathura date from *c* AD 75 and are generally Bodhisatvas (the Buddha before his enlightenment) probably indicating a transitional period before the ideological prohibition upon the human representation of the Buddha was fully overcome. With the present uncertainty in the dating of early Buddha images it is impossible to say whether Mathura or Gandhara can claim priority in the development. The Mathura Buddha image is stylized and is always shown larger than his companions.

MAUDSLAY, Alfred Percival (1850–1931) A pioneer in the study of the MAYA civilization, he visited many parts of Guatemala, financing his own expeditions during which he made detailed plans and drawings of CEREMONIAL CENTRES, monuments, buildings and inscriptions which were of fundamental value in the later translation of many Maya hieroglyphs. The result of his travels were published in his *Biologia Centrali-Americana* on the flora and fauna of Mexico and Central America (1889–1902).

MAURYAS The ruling dynasty of MAGADHA, north India, from the late 4th century BC. The first of the line, Chandragupta, drove ALEXANDER's successors from India and carved out an empire to which his son, Bindusara, and grandson, AŚOKA, added. Under the latter Buddhism

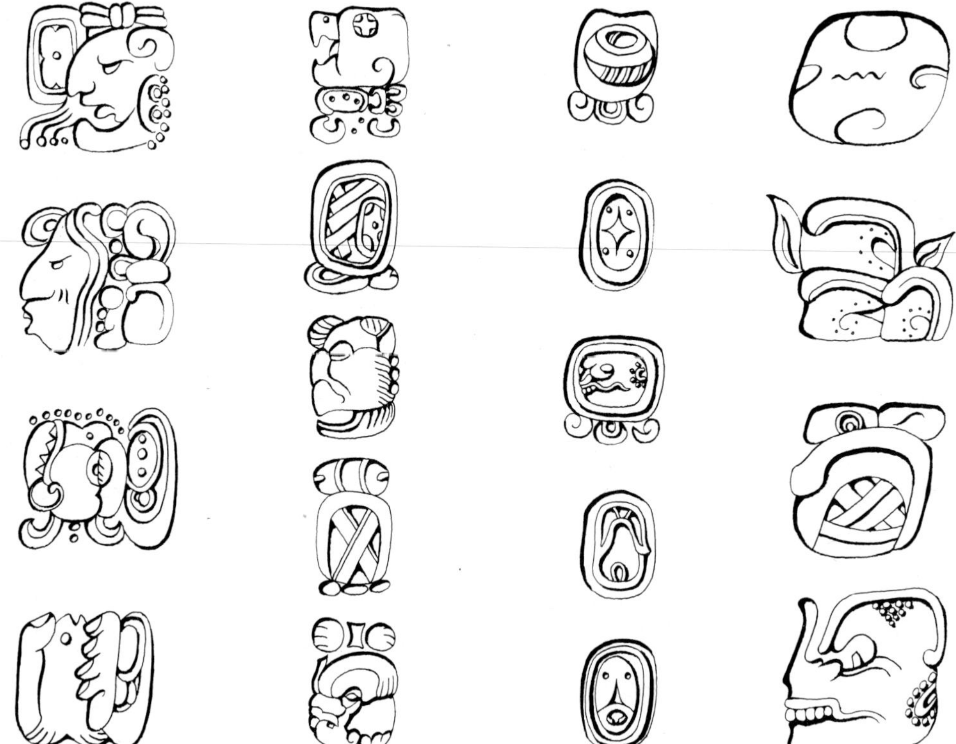

became the state religion. The succeeding Mauryas were lesser men and their dynasty was overthrown *c* 185 BC.

MAUSOLEUM A type of Roman funerary structure originating in that of AUGUSTUS, whose form was derived from ETRUSCAN tumuli. This was an elaborate concrete tomb covered with an earth mound, which was revetted with a decorated stone wall, planted with trees and crowned by a statue. It was emulated by others, notably HEROD THE GREAT and HADRIAN, but later the term is applied to any substantial tomb above ground level.

MAYA This civilization which developed in the lowland regions of central Guatemala, Belize, western Honduras and eastern Campeche was based on the construction of great CEREMONIAL CENTRES which acted as the social, political and religious foci for a scattered rural population (*see* TIKAL; PALENQUE; UXMAL). The Maya are best known for their unique and beautiful art style which flourished in the medium of elaborate stone sculptures of jade, mosaics of turquoise and serpentine, fine polychrome pottery and models or relief carving in stucco or stone. They possessed sophisticated hieroglyphic writing systems and CALENDRICAL computations were facilitated by the use of Long Count. They knew the 365-day solar year, had calculated the Venus cycle and, it is said, could even predict eclipses of the sun.

The origins of the Maya civilization are obscure, but archaeology shows that those features most characteristic of Maya culture had coalesced some time in the late Preclassic (*see* MESOAMERICA) to give rise to the ceremonial centre tradition by AD 300. This tradition shows the use of the CORBELLED vault in architecture, the erection of commemorative STELAE, the use of hieroglyphic writing, calendrics and the Initial Series or Long-Count calculations, a distinctive art-style and certain pottery types. The centre of this phenomenon was the Petén (lowland Guatemala), where some of the oldest and largest ceremonial centres such as TIKAL and UAXACTUN are to be found. From here Maya civilization radiated outwards to peripheral areas in north Yucatan, east Campeche, highland Guatemala and western Honduras. In the Maya lowlands especially, the Classic Period is to be divided into early (AD 300–600) and late (600–900) phases. During the late period, the Maya cultural focus moved progressively north and east, and distinctive regional architectural variations became important – characterized by Puuc, Chenes and Rio Bec types. Between early and late Classic, there is a 40-year hiatus in the erection of stelae, probably when the Maya lowlands were subjected to the first strong influences from TEOTIHUACAN in highland Mexico. These are best demonstrated in the depiction of two Mexican warriors carved on stela 31 at Tikal. After this, in the Late Classic, Maya civilization reached new heights, until its sudden mysterious decline and collapse in the 9th century.

The last Long-Count date recorded on a stela is AD 889, and, soon after this, activity at the major ceremonial sites in and around the Petén ceased and was followed in some areas by significant depopulation. The succeeding Post-classic period saw power move to north Yucatan with the rise of CHICHEN ITZA. At this time, there is a further period of strong impulses from highland Mexico, brought first by the Itzas and soon after by an actual colonization of TOLTEC peoples led by Kukulcan in 987. Maya civilization became progressively decadent and by the time of the dominance of the fortified city MAYAPAN in the 14th century, much of the

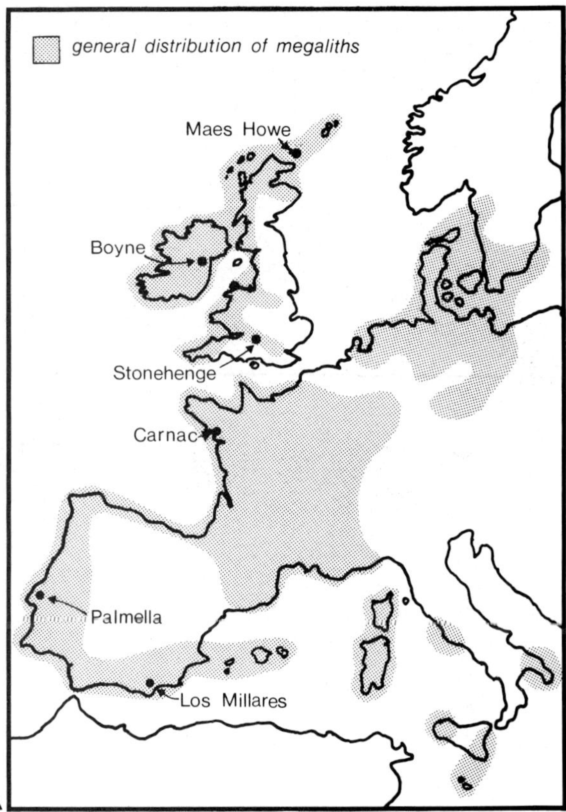

glory of the lowland tradition had been lost. Many of the late Postclassic towns were fortified against increasing unrest. The Mexican principles of extortion and tribute were rife amongst the petty warring city-states in existence at the time of the Spanish Conquest early in the 15th century. By this time, the rulers of the region claimed descent from Mexico, and Maya culture was already part of history and legend.

MAYAPAN A fortified MAYA town of the Postclassic period (*see* MESOAMERICA) and the capital of northern Yucatan between 1283 and 1441, when Mayapan was destroyed. It was founded by Itzas from CHICHEN ITZA who under the Cocom dynasty maintained an effective centralized government and a vigorous economy based largely on extortion and tribute. The town covers 5 square km with 9km of encircling defences and a maximum population estimated at 12,000.

MEARE, Somerset An IRON AGE 'Lake Village' in the SOMERSET LEVELS, 6km from GLASTONBURY, with similar ROUND HOUSES, palisade, and the same range and good preservation of objects. In the 3rd century BC, about forty wooden circular buildings were built on dessicated peat. The settlement was flooded in the 1st century AD and moved to higher ground.

MEDES A little-known people who inhabited north-west Iran. HERODOTUS mentions a certain Phraortes who *c* 670 BC united the tribes in west Iran and gained control of the Persians to the south. Their capital Ecbatana (modern Hamadan) has not been excavated. They were constantly fighting the SCYTHIANS in the east, and in the west they conquered the ASSYRIAN capital NINEVEH in 612 BC. The Median empire passed to the ACHAEMENID Cyrus the Great.

● **MEDINET HABU, Egypt,** Western Thebes. Ramesses III (Dynasty XX), last great warrior-king, built this multipurpose construction. A University of Chicago expedition excavated the royal palace adjoining a temple within surrounding battlements. They found the Audience Chamber with its throne, rooms leading to ceremonial window for royal appearances, bedroom, bathroom and harem-quarters.

The temple was influenced by the RAMESSEUM. It has a pictorial record of the land and naval combat against the Sea Peoples attempting to invade the Nile delta (1176 BC), and also of Ramesses III inspecting hands and phalli cut off from killed Libyan invaders.

Towards the end of the king's reign the complex was enclosed by a rampart with huge fortress-gates.

▲ **MEGALITH [Adjective megalithic]** From the Greek for 'large stone': any such stone arranged by man in some way. Frequently left in their natural, irregular shape, megaliths can be free-standing (individually, in a circle or in a row or alignment) or part of a larger structure such as a megalithic tomb. Single standing stones are sometimes referred to as 'menhirs' (Breton for 'long stones'). 'Dolmen', of similar derivation, refers to a megalithic tomb; a 'cromlech' (Welsh for 'bent flat stone') can be either a tomb or a standing stone. The main European types of megalithic tomb are CHAMBER TOMBS, GALLERY GRAVES and PASSAGE GRAVES. *See:* AVEBURY; CAPSTONE; CARNAC; CORBELLING; MAES HOWE; ORTHOSTAT; PERISTALITH; STONEHENGE; *also* SOUTH INDIAN MEGALITHS.

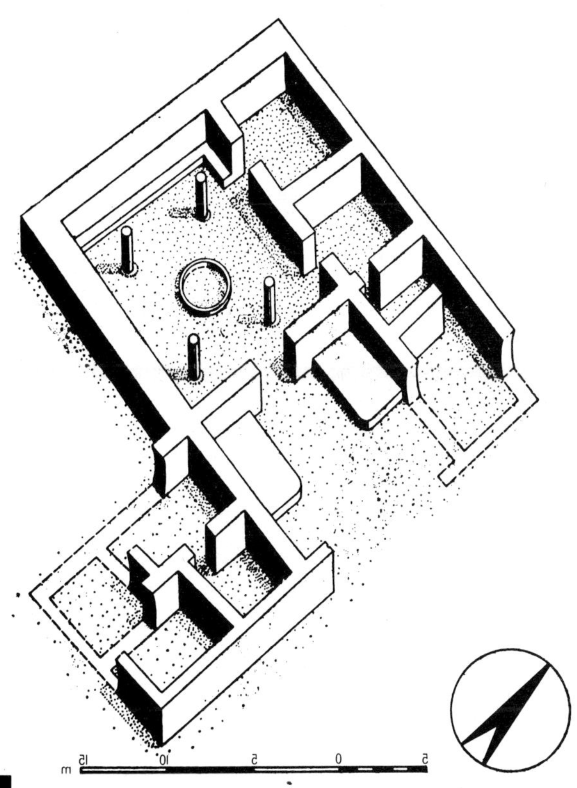

MEGARON A building with a basic design made up of a rectangular room, often containing a central hearth, and a porch formed between projecting walls of the main room. Pillars often supported the roof of the porch and the main room. As can be seen in the example which was found at KULTEPE, from about 2300 BC additional rooms can be added. Another early example is found at Troy (*see* SCHLIEMANN). The design is common in MYCENAEAN palaces some time later.

MEGIDDO, Israel A large TELL in northern Palestine, strategically situated at the entrance of a pass which crosses the Carmel range. Many battles have been fought on the plain at Megiddo. The site has been extensively excavated, revealing many structures including a number of temples of the 2nd and 3rd millennia. After 1900 BC the city was heavily fortified, and when captured *c* 1469 BC by the Egyptians provided much booty. It recovered and continued as a strong CANAANITE city; a 70m long water-tunnel was built to provide the city with water in time of siege. The ISRAELITES probably took control *c* 1000 BC. Many buildings of this occupation have been found including a gate (*see* GEZER), a shrine, two palaces, some unidentified structures and some buildings which are either stables or store-houses.

MEIDUM, Egypt South of MEMPHIS, a colossal structure on the desert edge identified as a pyramid of Sneferu (Dynasty IV) – perhaps, with two pyramids at DASHUR, it is a completion of his predecessor's. The archaeologists MARIETTE and PETRIE excavated here. Mastaba tombs of Dynasty III and IV surround it; from one came the exquisite pair-statue of Sneferu's relatives, Rahotep and Nofret. Information on the techniques of pyramid-construction come from this site – e.g. the causeway for hauling building materials. Originally it was a MASTABA, transformed into a pyramid of seven steps which were finally filled in with limestone, making it a true pyramid. The outer casing collapsed, forming the surrounding debris. Petrie discovered coffin fragments and socket-holes for crossbeams.

MEMNONIUM, Egypt The Greek geographer Strabo's name for the Temple of Sethos I (Dynasty XIX) at Abydos. A monument in fine limestone and sandstone with chapels dedicated to the god Osiris, and to the all-powerful Amun. The sun god of Heliopolis and Ptah of Memphis were incorporated as well as a chapel to Sethos I himself. One of the galleries behind the central sanctuary contained a King list, one of the most valuable documents for establishing the succession of the pharaohs. The reliefs (Sethos sacrificing to the gods) are among the finest surviving from Ancient Egypt for colour and craftsmanship. Ramesses II finished and made his own additions to his father's temple.

MEMORIAL STONES Inscribed pillar-stones, usually unworked, are found as grave markers in the Celtic parts of Britain. They were erected in the 5th and 6th centuries AD and bear inscriptions in Latin in Late Roman script, sometimes duplicated by an Irish version in OGAM. Most of the personal names are Irish in origin and are thought to refer to FOEDERATI settled in western Britain to protect local inhabitants from Irish raiders. The formulas of the inscriptions and the carved symbols usually indicate that the commemorated person was Christian.

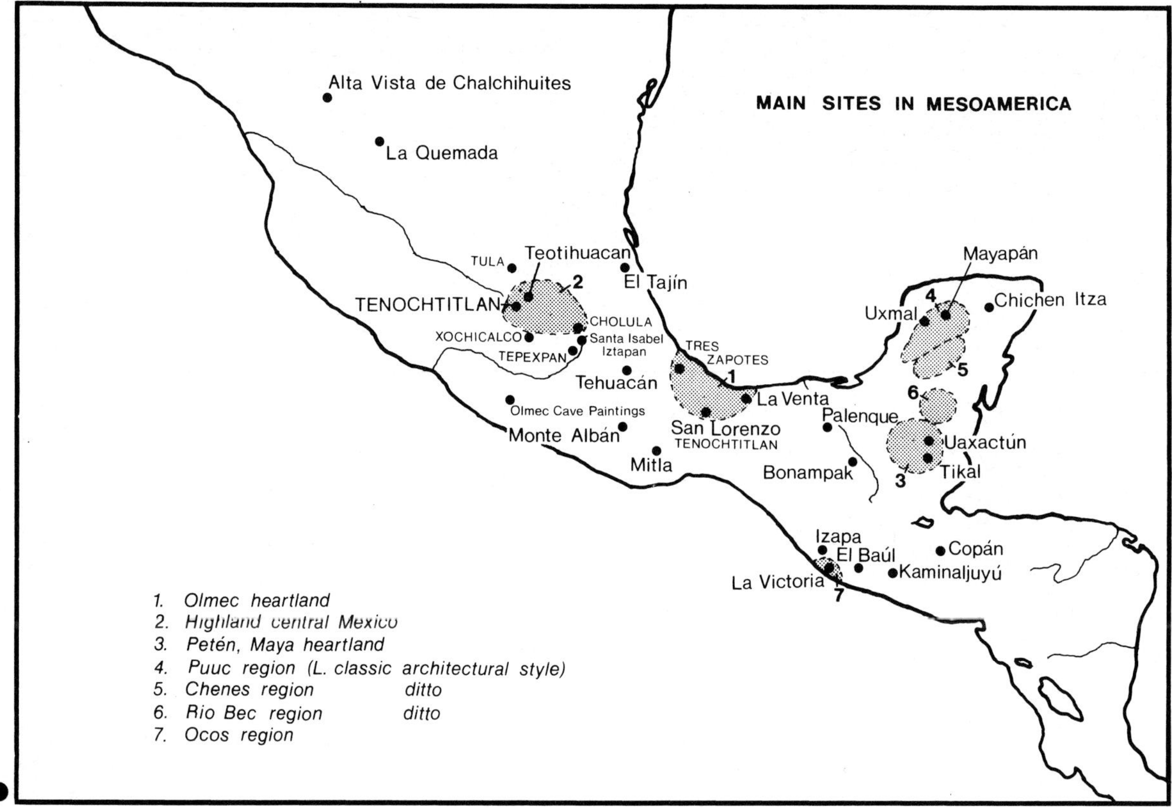

MEMPHIS, Egypt Below the apex of the Nile delta, this capital of Old Kingdom Egypt was established, at least as a fort, after the unification of north and south by the first pharaoh Menes (Narmer). It was called the White Walls after the plastered mud brick of the archaic Royal Palace – also symbolically the colour of the crown of the conquering Southern ruler. Memphis held a prominent political and religious status despite the rise of Thebes and the later commercial attractions of Alexandria. It became an international metropolis with settled communities from the Aegean and Middle East.

Little is left except for a colossal statue of Ramesses II and an alabaster sphinx possibly guarding the Temple of Ptah (creator god of Memphis) whose southern boundary wall was traced by PETRIE.

MENAT Counterpoise strung from terminals of an Egyptian bead collar or necklace, designed to keep the jewellery in position on the wearer. The material was metal, stone or faience. Closely connected, from at least the Middle Kingdom, with the cult of the cow-goddess Hathor. Queens, priestesses and female worshippers are depicted carrying ceremonial necklaces in processions in the temple. If shaken, the collar and counterpoise would produce rhythmic musical percussion to accompany the rituals. The amuletic value of the Menat comes from its association with great goddess Hathor who suckles the pharaoh; therefore it might magically bring fertility to the woman carrying it. Its popularity might also derive from Hathor's role as goddess of sexual delights – the Menat, it has been pointed out, bears a striking resemblance to the shape of paddle-dolls which were buried as concubines for the dead man's enjoyment.

MENHIR
see MEGALITH

MERCIA A kingdom of the Anglo-Saxons in the north and west Midlands of England. It rose to power in the 7th century AD after the defeat of Ecgfrith, King of NORTHUMBRIA in 674 and continued to dominate the political scene until 825, when it was assimilated into WESSEX by Egbert. Mercia's most famous king was OFFA. From the mid 9th century Mercia was occupied by the Danes and formed part of the DANELAW.

MERIDA, Spain A Roman colony in Lusitania, founded by Augustus in 25 BC and called Augusta Emerita. It became the capital of the province. Chief visible remains are the circus, amphitheatre and theatre, the aqueduct of 'Los Milagros' which influenced Moorish architecture and the bridge, nearly 1km and still in use. Merida was one of the richest cities in the western Roman empire.

MEROE, Sudan Site downstream from the Sixth Cataract, it was from 295 BC to AD 350 the capital of the Nubian state previously centred further north at Napata (*see* NUBIA). The royal necropolis consists of sandstone and mudbrick pyramids mostly now ruins. Before REISNER'S scientific excavations, some of these pyramids had been hacked to pieces by the 19th-century Italian treasure-hunter Ferlini. Compared with an Egyptian PYRAMID COMPLEX their dimensions are paltry: bases 14m square, height 20m. The angle of elevation is sharp: 65–70°. A chapel on the south-eastern side usually had Pylons showing reliefs of the ruler, in true pharaonic style, about to slay enemies grasped by the hair.

Date	Period	Mexico	Maya Zone
1500–1000	POST-CLASSIC	AZTEC EMPIRE CHICHIMEC INVASIONS TOLTECS at TULA; MIXTECS in OAXACA	MAYAPAN DOMINATES YUCATAN TOLTEC-MAYA at CHICHEN ITZA
1000–500–A.D.	CLASSIC	ZAPOTECS at MONTE ALBAN CLASSIC TEOTIHUACAN CIVILISATION EL TAJIN	BONAMPAK, PALENQUE, TIKAL, UAXACTUN; PUUC Architecture; UXMAL, OLD CHICHEN
B.C.–1000–2000	PRE-CLASSIC	Earliest remains at MONTE ALBAN, TEOTIHUACAN TLATILCO, OLMECS at LA VENTA, SAN LORENZO, TENOCHTITLAN OCOS	Earliest remains at TIKAL, UAXACTUN etc.
2000–3000–4000–5000	FIRST FARMERS	TEHUACAN VALLEY SITES	*no information*
5000–6000–7000–8000–9000–10,000	PRE-AGRICULTURAL HUNTERS AND PLANT COLLECTORS	TEPEXPAN BURIAL SANTA ISABEL IZTAPAN MAMMOTH KILL TLAPACOYA *c.* 19,000 B.C.	

Meroe had a royal palace and an impressive temple built to the Egyptian state-god AMUN. This yielded a fine bronze head of Augustus, the whole statue having been captured during a Meroitic attack on the Roman garrison as far north as ASWAN in 24 BC. Then a treaty regularized relations with Rome, much to Meroe's advantage politically and commercially. Juvenal (*c* AD 60–130) sarcastically upbraids the Roman world for ritual excesses of mystery cults: female devotees go as far as Meroe to bring back pure water for the Temple of Isis on the Campus Martius in Rome.

Recent excavation tells more of the complex Meroitic civilization, highlighting Meroe's importance for African archaeology in its capacity as an iron-smelting nucleus. Besides the mixture of African and Egyptian iconography (corpulent Meroitic queens seated on thrones like their slender Egyptian counterparts) and religion (Isis protecting the ruler with her wings, and a temple at nearby Musawaret dedicated to the African lion-god Apedemak), Meroe had trade links with Ethiopia, Arabia and the Middle (possible Far) East. Meroitic pottery has a decoration and quality hard to rival in Nile valley archaeology. The native script of 23 characters is related to cursive HIEROGLYPHS. It can be transliterated, but the language is not yet understood. The expanding Ethiopian kingdom of Axum seems to have encroached upon Meroe's trading interests and monopolies until the Axumite king could claim the title Ruler of Kush, i.e. the Meroitic state, in AD 350.

● **MESOAMERICA** Mesoamerican prehistory is divided chronologically into three main periods: Preclassic or Formative (*c* 2300 BC–AD 300), Classic or Florescent (AD 300–900) and Postclassic or Decadent (AD 900 until the Spanish conquest in 1519).

The Preclassic era is divided into early, middle and late sub-phases and sees the crystallization of the Mesoamerican cultural tradition which has its foundation in the settled villages with agricultural economy evolved through several millennia (*see* TEHUACAN). Monumental architecture in stone and ADOBE characterized the first CEREMONIAL CENTRES with PLATFORM MOUNDS, temples and PYRAMIDS. Pottery was introduced *c* 2300 BC and the first small towns grew. On the gulf coast, the OLMEC culture of SAN LORENZO and LA VENTA predominated throughout much of the Preclassic period and spread its influence quite widely throughout much of Mesoamerica. In central Mexico, other Preclassic cultures existed, such as that of TLATILCO with its local styles of FIGURINE. On the Pacific coast, the OCOS Phase bears witness to similar developments.

C 100 BC–AD 300, the Preclassic evolved into the Classic phase. Ceremonial centres and large towns (e.g. Cuicuilco in central Mexico) ruled over small states. The full Classic saw the rise of the major city states with political leadership centred on large urban centres like TEOTIHUACAN in the valley of Mexico. MONTE ALBAN in Oaxaca and EL TAJÍN on the Gulf coast were similar developments in these different regions. In Guatemala, Honduras and the Yucatan peninsula, the MAYA civilization achieved its climax during this time, with the flourishing of the great ceremonial centres such as TIKAL, PALENQUE and COPAN. The Classic period is usually divided into two parts, early (AD 300–600) and late (AD 600–900).

The Postclassic period brought several dynamic changes in the cultural tradition of Mesoamerica. Mexico was

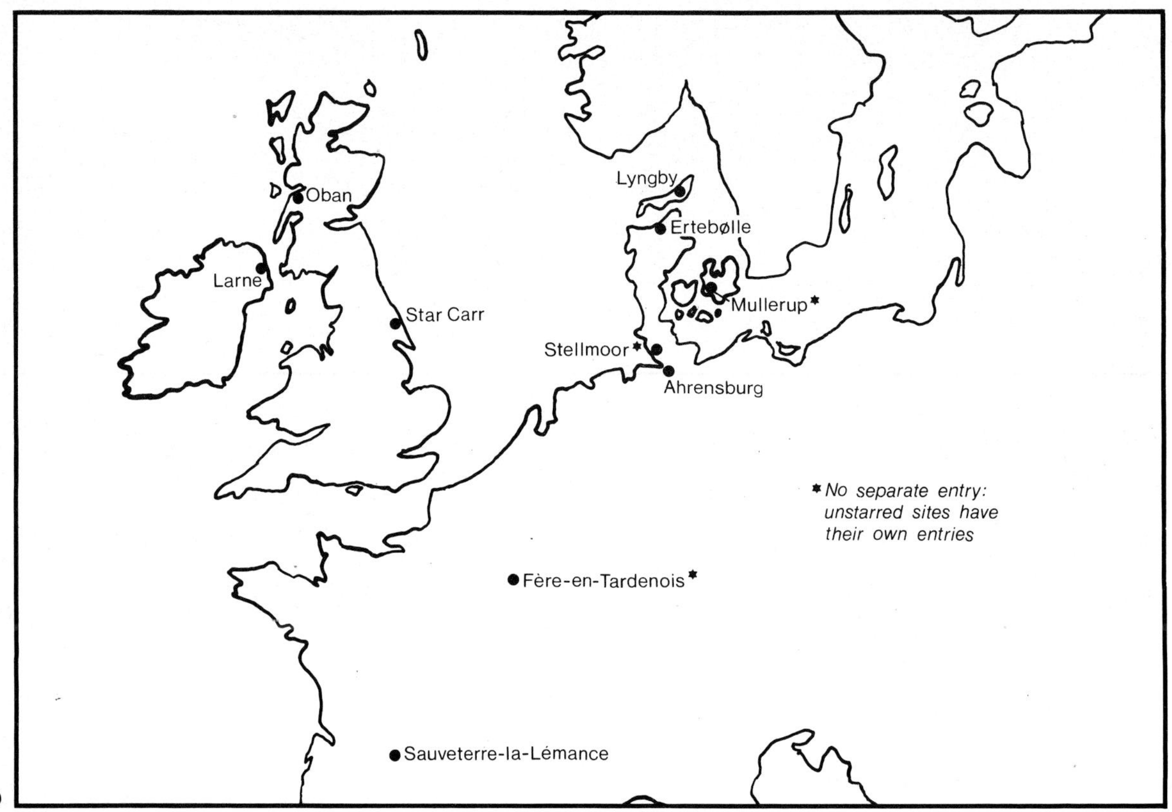

overrun by invasions from the less settled and civilized tribes of the DESERT cultural tradition living on its northern borders. The most significant of these were the TOLTECS who set up their capital at TULA. A new spirit of militarism pervaded this era, with such rituals as human sacrifice having importance for the first time (*see also* MIXTEC). Another wave of invasions from the north in the later part of the Postclassic in the 12th century brought the AZTEC or Mexica tribe to rest on Lake Texcoco, later the site of their capital city TENOCHTITLAN. In the Maya lowlands, the Classic Period ceremonial centres fell in the 9th century, and the political leadership passed to the north with the rise of CHICHEN ITZA. The end of the Postclassic period saw much of Mesoamerica held under the tyrannical dominion of the Aztecs, before the arrival of Spanish adventurers brought European culture and religion to the New World and with it, the end of native American civilization.

● **MESOLITHIC [Middle Stone Age]** The period between the PALAEOLITHIC and the NEOLITHIC (the word Mesolithic was coined by Westropp in 1886). As the great PLEISTOCENE ice-sheets retreated northwards for the last time (*c* 8–9000 BC), human communities were forced to adapt to a very different environment from that of previous millennia. A rising sea-level meant a shrinking land surface. In Europe tundra and steppe vegetation, supporting large herds of reindeer, was gradually replaced by forest. Hunting bands became smaller, and exploited a greater variety of animals. Similarly, the range of useful plants – for foods, fibres, timber, etc – was vastly increased. The ecological changes are reflected in the stone industries, which are commonly MICROLITHIC. In the Near East, where the environmental change was less dramatic, the climate becoming drier, the Mesolithic period is less clearly defined than further north; and a Neolithic (farming) economy began to develop soon after the close of the Pleistocene. It was not until the 4th millennium BC that agriculture reached Britain, and the Mesolithic ended.

▲ **MESOPOTAMIA** The area contained in the eastern half of the FERTILE CRESCENT, today known as Iraq. The name 'Mesopotamia' is derived from its position 'between the two rivers', the Euphrates and Tigris. The mineral wealth of the mountainous areas to the north and east is absent from the plains of Mesopotamia. Instead the area has relied for its prosperity on irrigation from the two rivers and their tributaries, the Habur, Zab and Diyala. While the slopes of the Zagros mountains in the north-east had climate and vegetation which encouraged agriculture (*see* JARMO), the plains of the south required a degree of organization in agriculture only obtainable by a people capable of writing. So it was in order to survive on the hot, dry inhospitable plains that Near Eastern civilization began at SUMER. The comforts developed in this area attracted other peoples. The nomads (*see* AMORITES) who inhabited the desert west of Sumer constantly infiltrated the cities until they gained control in the empire of AKKAD. The Elamites (*see* SUSA) from the east attacked in force and overthrew UR in 2006 BC. During the next 3000 years many peoples were to invade Mesopotamia from the east – Kassites, MEDES, SCYTHIANS, Persians (*see* ACHAEMENID EMPIRE), PARTHIANS, SASSANIANS and SELJUK Turks. From the west came the ARAMAEANS, the Greeks (*see* ALEXANDER) and the Moslems (*see* OMAYYAD) and from the north the HURRIANS. Outside attacks curtailed the lives of the empires of ASSYRIA and BABYLON.

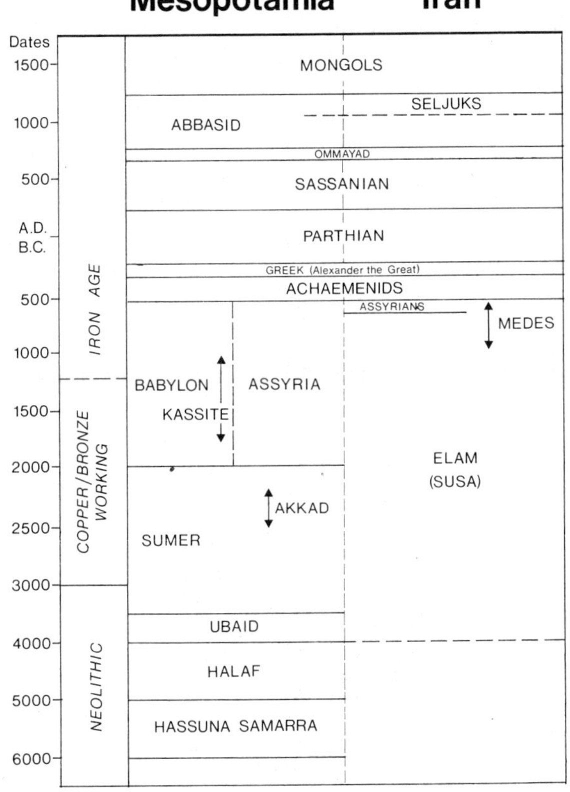

▲

■

MICHELSBERG A NEOLITHIC culture centred on the area between the Rhine and the Danube, bordered by three major groups: the FUNNEL BEAKER culture to the north, the later LINEAR POTTERY groups to the east and the WESTERN NEOLITHIC complex to the south and west. Hunting was important in its economy. Characteristic pottery includes the flaring-rimmed 'tulip beaker' and flat disc or 'baking plate'. The TYPE-SITE is a HILLFORT at Michelsberg, overlooking the Rhine near Baden. Settlements surrounded by ditches with many causeways have been compared to the CAUSEWAYED CAMPS of the WINDMILL HILL culture of Britain, as have the flint-mines, e.g. at Spiennes, Belgium.

MICROBURIN TECHNIQUE If a notch is deliberately worked in the side of a BLADE, continual percussion eventually causes the blade to snap. 'Microburin' refers to the waste-product (usually the bulbar end of the blade – *see* FLAKE) which was originally thought to be a small BURIN, an idea discredited by modern experiments. The main section of the blade is then made into a MICROLITH.

MICROLITH A very small piece of stone, usually produced by the MICROBURIN TECHNIQUE, which could be hafted as the working part of an implement (e.g. the barb on a HARPOON). Sometimes several microliths are mounted together (e.g. for a SICKLE) producing a composite tool. If the pieces are of a symmetrical shape, such as a triangle or a trapezium, they are known as geometric microliths. At one time microliths, a favourite with collectors, were known in Britain as pygmy flints. Microliths and the microburin technique are especially characteristic of MESOLITHIC assemblages.

MIDDEN A deposit of domestic rubbish, usually consisting of food remains and debris such as broken pottery. Shell middens like those of the ERTEBØLLE culture are found on certain maritime sites.

■ **MILDENHALL TREASURE** A hoard of lavish late Roman silver plate, probably buried in the 4th century AD. It comprises 39 pieces, including the remarkable Neptune Dish, a great dish with the face of Oceanus in the centre, surrounded by dancing sea-nymphs. An outer zone of decoration depicts the drinking-contest between Bacchus and Hercules. This classically pagan scene is balanced by the presence in the hoard of silver spoons probably connected with baptism. The treasure also includes bowls and goblets of various sizes. It has considerable importance in the development of late Roman art, and the style is an influence upon the art of the barbarians who were to inherit so many Roman traditions.

MILLEFIORI To make this mosaic glass a tube or cane of glass was cased with several layers of different coloured glass, then re-heated and drawn out. Sometimes the sticks of glass were rolled on a corrugated surface, producing a flower-shaped cross section. Occasionally square-sectioned chequered designs were made. The multi-coloured rods were then cut into short sections and inlaid in individual cells or CLOISONNÉS. Millefiori was often used in the polychrome jewellery of the Dark Ages in England, as at SUTTON HOO, and used combined with CHAMPLEVÉ ENAMEL in Irish decorative metal-work.

MILPA Mesoamerican term for a field (usually a maize field) cultivated by the SLASH-AND-BURN method.

MINDELHEIM
see SWORD

●**MINOAN** The excavations at Knossos by Sir Arthur EVANS first revealed evidence of an advanced civilization in Crete during the Bronze Age. To this civilization Evans gave the name 'Minoan' after the legendary King Minos and the story of the Minotaur. The Minoans dominated the Aegean in the period *c* 2000–1450 BC and built up a powerful trading network with colonies at THERA, Miletus, Kythera and PHYLAKOPI. Large palaces were built on Crete from *c* 2000 onwards (*see* KNOSSOS, MALLIA, PHAISTOS), and the labyrinth of the Minotaur legend perhaps alludes to a palace complex of this kind. Surviving Minoan remains include advanced engineering works such as water-supply systems, multi-storey dwellings etc. Fresco painting was a common form of decoration, and fine examples can now be seen in Herakleion museum. Religion is documented by FIGURINES and engraved SEALS. Sacred objects were the bull (or its horns) and the double-sided axe, with which are associated a bull-leaping game in which acrobats vaulted over the horns of a bull onto its back. The TABLETS inscribed ▲ in the LINEAR A and LINEAR B scripts give information about economic organization and the goods held in the vast magazines under the palaces. The decline of Minoan culture was probably sparked off by the explosion of the volcanic island THERA in *c* 1450. Crete suffered much as a result, and the blow to her shipping enabled foreign invaders (or a local revolt) to take over the island. Henceforward only Knossos was heavily populated, and by people with a markedly MYCENAEAN type of culture. After a few hundred years the whole culture had sunk into obscurity.

MISENUM
see RAVENNA

MISSISSIPPI TRADITION Cultures in the Mississippi, Ohio and Missouri drainages of the eastern woodlands of North America evolved from the earlier WOODLANDS tradition around AD 700. The Mississippian Indians practised maize agriculture supplemented by hunting and collecting and lived in fairly settled villages and towns, sometimes fortified. These frequently had large temple platform mounds. Artefacts include chipped stone arrow points and a great variety of pottery forms.

MITANI This kingdom occupied the area between the Euphrates and the Tigris rivers immediately south of the Taurus mountains. It was established by King Paratarna *c* 1480 BC and its capital was Washukkanni, the site of which has not yet been found. HURRIANS had moved into the cities in northern Syria from the mountains of eastern Turkey during the preceding 500 years, and it seems that they were the major ethnic group of the kingdom. The ruling class however appear from their names and gods to be INDO-EUROPEAN. The ASSYRIANS were vassals to the Mitanians 1500–1360 BC. During this period Mitani vied with Egyptians and HITTITES for control of Syria. *C* 1360 BC the Hittite king, Shuppiluliumash I, attacked Mitani from the north and plundered Washukkanni.

MITHRAISM A religious cult, particularly common in the Roman empire in the first two centuries AD, and traditional among soldiers. The cult is originally from Persia, and is one of a number of Oriental mystery-cults common in the empire. It centres around Mithras, god of

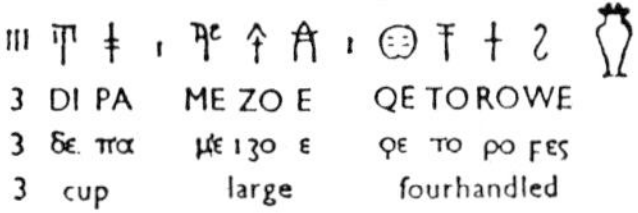

light, identified with the Unconquered Sun, and born out of a rock, who kills the great bull from the body and blood of which sprang all the life on the earth. The religion involved a secret meal and had several degrees of initiation, culminating in baptism in bull's blood. A Mithraic temple is called a Mithraeum; there are several at OSTIA and one in LONDON at Walbrook. Typical features include a nave flanked with earthen banks, an apse for rituals and a pit for the ordeal of baptism in blood.

MITLA, Mexico A large town and CEREMONIAL CENTRE in Oaxaca, dating from the Preclassic period (*see* MESOAMERICA), which continued as a major political and religious focus from the early Postclassic down to the Conquest when it was held to be the residence of the ZAPOTEC high priest. The plan of the city and its ceremonial buildings are typical of late Mexican architecture, with temples, palaces and PYRAMIDS set around paved PLAZAS and ornately decorated with geometric carved stone reliefs on the outside and the remains of painted frescoes on the interior walls.

MIXTEC Late Postclassic Mexican people (*see* MESOAMERICA) centred in the Mixteca Alta, Oaxaca. Mixtec codices indicate a genealogy going back to the 7th century AD, with early dynasties located at Tilantongo. Towns and buildings were architecturally less impressive than those of their ZAPOTEC or AZTEC neighbours, but the Mixtecs were renowned for their exceptional craft skills in metallurgy, feather-working and the cutting and polishing of precious and semi-precious stones such as jade, turquoise, jet, amber, coral and obsidian. They were also responsible for the production of exceptionally fine lacquered polychrome pottery. After the abandonment of the great centre of MONTE ALBAN by its Zapotec builders, the Mixtec people took over the site as a burying ground for their dead. It is here that one of the richest and most famous tombs in all Mesoamerica was found, probably the grave of a high priest, containing many gold and silver objects together with finely worked jewellery and semi-precious stones. The Mixtecs partially overlapped with the Zapotecs in Oaxaca, although culturally they remained distinct. They were fiercely independent and fought hard to resist Aztec expansion, then engulfing much of Mesoamerica. In the 15th century, however, the greater part of the Mixteca Alta fell under the dominion of Tenochtitlan, but the Mixtecs were never fully subdued and after 1519 allied themselves with the Spaniards to help crush the Aztec tyranny.

MOBILIARY ART Decorated objects, usually engraved antler, bone or ivory, found in Upper PALAEOLITHIC contexts. Their portability leads to their incorporation in stratified deposits, enabling more accurate dating than is possible for CAVE ART. Typical examples would include BÂTONS DE COMMANDEMENT, FIGURINES, HARPOONS and SPEAR THROWERS. Mobiliary art is particularly found in MAGDALENEAN contexts.

○ **MOCHE, MOCHICA** Emerged in PERU *c* AD 200 and lasted until the spread of the HUARI style around AD 700. Centred on the Moche and Chicama valleys of the North Coast, at the height of its influence, the Moche culture spread farther north to the Pacasmayo valley and south to Santa and Nepeña, probably through military conquest. Responsible for the building of huge ADOBE temples, palaces and fortresses, the Mochica also constructed large

irrigation systems in the river valleys. The culture is best known for its sophisticated pottery: STIRRUP-SPOUTED bottles modelled to represent the heads of chieftains or myriad scenes of daily life. Others are decorated with similar scenes of religious, military or social nature in red on a white or buff background.

MOGOLLON A culture of the SOUTHWESTERN tradition developed from COCHISE antecedents in south-eastern Arizona and south-western New Mexico, USA, dating from 100 BC to the 14th century AD. It has links with both the ANASAZI and HOHOKAM cultures, being partially agricultural with supplementary hunting and gathering. The first settlements were small sedentary hamlets with oval subterranean houses later developing into larger PUEBLO villages. Pottery is best represented by the Mimbres painted ceramics decorated with complex geometric and finely executed animal designs. Artefacts include MANOS, METATES, ground stone tools, smoking pipes and dishes, together with basketry and cotton textiles.

1 **MOHENJO-DARO, Pakistan** Situated on the right bank of the indus, this was, with HARAPPA, one of the twin 'capitals' of the INDUS CIVILIZATION. Excavations were undertaken by the Archaeological Survey 1922–31 and by Wheeler after 1947. Little is known of its earliest stages as the high water-table has prevented deep excavation. The citadel has revealed monumental structures of which the most remarkable is the great bath in the northern part, a brick structure entered by steps at either end. In the light of later Indian culture it is likely that this structure had a ritual significance. In the southern area a rectangular hall with brick piers for wooden pillars was found, surrounded by rooms in one of which a seated male statue was found. These suggest it was a temple. To the west of the bath was a brick-work block structure ventilated by narrow shafts, thought to be a granary.

MONSOON The monsoon winds allow a direct two-way sea-crossing between Arabia and South India. Although the route may have long been known to the Indians and Arabs, the route was not discovered by the Romans until *c* 1st century BC when it led to a great opening up of trade with south India. *See also:* ARIKAMEDU, ARRETINE WARE, BROACH, COIMBATORE, PERIPLUS.

MONTE ALBAN, Oaxaca, Mexico Built on an artificially levelled mountain spur, the site was a large city and a major ceremonial centre. There were five phases of cultural development, the first three belonging to its occupation by its ZAPOTEC builders. Period I *c* 600–300 BC marks the construction of the site and is important for the early presence of hieroglyphic inscriptions and bar-and-dot numerals (*see* CALENDAR). At the close of Period II *c* AD 150, there is a transitional phase until AD 300 with increasing influence from TEOTIHUACAN which reaches its maximum AD 300–600 in IIIa. The following phase IIIb initially saw the climax of the centre, but this was succeeded by a regression after which the site was abandoned *c* 700. In the final phase it was used as a burying place by the MIXTECS. The site has a huge paved PLAZA 300m × 200m towards the centre, around which are planned PLATFORM MOUNDS, PYRAMIDS and a large BALL COURT. In the earliest period, strange human figures (Dancantes) were carved in relief on stone slabs.

MONTELIUS, Oscar (1843–1921) Swedish prehistorian who developed the possibilities of cross-dating, a technique of dating prehistoric material by tracing supposed relationships with historic societies. In his works he described four subdivisions of the NEOLITHIC and five of the BRONZE AGE. His primarily TYPOLOGICAL classification, broke new ground by numbering rather than naming his stages. The basis of his scheme was that all European culture was derived from the Ancient East (an approach followed in a less extreme way by CHILDE). Now that independent dating evidence in the form of RADIOCARBON dates is available, many of Montelius's dates are seen to be in error and the supposed connections with the Near East and Egypt have been called in question.
Main books: *Orient and Europe* (1899); *Die Chronologie der ältesten Bronzezeit in Nord-Deutschland und Skandinavien* (1900).

MONTMAURIN, France A huge Roman VILLA in southern Gaul, just north of the Pyrenees. The villa itself covered 4 hectares, and included almost 200 rooms. A small villa had been on the site *c* AD 50, but the most lavish phase dates from *c* AD 350. The approach is through a huge U-shaped portico with a shrine to a native deity; other features include winter rooms heated by HYPOCAUSTS, and walls with beautifully intricate MOSAICS. Excavation of the working areas of the villa has also underlined its economic self-sufficiency: the end came however in the early 5th century when the villa was burned down, perhaps by the VANDALS.

MORTARIUM A common item of Roman coarse household pottery, used for grinding food. It takes the form of a flat-bottomed bowl the inside of which is hardened and roughened by large pieces of grit embedded into the surface; there is often a lip for pouring, and the rim usually has a pronounced flange. Mortaria may be stamped with the name of the potter. A distinctive form is in SAMIAN pottery, with a spout in the form of a lion's head with open mouth. Corresponding pestles are rare, and were probably of wood.

MOSAIC A form of decoration chiefly used in the Roman world. It consisted of small stones or *tesserae* of different colours set in patterns. It originated in HELLENISTIC Greece as pebble mosaic, but became very popular from the 1st century AD in the Roman empire. Geometric black-and-white styles were the first trend, later more coloured and figurative patterns came in. In the 4th century wall mosaics are often found and this becomes the chief use of mosaic in BYZANTINE times.

MOUNT CARMEL, Israel On the western slopes of the Carmel range in Palestine are a number of caves containing a long STRATIGRAPHIC sequence of Palaeolithic occupation. It begins in the lower Palaeolithic with TAYACIAN flake tools and later ACHEULEAN-type hand-axe industries are added. Next is found a MOUSTERIAN flint industry in which CORES are prepared specifically for the production of flint tools. It is a technique used by NEANDERTHAL man, a number of whose skeletons were found in the caves. Finally an AURIGNACIAN type industry with characteristics unique to Palestine develops into an indigenous culture called the Natufian. Small flint flakes with one straight edge and a crescent-shaped back are characteristic of the Natufian. The Natufians, who also lived in rock shelters elsewhere in Palestine, hunted gazelles and fished. Flint-bladed sickles were found testifying to the gathering of wild grain. The dead were buried in tightly-flexed positions with ornaments of shells under the living area in the cave or at its entrance.

MOUSTERIAN A widespread Middle PALAEOLITHIC industry, lasting between 70,000 and 30,000 BC. It is found throughout Europe (including Spain, Italy, Greece and European Russia), and in various related forms in north Africa and Asia, including China. It is associated with NEANDERTHAL man, whose culture for the first time shows features traditionally regarded as typically human, such as active concern for the dead and the living. The burnt and broken remains of at least 13 individuals at Kraphina, Croatia, testify the practice of cannibalism. The first clear indications of regular dwellings of any kind also date from the Mousterian. These include an apparently circular hut or tent-like structure at Molodora in western Russia. Like the later structure at DOLNÍ VĚSTONICE, mammoth bones appear to have formed a structural element, possibly to weigh down a skin covering. The Mousterian is named after two ROCK SHELTERS at Le Moustier (Les Eyzies, Dordogne, France).

MUCKING, Essex An early Anglo-Saxon village site overlooking a bend in the Thames estuary. More than 100 2-post GRUBENHÄUSER measuring about 4m by 3m have been found containing much household rubbish. There is an associated cemetery with rich grave goods. The sub-Roman metalwork and 4th–5th century AD pottery with strong Germanic links suggests that Mucking may have been an early settlement of FOEDERATI or LAETI troops before the mass migrations of the 5th century.

MUD-BRICK Where stone proved too expensive or unobtainable, buildings often were constructed from mud-bricks. Bricks were moulded out of a mixture of clay, sand and water, tempered with straw and dried in the sun. A mortar such as gypsum or bitumen sometimes bonded the bricks, and the surface both inside and out was often plastered. Mud-brick buildings required annual maintenance, without which they soon deteriorated and collapsed. The debris formed from collapsed mud-brick houses is largely responsible for the forming of Near Eastern TELLS. Because of the expense, bricks fired in a kiln were not used regularly until Roman times. The earliest mud-bricks were found at JERICHO. In MESOPOTAMIA mud-bricks of plano-convex shape were often used *c* 2000 BC and were laid in a herring-bone fashion. When formwork is used so that mud can be formed directly into a wall rather than as separate bricks, the material is called *pisé*.

MULTIVALLATE Having more than one rampart and/or ditch. Used particularly for HILLFORT defences.

● **MUMMIFICATION** Generic name for various methods employed by ancient Egyptians to keep the corpse looking as life-like as possible. (The word 'mummy' derives from Persian, referring to the black colour of the treated corpse and bandages, thought to be due to bitumen.) Belief that the spirit preferred to inhabit a tangible, recognizable form led to the attempt to preserve the features of the dead person. It had been observed that decomposition was worse in sophisticated burials than when the body was merely placed in direct contact with dessicating sand (where speedy dehydration resulted in reasonable preservation). In the earliest burials, linen bandages were moulded to the external features of the dead person, but by Dynasty IV it was realised that internal organs caused putrefaction, and these were therefore removed from the corpse. Summary and various degrees of mummification were practised in the Old and Middle Kingdoms, but the best examples belong to the late New Kingdom. From scientific examination of mummies, and from Herodotus, the costliest and most complete process can be outlined:

(1) The embalmers put the corpse on a slab which slanted towards a basin in which the body juices were caught. The brain was removed by curved hooks (usually inserted via the nose) and with liquids which dissolved the tissues.

(2) An incision was made in the left side of the abdomen for the removal of the contents of the thoracic and ventral cavities, except for the heart (which was the source of intellectual and emotional feelings, and therefore necessary for judgment in the underworld). Occasionally the kidneys were also left in place.

(3) Solid natron (a sodium bicarbonate compound) was applied. The basic principle underlying the whole process was the removal of all body moisture.

(4) The corpse was washed and rubbed with fragrant ointments.

(5) The body cavities were stuffed with linen (to preserve a life-like bulk) and with myrrh, cassia and other aromatic substances. During Dynasty XXI the body was packed with sand and mud to keep the features fuller, and the dehydrated internal organs were packaged and returned to the corpse instead of being placed in CANOPIC JARS.

(6) The corpse was heavily bandaged and amulets were wrapped onto it. (Tutankhamun had 16 linen layers.)

During and after the above process (taking 70 days in all) priests recited rituals. All materials (linen swabs etc.) that had come into contact with the corpse were buried in a pit near the tomb. *See also* CANOPIC JARS.

MUNDIGAK
see AFGHANISTAN

MUNICIPIUM A Roman town, the people of which were Roman citizens (a very real distinction until AD 212, when the citizenship was extended to all). It differs from a COLONIA in that the name was usually bestowed upon a settlement already existing. The municipium was self-administrating, in much the same way as the *colonia*. Although usually based upon native settlements, municipia can often be distinguished where the name lacks a tribal suffix: thus, the tribal capital of the Catuvellauni appears to have been a municipium, but was usually referred to simply as VERULAMIUM. Many of the leading figures in the municipium would have been the native aristocracy fitting into a Romanized, urban, way of life.

MURUS GALLICUS A type of fortification developed in Gaul in the 1st century BC in response to Roman siege tactics, and called *murus gallicus* (Gallic wall) by JULIUS CAESAR. It was a wall of stone and earth reinforced by a horizontal box framework of wood, fastened with iron nails. It is calculated that the walls at MANCHING used 300 tonnes of iron nails. This technique was used in the defence of OPPIDA from Czechoslovakia to France, but proved to be no protection against the Roman armies.

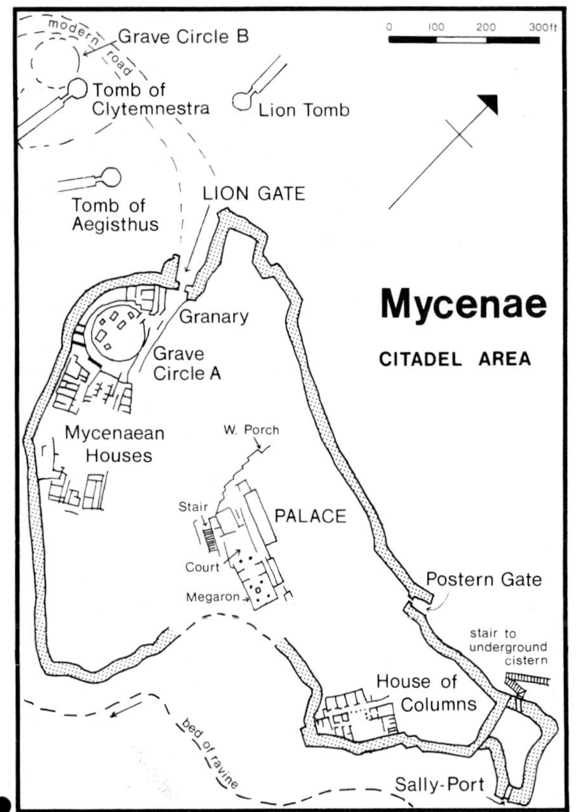

MYCENAE, Greece This, one of the earliest fortresses of the MYCENAEAN culture, was built *c* 1600 BC. The walling is of massive stone. (Cyclopean masonry), and the Lion Gate entrance has a carved tympanum with two lions. The buildings inside were halls on the MEGARON plan. The main feature of the site is its tombs. Two shaft-grave circles have been found. The later, richer one was excavated by SCHLIEMANN in 1876. Very rich finds were made, including gold face masks (the 'mask of Agamemnon'). Later burials were in tholos tombs, or underground vaulted, burial chambers, notably the 13th century example known as the Treasury of Atreus. The fortress survived the 13th century invasions by the DORIANS, but fell *c* 1190 BC.

MYCENAEAN This is the late Bronze Age culture of Greece, centred on the mainland but spreading *c* 1450 BC to take over the MINOAN and CYCLADIC cultures. Its power was based on shipping and trade and on colonies in RHODES and CYPRUS, Cyprus being most important for trade with the Near East. Other trade routes extended north to the Baltic for amber. Mycenaean culture declined suddenly at the end of the 13th century, perhaps as a result of DORIAN invasions. The main sites are fortified (e.g. MYCENAE and TIRYNS) and were richly appointed. Other sites (e.g. LERNA, PYLOS) were also rich. All had palaces and presumably were centres of local fiefdoms. The language was Greek. The Mycenaeans were the first speakers of that tongue in the country; they wrote in LINEAR B. The stories of the *Iliad* and the *Odyssey* refer to this period, although written later, and they contain much information on the Mycenaean way of life.

MYCERINUS' PYRAMID, Giza, Egypt Smallest of the three major pyramids at Giza: 66m high by 108m base-length. Mycerinus (Egyptian, Menkaure) of Dynasty IV before its completion. His son Shepseskaf made extensive economic cuts in the pyramid complex. The lower burial chamber (with a vaulted ceiling) contained the royal sarcophagus with an exquisitely carved imitation in miniature of palace architecture. It was lost at sea en route to England and only a drawing survives. REISNER discovered in a storeroom of the pyramid's valley temple ▲four fine slate statues of Mycerinus with his queen or tutelary goddesses.

NABATAEAN
see PETRA

NAGADA, Egypt PETRIE'S discoveries at Nagada, El-Ballas and Diospolis Parva downstream from Thebes brought to light the hitherto unrecognized predynastic periods of Ancient Egypt. These cultures are usually (not universally) referred to as stages of the Nagada civilization: Nagada I (also Amratian after site of early predynastic material); Nagada II (also Gerzean after site of middle to late predynastic artefacts).

Although these civilizations existed in the fourth millennium BC the chronology can only be given in terms of successive cultural stages based on Petrie's analysis of the pottery found in tombs. This system, known as Sequence Dating (SD), provides an outline to the period but there is a need for archaeological excavation of stratified sites to corroborate the cultural development based on typology.

Nagada I (SD 30–37): These people lived in fortified settlements. Their grave-goods include jewellery (shell, soft stone and pottery beads), combs, and slate palettes on which to grind minerals for eye make-up. The shapes of the

palettes are generally rhomboid but some occur carved like turtles or hippopotami. White cross-lines on polished red pottery is characteristic, showing geometrical patterns analogous to designs found in Western Asia.

Nagada II (SD 38–63): The culture of Nagada I received a vigorous input from foreign traders who had then decided to colonize the fertile Nile valley. The incursion could have been via the Wadi Hammamat which leads from the Red Sea coast to the Nile. Archaeological finds, and the idea of picture-writing (*see* HIEROGLYPHS) and the structure of the Egyptian language suggest that this stimulus came from the Middle Eastern civilizations (Mesopotamia or Elam). Possibly the Delta and Lower Egypt were more subject to the influence of Bronze Age Palestine. The more sophisticated of the Nagada II tombs show the body placed in contracted position in a recess of the burial pit which then was filled with grave goods. Matting and wooden planks foreshadow the sarcophagi of the Dynastic period. Beads and amulets are made of more varied materials, some imports such as lapis lazuli (originally from Afghanistan). Advanced stone-working techniques are seen in the vases of alabaster and limestone. Copper is fairly common for knives, rings or beads. For some of the pottery the wheel has been used. Brick-red pots of high-quality clay show patterns and pictures (e.g. rows of antelopes or mountains) in dark red closely resembling motifs found in particular on pottery and seals from the predynastic JEMDAT NASR culture of Iraq. Other designs however show a completely Egyptian source, e.g. the observation of papyrus boats with shrines and poles bearing an emblem of a god or particular district. Other notable artefacts are rippled flint-knives with ivory handles elaborately carved to show animal files or in one case a naval battle, chisel-tipped arrow heads, and pear-shaped mace-heads. There are also large slate palettes decorated with scenes thought worth commemorating for dedication in a temple. The Hunters' palette in the British Museum shows in relief two contingents, one hunting antelope with a lasso, the other armed with bows on a lion hunt. Narmer's palette found at HIERAKONPOLIS celebrates the southern ruler's victory over the northern confederation about 3100 BC, marking the unification of Egypt into one state.

NAHUATL Principal language spoken by the AZTECS and various other Precolumbian Mexican tribes.

NAPATA
see NUBIA

NARSIK
see ROCK-CUT ARCHITECTURE

◀ ■ **NASCA CULTURE** Evolved in Peru from the PARACAS culture in the Ica, Nasca and Acari valleys of the south coast. Whilst incorporating similar themes to the late Paracas pottery, including 'cat demons', technological innovation is marked by the application of polychrome design *before* firing. In addition to cat demons, later Nasca themes include figures of animals, plants, fish and birds, together with fantastically rendered and sometimes headless torsos of humans or demons.

NATSUSHIMA SHELL-MIDDEN, Japan Near Tokyo Bay, with material dated to before 7000 BC, this is an early example of the remains of the JOMON culture.

NATUFIAN
see MOUNT CARMEL

NEANDERTHAL MAN In 1857, a skull-cap and the remains of a complete human skeleton were recovered by some workmen in a limestone quarry in the Neander valley (*thal*) near Düsseldorf, Germany. Since then about 60 individuals have been found in various parts of the Old World, dating from the Riss–Würm interglacial or the final (Würm) glaciation of the later PLEISTOCENE.

There is some debate about the Neanderthals' position on the evolutionary tree. One view is that they represent a distinct species of HOMO, but more generally they are regarded as a 'sub-species' of HOMO SAPIENS and called *Homo sapiens neanderthalensis*. Despite the impression given by a large brow ridge, flattened nose and chinless face, Neanderthal man's brain capacity was as great, or even greater, than that of modern man. It has been suggested that his large skull made childbirth a more than usually hazardous process and may have been partly responsible for his ultimate extinction. One of the early reconstructions, showing Neanderthal man with a pronounced stoop, was based on a burial from La Chapelle aux Saints in France. This skeleton has since been recognized as severely arthritic, and there is every reason to assume that he walked fully upright. Neanderthal man is associated with MOUSTERIAN deposits. He has left behind the earliest evidence for the ritual burial of man by his own kind. At Teshik-Tash in Uzbekistan, a child was buried with several goat-horns. *See also:* SHANIDAR.

NEA NIKOMEDIA, Greece An early NEOLITHIC settlement in west Macedonia, dating from about 6000 BC.

NEBI MEND, Tell
see KADESH

NECROPOLIS Literally 'City of the Dead', a term sometimes applied to cemeteries or CATACOMBS.

NEGATIVE PAINTING [or resist painting] A type of pottery decoration common in certain parts of the New World. The intended design is blocked out on the surface of the vessel by means of applied wax or clay. The vessel is then slipped in black or dark red and fired or baked in smoky or reducing (oxygen-starved) conditions. When the wax or clay is removed, the pattern is left in the original colour of the pot against the darker background.

NEKHBET Vulture-goddess, protectress of southern Egypt, her sanctuary was at El-Kab. She was the guardian of the predynastic rulers of Upper Egypt whose capital, HIERAKONPOLIS, was across the river from her sanctuary. After the unification of Egypt she became important element in the King's regalia – placed alongside the URAEUS on his headdress, she symbolized his control over Upper Egypt under her auspices. Tutankhamun's tomb revealed splendid representations of Nekhbet: solid gold vulture's head on the funerary mask; large vulture collar (250-segments of polychrome glass) covering the chest of the mummy; gold pendant inlaid with lapis lazuli of Nekhbet, wings slightly opened then turning downwards.

NEMAUSUS [modern Nîmes], France A town in southern Gaul important in Roman as well as modern times for its

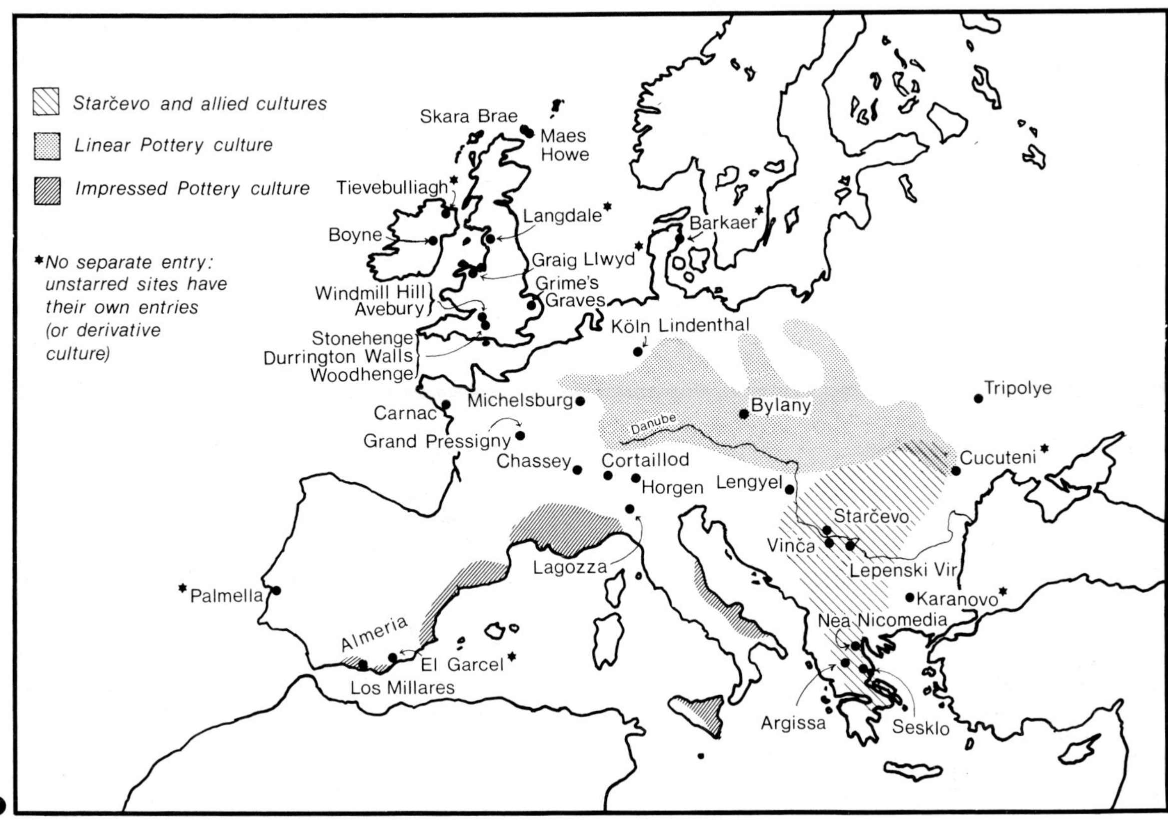

healing springs, which were certainly known in 25 BC; the town was named after the god of these springs. There are several temples, including a beautiful barrel-vaulted Temple of Diana built in the early 2nd century AD, and a temple of the late 1st century BC dedicated to Rome and Augustus, perhaps the best-preserved temple in France. The town walls include the Tour Magne, a tower still standing to over 40m. There is an AMPHITHEATRE, the twin of that at ARLES. Water was supplied by an AQUEDUCT which includes the spectacular PONT DU GARD.

NEMES Linen headcloth, usually striped, worn by pharaohs. The two horizontally-pleated lappets draped down behind the ears onto the collar-bones. The rest of the nemes fitted closely over the crown of the head, spread out and was gathered into a hanging plait (symbolic of the tail feathers of the hawk-god?) just below the nape of the neck. A styled band between the linen and the forehead prevented rubbing.

Modern attempts to recreate this linen headgear resulted in the nemes keeping its shape only for a very short time. This led to the suggestion that maybe the material was a soft leather.

NEOLITHIC [New Stone Age] Like PALAEOLITHIC, a term coined by John Lubbock in 1865. Following the MESOLITHIC, it lasted until the introduction of metal-working. The major feature of the Neolithic is the presence of an economy wholly or partly dependent on domesticated crops or animals, or both. CHILDE described the development of such an economic system as the Neolithic Revolution. It is now realized that the domestication of plants and animals occurred in a number of unrelated places throughout the world, and far from being a revolution was in some areas a very drawn-out process. The Neolithic is frequently associated with the development of various home crafts, including the manufacture of pottery. Crop-growing necessitated a less mobile existence than was possible before, and permanent settlements of any size usually do not appear before this period, in south-west Asia beginning 9–6000 BC.

NEUSS, Germany A Roman fortress on the Rhine. It was built *c* 12 BC and held a variety of legions until AD 92 when it became an auxiliary fort. It was abandoned after the FRANKISH invasion of 276, restored in the early 4th century and abandoned again in 378. It is the only legionary fortress to have been almost completely excavated although nothing now remains to be seen. In the centre was the headquarters, and barracks were spaced around the outside. Other buildings included a hospital with operating theatre, officers' houses, workshops and stables.

NEW STONE AGE
see NEOLITHIC

NIAH, Sarawak Excavations of the limestone massif of Niah, from 1954, have yielded rich remains dating from *c* 40,000 BC to AD 1300. The 'Great Cave' of Niah is especially important, covering a vast area and containing among the burials skull fragments of an early HOMO SAPIENS, dating to *c* 40,000 BC. The skull is of a lightly-built individual of late immaturity. Extensive animal bones have been recovered from the stone age periods of the site; only one extinct species is represented, a giant anteater. Stone tools are relatively scarce at Niah; however the deeper levels

yielded small flakes of quartzite, which continue into later levels, and by *c* 8000 BC edge-grinding on axes appeared, followed several thousand years later by quadrangular adzes, fine decorated pottery, and, in the latest levels traces of bronze, along with beads and iron tools. Typical HOABINHIAN tools are absent from Niah, as they often are in the islands of south-east Asia. Several types of bone tool are preserved at the site.

NICOPOLIS, Greece A Roman town set up by AUGUSTUS in 31 BC to commemorate the near-by battle of Actium. The name means 'city of Victory'. The town flourished until sacked by Genseric the VANDAL in AD 475. Standing remains at present consist of the THEATRE, CIRCUS, odeion (indoor theatre), a BASILICA and the BYZANTINE town walls.

NIELLO Engraved lines on silver and gold objects are sometimes filled with a black silver sulphide, niello, in order to give the design a bigger contrast with the shining metal.

NIHON SHOKI The 'Chronicles of Japan' written in the 8th century AD. The contents are part fact, part legend, describing events in those islands' history, as well as customs. Much of the information had been transmitted by centuries of oral tradition. Some of the descriptions have been substantiated by archaeological investigation.

NIMRUD [Ancient Kalhu, Biblical Calah], Iraq An ASSYRIAN capital city about 38km south of NINEVEH on the east bank of the Tigris river. It was excavated by LAYARD 1845–8, by the British 1949–61, and at present by the Iraq Department of Antiquities. Although the TELL was occupied from prehistoric to Greek (*c* 300 BC) times, excavations have centred on the remains of the cities built by Shalmaneser I (*c* 1250 BC) and Ashurnasirpal II in 879 BC. Within the 8km-long city wall are palaces, temples and housing for an estimated 60,000 people. In the north-west corner was a ZIGGURAT and in the associated temples and palaces many scuptures in stone and ivory were found, ● including the Black Obelisk (now in the British Museum) which records King Jehu (841–814 BC) of Israel bringing tribute to Shalmaneser III. In 612 BC Nimrud fell to the MEDES and BABYLONIANS.

NINEVEH [modern Kuyunjik], Iraq A TELL across the Tigris river from Mosul excavated many times. The most important finds, made by LAYARD and Rassam in the 1850s, consist of 25,000 inscribed TABLETS which formed the libraries of Sennacherib and Ashurbanipal (*see* ASSYRIA). ▲ They also found many RELIEFS, such as that of the lion hunt of Ashurbanipal, which decorated the walls of the palaces. The libraries contain epics, e.g. Gilgamesh, histories, grammatical and scientific texts collected by the two kings which are instructive of the history and literature of the Assyrian Empire. The tell was occupied as early as the HASSUNA period *c* 5000 BC, but it was not until it became joint capital of Assyria with ASSUR and NIMRUD that it became important. Like Nimrud, Nineveh fell to the combined MEDES, SCYTHIANS and BABYLONIANS in 612 BC.

NINTOKU TOMB, Japan The late 4th century-early 5th century AD tomb near Osaka of the Japanese Emperor Nintoku, who according to the later NIHON SHOKI began its construction 20 years before he died. The tomb covers approximately 35 hectares, is of the 'keyhole' style, and is

surrounded by three moats. The Nintoku tomb is the largest of those monumental structures built during the TOMB PERIOD.

NIPPUR [modern Nuffar], Iraq This site, about 160km south-east of Bagdad, was a city-state and an important religious centre in SUMER. Excavations were conducted 1888–98, resumed 1948. The earlier excavations cleared a series of temples belonging to the Sumerian god Enlil. Nippur itself was found to have a continuous history from Early Dynastic (*c* 3000 BC) to PARTHIAN (AD 226) times, More recently a series of temples belonging to Inanna, and another dedicated to ISHTAR the goddess of love and war, have been excavated. Many inscribed TABLETS have been found in the temples and it is from these that much of our knowledge of Sumerian religion comes. Although the tablets were written in the late 3rd millennium, they are thought to contain traditions were originally passed on by word of mouth.

NON NOK THA ['Partridge Mound'], Thailand Site in north-east Thailand excavated in the 1960s. Along with the more than 200 burials were artefacts of stone, copper, bronze, iron and pottery, as well as animal remains. The two dozen dates obtained from the site do not form a consistent pattern. Instead, they have been grouped into an 'early' and a 'late' sequence, with some controversy as to whether the 'early' dates can be accepted without reservation. If the 'early' sequence is accepted, the oldest levels go back beyond 7500 BC, and abandonment was *c* AD 1400. Pottery, abundant at the site, is incised, painted or cord-marked, with forms such as flat-bottomed jars, round-bottomed vessels, bowls and footed specimens. Some of the pottery, even in the earliest levels, had impressions of rice, and in one case a carbonized rice grain which had been used as temper. This may indicate rice agriculture. Animal bones associated with burials included the articulated limb bones of pigs, dogs and cattle, some from the earliest levels. The bovine remains may possibly be those of domesticated animals.

It is the evidence of metal-working however which may prove the most important feature. A copper implement, found with one of the burials, is from the end of the early period, and is the only metal object during that phase. It is a socketed tool of a great antiquity, not only for south-east Asia, but for the world. By the middle period, beginning *c* 2500 BC, evidence of a well-developed bronze industry is apparent in the form of socketed axes, bracelets, sandstone moulds and earthenware crucibles. The dating here is crucial: if accurate, it argues for an early and indigenous bronze-working technology. If this is the case, traditional thinking regarding the diffusion of such techniques from the Near East, India or China must be re-assessed, and with it the role of what was previously considered the 'backward' area of south-east Asia in prehistory (*see also*: SPIRIT CAVE). Iron, mainly in the form of tanged knives, does not make its appearance at Non Nok Tha until *c* AD 1000; other drastic changes after this point include replacement of inhumation practices by jar cremations, and a shift from funerary offerings of large animals to those of fowl and pig; the remains of post-holes seem to indicate a pile-dwelling.

NORTHERN BLACK POLISHED WARE is the predominant fine ceramic of the Early Historic period in the Ganges area of India (*see* GANGES CIVILIZATION). It

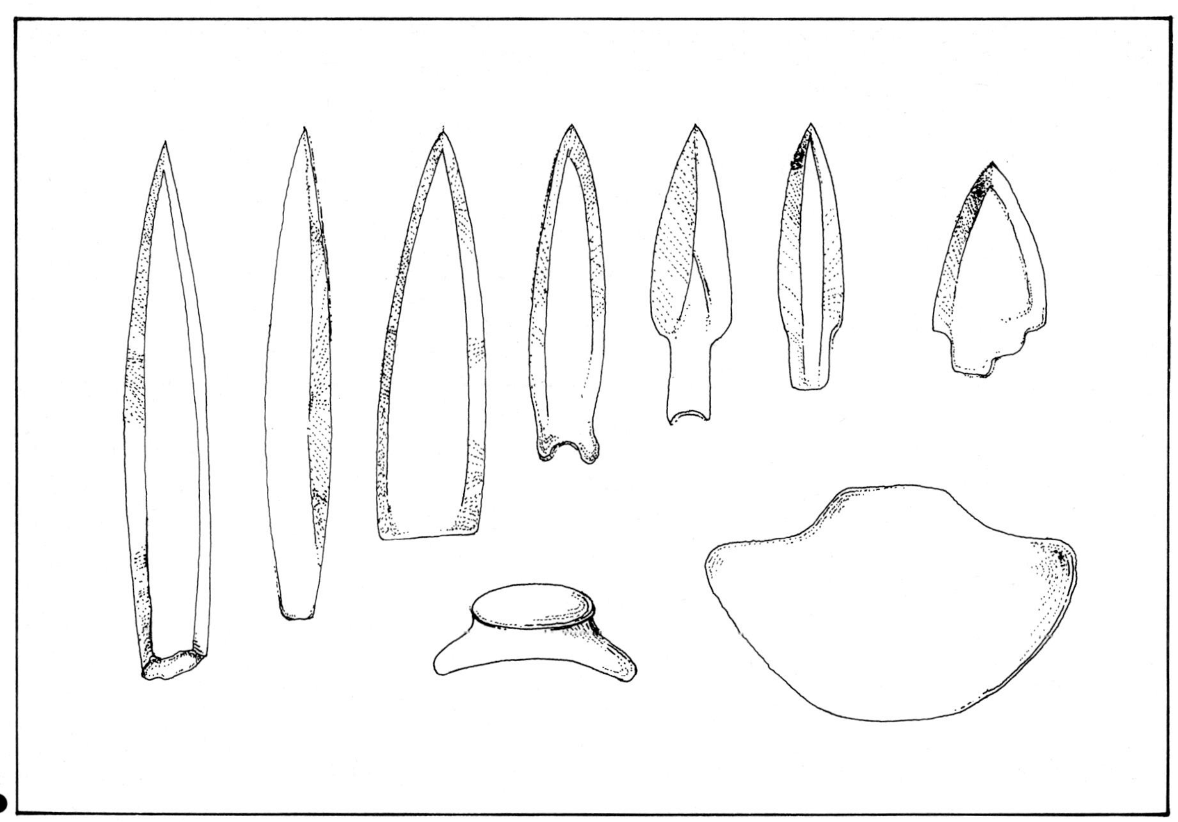

continues the tray and bowl forms of the preceding PAINTED GREY WARE pottery. The decorative technique used to produce the shiny black surface is similar to that employed in the manufacture of Greek black ware (*see* GREEK POTTERY).

NORTHUMBRIA An Anglo-Saxon kingdom, sometimes divided into two parts, Bernicia between the Tees and Forth, based on Bamburgh, and Diera between the Humber and the Tees with a capital at York. During the 7th century AD the kingdom nearly achieved hegemony over all England under Edwin, Oswald and Oswiu, whose palaces have been excavated at YEAVERING. Although eclipsed by the rise of MERCIA after 658, it continued as an important centre of art and learning, as is shown by exquisite illuminated MANUSCRIPTS produced at LINDISFARNE.

● **NORTHWEST COAST TRADITION** Emerged in the 1st millennium BC on the north-west coast of America between northern California and southern Alaska from OLD CORDILLERAN antecedents. Indian communities living in settled and semi-settled villages close to the shore had a rich economy based on salmon, hunting of marine mammals and littoral collecting. Communities were materially wealthy and artistically skilled, especially in the carving of totem poles, dug-out canoes and embellishments for log cabins. Equipment includes a large proportion of bone harpoons and barbed points, chipped stone lance heads, polished stone axes, adzes and hammers. The tradition continued down to historic times, when fur-trading with the first European settlers gave the Indians iron tools and woollen textiles.

NOVGOROD, Russia By AD 900 Swedish influence was a very important factor in eastern Europe. A network of river routes had been established and two Scandinavian Khaganates (trading centres) set up at Novgorod and Kiev. Swedish traders used the route from the Baltic to the Dnieper, to the Black Sea and on to BYZANTIUM and the east. Although there is little archaeological evidence of the Swedish colonization at Novgorod, there are traits in house construction and funerary rites linking the areas. In the 11th century the Khaganates combined into an increasingly Slav Christian west Russian empire.

NUBIA, Egypt General name given to the regions south from the First Cataract of the Nile down to the Sixth. Ancient Egyptian names are found which can be approximately attributed to geographical areas:

First to Second Cataract – Wawat. (This region no longer exists, submerged by Lake Nasser as a consequence of the building of the new Aswan High Dam).

South of Second Cataract – Kush.

Probably upstream from Third Cataract – Yam. The native Nubian cultures coeval with Dynastic Egypt begin with the A-Group, contemporary with the Archaic Period and Old Kingdom. This culture, remarkable for extremely thin pottery reminiscent of the best productions found in Egypt during BADARIAN civilization, was superseded at the end of the Old Kingdom by the C-Group, specialists in cattle-breeding. The involvement of Egypt in Nubia was political, strategic and commercial, ranging over the lifespan of pharaonic civilization.

The temples of Nubia are impressive propaganda-monuments built in the name of the king and gods of Egypt (*see* ABU SIMBEL, BEIT EL-WALI, KALABSHA and SOLEB). Also

▲

immigration-control, custom-posts and the headquarters of military intelligence (e.g. reconnoitring the movements of hostile African tribes into sphere of Egyptian influence) were combined in the massive fortresses on the banks of the Nile, especially near the Second Cataract (*see* BUHEN). Any weakness in the centralized authority far to the north in Egypt led to a power-vacuum in Nubia and local chieftains becoming controllers of the rich produce coming up from Africa. The Kerma culture (capital upstream from the Third Cataract), which created some of the finest ceramics in the Nile valley, was due to local rulers taking advantage of the confused political situation in Egypt at the end of the Middle Kingdom. Their power lasted until the Theban pharaohs of the New Kingdom expanded the Egyptian sphere of influence as far south as the Fourth Cataract. ▲ Tomb paintings and pharaonic annals give some idea of the wealth and luxury goods that reached the Egyptian court as a mixture of tribute and trade from Africa: gold (either as ingots or as rings), ivory-tusks, ostrich feathers and eggs (for decorating), cones of incense (for temple-rituals), leopard skins (worn by priests). Live animals also figure prominently, e.g. giraffes, panthers, and baboons. We know from as far back as an Old Kingdom tomb inscription at ASWAN that captured pygmies were popular at the Egyptian court. After the New Kingdom a principality independent of Egyptian rule formed in the region of Napata near the Fourth Cataract.

The kings of this state naturally had many Egyptian elements in their culture, the most significant being strong adherence to the Egyptian god AMUN. The fragmentation of pharaonic authority in Egypt at the end of Dynasty XXII enabled this Nubian kingdom to invade in 730 BC and to quickly establish itself as de facto government (Dynasty XXV). Its rule marked a revival of Egyptian sculpture and an intensified building programme, together with an interest in preserving Egyptian culture and beliefs (*see* PTAH – account of Shabaka stone). But these kings continued to be buried in their native cemeteries near Napata.

Dynasty XXV collapsed under the invasions of Assyria and its last ruler retreated to the Fourth Cataract.

This state maintained its independence, first with its capital at Napata (655–295 BC) and then for greater security moving it further south to MEROE, towards the Sixth Cataract. The small pyramids of the royal rulers of both these capitals were excavated by REISNER who attempted to form a sequential king-list from cartouches and cultural traits and artefacts in the pyramids. *See also* BALLANA; MEROE.

NUMANTIA, Spain This IBERIAN town was besieged by the Romans in the 2nd century BC. It is surrounded by a continuous wall and a series of forts, the most famous at Renieblas (occupied 195–133 BC). Some of these forts give evidence of the organization of the early Roman army. The fort-plan resembles in a loose way the more conventional Imperial forts such as NEUSS or HOUSESTEADS.

NUZI [modern Yorghan Tepe], Iraq TELL near Kirkuk. Excavations in 1925–31 found that the main levels of occupation belonged to the 15th–14th centuries BC when the town was controlled by HURRIANS. In the palace and private houses of this period were found about 20,000 tablets which deal with business and family transactions.

NYMPHAEUM A colonnaded garden found in the richer Roman houses: the central feature is an ornamental

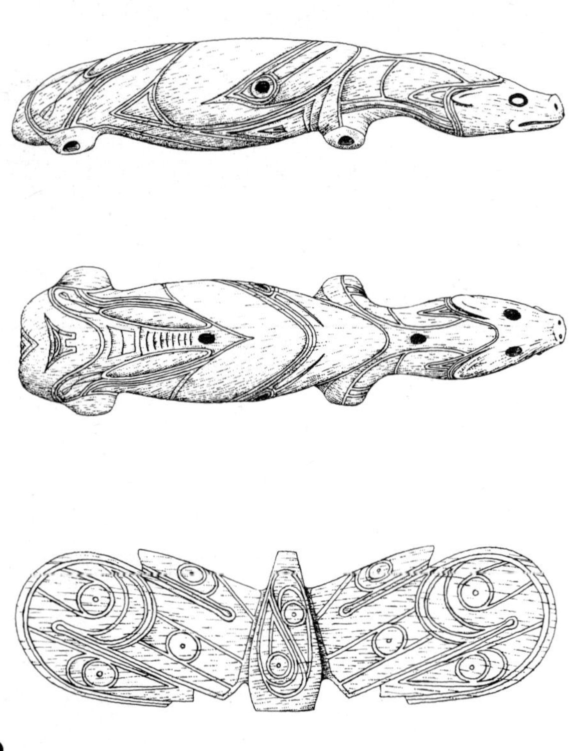

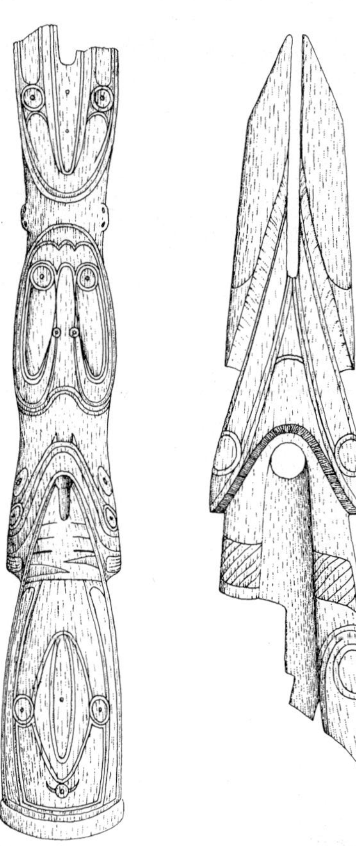

fountain, and statues are usually placed in niches around the circuit. The original idea was of a shrine to the water-nymphs, but the result was more often merely an ornamental bower.

OBANIAN A MESOLITHIC culture found along the west coast of Scotland *c* 4–3000 BC, named after Oban, Argyll. Sites are typically ROCK SHELTERS or shell middens, where bone and antler are particularly well preserved.

OBELISK A long shaft surmounted by a pyramidion, symbolically representing the 'benben' stone at Heliopolis where the sun-god emerged from the primeval waters. Two of these solar emblems usually formed an architectural unit outside the entrance to temple courtyards – possibly a hangover from the god-poles in front of archaic shrines. The best-preserved obelisk in situ is Queen Hatshepsut's at KARNAK, mainly due to Tuthmosis III, her successor, who unwittingly gave it protection against the centuries when he walled it up to hide the name of the queen who had kept him out of power for twenty years. The granite quarries at ASWAN show an obelisk in the stages of being cut out from the rock before flaws stopped it being the largest one erected in Egypt. Obelisks weighing up to 500 tonnes were transported from Aswan hundreds of miles by river to THEBES or farther north. When they reached their location, probably a ramp of sand built over-looking the spot where they were to stand helped to tilt and slide them into position. *See also:* HELIOPOLIS.

OBSIDIAN DATING A freshly-flaked obsidian surface absorbs water from its surroundings at a rate dependent on the surrounding temperature. This fact is utilized in the dating of obsidian. The absorption of water forms a 'hydration layer' which is of measurable thickness, though invisible to the naked eye. Where it can be assumed that the climate, and therefore the average temperature, of a region has remained constant since the manufacture of the obsidian artefact, the rate of hydration can be calculated by the measurement of the hydration layers on artefacts of known date. The rate of hydration can then be used to calculate the age of other obsidian artefacts from the same area.

OC EO, Vietnam An important mercantile port of the kingdom of FUNAN in the early centuries AD; its location on the south coast of the lower Mekong area of present-day south Vietnam made it a prosperous point in trade routes, as between India and China. Aerial photography of the Oc Eo region revealed irrigation and communication canals. Excavations of the city provided archaeological evidence for the Funan kingdom, long known from the Chinese texts. Among the finds were earthenware stamps (perhaps for fabric printing), coins, seals and medallions, bronze bells, gold jewellery (with stone moulds for its casting) and abundant tin jewellery. Some of the material is known to have come from China, India, the eastern Mediterranean, and the Near East, either directly or through links in the trade routes; at the same time, much of the locally manufactured jewellery exhibits fine craftsmanship.

OCHRE COLOURED POTTERY The worn condition in which this Indian pottery is generally found suggests that it has usually been carried for some distance in a river, which explains the lack of associated finds. It seems to have been related to the GANGES COPPER HOARDS. THERMOLUMIN-

ESCENCE dates suggest that it was contemporary with and survived the INDUS CIVILIZATION.

OCÓS, Pacific Coast, Guatemala Early Preclassic locality (*see* MESOAMERICA) giving its name to one of the earliest phases in the emerging Mesoamerican cultural tradition when pottery was first widely in use, 1500–1000 BC. The most important Ocós site is La Victoria, where there are finds of typical early Mesoamerican ceramic forms including the TECOMATE and the flat-bottomed pan-shaped bowl, with ROCKER-STAMPED decoration and sometimes bands of irridescent red paint.

OENPELLI, Australia Located in Arnhem Land, Northern Territory. Excavation of ROCK-SHELTERS in the area revealed the unusually early presence of edge-ground axes, some bearing features possibly related to hafting at a date before 20,000 BC. More than a dozen complete examples were retrieved, and all were made from igneous or metamorphic rocks. Sites in the area dated from 20,000 to 5000 BC also yielded assemblages including flake and CORE tools (e.g. heavy core-scrapers) along with edge-ground axes. Unifacial and bifacial points do not however appear here until after 5000 BC.

OFFA King of MERCIA AD 757–96. During his long reign the political stability of Mercia was increased and the once independent neighbouring kingdoms of EAST ANGLIA, Lindsey and Hwicce were reduced to subject status. Kent, Sussex and even WESSEX also came under strong Mercian influence. Perhaps the greatest of all Anglo-Saxon kings, Offa was the first to call himself *Rex totius Anglorum Patriae* (king of all the countries of the Angles), and negotiated with CHARLEMAGNE as his equal. For his consolidation of Mercia he ordered the construction of Offa's Dyke, a massive LINEAR EARTHWORK along the Welsh border from Prestatyn to Chepstow. In AD 780 the first silver PENNIES were struck in a major reorganization of the coinage, one of the most lasting effects of his reign.

OGAM [or Ogham] A writing system consisting of horizontal and diagonal lines of varying length meeting or crossing a vertical base line, often the straight edge of an upright stone slab. The script was invented in Ireland *c* 3rd century AD, and spread to the CELTIC areas of England and Wales where the most numerous examples are found on MEMORIAL STONES of 5th and 6th centuries AD. Later inscriptions are found on the symbol stones of the PICTS in eastern Scotland and in DALRIADA, where the alphabet continued in use until the 9th century AD.

OGDOAD Overall title given to the eight Egyptian creator-deities whose cult centre was at HERMOPOLIS. The cosmogony here not only offered an almost scientific explanation of the world's creation, but also attempted to outdo the ENNEAD devised by the priests at HELIOPOLIS. The Ogdoad were the four pairs (imagined as frogs or serpents) that made up the original elements present in the chaos before creation – the second of each pair being a shadowy counterpart to the male force:

Nut and Naunet	=	primeval watery expanse
Huh and Hauhet	=	infinite space
Kuk and Kauket	=	darkness
Amun and Amaunet	=	invisibility, or the breeze activating the chaos.

The god THOTH, already present in the theology of Heliopolis as a minor deity, was incorporated at Hermopolis as the chief god overshadowing the original members of the Ogdoad. It was explained that the eight deities were parts of the soul of Thoth, who in his form as an ibis produced the cosmic egg out of which the sun-god emerged to create the physical world.

● **OLD BERING SEA** An ESKIMO culture of the Northern Maritime tradition which flourished during the first 5 centuries AD in north Alaska and north-east Siberia and is best known for its distinctive style in carved ivory objects.

OLD COPPER CULTURE A culture of the ARCHAIC tradition which emerged in the Great Lakes and Upper Mississippi region 6000–4000 BC with an economy based on hunting and fishing. Metallic copper was mined around lake Superior and worked by hot and cold hammering into a variety of tools, especially spear points and knives. Smelting and casting were unknown and so were farming and pottery. The culture ended around 1500 BC.

OLD CORDILLERAN TRADITION Cultures located in the Pacific Northwest and Interior Plateau of north America whose economic activities depended on generalized hunting, fishing and gathering. It emerged by *c* 10,000 BC and was contemporary with the BIG-GAME HUNTING and ARCHAIC traditions, persisting in some areas down to *c* 5000 BC and giving way in others, for example the Great Basin region, to the DESERT tradition *c* 8000 BC. In the Northwest Coast and Interior Plateau area, it was replaced by the NORTHWEST COAST cultures and further south by the California Coast and Valley tradition. Diagnostic tool types of the Old Cordilleran tradition include leaf-shaped bipointed spearheads of flaked stone, oval flint knives and cobble pounders.

OLD CROW FLATS, Canadian Yukon A site with butchered bone and bone tools fashioned from caribou tibia yielding a radiocarbon date of 28–23,000 BC, one of the earliest reliable dates for man in America. The bone tools may possibly be of the oldest flake and bone tool tradition of North America. *See also* TLAPACOYA.

OLDOWAN A Lower PALAEOLITHIC stone industry consisting largely of rough implements fashioned from pebbles. It is found mainly in southern and eastern Africa (for example in the Omo Valley, near lake Rudolf, Ethiopia, and at OLDUVAI GORGE, the TYPE-SITE).

OLD STONE AGE
see PALAEOLITHIC

▲ **OLDUVAI GORGE, Tanzania** A site near Lake Eyasi, north Tanzania, which has produced the world's finest sequence of Lower PALAEOLITHIC artefacts and an important series of early man fossils. The deposits (mainly volcanic tuffs) in which the remains are preserved are over 100m deep, and have been divided into five 'Beds'. At the base, Bed I, dated by the POTASSIUM–ARGON method to 1.75 million BC, contained an OLDOWAN pebble tool industry and bones of HOMO HABILIS and AUSTRALOPITHECUS. Bed II yielded fossils of HOMO ERECTUS and Early ACHEULEAN tools. The HANDAXE tradition developed in Beds III and IV, the latter containing human fossils comparable to ►

Olduvai Gorge Sequence

Potassium-Argon Dates (millions of years before present)		BEDS	HOMINID REMAINS	INDUSTRIES
	UPPER PLEISTOCENE	Bed IV	HOMO	
		Bed III		OLD TO UPPER ACHEULIAN (Handaxe Tradition)
0·49	MIDDLE PLEISTOCENE	Upper Bed II	HOMO ERECTUS	
		Windlian Deposits		
1·1		Lower Bed II	HOMO ERECTUS (PITHECANTHROPUS)	OLDOWAN
1·75 1·85	FINAL AND UPPER VILLEFRANCHIAN	Bed I	HOMO HABILIS AUSTRALOPITHECUS (ZINJANTHROPUS)	OLDOWAN
		Basalt		

NEANDERTHAL man. Finally, a blade-and-burin industry was present in Bed V.

● **OLMEC** A late prehistoric – early historic tribe whose name translates as 'rubber people', living in the southern Veracruz and Tabasco region of the Gulf coast after migrating from central Mexico (*see* CHOLULA). Archaeologists have also given the name Olmec to the middle Preclassic (*see* MESOAMERICA) civilization which had its heartland there. These earlier 'Olmecs' were responsible for a unique art-style and iconography associated with the first CEREMONIAL CENTRES in Mesoamerica, notably sites like SAN LORENZO, TENOCHTITLAN and LA VENTA. Although Olmec cave paintings do exist, their art style is typically sculptural, as carved reliefs or full-round figures. Two themes pervade Olmec iconography: baby-like features which are frequently combined with the fanged and snarling attributes of the jaguar. These basic ideas, together with a general heaviness, slant eyes, full lips and thick nose characterize Olmec sculpture, whether as the monumental basalt heads measuring over 3m in height and weighing up to 22 tonnes, or the smaller and beautifully carved and polished jade figurines and celts. The origins of the Olmec tradition are still obscure, but radiocarbon dates from their earliest centre at San Lorenzo indicate that the typical style had emerged by 1200 BC. Not only does the presence of hieroglyphic inscriptions, together with the bar-and-dot Long Count (*see* CALENDAR) date of 31 BC on a stela at Tres Zapotes argue for an Olmec origin for Maya writing and counting systems, but in a NAHUATL legend the Mayan name of Tamoanchan is given to an early civilization which existed in the Olmec heartland and implies that the Olmecs were possibly ancestral to the great MAYA civilization. Monumental Olmec sculpture is limited to the central region of southern Veracruz and parts of Tabasco, but influences spread widely throughout Mesoamerica, down to Pacific Guatemala and as far as Salvador. At such sites as TLATILCO there are figurines with strong Olmec influence which cut across local and very different styles. The culture reached its climax in the 1st millennium BC and by 400 BC had disappeared.

OLYMPIA, Greece A Greek sanctuary to Zeus and Hera, famous for its four-yearly Panhellenic games and festival. 776 BC is the date of the first Olympiad and the area soon became cluttered with shrines and statues set up by successful athletes and happy worshippers. The games lasted 1200 years until AD 393. Its stadium (CIRCUS) is visible and held 40,000 people.

OMAYYADS The first dynasty of the Moslem empire after the death of Mohammad (called 'a Caliphate'). Following a civil war Moawiyah established himself as the first Omayyad Caliph in DAMASCUS in AD 661. From here Moslem rule expanded to include Syria, Palestine during the reigns of Abd-al-Malik (AD 685–705) and al Walid I (AD 705–45). Arabic became the official state language and Arabic coinage was introduced. Communications were improved and many fine buildings were constructed, e.g. in JERUSALEM. Religious and economic problems weakened the empire after the main Omayyad army had been defeated by the BYZANTINE ruler Leo III in AD 717; it finally fell to the Abbasids in AD 750.

ONAGER A nickname for a heavy catapult used by the Roman army. The name means 'the ass'; its lightweight

counterpart was known as 'the scorpion'. A vertical arm was drawn back against tension in a vertical plane and used to propel missiles against fortifications or massed troops.

ONION PORTAGE, Alaska One of the earliest sites in north-west Alaska with occupation dating back to 13,000 BC, where the Akmak and Kobuk industries show more affinity with Asiatic chipped stone tools than with north American types. The sequence continues down to historic times, firstly showing links to the ARCHAIC tradition and latterly to the Arctic Woodland ESKIMO.

OPPIDUM [plural oppida] Name for large European fortified settlements (e.g. MANCHING and TRISOV), which developed during the last centuries BC into towns. They often covered several acres of ground, with streets and MURUS GALLICUS fortifications, and were self-supporting trading and marketing centres. Goods produced and exported included salt, specialized pottery, metalwork, coins and glass objects (e.g. the dog from Wallertheim). Some oppida, for example ENTREMONT, were centres of worship; most were political centres. Possible oppida in Britain, including STANWICK, CAMULODUNUM and Hengistbury Head (Hants.), are much smaller and less sophisticated than those on the Continent.

OPUS INCERTUM A Roman building material found from the 2nd century BC. Walls were constructed of a strong concrete of lime and rubble, studded on the outer face with stones of irregular shape and size.

OPUS RETICULATUM A Roman building material, mentioned by the architect Vitruvius and especially characteristic of the time of AUGUSTUS. It consists of pyramidal blocks of stone set in a wall with their points inwards, their square bases making a diamond-pattern.

OPUS SECTILE A Roman type of floor decoration similar to MOSAIC but composed of slabs of marble usually laid in geometrical patterns. It is mainly an Italian style but does occur in most other provinces. 1st–3rd centuries AD are the main periods of production.

OPUS SIGNINUM A type of Roman concrete made from sand, lime and crushed tile, giving a red colour and a fairly waterproof finish: for this reason it was often used in bath houses, for the floors of plunge-baths.

● **ORACLE BONE** Any animal bone, but especially the shoulder-blade (scapula) of oxen or deer, or sometimes tortoise carapace, used in China for making predictions. The bones were heated, holes often drilled, and the resultant cracks used as the basis of prophecies. Though mainly a feature of the SHANG period, where questions and answers were written directly on the bone and are examples of their early writing, divination with oracle bones has been noted earlier (but without writing) in the pre-literate LUNGSHAN period. This practice of using animal bones for predictions is known as 'scapulimancy'.

ORANIAN An Upper PALAEOLITHIC culture of north-west Africa, which succeeds ATERIAN industries in caves of Mediterranean coastal areas. The TYPE-SITE is La Mouilla (in Oran, Algeria). Later Oranian industries are contemporary with the appearance of the CAPSIAN.

ORDOSIAN CULTURE The northern zone of the Ordos region includes sections of modern Inner Mongolia, north Shensi and north-east Shansi, in China. PALAEOLITHIC tools have been found throughout the area since the 1920s, mainly in the region of the Yellow River and Sjara-osso-gol valleys, and form the Ordosian culture. By the Upper Palaeolithic, the stone industry included triangular flakes made from prepared cores, PEBBLE tools, BLADES and points, some of them with secondary retouch, SCRAPERS and BURINS. MICROLITHIC implements were to become especially prominent in the early post-glacial period (*see* GOBI MICROLITH). Human remains associated with the Upper Palaeolithic industries in the area include an incisor tooth, skull fragments, and a femur. Though the sample is small, the physical characteristics of Ordos man are modern in appearance. Animal remains indicate moister conditions than prevail today, providing a basis for hunting.

ORDOS MAN
see ORDOSIAN CULTURE

ORISSA, India There are rock-cut caves at Udayagiri and Khandragiri. *See* ROCK-CUT ARCHITECTURE.

ORTHOSTAT From the Greek words meaning 'standing straight'. Any large stone or MEGALITH erected into an upright position, frequently incorporated into the structure of a CHAMBER TOMB.

ORVIETO, Italy This site lies 25km north-east of lake Bolsena and overlooks the valley of the Tiber. The ETRUSCAN city flourished from the 6th to 4th centuries BC. Finds from within the city include many fragments of votive and architectural terracottas. The cemeteries (Cannicella and Crocefisso del Tufo) are notable for the regular alignment of architectural CHAMBERED TOMBS, forming streets. It has been suggested that Orvieto may be the true site of Etruscan VOLSINII, as the richness of its cemeteries indicates a site of importance.

OSEBERG, Norway A very well preserved VIKING ship of *c* AD 800 was found in a TUMULUS by the Oslo Fjord in 1903. It was made of oak, 24m long, 6m wide, with mast and sail as well as oars. Its lines are remarkably elegant and the carving of the prow is a superb example of Viking art. A timber burial chamber situated in the stern contained the remains of two women, one old and one young. The younger woman may be Queen Asa who died *c* 850. Like the GOKSTAD ship, Oseberg was well provided with luxurious grave goods: beds, pillows, eiderdowns, wall-hangings and looms along with astoundingly carved ▲ and decorated wooden carts, sledges, tent posts, beds, a chair and a hand-loom. There was also a RUNIC inscribed stave and four posts carved with grotesque human figures. This SHIP BURIAL is outstanding for the excellent wood preservation which has provided a marvellous fund of wood-carving, an artistic technique whose importance and achievement was only guessed at before this excavation.

■ **OSIREION, Egypt** The cenotaph of Sethos I (Dynasty XIX) at ABYDOS, symbolically reproducing the tomb of the god Osiris as well as corresponding to Sethos' chapel in the MEMNONIUM on the same axis in front of it. The British Egyptologist Margaret Murray discovered and began excavations of this unusual, partly-underground, building cut into the hillside. A descending corridor led to a stone platform on which stood ten pillars of granite, with a surrounding ditch which could be filled with water. The reliefs relate to the pharaoh's journeys in the afterlife.

■

OSIRIS The Ancient Egyptian myths surrounding the god Osiris make it hard to determine whether he was always a god of the dead and underworld to whom a legendary life on earth was attached fitting into the pharaonic cult, or whether his role in the afterlife was an extension of his earthly existence brought about by amalgamating with him necropolis deities such as the jackal-god Khentiamentiu. From references in Egyptian texts and rituals supplemented by the account given by Plutarch (AD 46–126) we can reconstruct the myth: Osiris was a predynastic ruler in the Delta – absorbing the god Anedity of Busiris (possibly a deified chieftain) into his own personality. His rule was just, and the country prospered until his murder was cunningly arranged by Seth his jealous brother (*see* HORUS). His body was thrown into the Nile and carried out of Egypt along the Mediterranean coast to Lebanon. ISIS, his wife, was the epitome of loyalty and devotion. She retrieved Osiris's body from Byblos only to have it stolen from her by Seth who cut it into 14 or 16 pieces then scattered them throughout Egypt. Undaunted, Isis helped by her sister Nephthys found nearly all her husband's body (we now have the four deities incorporated for political reasons into the totally unrelated cosmogony of HELIOPOLIS). She failed, however, to get back his penis which had been eaten by a fish (*see* OXYRHYNCUS). By magic she restored his body to its original shape (innovating MUMMIFICATION) and was even able to become pregnant by Osiris. He did not resume life on earth but became the god controlling the underworld, leaving his posthumous son Horus to avenge his murder and regain the throne of Egypt.

The pharaoh (*see* EGYPT society) was regarded as Horus while alive, but on dying became united with Osiris as ruler of the underworld. A gradual usurpation of royal prerogatives and a democratization of religious beliefs meant that everyone could hope for an afterlife united with the god Osiris. *See also* ABYDOS, BOOK OF THE DEAD, PYRAMID TEXTS.

●

OSSUARY A receptacle for human bones. The flesh of the corpse is removed or allowed to decay, leaving only the bones which are then interred in the ossuary.

OSTIA, Italy A town by the mouth of the river Tiber, and the port of ancient ROME. It was sacked by Marius and rebuilt by Sulla. CLAUDIUS had a new large harbour built opposite the ancient, silted one; this was enlarged by Trajan. The town was abandoned during the time of CONSTANTINE because of a malaria epidemic. Existing monuments include a good theatre and a number of temples (one to Mithras) as well as the colonnaded FORUM and the baths of Neptune.

OSTRACON [plural ostraca] A broken piece of pottery (potsherd) which is written on with a pen or brush and ink. The availability and cheapness of ostraca made them ideal for writing memoranda and records. Ostraca have been found at SAMARIA and ARAD and in Egypt. In Greece they were employed for voting.

▲

OSTROGOTHS Suffering from the effects of poor farming techniques and consequent population pressure, the Ostrogoths began to move westwards across the Danube into the Balkans in the middle of the 5th century AD. During the 470s and 480s they rampaged throughout the area and even threatened Constantinople. In 488 the emperor commissioned Theoderic, their greatest king, to rid Italy of Odovacer, a Germanic usurper of Imperial power. Many Ostrogoths remained in the Balkans, others accompanied him to Italy where Odovacer was deposed and Theoderic proclaimed king in 494. The Ostrogothic kingdom was very heavily Romanized and in close contact with BYZANTIUM. Much of their metalwork stems from the same Germanic inspiration as that of the FRANKS: radiate fibulae, CLOISONNE jewellery and bird fibulae are some of the common types. The influence of Rome is evident most clearly in the superb mosaic decoration of the churches in Ravenna. The Ostrogothic period in Italy ended *c* 560.

OXYRHYNCHUS, Egypt City on the Bahr Yusuf, sacred to the god SETH, especially under his form as the oxyrhynchus fish, devourer of the PHALLUS of Osiris. Beside architectural and sculptured fragments of HELLENISTIC style, its importance lies in the mounds of rubbish thrown out by the townspeople. Vast quantities of PAPYRUS fragments relating to the Roman period of Egypt's history have been recovered. They are still being studied by scholars and are giving valuable information on the administrative and financial organization of the country.

PACHACAMAC, Lurin valley, Central Coast of Peru A CEREMONIAL CENTRE dating at least from the Early Intermediate Period (*see* PERU) and later on in the Middle Horizon, evolving into a city of important status under the influence of the HUARI empire. At this time and after the fall of Huari, it may even have controlled a state in its own right as implied by the spread of its own distinctive polychrome pottery up into the north coast and down to the south. Although later declining in size and political prestige, Pachacamac remained important between 1476 and 1534 as the seat of the famous INCA oracle.

■ **PAESTUM, Italy** A Greek colony in ancient Posidonia, founded as a rival to nearby CUMAE *c* 700 BC. It is a good example of HELLENISTIC town-planning with its parallel streets and administrative and religious centre. The three temples, (all DORIC), the fame of Paestum, are the Basilica (mid 6th century BC), the Temple of Hera (mid 5th century BC) and the Temple of Ceres or Athena (late 6th century BC).

PAGUS A sub-division of the CIVITAS, the unit constituting the inhabitants of a small, usually rural area. Gaulish *civitates* are known to have been divided in this way for administrative purposes, and although there is no direct evidence it is likely that this was also done in Britain and elsewhere.

PAINTED GREY WARE A fine, well-fired, wheel-thrown ware found in India. It is dominated by two major forms, a shallow tray-bowl and a deeper bowl and is decorated with a limited repertoire of geometric designs. It is found in the area of later ARYAN settlement, and its dating corresponds with that of the later VEDIC Age. These facts suggest that it was the predominant pottery of the Aryans in the Ganges–Jamuna Doab *c* 1100–600 BC.

Upper Palaeolithic Sequence in W. Europe

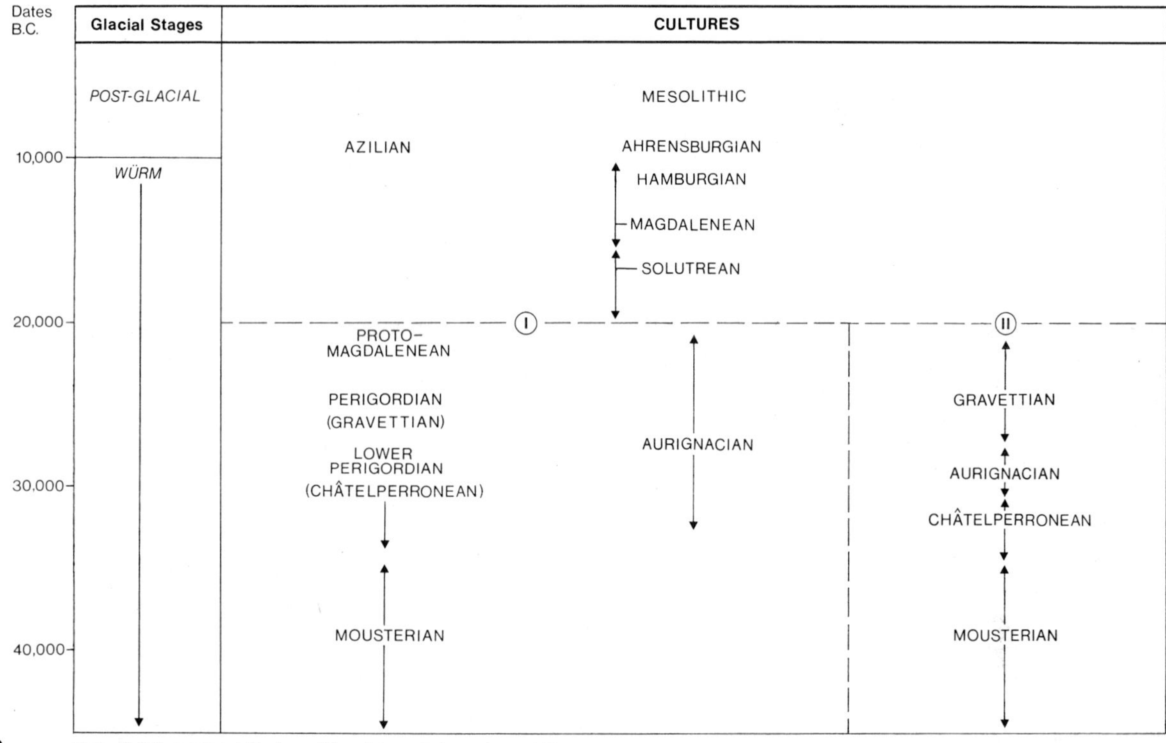

Note: Ⓘ & Ⓘⓘ represent the two different accepted versions of the sequence.

PALAEOBOTANY The study of the history of plants from fossilized and otherwise preserved material. Especially important to archaeology is the study of the early history and domestication of food crops. *See also* CARBONIZED GRAIN, CULTIVATION, GRAIN IMPRESSION, POLLEN ANALYSIS.

PALAEOCLIMATOLOGY The study of past climates, particularly important to archaeology because climatic changes may well have influenced cultural or economic developments. Such study also aids understanding of current climatic fluctuations. *See also* DEEP SEA CORE, GLACIATION, PLEISTOCENE, POLLEN ANALYSIS, POST-GLACIAL PERIOD.

PALAEOECOLOGY The study of ancient plant and animal communities as ecosystems. This subject utilizes information from many other fields, including archaeology, PALAEOBOTANY, PALAEOCLIMATOLOGY and PALAEONTOLOGY. The most detailed studies in this field concern late glacial and postglacial times; it is from these periods that information is most easily obtainable. *See also* GLACIATION, POLLEN ANALYSIS, POSTGLACIAL PERIOD.

PALAEOLITHIC [Old Stone Age] Lubbock (Lord Avebury) divided the Stone Age into the Palaeolithic and the NEOLITHIC in 1865, associating the Palaeolithic with what is now known as the PLEISTOCENE period. By 1895 the European Palaeolithic had been divided into 'epochs' (mainly by the Frenchman, Gabriel de Mortillet), most of them now recognizable as more restricted INDUSTRIES or CULTURES. These were the Thenaisian (or EOLITH epoch: both terms are now obsolete), CHELLEAN, ACHEULEAN, MOUSTERIAN, SOLUTREAN, and MAGDALENEAN. The Palaeolithic begins with the emergence of man and ends with the close of the Pleistocene, covering 3 million years. It is divided into Lower (characterized by CORE TOOLS), Middle (when FLAKE TOOLS are prominent), and the Upper Palaeolithic (with BLADE-and-BURIN INDUSTRIES). Throughout this period agriculture and the rearing of animals were unknown.

PALAEONTOLOGY A general term for the study of fossil remains of all ancient or extinct forms of life.

PALAEOPATHOLOGY The study of disease and injury in ancient individuals (animal and human). The nature of many diseases and accidental injuries can be determined by a study of the abnormalities displayed in the bone structure. In exceptional circumstances where body tissue other than bone survives (for example, MUMMIFICATION) more detailed pathological studies can be undertaken.

PALATINE, Rome One of the seven hills of ROME. It was the heart of the early city and has traces of Iron Age occupation. Under the empire it was the area where, in succession, imperial palaces were built by Tiberius, Nero and Domitian. It was also the site of several important TEMPLES, such as those of Apollo and Cybele.

PALENQUE, Chiapas, Mexico An important MAYA CEREMONIAL CENTRE of the Classic period (*see* MESOAMERICA) located in the forested foot-hills of the Chiapas mountains and best known for the fine stucco sculptures and bas relief carvings. One of the richest Maya burials was discovered here in the Temple of the Inscriptions, where the body was interred with quantities of jade and the face covered with a mosaic mask with eyes of shell and obsidian. The palace at Palenque is remarkable for its four-storeyed tower resting on horizontal wooden beams.

PALMIFORM COLUMN Classification of an ancient Egyptian stone column according to its capital which shows, in a fairly stylized way, the leaves of the date-palm tree. Conventional imitation in stone, of original wood and vegetation used in architecture – in this case, where the roof was supported by actual palm trunks. Good examples (cut from hard granite) of this column are found as early as Dynasty V in the funerary temple of King Sahure at ABUSIR.

● **PALMYRA [ancient Tadmor], Syria** A site in the desert mentioned in the KULTEPE texts and many later records. As an oasis it has long been a centre for nomads such as the AMORITES and ARAMAEANS. Its importance is primarily as a trading centre and in this capacity it expanded under Greek and Roman administration of Syria. Although it became a Roman colony in AD 212, Queen Zenobia and an indigenous army, probably descended from the Aramaeans, revolted in 271. The revolt was soon crushed and Zenobia captured. The most impressive building is the Temple of Bel (BAAL), founded in AD 32. The Palmyrenes ○ had an unusual practice of burying their dead in compartments of towers.

○

PALSTAVE A type of unsocketed AXE common in the BRONZE AGE of Europe.

▲ **PAN-P'O, China** The best excavated and described of all the YANG-SHAO Neolithic sites. Dated to approximately 4000 BC, this agricultural village in Shensi covers 70,000 square metres of loess land. The site consists of 46 semi-subterranean dwellings with wooden supports and walls of earth, and roofs of clay and straw. Packed earth formed benches and other interior features. Typical Yang-shao painted pottery was found, in addition to pottery bearing a variety of cord and mat impressions. The houses were surrounded by deep pits for storing grain. Special areas were used for pottery kilns and for burials. The dead were interred in extended positions, accompanied generally by three pots and sometimes beads or ornaments of shell; children were buried in urns near the dwellings. *See also:* LUNG-SHAN.

■ **PAN SHAN** A phase of the YANG-SHAO Neolithic period, located in the hills of east Kansu, China, considered to be probably somewhat later than more central Yang-shao sites. In the 1920s burial areas were unearthed. Along with the inhumed bodies were found characteristic sophisticated pottery, painted red and black and decorated with spiral patterns, or with 'death-patterns' in which the main lines of the design were surrounded by lines of small 'teeth'. Common are jars with a wide belly, two loop handles, and flat bottoms.

■

PANTHEON, Rome A temple for all the Gods, originally built by M. Vipsanius Agrippa, it was remodelled by HADRIAN AD 118–128 in the form of a rotunda and dome, 45m in diameter and height, with a rectangular colonnaded porch. The whole is built of concrete, faced with marble, limestone and stucco, and is the best surviving example of Roman architecture in that medium.

PAPYRUS A plant of the sedge family – a main feature of marsh landscape in ancient Egypt (especially in the Delta). It is now not found north of Khartoum, Sudan. Its versatility led to thorough exploitation – for boats, sandals, ropes, stools, domestic architecture (imitated in stone papyriform columns, e.g. of the STEP PYRAMID complex). Its predominant use was for writing-sheets which are attested in the Archaic period, but the first example with hieroglyphic and hieratic signs belongs to Dynasty V. A Royal monopoly under the Ptolemies, papyrus was only gradually replaced by parchment and paper (*c* 8th century AD).

In the process of manufacture, papyrus stem was cut off a short way above waterline, the rind peeled off and the pith sliced into strips laid each slightly overlapping to cover the area of sheet required, with top layer of strips crosswise to those below. The whole was beaten so that plant-juices welded fibres together and rubbed smooth with pebble. It could then be joined by adhesive to other sheets (longest series is the Great Harris Papyrus in the British Museum – over 37m) to form a papyrus-roll, an extremely portable means of communication and recording.

PARACAS CULTURE Named for the Paracas peninsula, south coast of Peru. It is divided into 10 phases, the first 8 of which show marked Chavín influence (*see* CHAVÍN DE HUANTAR) and span much of the Early Horizon Period (*see* PERU). Unlike Chavín, Paracas pottery is decorated in bright resin-based paints applied after firing. The last two phases are contemporary with the rich burial grounds of the Paracas Necropolis and Cavernas cultures where mummified bodies decked in finely woven and bright coloured textiles have been found, preserved in the prevailing desert conditions of the region.

PARIS, France Originally the capital of a Gallic CIVITAS, the Parisii, Paris was attacked by JULIUS CAESAR's deputy, Labienus, and destroyed; it was rebuilt as a Roman town but never became a major centre under Roman administration. It did however have the usual attributes of a Roman town in Gaul: an amphitheatre, a small theatre and at least three sets of public baths, including a very fine one of the 2nd or 3rd century AD, the vaulted roof of which is still intact. A temple to Mercury stood in Montmartre, and pillars of this can be seen in the fabric of the church of St Pierre.

PARTHENON
see ACROPOLIS

PARTHIANS A semi-nomadic people who migrated from the region east of the Caspian Sea *c* 250 BC into Iran and founded an empire independent of the Seleucids (who were previously established by ALEXANDER THE GREAT). Their capital was at Ctesiphon on the middle Tigris and from here their empire was loosely ruled. They constantly warred with Rome, halting her expansion in the east until in AD 226 they were finally taken over by the SASSANIANS.

● **PASSAGE GRAVE** Basically a CHAMBER TOMB at the end of a corridor or passage (hence the alternative name chamber-and-passage tomb) the whole covered by a mound. The tomb may be built of ORTHOSTATS and roofed with CAPSTONES (usual for the smaller tombs); built of drystone walling with a CORBELLED roof (*see* MAES HOWE); or cut out of the living rock (e.g. the cemetery of such tombs near Lisbon, in Portugal, at Palmella, of COPPER AGE date). The covering BARROW may be skirted with PERISTALITHS.

PATALIPUTRA
see PATNA

PATINA A change in the surface texture or appearance of an object caused by weathering or by chemical activity during burial. The most common examples of patinated materials are bronze, which acquires a green covering of copper salts, and flint, which may become opaque and white or brown on the surface following flaking. The extent of the patina cannot be used as an aid to the dating of an object, as the rate of patination is affected by a number of different factors and is extremely variable.

PATJITANIAN The central Javan regional variety of the Lower PALAEOLITHIC industry known as the CHOPPER–CHOPPING TOOL complex.

PATNA [ancient Pataliputra], India This city postdates the BUDDHA, who prophesied its future greatness: it became the royal city of MAGADHA from the mid 5th century BC. Archaeological remains include NORTHERN BLACK POLISHED WARE, terracottas, iron tools, punch-marked and cast copper coins and seals. A hall supported by 80 pillars and approached by a ramp fits Megasthenes' description of the MAURYAN hall of public audience. It bears a striking resemblance to ACHAEMENID halls, and it has been suggested that some Achaemenid craftsmen fled to India after their defeat by ALEXANDER. Megasthenes, who was Achaemenid envoy at the Mauryan court, also described the defences of the city: a wooden palisade pierced with loop-holes for shooting arrows. Due to exceptional conditions of preservation, part of this remains.

PATTERN WELDING A method of twisting bands of iron together and beating the resulting plait into a thin blade which was then edged with hard steel. The faces of the blade were often highly polished, giving a marbled effect. This technique was used during the Anglo-Saxon and VIKING periods to produce thin, straight yet very flexible swords.

PAULINUS Sent to NORTHUMBRIA in AD 625 as a missionary of the Roman Church, St Paulinus achieved the conversion of King Edwin in 627 when he baptized him at York. Moving to the royal estate at YEAVERING he continued his ministry to the Bernicians with great success. He was consecrated Archbishop of York, and Christianity seemed well established in the kingdom. The sudden death of Edwin in 632 checked this progress, and the country relapsed into paganism. In the second half of the 7th century the Celtic church made much progress in Northumbria from bases at IONA and LINDISFARNE.

PAZYRYK, USSR The site in the Altai Mountains, Central Asia, of 8 BARROWS or KURGANS. Permafrost and ice preserved organic remains: wooden furniture, and a ▲ waggon; fur, leather, and felt ornaments in the SCYTHIAN ▶ art style; embroidered silk from China; and woollen carpets. There were also metal objects. One goatskin pouch still contained cheese. 8 human corpses and 12 horse bodies were preserved by embalming; tattooing can

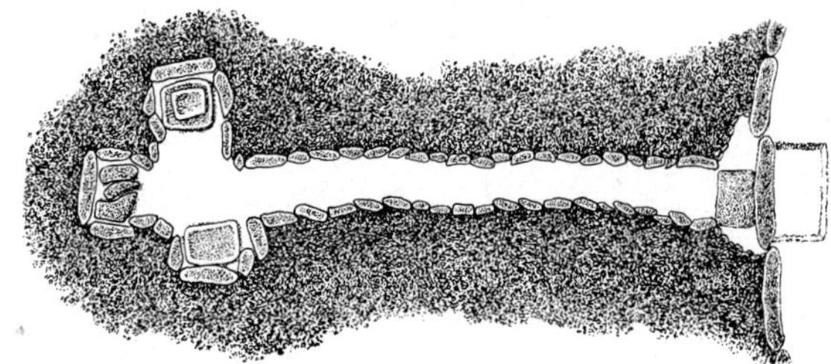

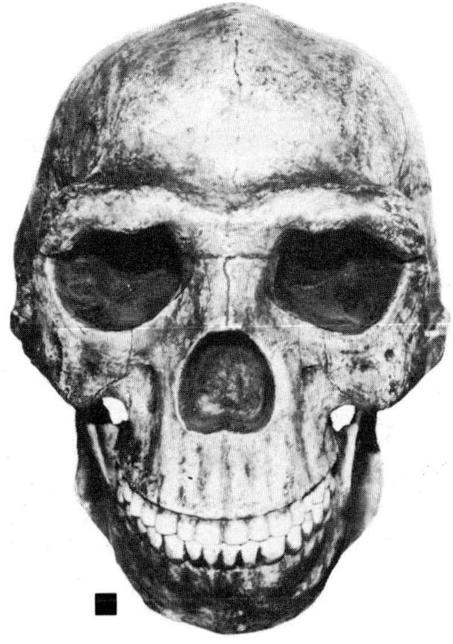

be seen on the skin of one male body. The barrows cover a period of 50 years at *c* 400 BC.

PEKING MAN The name given to specimens of HOMO ERECTUS found at CHOU-K'OU-TIEN, near Peking, China. The first was discovered in the 1920s. Dating to the Middle PLEISTOCENE, the Peking remains were formerly known as *Sinanthropus pekinensis* or *Pithecanthropus pekinensis*.

PELTA A decorative motif based on the shield of the Amazons, crescentic in form. *Peltae* are found in Greek, Etruscan and Roman art, and are an essential element in LA TÈNE art. They are common on Roman inscriptions.

PENNY Soon after the middle of the 8th century AD SCEATTA coinage was replaced throughout Anglo-Saxon England by the new silver penny introduced by OFFA. The new coin was larger and thinner with a standardized weight of 22 grains, and bore the name of the king and (generally) a portrait bust on the obverse, the name of the moneyer on the reverse. The stability and high quality of the silver penny was maintained through regular recall of the coinage and reminting every six years, a system which has provided much archaeological evidence since the coins can be dated very accurately. Because of the high standards controlled by the crown, the penny was a recognized medium of exchange from the Balkans to Scandinavia and, though modified in design, remained essentially unchanged until the 12th century.

PERGAMUM [modern Bergama], Turkey City impressively situated on a large hill in western ANATOLIA. Little is known of its early history, except that it was not Greek. When ALEXANDER's general Lysimachus was killed in battle in 281 BC his wealth was used by Philetaerus, the ruler of Pergamum, to build much of the city. Pergamum became capital of Asia Minor in 230 BC when its king Attalus defeated the CELTS. As Rome expanded eastwards, Pergamum became its ally and eventually bequeathed its territory to Rome in 133 BC. One of the two great libraries of the ancient world was situated here with 200,000 volumes. Among many remarkable buildings was the theatre and the altar of Zeus, which has been reconstructed in East Berlin.

PERIGLACIAL The term used to describe the area immediately surrounding an ice sheet. Permafrost conditions prevail in periglacial areas. During the summer the upper layers of soil may thaw, but the lower layers remain permanently frozen. Vegetation is non-existent nearest the ice sheet, but further away sparse plant cover of the tundra type may be found. *See also*: CRYOTURBATION STRUCTURE; ICE WEDGE.

PERIGORDIAN A typological sequence of Upper PALAEOLITHIC flint industries following the MOUSTERIAN. The Early Perigordian (or CHÂTELPERRONIAN) gives way to a series of Upper Perigordian stages, the earliest of which is called the GRAVETTIAN. The sequence ends with the arrival of the SOLUTREAN, whose origins are uncertain. The Perigordian is sometimes split stratigraphically by the AURIGNACIAN, thus requiring the two to have co-existed independently for several millennia.

PERIOD OF WARRING STATES The period during which internal warfare among the states of the Chinese

CHOU dynasty resulted in great disorder and political upheaval. Beginning some time during the 5th century BC, it lasted for the last few centuries of the Chou period, and ended with the unification of all China under the CH'IN Emperor, Shih Huang Ti, in 221 BC.

PERIPLUS OF THE ERYTHRAEAN SEA A work written in the later 1st century AD describing the trade routes through the Red Sea and the Indian Ocean. It appears in the main to be an accurate first-hand account. From BARBARICUM at the mouth of the Indus the writer travelled down the Gujurat coast to BROACH and on to the Malabar coast whence came pepper, pearls, ivory, silk cloth, cinnamon, diamonds, sapphires and tortoise-shell. Continuing, the Periplus describes ports on the east coast (*see* ARIKAMEDU) as far as the mouth of the Ganges. *See also:* MONSOON.

PERISTALITH From the Greek for 'stones standing round', and so a circle of standing stones or MEGALITHS. It usually refers to the ring of stones sometimes erected around the edge of the BARROWS of CHAMBER TOMBS.

PERSEPOLIS
see ACHAEMENID

PERSIAN
see ACHAEMENID

● **PERU** Before the widespread introduction of pottery 1800–1500 BC, there are six main phases of Preceramic cultural development beginning before 10,000 BC. The first three of these are represented by advanced stone age hunting and gathering economies. Men preyed on the mastodon, giant ground sloth and horse which all became extinct after 8000 BC. Deer and guanaco were hunted in the *lomas* (foothill) regions between the desert coast and the Andes mountains. Along the shore, early fishing communities lived off the rich sea and littoral resources. The latter periods 6000–1800 BC witness the emergence of settled communities along the coast (*see* HUACA PRIETA). At first they still depended on the rich marine environment, later on the cultivation of such crops as squash, lima and jack beans, chili, maize, guava and sweet potatoes, many of which were first domesticated in the highlands. The bottle gourd and cotton were cultivated before *c* 4000 BC, whilst in the Andes crops such as the grain quinoa and the potato were first domesticated along with the llama, alpaca and the guinea pig.

Following the introduction of pottery in the Initial Period, together with the development of the first irrigation systems, large settled communities developed, and societies became more complex with the emergence of the Peruvian Cultural Tradition. Peculiar to this tradition is the alternation of so-called Horizons and Intermediate periods. When one culture or art-style, either through military or religious influence, cuts across the local regional diversities to appear more or less uniformly over a wide area it is termed a Horizon style (*see* CHAVÍN DE HUANTAR for an example). The waning of such influence culminating in the return of different regional styles is termed an Intermediate phase (as in MOCHE and NASCA). Between *c* 1000 and *c* 200 BC, the first of these Horizon cultures (called Chavín, after Chavín de Huantar) unites much of both highland and coastal Peru with its distinctive art style. The Early Intermediate period, *c* 200 BC–*c* AD 600, follows the

Peru and Bolivia

Dates		N. COAST	C. COAST	S. COAST	HIGHLANDS	TITICACA BASIN
1500	*LATE HORIZON*	← INCA EMPIRE →				
	LATE INTERMEDIATE PERIOD	CHIMU				
1000	*MIDDLE HORIZON*		PACHACAMAC		HUARI	TIAHUANACO
500	*EARLY INTERMEDIATE PERIOD*	VICUS MOCHE		NASCA	RECUAY CAJAMARCA	OLDEST TIAHUANACO PUCARA
A.D. B.C.						
	EARLY HORIZON			PARACAS	CHAVIN DE HUANTAR	
1000	*INITIAL POTTERY PERIOD*					
2000		HUACA PRIETA & SIMILAR COASTAL SITES				
3000	*FIRST FARMERS*					
4000					AYACUCHO CAVES	
5000						
6000						
7000						
8000	*PRE-AGRICULTURAL HUNTING AND COLLECTING OF WILD PLANTS*	PATAGONIAN CAVE SITES (Fell's Cave, Palli Aike)				
9000						
10,000						
		PIKIMACHAY (Flea Cave) AYACUCHO – 14,000 B.C. or earlier				

break-up of Chavín with the return of distinctive regionalism, when many valleys had their local styles. Two important cultures of the Early Intermediate Period are the MOCHE of the north coast and the NASCA of the south coast region. The succeeding Middle Horizon Era, *c* AD 600–1000 saw the spread of the primarily religious influence of TIAHUANACO via the military intervention of a nearby city in the south highlands called HUARI. These Middle Horizon empires continued to influence the stylistic development of the later regional traditions long after the fall of the two cities (*see also* PACHACAMAC). The Late Intermediate Period beginning *c* AD 1000 witnesses the upsurge of several distinctive cultural traditions which incorporated much of earlier Middle Horizon elements into their own art styles. The most important of these was the CHIMU on the north coast who at one time rivalled the INCAS until conquered by the latter. The Late Horizon dating from the 15th century witnesses the expansion of the historically documented Inca empire which lasted until its conquest by the Spanish in 1534.

PERUGIA, Italy This ETRUSCAN city, 30km east of lake Trasimeno, was most prosperous towards the end of the Etruscan period, that is, 4th–2nd centuries BC. Its major monuments are the long stretches of city wall and the arched gateway, the Arco d'Augusto. Typical funeral vessels from the area are small urns of TRAVERTINE or terracotta decorated in relief.

PESCHIERA, Italy A Bronze Age settlement on the side of Lake Garda, northern Italy, dated to *c* 1250–1100 BC. It was a prolific site which yielded more than 2000 bronze, bone and pottery objects. The earliest European FIBULA, known as the violin bow or Peschiera fibula, is named after this site. Like the settlements of the TERRAMARA culture to the south of Peschiera, the sites in this area were probably established by URNFIELD immigrants from Hungary.

PETERBOROUGH WARE The elaborately decorated pottery of the British Later NEOLITHIC developing from the plainer round-based pottery of the earlier WINDMILL HILL culture, perhaps from as early as 3000 BC. All the sub-styles were found in the filling of the CHAMBER TOMB at WEST KENNET. *See also* AVEBURY, GRIMES GRAVES, GROOVED WARE, SILBURY HILL.

PETRA, Jordan A site magnificently situated in a deep valley east of the Wadi Arabah in southern JORDAN. It is identified with the Biblical Sela (Rock) which was an Edomite (*see* JORDAN) capital. The present name was given to the city by Greek merchants who visited it in the 1st and 2nd centuries BC when it was an important trade centre. At this time it was inhabited by the Nabataeans, a group of people of nomadic origin. Their relationship with the Edomites is unknown, partly because the remains found at Petra belong to the Nabataean period or later. The tombs cut into the sandstone cliffs around Petra are the most spectacular relics of the Nabataeans and of these the ● Khasneh (or Treasury) is one of the finest. In AD 106 Petra was annexed to the Roman empire and a temple and theatre from that period remain. Little is known of its later history except that the CRUSADERS had a fort there.

▲ **PETRIE, William Matthew Flinders (1853–1942)** One of the giants of modern archaeology. his early training was in British archaeology, and he only came into contact with

Egypt through reading a book on the Great Pyramid containing some extremely strange notions. In 1880 he went to survey the pyramids, and his career as an archaeologist began in earnest. His independent mind and character created difficulties at times, but for over 40 years his excavations produced the first systematic archaeological recording in this area. At Tell el Hesi (Palestine) in 1890 he demonstrated the importance of STRATIGRAPHY. A few years later at the cemetery of NAGADA he developed a method for dividing up the Predynastic period of Egyptian history, basing his system on the development and TYPOLOGY of painted and decorated pottery. This system (known as Sequence Dating) is, with recent improvements, still useful. In Egypt, Petrie also excavated at TANIS, Naucratis, Daphnae, Kahun, MEIDUM, AMARNA, MEMPHIS, ABYDOS and at the RAMESSEUM.

In 1893 he became Britain's first professor of Egyptology, at University College London.

Main books: *Diospolis Parva* (1901); *Arts and Crafts of Ancient Egypt* (1909); *Social Life in Ancient Egypt* (1923); *Seventy Years in Archaeology* (1931).

PHAISTOS, Crete A MINOAN palace, second only to KNOSSOS in importance. It is a courtyard palace with much the same layout as Knossos itself. Imposed on a NEOLITHIC and Early Bronze Age town *c* 1900 BC, it lasted until the THERA eruption of *c* 1450. After this it was replaced by Haghia Triada, 2km away, a smaller palace which had been founded *c* 1600 BC. Phaistos Disk is in an unknown script of HIEROGLYPHS. *See also* LINEAR A, LINEAR B.

PHALLUS The erect male organ, representations of which have been revered by many peoples at different times. The Greeks and Romans had a considerable array of phallic gods: the Greeks placed phallic effigies, or Herms, beside their doors, while the Romans preserved a very ancient stone phallus. In the CELTIC world, the phallic cult is linked with the cult of the severed human head, which when placed on a post represented also the phallus. Phallic pendants and amulets are common finds in Roman contexts: called *fascinae*, they were believed to be a protection against the evil eye. Phalli are also commonly found carved upon building stones or represented on pottery. In India the stone phallus or *lingam* is still a familiar sight. *See* CERNE ABBAS.

PHARAOH
see EGYPT society

■ **PHILAE, Egypt** Island just below Aswan, site of some of the finest architecture from Ptolemaic and Roman times. Its monuments have escaped permanent submersion in Lake Nasser. Philae was the major cult centre for the goddess Isis. Her Great Temple, begun under Ptolemy II, was still added to by Roman emperors. It incorporated a sanctuary for cult-image of Isis, colonnades with reliefs of Augustus and Tiberius in temple rituals, two pylons with Ptolemy XII depicted (unjustifiably) as a warrior-pharaoh. ▶

The Mammisi is a building with elaborate floral capitals and Hathor-heads on columns, celebrating Isis-Hathor and birth and upbringing of her son Horus.

The Kiosk of Trajan has exquisite floral architecture and is situated close to the Nile for Isis worship.

PHILISTINES A branch of the SEA PEOPLE who settled in south-west Palestine *c* 1150 BC. They are well known as the

enemies of the ISRAELITES; Goliath, who was killed in a duel by David (1 Samuel 17), was a Philistine. From *c* 1200 BC a form of MYCENAEAN pottery from Greece is found on sites in the coastal area of Palestine. It is thought that this type of pottery was brought by the Philistines, who therefore must have been Greek in origin. The anthropoid sarcophagus found at BETH SHAN is also thought characteristic of the Philistines. They had five main cities: Gaza, Ashkelon, Ashdod, Ekron, and Gath. Excavations at Ashdod have unearthed objects associated with religious practices in the Philistine levels. At Tell Qasile, near Tell Aviv, a temple probably used by the Philistines was found.

PHOENICIANS The Greek name given to the CANAANITES who inhabited the narrow coastal plain of Lebanon (Phoenicia) and Syria in the 1st millennium BC. Their geographic position forced them to become seafarers and traders operating from MESOPOTAMIA to Spain. Their name is thought to derive from one prized commodity which they produced and traded, the purple dye extracted from the Murex shell. To facilitate trading they established colonies around the Mediterranean, the most important CARTHAGE. In the west the Phoenicians were known as Punics. Because of their seamanship, they were often enlisted as mercenaries, using warships such as those depicted on an ASSYRIAN RELIEF. They were also often enlisted as craftsmen for building and manufacture. The carved ivory objects from Nimrud are some of their best work and include such subjects as a lion guarding the sacred tree. The development and diffusion of the ALPHABET is their greatest contribution to world culture. The major cities in Phoenicia – Arvad, Byblos, Sidon, and Tyre – always remained independent of each other and their rivalry at times led to conflict. Arvad and Tyre were situated on islands which provided security and good harbour facilities. When Tyre was captured by ALEXANDER THE GREAT *c* 332 BC he built a causeway to the island which still remains. Extensive excavation since 1930 at Byblos shows that the occupation of the site began *c* 5500 BC.

PHRYGIANS A people who inhabited the area of west central Asia Minor and are referred to by the Greeks and Persians (*see* ACHAEMINID). They succeeded the HITTITES *c* 1000 BC on the ANATOLIAN plateau and had their capital at Gordion. Excavations there since 1950 have revealed Hittite, Phrygian, Persian and Graeco-Roman occupation. The Phrygian kingdom seemed to consist of an INDO-EUROPEAN aristocracy ruling an indigenous agricultural population. In 547 BC Cyrus the Great took control of Gordion ending Phrygian independence. The royal road of the Persian empire which ran from SUSA to SARDIS has been found near Gordion. Burials were made in large TUMULI and rock-carved buildings were used as religious centres.

PHYLAKOPI
see CYCLADIC

PHYTOLITHS Silicified cells which occur in the structure of grasses and some other plants. Phytoliths, or 'grass opals', are in some cases identifiable to the genus from which they came. As they are often preserved, it is possible that their study could make a useful contribution to ENVIRONMENTAL ARCHAEOLOGY.

PI Circular discs carved of jade with a wide central perforation, at times with grain patterning or stylized

animal ornamentation; dating mainly from the SHANG and CHOU period of China. Neolithic examples have been found as well. Early texts describe their use by the emperor in performing sacrifices to heaven.

PICTS First called 'Pictae' (the painted people), thistribe living north of the ANTONINE WALL was given the name by the Romans in the 3rd century AD. With the SCOTS they made many raids on northern Britain in the 4th century encouraging the Roman government to bring FOEDERATI into England. the Picts remained independent until the 8th century when they were absorbed into DALRIADA. Little is known of them archaeologically; the only artefacts attributable to them are the symbol stones. These upright slabs of stone carved with complicated geometrical patterns, animals and human figures occasionally have OGAM inscriptions in an unknown language of Celtic origin. They may be memorials or possibly boundary markers. Later Pictish stones have elaborate crosses carved on them.

PILTDOWN, Sussex A village near Lewes where a series of famous finds were made in a gravel pit by Charles Dawson, a keen amateur archaeologist and geologist, between 1908 and 1915. The finds included the bones of extinct animals, EOLITHS, a carved bone 'knife' and a modern-looking human skull with an ape-like jaw – which was quickly acclaimed as the 'missing link' in the human evolutionary tree. However, in 1953 tests showed the whole affair to have been an elaborate hoax (*see* FLUORINE TEST). The skull was of HOMO SAPIENS, the jaw of an orang-utan suitably doctored to conceal its true nature; the bone 'knife' had been carved with a metal tool; and the animal bones were foreign to the site. The perpetrator(s) of the hoax remains unidentified.

PISÉ
see MUDBRICK

PITHECANTHROPUS
see HOMO ERECTUS

PITHOS [plural Pithoi] A large storage jar up to 1.5m high, used mainly in MINOAN times. It chiefly stored grain, olives, oil and wine, these being the important bulk goods. The magazines at KNOSSOS, PHAISTOS and MALLIA all held rows of pithoi for storing tribute.

△ **PITT-RIVERS, Lt-General (1827–1900)** The first field archaeologist in Britain to dig in a professional manner. Prior to his inheritance in 1880 of a large estate in Dorset, he had a distinguished career in the army. During this period he collected many objects of ethnographic interest, which became the basis of the Pitt-Rivers Museum in Oxford. His meticulous and complete excavations of sites on his estate were unparalleled in their thoroughness. He published privately the results in 4 volumes of *Excavations in Cranbourne Chase* (1898). Modern scientific excavation owes a great deal to his work.

PLAINS INDIANS People living in the Great Plains of north America down to historic times whose way of life descended earlier from BIG GAME HUNTING and ARCHAIC traditions. Economy revolved largely round the hunting of bison, trapping, fishing and collecting of wild plants, supplemented in some area by maize agriculture. Settle-

ments were permanent and semi-permanent villages with both pit-dwelling and timber and earth houses. Artefacts include chipped stone points, knives, spades and hoes of bison shoulder blades and pottery. In the early historic period, some of the Plains Indian tribes such as the Pawnee, Arikara, Cheyenne, Dakota, Blackfoot and Apache groups took up an almost exclusive nomadic life with their adoption of the horse to pursue the great bison herds.

PLATFORM MOUND In the Americas, these structures are closely allied to PYRAMIDS. They were built of either ADOBE or earth and rubble faced with stone and are common both in MESOAMERICA and South America. They were flat-topped and usually supported temples or important residences.

● **PLAZA** A major feature in the planning of Mesoamerican Preconquest CEREMONIAL CENTRES. Palaces, PYRAMIDS and temples were organized around an open court which served a predominantly ceremonial function. In the large centres such as TEOTIHUACAN and TENOCHTITLAN, there were several plazas.

PLEISTOCENE The present geological epoch, which began about 2 million years ago. The earliest phase of the Pleistocene is the VILLAFRANCHIAN, the start of which is marked by a general cooling of the northern hemisphere, and the extinction of many species of plants and animals associated with the preceding *Pliocene* period. In many parts of the world the Villafranchian is followed by a succession or GLACIATIONS which alternate with warmer periods of interglacials (during which the ice sheets retreated). The glaciations themselves were interrupted by shorter warm periods or interstadials.

Although the dates of most of the glacial and interglacial episodes are not accurately known at present, the last glaciation and its phases can be dated by RADIOCARBON techniques and the fluctuations within the glaciations have been studied in some depth. The period following the most recent withdrawal of the ice sheets (*c* 8000 BC) has been termed the *Holocene*. This term is no longer in use and the period is now properly known as the POSTGLACIAL or Flandrian. *See also* POLLEN ANALYSIS.

PLOUGH The most primitive type was the ARD, consisting of a wooden beam and a share to cut the furrow. Ards produced only shallow furrows and frequently, cross-ploughing had to be adopted (e.g. at GWITHIAN). Later a coulter was added to cut the soil vertically, while the share was fitted with side wings for undercutting. A mouldboard turned the slice over. In Europe these mouldboard ploughs were introduced in the late IRON AGE or Roman period. Wheels sometimes were added to Roman ploughs. *See also* DONNERUPLUND ARD, PLOUGH MARKS, PLUMPTON PLAIN.

PLOUGH MARKS Marks left in the subsoil by the point of a primitive plough. They normally appear as criss-cross shallow grooves filled with top-soil. Plough marks are usually found on sites where the original soil has been buried – either by a BARROW, as at South Street, Wiltshire or by LYNCHET formation – and therefore has survived despite modern cultivation. They have been found on a number of NEOLITHIC and later sites and are a useful indication of primitive ploughing techniques.

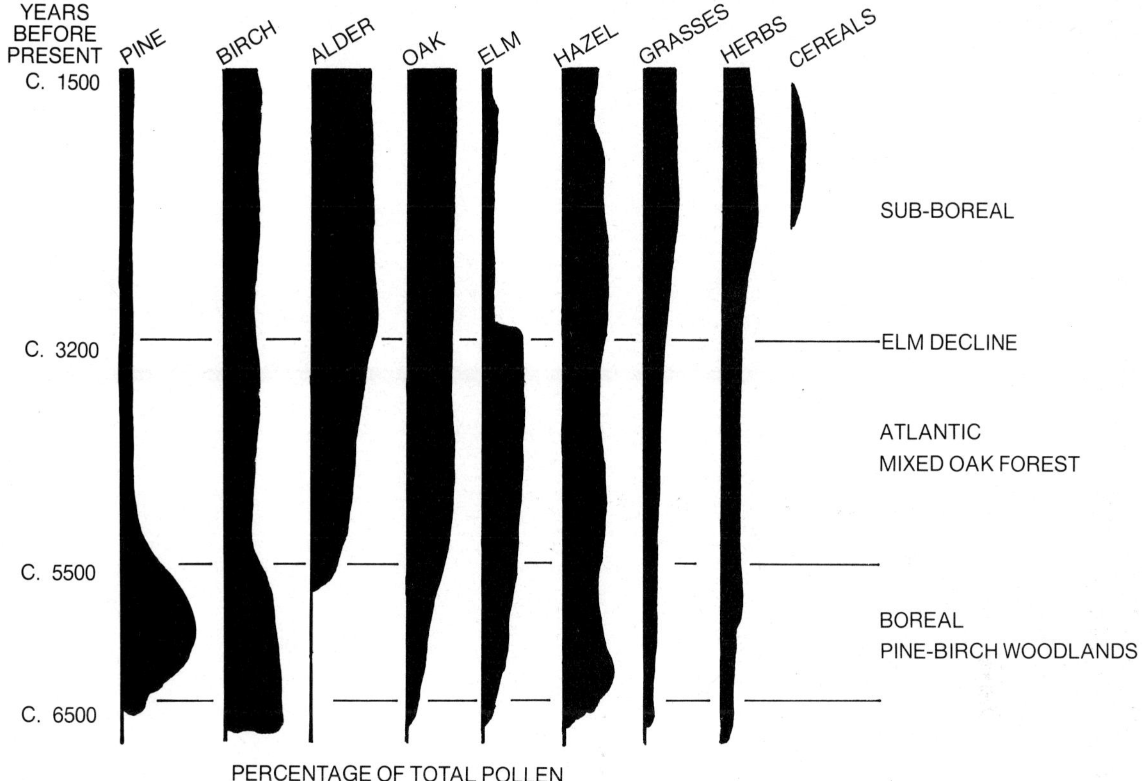

▲

PLUMBATE WARE A distinctive fine-textured pottery the surface of which gains a hard metallic sheen upon firing owing to the high percentage of iron compounds in the clay. The ware was first recorded from the Pacific side of Guatemala in the Late Classic period (*see* MESOAMERICA) whilst a different type of pottery of the same composition was traded widely in the early Postclassic and was a distinguishing feature of the TOLTEC period.

PLUMPTON PLAIN, Sussex A Bronze Age settlement consisting of a complex of banked enclosures with ROUND HOUSES and STORAGE PITS within them. Like ITFORD HILL, the village is associated with a CELTIC FIELD system. The earliest pottery is in the DEVEREL–RIMBURY tradition, and settlement continues into the Late Bronze Age, when exotic pottery was imported from France.

POCHTECA AZTEC professional long-distance merchants who also acted as spies and emissaries in tribute territories for the government in TENOCHTITLAN. Spanish colonial reports and Preconquest codices list some of the important products they traded for, which included bright feathers and skins from the tropical forest areas of Veracruz and Guatemala, jade, obsidian, serpentine and turquoise, cotton, honey, and cacao, which was important enough to be used as currency in most parts of Mesoamerica. Raw materials were converted by craft specialists into luxury items – featherwork, mosaics and jewellery to supply the court or for retrade as finished products.

▲**POLLEN ANALYSIS** All flowering plants produce pollen grains in considerable quantities. The grains are dispersed by wind and/or insects to fertilize other flowers of the same species. Vast numbers of the grains fall to the ground after release, and become incorporated in the soil, lake sediments or peat bogs. Because the outer skin of pollen grains is exceptionally resistant to decay, the minute grains (visible only under powerful microscope) are often preserved over many thousands of years, particularly in the favourable conditions of acidic soils or peat bogs. Many of the grains are identifiable to the species or genus from which they came.

Samples of material containing pollen for analysis are usually taken in a vertical series or column through the BURIED SOIL or peat deposit, thus enabling vegetational changes over a period to be studied. Analysis of the samples involves extracting the pollen grains from the soil or peat, identifying a representative number of the grains (usually 200 or more), and interpreting the information obtained. These results are normally expressed in diagrammatic form, in which the frequencies of the different pollen types are recorded as percentages of the total pollen present in each individual sample. The generalized pollen diagram illustrates this treatment of results; it also shows clearly how climatic phases and changes are observed in such analyses. In addition to climatic changes, pollen analyses have demonstrated man's effect on the vegetation, especially the effect of NEOLITHIC clearances (*see* ELM DECLINE, LANDNAM). Pollen analysis has proved the most useful tool of ENVIRONMENTAL ARCHAEOLOGY and its application to buried soils in the last twenty years has contributed much to our knowledge of prehistoric agricultural practices and the development of the vegetation we know today.

● **POMPEII, Italy** Founded in the 6th century BC as a native town, it was conquered by the Samnites and Romans, and became a Roman colony *c* 80 BC. The town grew into one of the richest in the Roman world until its complete destruction by ash-falls and volcanic mud from the eruption of Vesuvius AD 79. This event has created a unique opportunity for archaeologists to study and recreate the life of a Roman town of the 1st century. Remarkable evidence of the hasty evacuation of the town is provided by the bodies of dogs, old people and prisoners buried in the ash before they could escape, loaves of bread ready for baking, and so on. The buildings are well preserved, some up to the second storey, and the state of the wall-plaster and the sculpture make it essential to the study of Roman art. Most of the town, especially the richer parts and the municipal buildings, is now uncovered. Work continues on the undug portions but the problem of conserving vast numbers of finds makes progress slow.

PONT DU GARD, France Probably the most spectacular section of AQUEDUCT in the Roman world, it crossed the river Gard 50km from NÎMES. The aqueduct has been calculated to have supplied 400 litres of water per day for each person in the Roman town. The Pont consists of three tiers of arches, the lowest of which carried a road while the uppermost tier contained the channel which carried the water. The entire construction was built without mortar.

POSTCLASSIC [or Decadent Period]
see MESOAMERICA

POSTGLACIAL PERIOD This period started *c* 8000 BC when the ice sheets of the last GLACIATION had fully retreated. Extensive research has identified a number of different climatic episodes within this period. These phases are partly reflected in changes in sea level (*see* RAISED BEACH) and partly in vegetational changes observed through POLLEN ANALYSIS. *See also* PLEISTOCENE.

POTASSIUM–ARGON DATING This technique is based upon the fact that the radioactive isotope potassium-40 decays to calcium-40 and argon-40. The method can date any minerals which contain sufficient potassium. Following the formation of the mineral, a proportion of the radioactive potassium changes at a known rate into argon-40, and measurement of the ratio of potassium-40 to argon-40 in the specimen enables its date of formation to be calculated. Two principal causes of error inherent in this system are the presence of argon-40 in the mineral at the time of its formation, and the change of the potassium–argon ratio by chemical or physical means. Fortunately, microscopic examination of a specimen can usually determine whether it is suitable for dating. This technique is of limited use for the dating of purely archaeological sites. It has however been used at OLDUVAI GORGE, where strata containing artefacts are sealed by lava flows datable by this method. The age range for which this technique is most useful is 1–10 million years BC.

POTIN COINS British IRON AGE coins dating to 100 BC–AD 50, made of an alloy of tin and copper; the name comes from the French word for pewter, or white metal. Unlike other British coins, they were cast in moulds in strips and then separated. Each mould was used only once. They are derived from Gaulish potin coins and found particularly in northern Kent. They have no alphabetic inscription, but

only the design of a head on the obverse, and a stylized bull on the reverse. *See also* GALLO-BELGIC, SNETTISHAM.

POVERTY POINT Northern Louisiana, USA A group of large mounds and earthworks of late ARCHAIC or early WOODLANDS tradition in the lower Mississippi valley. The two principal structures are a massive earthen mound 200m long and 20m high, and an octagonal structure 1200m across with six rows of earthen ridges which possibly enclosed a large planned settlement of 600 or more houses. Radiocarbon dates span a period 1200–100 BC. A simple fabric-tempered pottery was produced.

POZZUOLANA A grey or red volcanic dust from the Roman Campagna between Rome and Pozzuoli, used to create a high-quality hydraulic cement. Its capacity to set under water and its durability enabled the construction of concrete harbour installations, bridge foundations and weather-resistant vaulted buildings.

PRECLASSIC [or Formative Period]
see MESOAMERICA

PROTO-GEOMETRIC
see GREEK POTTERY

▲ **PTAH** A major Ancient Egyptian creator-god with his main temple at the capital MEMPHIS, where he was known as 'Ptah, South-of-his-wall'. His appearance is austerely anthropomorphic – usually wrappped in a tight shroud with only his head (closely-shaven or wearing skull-cap) and hands visible. To satisfy the Egyptian predilection for gods as families and also to incorporate prominent neighbouring rival deities into the cult, Ptah was given as his wife the ferocious lioness-headed goddess Sekhmet who represented the scorchingly-destructive aspect of the sun. Their child was a symbol of flower-power, Nefertum, god of the lotus. By a natural extension the creator-god Ptah became the patron deity of craftsmen, identified by the Greeks with their smith-god Hephaistos.

Ptah's role in the creation of the universe, often called the 'Memphite Theology', was evolved at least as early as the Old Kingdom. Religious prominence was claimed for Memphis over its nearby rival sanctuary at HELIOPOLIS, not only by equating Ptah with Horus, Egypt's rightful ruler and by drawing attention to Memphis itself as a politically ideal focal point for northern and southern Egypt, but also by attributing to Ptah the creation of the gods comprising the Heliopolitan ENNEAD. Atum was described as the heart and tongue of Ptah. The most interesting feature is the metaphysical account of the creation where Ptah's heart devised the plan and his tongue repeated the words that brought all the gods and organized human society into being. *See also* APIS; MEMPHIS.

PUCARA, Bolivia An important CEREMONIAL CENTRE and town in the north Titicaca basin, at a height of 3800m, occupied for a brief 200 years during the beginning of the Early Intermediate Period (*see* PERU). With HUARI and TIAHUANACO, it was one of the largest cities of the time and is best known for its large ceremonial buildings of dressed stone and its monumental sculptures. Statues and STELAE were carved in low relief, often to represent human beings with trophy heads or serpents, fish and a variety of geometric designs. The pottery from the site is a distinctive black and yellow on red fired onto the vessel with motifs

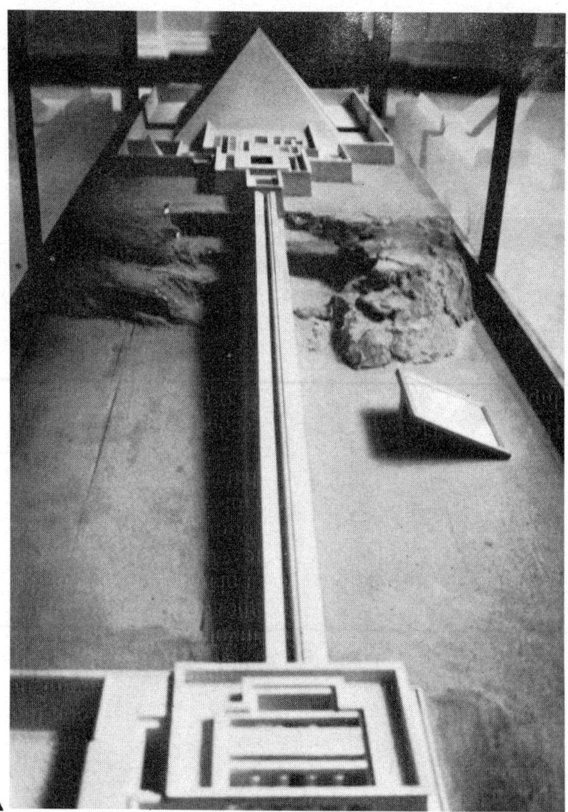

including cat faces and human heads. The similarity to the later Middle Horizon styles may suggest Pucara as the place of origin for the Tiahuanaco type, although the city had been abandoned some time before the rise of the empires of Huari and Tiahuanaco.

PUEBLO A distinctive type of settlement characteristic of the SOUTHWESTERN-tradition ANASAZI, HOHOKAM and MOGOLLON peoples of North America. Pueblos comprised large rectangular or semi-circular stone or ADOBE apartment-like houses with up to several hundred rooms and sometimes multi-storied. *See also* KIVA.

PUNCH-MARKED COINS
see INDIAN COINS, SILVER BAR COINS

PUNIC WARS A series of wars fought between 264 and 202 BC between the ROMANS and CARTHAGE, trading rivals in the Mediterranean. In the First Punic War the Romans gained control of Sicily and won initial victories at sea, but were defeated in Africa. In 241 BC the Carthaginians were forced to evacuate Sicily. An uneasy peace led into the ● Second Punic War in which Hannibal advanced across the Alps towards Rome, devastating much of Italy. He was recalled, and the Roman general Scipio won victories in Africa and Spain. Carthage was eventually crushed at the battle of Zama.

PUSHKALAVATI
see CHARSADA

PYLOS, Greece This MYCENAEAN site was first occupied in the early 2nd millennium BC. The principal remains date from the 13th century BC when the palace, attributed to King Nestor of the Iliad, was built. It is similar in plan to TIRYNS but was destroyed by fire *c* 1100 BC probably by the DORIANS. The excavated remains are housed indoors and include the throne room with depressions where the thrones themselves stood and many store-rooms for tribute. A large cache of LINEAR B TABLETS was found here and the discovery hastened the decipherment of the language.

PYRAMID [American] In the Americas, the pyramid is principally ceremonial, rather than funerary as in Egypt, and is constructed of ADOBE or earth and rubble faced with stone (*see* TEOTIHUACAN). It is square at the base, but is truncated in a flat surface rather than meeting in a point at the apex. Temples either of stone, adobe or wood and thatch were constructed at the summit and were reached by flights of steps up the sides.

▲ **PYRAMID COMPLEX [Egyptian]** It is essential not to see the Ancient Egyptian pyramid as an isolated structure, but as forming part of a funerary complex of temples and subsidiary buildings playing a vital role in the cult and afterlife of the pharaoh. The format (as in Dynasty IV) is basically:

(1) Pyramid – which developed out of the MASTABA into the step pyramid (Dynasty III) then to true pyramids (Dynasty IV). The motivation for the change was probably religious, the pyramid representing a stairway for pharaoh to join the sun-god. The shape also imitates in stone the pattern of the sun's rays breaking through clouds.

(2) Mortuary temple on the east face, for daily cult.

(3) Small pyramid off the southern face – of uncertain

purpose, but possibly to contain viscera, or (at ABYDOS) to represent a cenotaph tomb.

(4) Boat-pits cut into rock; two boats were for the king to accompany the sun-god by day and night. (*see* CHEOPS' PYRAMID).

(5) Causeway from the pyramid in the desert to the edge of cultivation.

(6) Valley temple at the end of the causeway, marking the entry to the whole complex. Here the king's corpse was ritually washed and mummified. *See also* DASHUR, GIZA, HAWARA, LAHUN, LISHT, MEIDUM, SAQQARA.

PYRAMID TEXTS [Egyptian] Not found in pyramids before the reign of Unas (Dynasty V). Inscriptions in hieroglyphs occur on walls of burial chambers and connecting corridors. The use of these kinds of inscriptions were a Royal prerogative during Dynasty VI (e.g. in pyramids of Teti, Pepi I and II, Queen Neith). Following decentralization of authority at end of Old Kingdom, inscriptions were appropriated by nobles and wealthy officials, forming by the Middle Kingdom a substantial portion of the corpus of funerary spells known as Coffin Texts.

The main purpose of Pyramid Texts was to safeguard the well-being of pharaoh in the afterlife and enable him to join the gods in the sky. The texts are a heterogeneous compilation of about 700 spells, incantations and lists of ritual necessities (e.g. festival perfume, cedar-oil). Some primitive elements antedate Dynasty V by many centuries, e.g. the spell describing how the pharaoh absorbs magical strength by eating inhabitants of the sky. Other spells illustrate the diverse and apparently conflicting nature of Egyptian religion – Osiris god of the underworld versus Re and Horus, gods of sun and sky. Pyramid Texts have been used to reconstruct beliefs and political events occuring before the beginning of Dynastic history.

QADESH
see KADESH

QUENTOVIC This town, which replaced Boulogne as the main port for Britain in the 5th–6th centuries AD, was the FRANKISH empire's main trading station on the North Sea. By the 7th century the quantity of goods passing through the port rivalled that at DORESTAD, and Quentovic also had a customs house and mint. Its precise location has been lost, though much documentary evidence suggests a site near modern Calais. Quentovic remained important despite the VIKING attacks of 842 and 900 and continued to trade with England, especially HAMWIH, until its harbour silted up and it was abandoned.

QUERN A stone for grinding corn into flour. The earliest were saddle querns, in which a rubber was pushed up and down a dished stone: these were used from the NEOLITHIC onwards. The rotary quern, in which one stone was turned on another, was in use in the 3rd century BC, and was introduced into Britain by the Romans. Stone for querns had to wear to a rough surface and yet be hard enough to prevent grit in the flour. Suitable stones were traded long distances. Nevertheless many skeletons of the prehistoric period have very worn teeth due to grit. Recent experiments have shown that rotary querns are more efficient if the handle is moved backwards and forwards rather than making a complete circle.

● **QUETZALCOATL** NAHUATL name for the plumed serpent deity common in MESOAMERICAN ideology from at least the Classic period. In various aspects he was the patron of priesthood and learning, god of self-sacrifice, life, the morning, the planet Venus and of twins and monsters. His associations with wind and rain (*see* TLALOC) go farther back into the Preclassic period (*see* MESOAMERICA; IZAPA) whilst during the Postclassic, TOLTEC period, he was associated with a priest-king ruler who was deposed and exiled. The appearance of feathered serpent images at CHICHÉN ITZÁ corresponds with this legend, when Kukulcan – Mayan for feathered serpent – arrived with a group of Mexican followers here. The legend stated that one day this god-king would return from the east to rule Mexico again.

QUIPU The INCA mnemonic device for keeping economic and political accounts. The information was coded by tying knots in strings of different lengths and colours.

▲ **QUMRAN, Israel** The site of a Jewish monastery on the north-west shore of the Dead Sea. Here *c* 130 BC–AD 70 a group of religious men, probably the Essenes, had a settlement and a water system which enabled them to live and regularly participate in ritual washings in spite of desert conditions. Excavations of the settlement found jars identical to those in nearby caves containing the famed Dead Sea Scrolls. The Essenes devoted themselves to copying Old Testament and Jewish writings. When their community was threatened they hid their scrolls in surrounding caves. The even temperature and constantly low humidity of the area preserved the scrolls until in 1947 a shepherd boy found the first of many scrolls in the caves.

RADIOCARBON DATING Over the last 30 years the radiocarbon method has become the standard – and not infrequently the only – means of dating prehistoric deposits. It can be applied to any organic matter, including wood, peat, bone and the charcoal ubiquitous in archaeological deposits. The theory on which the system is based is simple: the proportion of carbon-14 (the radioactive isotope formed by the action of cosmic radiation on nitrogen in the air) to that of the more common isotope, carbon-12, is fairly constant in the atmosphere and thus in living plants and animals. After the death of any organism the carbon-14 in its tissue decays at a known rate. The time that has elapsed since an organism's death can therefore be calculated by measuring the amount of carbon-14 remaining.

Since radiocarbon dating was first introduced in 1946, two major sources of error have been found in the system. First of all the original calculation of the HALF-LIFE of carbon-14 was too low (the 'Libby' half-life, named after the pioneer of radiocarbon dating W. F. Libby). However, no new figure for the half-life has been decided upon, and the old half-life of 5,568 years is still being used. Secondly, it was assumed that the ratio of carbon-14 to carbon-12 in the atmosphere was constant. However, recent dendrochronological work with BRISTLECONE PINE trees has shown that in antiquity there was a greater proportion of carbon-14 in the atmosphere. Both these sources of error led to underestimates of the age of a sample. Uncorrected radiocarbon dates generally suggest an object is less old than it really is; the older the object, the greater is the discrepancy. Fortunately the complexities of these and other sources of errors are gradually being understood, and it is becoming possible to correct radiocarbon dates.

Radiocarbon has made it tolerably cheap and easy to date much archaeological material previously difficult or impossible to date. Much exciting progress in archaeology in recent years has been made possible only through radiocarbon; among these advances have been the dating of the last glaciation and the early advances towards agriculture which followed it, and the discovery that the beginnings of agriculture, metal-working and other advances took place in northern Europe and elsewhere at a far earlier date than had long been thought.

As other dating methods are developed, radiocarbon is becoming less crucial, but it is certain to play a major part in archaeological dating in the future.

RAISED BEACH Evidence of the changing sea levels of the PLEISTOCENE remains in a number of areas in the form of raised beaches, formed when sea levels were higher than at present. Differences in sea level may be caused by melting or refreezing of the world's ice caps, or by movement of the earth's crust, resulting in depression or raising of certain land masses, which both occurred during the Pleistocene.

RAJAGRIHA [modern Rajgir], India Capital of MAGADHA, often visited by the BUDDHA. A series of elliptical structures may be the Jivikarama monastery of the Buddha but dating evidence is lacking. The rubble wall surrounding Old Rajgir is traditionally linked with the Śiśunaga dynasty who ruled from the later Vedic period (*see* GANGES CIVILIZATION) until the time of the Buddha when the wall was repaired.

RAJGHAT, India The earliest occupation, 800–600 BC, is characterized by BLACK-AND-RED WARE and by unpainted grey ware similar to PAINTED GREY WARE. This period sees the earliest iron and the beginnings of the massive brick rampart. In the following period, 600–200 BC, Black-and-Red Ware is replaced by NORTHERN BLACK POLISHED WARE; otherwise there is continuity in the material culture. Cast copper coins appear, and structural remains including RINGWELLS. A channel was dug connecting the rivers Ganges and the Varuna to encircle the site. *See also* ARYANS; GANGES CIVILIZATION.

■ **RAMESSEUM, Egypt** Western Thebes. Ruined funerary temple of Ramesses II ('the Great', Dynasty XIX). The battle of KADESH which Ramesses II fought against the HITTITES, nearly at the cost of his own life, is recorded in scenes on First Pylon (68m wide). A ruined granite statue of the king stood originally 17m high, weighing over 1000 tonnes. Statues of Ramesses as pillars, identify the pharaoh with god of the dead OSIRIS. The large hall has only 29 out of 48 pillars standing. Processional boats with images of Amun, the King-god and family were taken to rooms at rear of temple. Vaulted brick buildings (storehouses and stables) surround temple. Papyri and OSTRACA are evidence that a scribal academy was attached to the temple.

RAMS HILL, Berkshire A site overlooking the Vale of the White Horse, which was occupied in the Early Bronze Age with a cattle compound and developed into one of the earliest British Bronze Age settlements. By the DEVEREL–RIMBURY period, *c* 1000 BC, ROUND HOUSES, pits and 4-post structures (probably barns) were built, and a palisaded rampart and ditch surrounded the settlement. Occupation continued into the Late Bronze Age and the enclosure was enlarged in the Iron Age to form an early HILLFORT.

RAPIER A weapon (like a long dagger) used for thrusting; introduced into Britain from the Continent in the Middle Bronze Age, before the earliest URNFIELD swords. These Bronze Age rapiers were riveted to their handles.

RAS SHAMRA
see UGARIT

RATHS Name of very small HILLFORTS in south-west Wales. Of 580 hillforts in Wales, 230 are less than 0.4 hectares in area. The earthen ramparts were faced with timber and contained a cluster of ROUND HOUSES with granaries, usual in IRON AGE settlements. In Ireland the term is used of small fortified farming settlements. Sometimes (as at TARA) within hillforts.

● **RAVENNA, Italy** A Roman town at the head of the Adriatic, first known as the station for the Roman fleet, along with Misenum near Naples. However, it is best known as the Imperial capital in the late 4th century and 5th century AD and for magnificent late Roman wall MOSAICS, especially in the Mausoleum of Gallia Placidia, the apse of San Vitale and the two Baptistries.

RECUAY Name given to an art style which flourished during the latter part of the Early Intermediate Period (*see* PERU) in the Callejon de Huaylas in the northern highlands of Peru. Designs represent stylized cats, condor birds, snakes and geometric figures, sometimes interlocking, and all in two- or three-colour NEGATIVE PAINTING in dark grey pigment against a white background. Shapes of the pottery show links to the North Coast MOCHE and Far North Coast VICUS styles and include STIRRUP SPOUT, figured BRIDGE AND SPOUT and tripod bowls, often with modelled figures of humans or animals. Monumental stone sculpture is rigid and angular showing warriors with maces and shields.

RED FIGURE
see GREEK POTTERY

RED HILLS Low mounds of ashes and red burnt clay found along the coasts of Essex and Lincolnshire, dating to the Iron Age and Roman period. They contain BRIQUETAGE, consisting of broken clay pans and ovens for the evaporation of sea water in salt-making processes, and also containers into which the salt was packed.

▲ **REISNER, George Andrew (1867–1942)** One of America's greatest Egyptologists. A Harvard law graduate, he went to Berlin where he studied Egyptology. Fieldwork for University of California showed his capabilities, and he was appointed Director of the important Nubian campaign to survey threatened monuments in 1907–9. From 1914 till his death he was professor of Egyptology at Harvard.

A meticulous attention to detail, and the comprehensive nature of his site records meant that his excavations were more documented than previous work done in Egypt. His publications of his digs show a high standard of archaeological recording. Failing eyesight and the gigantic task of turning his fieldnotes into published reports left much work incomplete.

His work in Nubia revealed much information on the pyramids of the kings of Dynasty XXV and of MEROE. In Egypt itself his most exciting work was reconstructing the gilt furniture from the tomb of Hetepheres, mother of

CHEOPS. He also excavated the Valley Temple of MYCERINUS and many private tombs at GIZA.

Main books: *Mycerinus* (1931); *Development of the Egyptian Tomb down to the accession of Cheops* (1936).

RELIEFS A form of decoration regularly used, especially in the Near East, on rock walls, STELE, tablets and in furniture. Instead of being drawn or painted, objects are carved so that the picture is clear when lit obliquely.

REMANENT MAGNETISM
see ARCHAEOMAGNETISM

■ **REPOUSSÉ** A method of decorating bronze, silver or gold work, used particularly in the European BRONZE and IRON AGES, e.g. for this gold bowl from Kuloba. Using a punch the design was raised from the back so that it stood out in relief.

RESISTIVITY SURVEY A system used to investigate archaeological sites prior to excavation, based upon the fact that the resistance the earth offers to the passage of an electric current depends upon the moisture content. Resistivity survey, therefore, involves the use of an instrument to measure the resistance of the soil. Readings taken over a site are plotted on a plan. Anomalies in the resistance of the soil may indicate walls, floors, ditches or other features. The results obtained from such an investigation are not always reliable, however, as anomalies may be caused by natural changes in the soil type.

RETOUCH The scars left by 'secondary working' on a chipped stone implement. *See* FLAKING.

RHODES, Greece This town, first laid out in 408 BC by Hippodamus of Miletus, is one of the earliest examples of a regular town plan. It was large, growing to hold some 80,000 people. The Colossus, a gigantic statue and one of the Seven Wonders of the ancient world, stood in Rhodes. It was later melted down. Visible remains include the stadium, the odeion (covered small theatre) and other municipal buildings.

RICHBOROUGH, Kent The landing point of the Roman invasion force in Britain in AD 43 and subsequently a major port of entry to Britain. Roadside development was the characteristic of early occupation and the main feature was a massive four-way TRIUMPHAL ARCH with bronze ornamentation which commemorated the conquest of Britain. However, in the 3rd century the arch was turned to a useful purpose, becoming a probable signal station defended by triple ditches. By the end of the century it was razed to make way for the stone-walled SAXON SHORE fort, the main feature to be seen today.

RIDGE AND FURROW An arable technique in which ridges are deliberately formed using a mouldboard PLOUGH. In Britain this technique was first employed in late Saxon times though most of the ridge and furrow that can be seen today is of later medieval date. The purpose of ridge formation is not always clear; it may have been either to delimit individual land holdings or to drain wet low-lying land. In the latter case the furrows were drainage channels and the tops of the ridges were cultivated.

RIGVEDA An Indian religious work not committed to writing until 14th century AD, but strictly remembered and

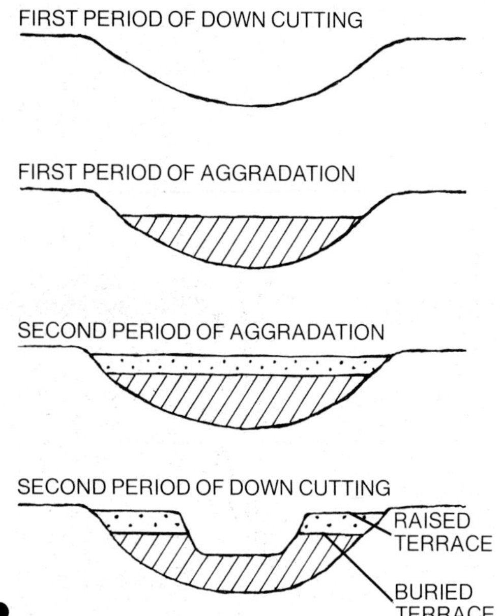

●

▲

handed down from the time of its composition before 1000 BC. It portrays a nation of horse- and cattle-keepers, growing wheat, barley and later rice, using light chariots and practising both inhumation and cremation. *See* ARYANS, VEDAS.

RILLATON, Cornwall An INHUMATION burial under a BARROW, famous for the gold cup of WESSEX culture date (*c* mid 2nd millennium BC). It has been cited as proof of trading contacts between Britain and MYCENAE, where other examples occur in the Shaft graves.

RINGWELLS Wells and soakage pits lined with pottery rings, frequent in sites of the GANGES CIVILIZATION of north India. A less common variant is the well lined with superimposed baseless vases.

RINYO-CLACTON
see GROOVED WARE

● **RIVER TERRACES** The PLEISTOCENE saw numerous sea level changes due to melting ice or uplift of the land. During the periods of high sea level, rivers deposited sediments in the valleys (termed aggradation). During periods of low sea level the rivers cut down through such sediments. Alternate aggradation and down-cutting led to the formation of river terraces, which are left standing above the present river level or buried beneath later sediments. A number of methods are used to date such terraces and their contents. Certain PALAEOLITHIC sites, such as SWANSCOMBE, have been roughly dated from the river terraces within which they occur.

RIXHEIM
see SWORD

▲ **ROCK-CUT ARCHITECTURE** The earliest Indian rock-cut cave temples were excavated in the Barabar hills by AŚOKA for the Ajivika sect. Aśoka's grandson also dedicated temples in the Barabar hills, including Lomas Rishi dated 220 BC. A Jaina group of temples is known in Orissa, dating from mid 1st century BC to AD 100. These contain small STUPAS and monasteries. They were similar in design and symbolism to Buddhist examples. The majority are Buddhist. Over 700 are known in the western Ghats, their main distribution area. Both the temples (CHAITYAS) and the monasteries (VIHARAS) are carved out of the living rock, often basalt which is soft when first exposed but later becomes extremely hard. The origins of these rock-cut monuments lie in wooden architecture; numerous imitative features reflect this wooden ancestry. The early period of rock-cut architecture in the western Ghats dates between mid 1st century BC and 2nd century AD. Probably the earliest site is Bhaja which consists of rock-cut stupas, viharas with small arcaded cells and stone benches, and a chaitya hall with octagonal columns and a pegged-on wooden façade with a hanging balcony supported on four pillars. The interior of the chaitya was also once decorated with much woodwork. The chaitya hall at Kondane, of similar date, also had a wooden façade. This site also had an unusual vihara with a pillared hall.

An early chaitya hall at Ajanta also had a wooden façade but the façade of the other early example was of carved stone with a sun window and gallery. The Ajanta temples are unique in being decorated with frescoes showing JATAKA STORIES; these foreshadow the famous later

▲

frescoes which date after AD 450. Narsik is contemporary with early Ajanta: here the interior of the chaityas begin to be elaborated in stone instead of wood.

Bedsa and Karle show further elaboration. Each site is preceded by a large entrance in which stand decorated pillars. Beyond these are the elaborate façade and an inner screen leading into the chaitya. The interior pillars have a vase-shaped base, bell-shaped capitals with sculptured human and animal groups above them. At Karle the stupa in the temple is decorated with wooden umbrellas and imitation balustrades.

The latest group in this early series is at Kanheri near Bombay, where the complex of viharas, chaityas, single cells and cisterns are interlinked by rock-cut steps. A cemetery of brick stupas contains the ashes of dead monks.

ROCKER STAMPING A technique of pottery decoration in which a tool (often a shell edge) is rocked back and forth over the wall of the vessel before it is fired. This process produced a zig-zag line.

ROCK SHELTER A rock overhang. Many have evidence for human activity on their floors often in the form of domestic debris buried under successive roof falls. Deeper cave-shelters provide important STRATIGRAPHIC sequences for PALAEOLITHIC archaeology.

ROMAN ROADS From their inception, most notably with the building of the Via Appia in 312 BC, Roman roads were built as military communication and supply routes. Under the Republic their construction and repair fell to magistrates as army commanders; later, the emperors established an elaborate system of staging-posts and carriage of imperial staff and goods, placing the burden of repairs and maintenance on the towns.

The army surveyors who laid out the main roads usually chose as direct a route as possible between two points, with diversions for natural obstacles. Materials used depended on what was available and varied from volcanic blocks around Rome to the flint gravel of southern Britain. Construction depended on the type of terrain being traversed and the importance of the road. In mountainous country directness and width were often sacrificed for easy gradients and economy; this was especially so with the Apennine routes in Italy and in areas like Wales. As the army consolidated expansion into flat country, such as most of Gaul, the type of construction became more standard. There were main roads with widths of 27m and 19m between drainage ditches; an earthen embankment (agger) in the centre carried the road surface. This was usually rubble covered with gravel or some fine aggregate. The foundations varied from desert areas, where little was needed, to marshy areas, where massive causeways might be used as with the Via Appia, south of Rome.

Roman roads and bridges provided fast, easy routes for the movement of troops and information, without which the empire could not, by virtue of its extent, have been administered or defended; for trade, however, road transport always took second place to the cheaper sea transport.

ROMANS Much of the early history of the Romans is shrouded in myth and tradition. The traditional date of the foundation, *c* 753 BC, is borne out by archaeology, for by the 8th century BC a cluster of huts belonging to Latin farmers existed on the Palatine, one of the seven hills of

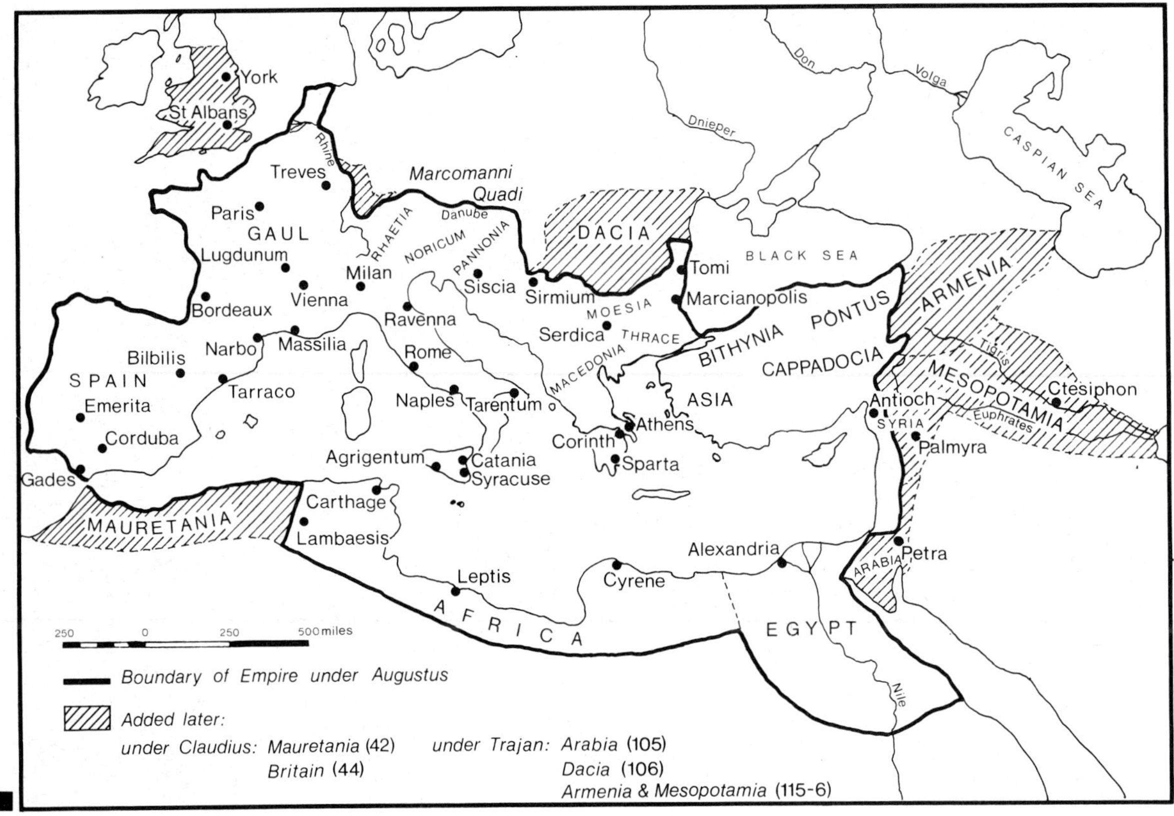

Rome; a little later the tribe was joined to that of the Sabines. During the 7th century BC Rome came under ETRUSCAN domination, and from this period one can speak of the City of Rome: the Etruscans ruled directly from *c* 550 BC. Despite this, the Romans maintained their individuality, and during the period of Etruscan rule Roman social and political institutions began to develop.

In 474 BC the Etruscans suffered a great defeat at the hands of the Greeks at Cumae, withdrew from Rome and Latium, and their dynasty was expelled from Rome. The Romans then began the period known as the Republic. The new constitution allowed for rule by two annual consuls, backed by numbers of other magistrates. Former magistrates became members of the important consultative body, the Senate. During the mid 5th century the law was codified for the first time.

During the Republican period, the Romans gradually became the dominant people of Italy. Already, during the period of Etruscan domination, they had occupied the lands of (among others) the Sabines, the Volsci and the Aequi: after a 10-year siege they also took the Etruscan city of Veii. Expansion was halted *c* 390 BC by an invasion of Gauls and the sack of Rome, but by 343 BC Rome conquered the Samnites in Italy. By the early 3rd century, Rome was mistress of Italy and an important Mediterranean power and after the PUNIC WARS with Carthage, took control of the province of Spain. By the 2nd century BC Rome had also dominated Greece.

At home, the Romans were far from settled; internal conflict led to reform. Between 90 and 82 BC were fought the Social Wars against neighbouring Italian tribes, culminating in the dictatorships of Sulla and Pompey. The final breakdown of the Republic came in the struggle for power between JULIUS CAESAR and Pompey, who was finally defeated at Pharsalus in 48 BC.

Caesar was succeeded by the first emperor, AUGUSTUS. The early years of the empire were of territorial expansion: Caesar had already carved an empire in Gaul and Germany, and this was increased. Roman COLONIAE sprang up in Africa, Spain and Gaul as well as Britain after the time of CLAUDIUS. The empire was expanded eastward into Asia under Trajan and HADRIAN.

The empire was often under pressure from expanding barbarian tribes on its frontiers; in the mid 2nd century AD German tribes pushed into northern Italy. Barbarian pressure ultimately dominated Roman policy. Before the end of the 2nd century, the Roman empire was on the wane. The decline may be seen in the debased silver currency, such as the DENARIUS and the ANTONINIANUS.

The 3rd century was a difficult period, because of economic problems and the increasing barbarian pressure (Germanic tribes devastated much of the empire). There were problems in the East and savage wars against the PARTHIANS. Some recovery followed the establishment of the TETRARCHY, and the social and economic reforms of Diocletian. At this time the centre of the empire was moved to CONSTANTINOPLE by CONSTANTINE the Great.

The shadow of destruction loomed over the empire in the 4th century. The Romans no longer controlled their borders, and desperate measures were taken to improve defences, especially against the GOTHS, HUNS and PERSIANS. In 410 the Visigothic king Alaric seized and sacked Rome: this was the real end of the Western Empire, and soon barbarians moved into Gaul, Germany, Spain, Britain, north Africa and Italy.

The Eastern Empire, governed from Constantinople, was under less pressure; perhaps, too, it was better ruled. It held out, a shadow of its former glory, until its destruction by the Ottoman Turks in 1453. Some recovery of the empire in the West was made by JUSTINIAN and his general Belisarius, but this was short-lived.

Even after its fall, a pride in Roman greatness was shared even by those who had destroyed it – who often adopted Roman institutions and considered themselves the heirs of the Roman tradition. After the Constitutio Antoniniano of AD 212, Roman citizenship was extended to all in the empire, and men would say with pride *Civis Romanus sum*. The Romans had dominated and ruled the world. Roman law had been generally administered, and apart from some sadistic excesses and the religious persecution general before CONSTANTINE, that law was fair: most Roman administrators had genuine ideals which they tried to practise. Roman artistic achievements were considerable, both in sculpture and architecture and in music, literature and philosophy: the epic verse of Vergil or the erotic poems of Catullus stand today as masterpieces, and Roman VILLAS are full of beautiful MOSAICS and sculpture. Public services and roads, fair laws and just administration were enjoyed by all.

In a sense, the Western and Eastern Empires live on as the Roman Catholic and Greek Orthodox churches.

ROME A city which developed at the lowest easily bridged point of the Tiber in a safe inland position, with access to the sea and central Italy via the river. Initially it was a small settlement dominated by Etruscan kings, but from *c* 500 BC, as the seat of the Senate, it expanded from its centre on the PALATINE hill as the influence and trade of the Roman republic grew in central Italy. By 300 BC the FORUM, which had been a swamp, was drained and surrounded by temples of Saturn, Castor and Pollux, and Concord, the Senate house and many houses, small shops and alleyways on the seven hills. During the 2nd century BC several BASILICAS were built there for business transactions.

During the Augustan period (27 BC–AD 14) the city spread from the hills to include the Campus Martius, the old army training ground. From then on the emperors channelled much of the wealth generated by the empire into embellishing their capital and power base. An elaborate administrative bureaucracy was developed for the city, with special emphasis on building programmes, water supply, fire control, food supply and policeing. Marble and limestone were used widely to beautify buildings, and concrete walls and vaults were used more and more to build, not only the massive spatial public buildings of the empire, such as temples, basilicas, AMPHITHEATRES, BATHS, THEATRES, but also the purely functional domestic and commercial buildings, such as Trajan's market complex. For several hundred years the wealth of the empire sustained an urban population in Rome of about 1 million people.

Although sacked on several occasions, especially in the 5th century AD, Rome survived as a major city until an Eastern Roman general cut her aqueducts in the early 6th century, although CONSTANTINE's shift of emphasis to CONSTANTINOPLE had already detracted from her pre-eminent position.

ROQUEPERTUSE, France A religious centre near MASSILIA and ENTREMONT. Like Entremont, it had a sanctuary with niches for human skulls, here cut into a

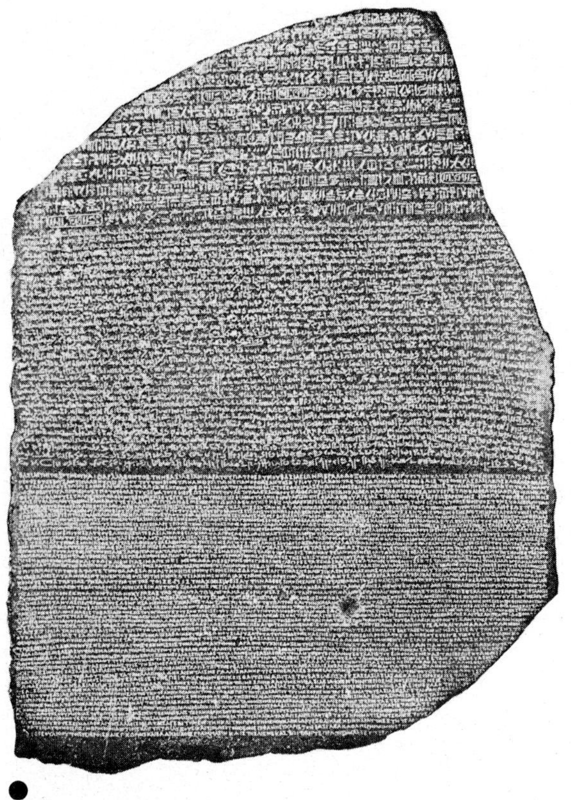

●

▲

○

portico of three stone pillars. In front of this were set five cross-legged stone figures. Above the portico was a fine double Janus head, carved in the round. The sanctuary was desecrated at the time of the Roman conquest (123 BC), to judge by the BALLISTA bolts on the site.

● **ROSETTA, Egypt** Arabic town on an older site on western branch of Nile delta. In 1799 the French army dug up the Rosetta Stone, and handed it over to conquering British forces in 1801. The inscription, in three scripts, was written in 196 BC acknowledging benefactions of Ptolemy V Epiphanes to Egyptian temples. The top section gives a decree in Hieroglyphic, the centre in Demotic – both scripts used for Egyptian language. The lower section was in Greek, for the benefit of the rulers and large mercantile community. The importance of this bilingual inscription was immediately realised, and it provided a key for the decipherment of Egyptian hieroglyphs, knowledge of which was lost in about the 3rd century AD. *See* CHAMPOLLION.

ROUND HOUSE From the Early BRONZE AGE until the Roman conquest, the traditional house in Britain was round. This is in direct contrast to the Continent where houses were long and rectangular. Although a few rectilinear buildings existing in the IRON AGE could be called houses, most are only 4- or 6-post structures, more suitable as granaries or barns. *See also* GLASTONBURY, LITTLE WOODBURY, MAIDEN CASTLE.

▲ **RUNES** A Germanic writing system with angular shaped characters derived from Mediterranean scripts which had been adapted to wood and stone-carving techniques. The oldest Runic alphabet was devised *c* AD 200 and consisted of 24 letters. Known as the *Futhark*, it was later reduced to 16 letters. Runes were thought to possess occult powers which could be released by the initiated for good or evil, and there are many inscriptions on weapons, jewels and tools. During the VIKING period many rune-stones bearing long inscriptions were erected in Denmark and Uppland as personal memorials to the dead, and these provide much information about trade, travel and social structure.

RUPAR, India Situated in the north Punjab, Rupar was occupied in the late Harappan period (*see* INDUS CIVILIZATION). After a hiatus, the site was reoccupied *c* 1000–700 BC by the makers of PAINTED GREY WARE pottery, who have left only a little iron and a quantity of pottery and bone points. The succeeding NORTHERN BLACK POLISHED WARE occupation, 500–100 BC, had a 4m wide enclosure wall and RINGWELLS and saw the introduction of silver coins and seals inscribed in the Brahmi or early Indian script. *See also* ARYANS; GANGES CIVILIZATION.

RYUTAIMON POTTERY
see FUKUI CAVE

■ **SABRATHA, Libya** A Roman town of CARTHAGINIAN origin. Well-known for its Roman Imperial theatre which has preserved the backdrop or *scena* behind the stage and which is the basis for most reconstructions of theatres elsewhere. Much of the rest of the town is visible.

○ **SAIS, Egypt** Ancient regional capital on western arm of Nile delta. Sanctuary of the war goddess Neith, whose temple impressed Herodotus. Its ruins cover a large area

but, as elsewhere in the Delta, the dampness of the ground makes excavation relatively unrewarding because of poor conservation.

Following the ASSYRIAN invasions, Sais was the capital for a new united Egypt during Dynasty XXVI. This Saite period, as well as modelling its art on traditions producing masterpieces in previous dynasties, opened up Egypt to the influence of Greek culture. The city lost much commercial importance to Alexandria but kept its religious prestige.

SAI YOK, Thailand Rock shelter and cave site in west central Thailand yielding a sequence of remains beginning with large CHOPPER TOOLS, HOABINHIAN material (especially unifacially-flaked pebbles) and extending through Neolithic (e.g. polished stone tools, pottery) to historic periods (exemplified by a Buddha figure). The only bronze in a prehistoric setting was a tiny bell. Animal remains, relatively rare, were exclusively of now living species and included bear, tiger, rhino, pig, deer, mountain goat; numerous mussel shels were found as well. The excavator interpreted the Neolithic remains as demonstrating contact with the LUNG-SHAN farmers of north China, a view that has been challenged.

SALAMIS, Cyprus A site near ENKOMI on the eastern coast of CYPRUS. Since 1965, tombs from the 8th and 7th centuries BC have been excavated. In these tombs were not only large jars and vases, but the remains of chariots and skeletons of horses which had been sacrificed. The wooden structure of the chariots had decayed, leaving impressions in the soil which when filled with plaster gave a cast of the original. Most of the buildings that remain at Salamis were built by the Romans after 58 BC although excavation would find earlier structures. A gymnasium and theatre are the main Roman remains.

SALONAE
see SPLIT

SALONIKA, Greece A town of Macedonian origin but mostly of the Roman period, whence the town plan, the FORUM and BASILICA. It was a centre from the 4th century BC, with an Imperial palace, CIRCUS and TRIUMPHAL ARCH to Galerius. Several important 6th century early BYZANTINE mosaics are to be found there.

SAMARIA, Israel A site in central Palestine founded by King Omri in 880 BC as the ISRAELITE capital (I Kings 16:24). Excavations have uncovered the palace King Ahab built for his wife Jezebel. This is called a 'house of ivory' in I Kings 22:39 because of the ivory the Phoenician workmen used in decorating it. Ivories found at NIMRUD were very similar to those at Samaria and were taken there when ASSYRIA captured Samaria *c* 722 BC. Samaria became an important city in the Greek and Roman period when HEROD THE GREAT constructed a temple to Augustus, a theatre, a stadium, a colonnaded street and fortifications. A collection of OSTRACA from *c* 800 BC illuminates ISRAELITE administration.

SAMARRA
see HASSUNA

SAMBAQUI Brazilian coastal SHELL MIDDENS dating from pre-agricultural human occupation in the 6th millennium BC and continuing to the late prehistoric period.

●

▲

● **SAMIAN WARE** A Roman red-glaze pottery in the tradition of ARRETINE WARE, and manufactured in huge specialized potteries, mostly in Gaul. This is the most important Roman pottery industry in Europe, and is especially useful for dating archaeological features. At its best, the slip is a glossy red, the colour and texture of sealing-wax, but it can be a dull and porous orange. As with Arretine ware, forms are standardized (with individual numbers) and are influenced by metal vessels. Decoration is usually moulded, or more rarely incised or slip-trailed: good early examples often have carefully worked-out scenes, although apprently random figures, animals and other devices are more common. Early varieties were made in south Gaul, especially around LA GRAUFESENQUE; by the second century the centre had shifted to LEZOUX in central Gaul; late Samian was made in TRIER. The ware was exported all over the Western Empire.

SAMPUNG BONE INDUSTRY The MESOLITHIC tool industry of east Java, of which GUA LAWA is the TYPE-SITE. The industry is characterized by its high proportion of bone tools, notably spatulas and awls. Often found with these are bifacially-trimmed arrowheads, shell scrapers, and flakes and blades.

▲ **SANCHI, India** Excavation suggests that an early brick STUPA was built contemporary with an AŚOKAN PILLAR there. By *c* 100 BC this stupa was encased in a stone envelope and surrounded by a railing. The four gateways were probably built 50–25 BC.

SANDIA CAVE, New Mexico, USA The TYPE-SITE for a kind of tanged spear point of lanceolate shape with a slight shoulder on one side of the base. They were found stratified below the FOLSOM type and are probably contemporary with CLOVIS points, dating to 12–8000 BC.

SANGOAN A central African PALAEOLITHIC industry, roughly contemporary with the European MOUSTERIAN. Its stone industry was suited to a forest environment.

SANKISA, India Scene of the BUDDHA's descent from heaven, marked by an AŚOKAN PILLAR with elephant capital.

SAN LORENZO TENOCHTITLAN, Mexico Located on man-made earth and clay platform raised 50m above the plain in southern Veracruz. San Lorenzo has a long history, starting *c* 1500 BC, and is important for the emergence of the OLMEC tradition. There are five main periods; the first two *c* 1500–1250 BC mark the construction of the earthen platform and some of the ceremonial buildings, although few of the smaller artefacts show marked Olmec influence. The third phase *c* 1250–1150 BC is demonstrably Olmec, with the production of the first typical figurines in fine white clay and the initiation of monumental stone sculpture. The climax of the site occurs in the fourth period *c* 1150–900 BC, when most of the ceremonial buildings and many of the stone monuments were built. The fifth phase *c* 900–700 BC sees the mutilation and burial of the great stone carvings and the destruction of the Olmec civilization at the site. Soon afterwards, the site is deserted until its final reoccupation much later in the early Postclassic period (*see* MESOAMERICA) *c* AD 900 by Villa Alta groups using PLUMBATE and Fine Orange (*see* TOLTEC) pottery. *See also* LA VENTA.

SANTA ISABEL IZTAPAN, Mexico Mammoth-kill site on the shores of old lake Texoco. With the remains of two mammoths, killed in a swamp by early hunters of the BIG GAME HUNTING tradition, were found flint blades and spear points, together with obsidian scrapers and knives. The site is dated to the Upper Becerra geological formation of *c* 8000 BC and is thus contemporary with finds at TEPEXPAN.

SAQQARA, Egypt Village giving its name to a necropolis on the west bank of Nile, just upstream from Cairo. It contains funerary complexes and burials covering all the important periods of ancient Egypt's history – from the First Dynasty mastaba-tombs on the escarpment through the Old Kingdom (Zoser's pyramid and tombs of nobles) the New Kingdom (tomb of the pharaoh Horemheb, rediscovered 1974) down to the last burials of the sacred Apis bull under the Ptolemies. *See also* ARCHAIC MASTABAS, SERAPEUM, STEP PYRAMID, STEP PYRAMID COMPLEX, TOMB OF TI.

■ **SARDIS, Turkey** A site in western ANATOLIA which was the capital of the Lydians. As little is known about the early history of the Lydians it is not possible to confirm the tradition that Etruria in Italy was colonized by them *c* 800 BC. About 100 years later a period of prosperity began in Sardis under King Gyges. It ended in 546 BC when the Persian king, Cyrus the Great (*see* ACHAEMENID) captured Sardis and its king, Croesus (who is credited with the invention of coinage). The wealth of Sardis came partly from alluvial gold from the river Pactalus which runs by the city. After the Persian invasion, Sardis continued as an important city until it was sacked by the Turks in AD 1401. Excavations and reconstruction began in 1910 with the Temple of Artemis. Recent excavations have revealed a gymnasium and associated buildings dating to the 2nd century AD.

SARNATH, India Scene of the BUDDHA's first sermon. A small temple of 3rd century BC date and an AŚOKAN PILLAR mark the site.

SARSENS Hard sandstone blocks which are found scattered over some areas of southern England and northern France. They are derived from Eocene (*see* PLEISTOCENE) sediments, the softer parts of which have been eroded away. These large blocks were used extensively in such famous prehistoric monuments of Wiltshire as AVEBURY, STONEHENGE and West Kennet LONG BARROW.

SASSANIANS A revolt led by Ardashir Papakan, a feudal lord, in about AD 226 against the PARTHIANS established this new Persian dynasty in Iran. The Sassanian kings were constantly at war with the Romans in the west, defeating Valerian in 260 and reaching the Bosphoros in 618. Iran was invaded by Emperor Heraclitus in 628 and the Sassanian empire was finally ended by the Moslems in 651. Their great building and town-planning skills can be seen in the cities of Firuzabed and Bishapur. Because of their position between Rome and China, they influenced the silk trade and adopted Chinese motifs in their own art.

SAUVETERRIAN A MESOLITHIC industry of south-west France and adjacent areas, which succeeded the AZILIAN and is characterized by a strong MICROLITHIC component, and the general lack of axes. In Britain a 'Horsham culture' was recognized in the Surrey and Sussex Weald, which was compared with the industry at the Sauveterrian TYPE-SITE of Sauveterre-la-Lémance, south-west France. The only relationship between the Horsham culture and the true Sauveterrian seems to be in a similar response to a comparable environment.

SAXON The Saxon phase of English history, which lasts from *c* AD 400 to the Norman Conquest in 1066, is subdivided into periods. The Early period runs from the settlement of England *c* 400 to the arrival of the Augustinian mission in 597. The Middle Saxon period embraces the establishment of England, the movement of political power from NORTHUMBRIA, to MERCIA and finally to WESSEX, where ALFRED achieved unification of the kingdoms in the late 9th century. The Scandinavian period overlaps the Middle Saxon period since the first VIKING raiders arrived in 793. Danish settlement spread rapidly and was recognized in 890 as the DANELAW.

SAXONS One of a group of Germanic tribes which first settled in England as FOEDERATI and later took part in the migrations of the 5th century AD. Their continental homeland was in north Germany, north of the River Elbe. Before coming to England there was much cultural contact with other tribes such as the ANGLES, FRISIANS and JUTES. According to BEDE the Saxons settled the areas now known as Essex, Sussex, Middlesex and Wessex. Cremation predominates in early cemeteries in these parts, and the distribution of saucer brooches in south east England and the Thames valley seems to bear him out.

SAXON SHORE A late Roman defensive system designed to protect the eastern and southern coasts of Britain against sea-borne raiding. The germ of the system was laid by CARAUSIUS, who constructed the forts at RICHBOROUGH, Lympne and Portchester, more likely as a precaution against possible Saxon raiders than against a force of loyal Romans. The system was extended by Constans, when Britain was recovered by Rome, the fort of Pevensey being a likely addition at this time. The office of Count of the Saxon Shore may have originated in this period. With the reorganization of Britain's defences under Count Theodosius *c* AD 369, signal stations in Yorkshire (and one near London) were added to the system, and Portchester was abandoned. *See* CLASSIS BRITANNICA.

SCAPULIMANCY
see ORACLE BONE

SCARAB Popular term for Egyptian ovoid seal, the convex upper section designed (with variable degrees of accuracy of legs, wings and head) as a sacred beetle, manifestation of the sun-god. Scarabs first occur after the Old Kingdom and were manufactured in countless thousands down to the Roman period – not forgetting numerous quantities faked in modern times. Main materials were glazed steatite, limestone, FAIENCE. Scarabs were worn as rings or on bracelets. Bases can show abstract designs (e.g. interlocking spirals), signs for good luck, or inscriptions including:

(1) Titles of government officials (mainly Middle Kingdom).

(2) Royal names – not always contemporary with pharaoh, e.g. name of Tuthmosis III (Dynasty XVIII) became amuletic for centuries after his reign.

(3) News bulletins promulgating pharaoh's acts throughout Nile Valley and Middle Eastern principalities. Amenophis III (Dynasty XVIII) during first twelve years of rule published commemorative scarabs about marriage to Tiye, cattle and lion hunts, arrival of Middle Eastern princess for his harim, construction of artificial lake for queen Tiye to sail on.

(4) Spell from the BOOK OF THE DEAD to help pass the ceremony of the Weighing of the Heart in the Underworld, scrutinizing the deceased's past life. These heart scarabs were placed on breast of corpses.

SCEATTA A silver coin struck when the Anglo-Saxons reintroduced silver coinage into England in the 7th century AD. The designs for these small coins were derived from Roman, Merovingian and northern sources and did not bear the king's name but an animal design. They are smaller and thicker than the later pennies and valued at one twentieth of a shilling. The earliest sceattas were struck in Kent *c* 625, though they were also produced in Mercia and Northumbria slightly later. *C* 730 the circulation peak was reached with sceattas minted in both England and in FRISIA with similar purity, weight and design. During the 8th century sceattas were common silver currency throughout the continent and have been found in places as far apart as Scandinavia and the south of France.

▲ **SCHLIEMANN, Heinrich (1822–87)** After retiring from a successful business career at the age of 41, Schliemann devoted himself to his boyhood dream – of excavating Troy. In four campaigns between 1871 and 1887 he excavated the small TELL of Hissarlik which he identified as Troy. Here he found seven successive cities which belong mainly to the period between 3000 and 1100 BC and two which belong to Greek and Roman times. Debate has surrounded the identity of the city, Troy, described in Homer's *Iliad*; some believe it to be the seventh city Schliemann found, others think it is the sixth, and yet others believe Homer's Troy never existed. Troy illustrates the development of civilization in Anatolia between 3000 and 1000 BC. Troy II for example is a strongly fortified city containing a MEGARON palace in which treasures of gold were found. Schliemann is equally well remembered for his excavations at MYCENAE in 1876 where he found great treasures in six shaft tombs. He also excavated at Orchomenos in Boeotia in 1880, and TIRYNS in 1884–5. He was the first archaeologist to recognize STRATIGRAPHY in a TELL and he set a high standard of recording of his work. Main books: *Mycenae* (1878); *Ilois* (1880).

SCOTS Together with the PICTS, the Scots attacked the Roman province of Britain in AD 367. At this time the Scots lived in Ireland and raided the west coast of Britain for slaves and plunder. In the early 4th century they may have established settlements on the coast of Wales, but *c* 450 Argyll was colonised and the kingdom of DALRIADA founded.

SCRAMASAX The single-edged long knife with a grooved blade and asymmetrical tang often found in male graves of the MIGRATION PERIOD through to VIKING times. Scramasaxes vary in length from 0.75–7.5m and were all-purpose tools usually carried in a sheath on the thigh suspended from the belt by small bronze loops. The finest examples have inlaid decoration in copper, bronze or silver.

SCRAPER A general term describing stone FLAKES or BLADES which have been RETOUCHED along the side, or more commonly, across the end. They are believed to have been used for removing fatty tissues from animal hides.

◄ ■ **SCYTHIANS** An INDO-EUROPEAN people on the Eurasian steppes north of the Black Sea, best known for their art, with its emphasis on animals, in metalwork and in perishable materials such as were found at PAZYRYK. The Scythians were described in classical writings as nomads, perhaps as head hunters. They were very dependent on the horse. Their burials were under TUMULI, often with horse sacrifices. They were an aggressive people, probably driving the CIMMERIANS south of the Scythian area in the 8th century BC. There is some evidence of Scythian raids on western European CELTIC communities, and perhaps even raiding in Egypt in 611 BC.

SEAL A small object made from a hard substance with a design carved into it. There are two basic types, the stamp seal and the cylinder seal. Cylinder seals are rolled to give an impression. They can be threaded onto a cord and worn around the neck or worn as a signet ring. Their usual purpose was to impress a softer substance such as clay to indicate authenticity or ownership and so they played a very important role in the organization of the ancient world. *See also* INDUS CIVILIZATION.

SEGOVIA, Spain A Roman town known for its aqueduct which still supplies water to the inhabitants. It is almost 1 km long, of 128 double arches and some 30m in height. It is probably of Augustan date (*c* 0 BC/AD).

SEINE–OISE–MARNE [SOM] CULTURE Originally defined on the basis of a group of final Neolithic–Copper Age MEGALITHIC TOMBS in the Paris Basin, SOM remains, strictly speaking, a local type of GALLERY GRAVE concentrated in an area rather than a full archaeological CULTURE. The SOM tomb, which has a porthole slab (a PERISTALITH with a large hole in the centre) at the entrance to the burial chamber, is also found to the west in Britanny and to the north in Belgium, southern Sweden and Westphalia. Similar rough, flat-bottomed pottery is found again in Britanny, in west France, Denmark and Switzerland (HORGEN culture). The origins of the SOM tombs are composite, and continued outside connections are demonstrated by the presence of traded copper, amber and GRAND PRESSIGNY flint.

SELJUKS The ruling family of the Turkman tribes who invaded western Asia in the 11th century AD. The tribesmen, who found plunder and holy war irresistible, moved westwards, establishing an empire including Iran and Mesopotamia by AD 1063, and Syria and Palestine by 1092. After defeating a huge Byzantine army at Manzikert in 1071, they added Anatolia. The strength of the empire was based in the religious and political training of officials which emphasized Persian rather than Arabic tradition. Family quarrels, revolts and attacks from central Asians (the Karakitai), CRUSADERS and Arab tribesmen left only Anatolia (the Caliphate of Rum) in Seljuk control by AD 1200. Although their empire was embattled with their BYZANTINE, Crusaders and Ayyubid neighbours, the sultans developed and administered Turkey well. Their capital, Konya, was endowed with many fine buildings. Although Konya owed allegiance to the Mongols after 1243 and became part of the Ottoman empire in 1467, the religious mystics who were established in their monastery in Konya by the Seljuk Sultans wielded much political power until this century.

SEMITIC Originally the adjective applied to a group of languages having the characteristic that almost all verbs, nouns and adjectives derive from words composed of three consonants. Arabic, Ethiopic and Hebrew are three modern examples. The term is also applied to people who speak these languages. In the BIBLE they are said to be the descendants of Shem, one of the sons of Noah. A group of ▲ Semitic princes from Syria are depicted in the illustration, an Egyptian tomb painting of *c* 1400 BC.

SERAPEUM, Egypt Underground burial chambers at SAQQARA for a series of Apis bulls, sacred to Ptah of Memphis. MARIETTE's work revealed an avenue of sphinxes (Dynasty XXX) as well as HELLENISTIC statues. In 1851 he reached the entrance to the bull-burials. Underground galleries with granite and basalt sarcophagi (some about 70 tonnes) flanking a central aisle. The earliest remains of Apis bulls from the New Kingdom were mummified, in wooden coffins. Later burials in catacombs range from Dynasty XXVI to the end of Ptolemaic period. From dedicatory inscriptions have come vital historical information on the dates of rulers. In 1970 EMERY discovered the badly-ruined Iseum – burial chambers for the cow-mothers of the Apis bulls. Much investigation remains to be done.

SESKLO, Greece A NEOLITHIC settlement at Souphli, near Larissa in Thessaly. The houses of the Middle Neolithic were built out of MUD-BRICK in the Near Eastern fashion, but already the MEGARON type of building was present. Sesklo pottery, painted with distinctive geometric designs, is found over much of Greece at this period, the 5th millennium BC.

□ **SESTERTIUS** A Roman coin first struck under the Republic, when it was a silver coin. Under the revised monetary system of AUGUSTUS, it became a brass coin of about one Roman ounce (25g) in weight.

SEVERED HEAD One of the most widespread cults in the CELTIC world. To the Celts, the head not the heart was the source of life. Numerous detached heads in the CELTIC ART style have been found, and there were sanctuaries at, e.g. ENTREMONT and ROQUEPERTUSE. Stories about severed heads abound in the later Celtic literature from Ireland, Scotland and Wales. Taking human heads as trophies was also common in Peru, where depictions of severed heads appear in the art of CHAVÍN, PARACAS, and NASCA.

SEVERUS, Septimius Lucius (AD 146–211) A native of LEPTIS MAGNA in north Africa, a town which owes much of its present grandeur to his patronage, Severus succeeded the ill-fated Pertinax to be Roman Emperor AD 193–211. Much of his reign was spent in conflict with the Senate, and he did much to seal the autocratic nature of the empire. He expanded the army and increased the empire's holdings on all fronts: Europe is dotted with forts of this period.

● **SHABTIS [also Shawabtis or Ushabtis]** Important element of Egyptian funerary equipment from Middle Kingdom

■

▲

S C

□

●

down to Roman period. Small statuettes in form of the mummified person – the earliest just have name of tomb-owner. Manufactured from wax, wood, stone and later especially from blue-green glazed composition (faience). By New Kingdom the figure holds working tools – hoes and baskets – and is inscribed with a spell from the BOOK OF THE DEAD, enabling it to become animated at any request for manual labour (cultivating fields, irrigation canal digging) made by OSIRIS, god of the underworld. By this device the dead man escapes being conscripted onto any afterlife equivalent of the compulsory work-force (corvée).

To begin with, only one shabti was necessary to deputize. Later, one was required for each day of the year, plus 36 overseers with whips. The tomb of Sethos I (Dynasty XIX) contained about 700 shabtis.

SHAIKHAN DHERI
see CHARSADA

SHAMASH [Sumerian Utu] The sun-god of the Near East. As the dispeller of darkness he was the one from whom nothing was hidden, therefore the god of truth and justice. On the top of the STELE of HAMMURAPI, Shamash is seen giving Hammurapi a rod and ring which denote straightness and completeness, i.e. right and justice. In ASSYRIA the symbol of the sun-god was a winged disk while in BABYLON it was a disk with a four-pointed star and rays. In statues, rays come from his shoulders.

● **SHANG DYNASTY** The earliest Bronze Age dynasty of China, beginning approximately 1500 BC, and ending with its fall to the CHOU dynasty in 1027 BC. It is sometimes known as the Yin. Excavations have shown that the early phases were centred at CHENG CHOU, Honan. The capital then shifted some 160km north, to the region of ANYANG, the city of Great Shang known from inscriptions. Excavations at Anyang have yielded the remains of the Shang dynasty from numerous sites, revealing palaces, tombs and workshops, as well as habitations. Archaeology, combined with written records, gives a picture of powerful government with an agricultural basis controlling a number of settlements.

The most distinctive feature of Shang civilization is the excellence of its metal-craft, specifically the complex designs and high skill displayed in its technology. No trace has been found of the rudimentary stages of bronze-work in China – instead bronze is first used here in sophisticated ways. In contrast are the primitive farming tools, where metal appears to have been used only rarely. Fine workmanship is seen in the bronze KO-halberds, spear-heads, axes and knives, as well as jade carvings. Elaborate bronze-cast vessels (mainly for aristocratic funerary use) reveal the Shang aesthetic sensibility; common motifs are the 'monster-mask', animal forms and geometric patterns, Pottery was both hand-made and wheel-produced. Affinities with the preceding LUNG-SHAN culture are seen not only in the many bronze shapes which echo the earlier pottery forms, but in a characteristic feature of Shang architecture, the building of walls and foundations by ramming and pounding of earth. Neolithic origins are also seen in the continuation and expansion of prophesying with oracle bones. More than 10,000 oracle bones have been excavated at the site of HSIAO-T'UN, near Anyang. They are the earliest examples of Chinese writing, as the questions and sometimes answers were inscribed on the bones. The royal tombs were pit graves, sometimes in the shape of a cross, and reveal the rituals of human and animal sacrifice that accompanied burials of the nobility. Chariot burials, as at Hsiao T'un, included both charioteers and horses, along with the trappings. At one site, though the wood of the chariots had rotted, the impression in the earth remained. More detailed 'moulds' of the later CHOU period have been seen.

SHANIDAR, Iraq A cave in the Zagros mountains with a long cultural sequence beginning *c* 50,000 BC. The first human activity is attributed to the MOUSTERIAN culture. The skeletons of seven of the occupants were buried in the cave, and it is possible that some at least were killed by a roof fall. The skeletons were of NEANDERTHAL type. One of the bodies had been covered with flowers (of which pollen remained to be identified by archaeologists). The Mousterian deposit was covered with an Upper PALAEOLITHIC Baradostian level, and this in turn by late Palaeolithic Zarzian debris. The stone industry of the Zarzian is marked by the presence of MICROLITHS, and with time an increasing emphasis on plant food becomes apparent. Further economic development is indicated at the near-by open-air site of ZAWI CHEMI SHANIDAR, with evidence of sheep management dating from as early as 9000 BC.

SHEIKH ABD el-QURNA, Egypt Western Thebes. Rock-cemetery for the highest officials during Dynasty XVIII. The typical tomb has a T-shaped plan and was cut into the mountainside, with a forecourt (for rituals), a transverse vestibule, and a corridor leading to a chapel with a burial chamber below. The decoration gives unparalleled insight into working life and recreations of the ancient Egyptians

Menna (responsible for estates and agriculture under Tuthmosis IV) hunts birds with a boomerang, spears fish, supervises harvesting. Workers have character of their own – girls squabbling, man asleep under tree.

Rekhmire (vizier of Tuthmosis III and Amenophis II) records kudos he gained from bringing to Egypt foreigners with gifts for pharaoh – Negroes, Syrians, Cretans: a delightful representation of monkey climbing up giraffe's neck. He also supervizes jewellers and sculptors working for temple of Amun.

Ramose (vizier under Amenophis III and Amenophis IV (Akhenaten)) has a splendidly sculptured tomb left unfinished at the move of capital to Amarna. Paintings show a funeral procession to the tomb; fine reliefs in Theban style illustrate ceremonial banquet of Ramose and relatives. In contrast, influence of Aten-worship and AMARNA art are seen where Ramose is decorated with gold by Akhenaten and Nefertiti.

▲ **SHIH-CHAI-SHAN, China** Site of rich burial ground in Yunnan province, on Lake Tien. Excavated 1955–60, it yielded 34 tombs furnished with 4000 artefacts including bronze and iron agricultural tools and weapons, and objects of clay and stone. A spectacular feature are large bronze kettle-drums, filled with thousands of cowrie shells. The lids of these drums are often decorated with figurines depicting rituals, battles, and market scenes. One of the tombs contained a golden seal of the King of Tien. Coins and mirrors had been imported from central China of the HAN period, dating the material to the centuries just before the time of Christ. Sophisticated decorative arts are evident, sharing animal motifs in common with the

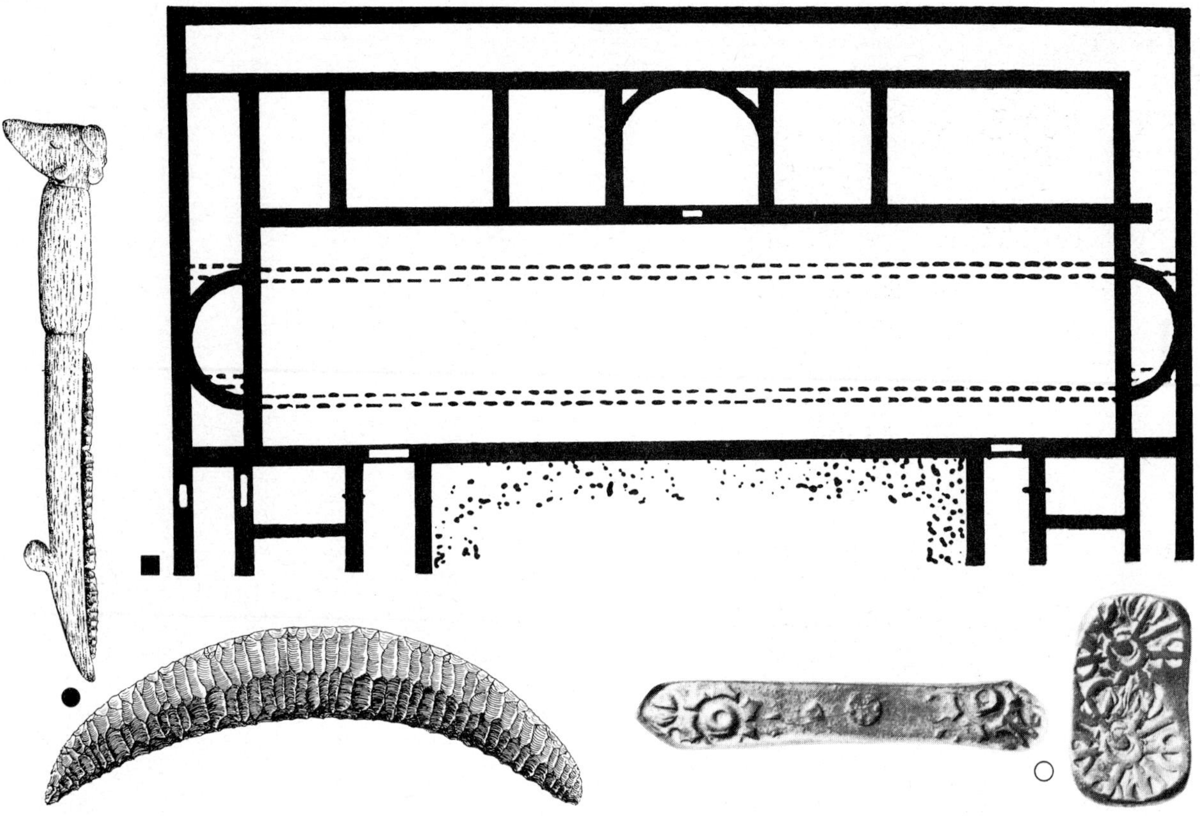

SCYTHIAN steppe imagery; in addition, similarities have been noted with the site of DONG-S'ON, 700km away in northern Vietnam. The connection with these various areas are not yet clearly understood. Historical records state that from the Late CHOU period the Lake Tien area was occupied by people described as prosperous farmers and stock-raisers of high cultural achievement.

SHIP BURIAL The ship of the dead carrying the soul far away into the ocean seems to have been a widespread belief in the Scandinavian-influenced parts of northern Europe. Boats were often carved on Viking gravestones, and boat-shaped graves outlined with stones have also been found. In the epic poem BEOWULF two ship burials are described; in one the body is placed in a boat and a pyre lit beneath it until all is burned and is covered with a BARROW, in another the body is placed in a ship which is then launched to drift on the sea. Several ship graves have been excavated, the most splendid ones at OSEBERG and SUTTON HOO.

SIALK, Tepe, Iran A TELL on the plateau south of Tehran excavated in the 1930s. It is the oldest site excavated in Iran having been settled in the 6th–5th millennium by people who built mud-brick houses and had black hand-made pottery as well as objects of bone, shell and copper. Their culture developed with the introduction of wheel-made pottery and finer metal work until it was replaced by the culture of SUSA and MESOPOTAMIA. Remains of the early 2nd millennium BC show that a people from the north-east settled the site, as happened at HISSAR. These may have been INDO-EUROPEAN. The inhabitants of the tell in the 1st millennium BC had belongings which certainly show them to be Indo-European.

● **SICKLE** Used archaeologically to describe any knife thought to have reaped cereals. Stone sickles were frequently unretouched BLADES, and only recognizable as such by the presence of SICKLE GLOSS. Some however were very finely worked by pressure FLAKING. Later bronze sickles tend to reflect the shape of their stone predecessors, but with the introduction of iron, the larger 'balanced sickle' became the norm. The balanced sickle is used with a sweeping stroke, unlike the smaller, straighter knives which were used with a cutting or sawing action.

SICKLE GLOSS A shiny surface on the working edges of some stone tools, produced by the cutting of cereals, reeds or grass. The polish is produced by the abrasive action of silica particles in the cut stems.

▲ **SILBURY HILL, Marlborough, Wiltshire** The largest artificial mound in Europe, it is 1.4km south of AVEBURY. Its construction (*c* 3000 BC) took place in four main stages, probably as a continuous process. The original plan was for a smaller mound than the existing one, but, reminiscent of events at STONEHENGE, plans were changed and the present earthwork was completed, some 40m high. Tunnelling into Silbury Hill at various dates has failed to reveal any burial or thrown light on its function.

SILCHESTER, Hampshire The deserted site of Roman Calleva Atrebatum. Little can be seen save the wall circuit (3rd century AD) and the amphitheatre, but it is the only Roman town to have been completely excavated (1864–78, 1890–1909). This has provided much detail on town layout and everyday life. However, the excavation methods of the time did not recognise all the wooden buildings and the

△

dating was not fully understood. Interesting features are the inn or MANSIO, the early defence circuit underlying the town, the layout of the streets beyond the walls (abandoned when the circuit was built), and the 4th century church near ■ the FORUM. The town appears very spacious and a recent population estimate goes for rather less than 1,000.

○ **SILVER BAR COINS** Punch-marked silver bar coins, struck on a standard related to that of the ACHAEMENIDS, are widely known in Gandhara, especially at TAXILA, and are probably the earliest coinage of the Indian subcontinent, dating back into the 5th century BC. The closely related silver round-and-concave coins complement them. Both types bear punched symbols largely identical to those found on certain Achaemenid coins. Later silver punch-marked coins often bear MAURYAN symbols.

SIN [pronounced Seen; Sumerian Nanna] The moon god of the Near East. He is recognized as the most powerful of the cosmic triad of gods which also includes SHAMASH and ISHTAR. He controlled the night. As the calendar was determined by the new moon, he ordered time. UR and Harran were the two chief centres of worship of Sin, and many other cities had shrines devoted to him. His symbol is △ a crescent-shaped moon such as can be seen on a STELE found in a small temple at HAZOR. It is also engraved with worshipping hands. His sacred number was 30.

SINJIRLI
see ZINJIRLI

SIRKAP
see TAXILA

SIRSUKH
see TAXILA

ŚIŚUPALGARH, India An important Iron Age site in Orissa, central India, with massive and elaborate defensive walls of late 1st millennium BC. The earliest occupation contains BLACK-AND-RED WARE dated *c* 600–500 BC. Unlike most Indian cities of this period, Śiśupalgarh has well developed town-planning. *See also* GANGES CIVILIZATION.

SKARA BRAE, Orkney A neolithic village excavated by CHILDE, after storms had removed its protective covering of blown sand in the 1920s. The pottery was GROOVED WARE. In the harsh environment of the Orkneys, no wood was available for building, flagstones being used as a raw material. Consequently a complete stone-built settlement was preserved: a collection of small, rectangular rooms huddled together, connected with covered passages. Interior furnishing, including shelves, was also made of stone. The main source of food was probably the sea, although cattle and sheep were raised.

SLASH-AND-BURN A system of agricultural land use in which the land was cleared by felling the trees and scrub, burning the wood and using the resultant ash to fertilize the soil. Such clearings soon lost their fertility and were usually deserted after two or three years. This clearance and burning of woodland has been detected in prehistoric contexts by POLLEN ANALYSIS. *See also* LANDNAM.

SLAVS The Slavs comprised a group of tribes occupying north Germany in the Elbe–Saale area and west Russia. Such peoples as the Wends and Obotrites on the Baltic

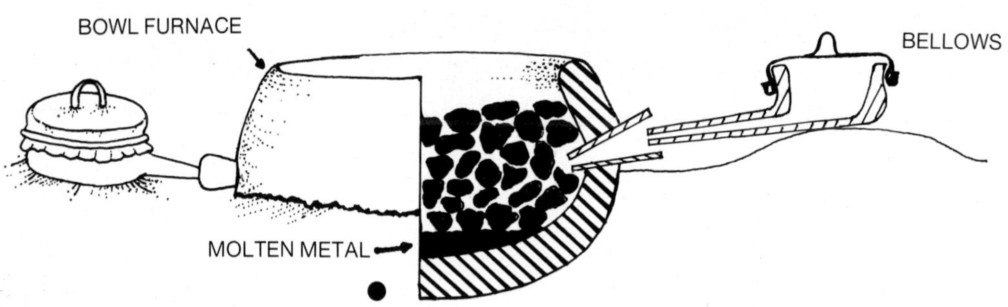

coast and the Kingdom of Moravia were included. During the VIKING period there was much contact between Swedish traders at towns like NOVGOROD and the Slavs, whom they captured and enslaved. Considered a threat to the eastern approaches to the FRANKISH empire, the Slavs were subject to Christian raids into their territory, partly as missionary activity but principally colonial in purpose.

● **SMELTING** Metal found in a pure state was used initially by ancient man. However most metals are found as chemical compounds and must be smelted, that is melted in the presence of carbon, to obtain pure metal. The temperature required for this process is about 1100°C. To obtain this temperature, ancient smelters used blow-pipes or bellows. The earliest furnaces from *c* 4000 BC were of simple bowl shape and were dismantled at the end of every smelt to obtain the pure metal. *C* 1000 BC a larger furnace with holes around the base for tapping the molten metal was introduced.

SMITHFIELD A late Stone Age industry of southern Africa, surviving as recently as AD 1000. It has been connected with rock-engravings in the same area.

SNAKETOWN, Lower Gila Valley, Arizona, USA Early HOHOKAM town. Sub-rectangular wattle and daub houses characterize the settlement which was occupied *c* 100 BC to its abandonment *c* 1100 AD. Complex irrigation systems are a feature of the valley.

▲ **SNETTISHAM, Suffolk** Spectacular group of IRON AGE metal objects, dating *c* 100–25 BC, and deposited *c* AD 10. The objects, probably all made in south-east England, include 7 gold TORCS, 48 gold alloy and 3 bronze torcs. 1 gold bracelet, and 14 gold and 145 POTIN COINS.

SOAN The pebble tool and flake industry of the Soan region of the Punjab, north-west India, provides the earliest evidence for man in India and Pakistan. In its later stages, it is contemporary with the Riss GLACIATION.

SOIL ANALYSIS The identification of soil or sediment types and the investigation of the processes that lead to their formation. Soil analysis uses mechanical and chemical methods to establish the origin of the deposits and the climate under which they were formed. Soil analytical techniques are frequently used to examine the soils on which archaeological sites occur or under which they are buried. They are of particular use to ENVIRONMENTAL ARCHAEOLOGY.

SOIL CONDUCTIVITY SURVEYING A technique being developed for application to archaeological prospecting: an electrical signal similar to a radio wave is transmitted into the soil, and is re-transmitted by metals present in the soil. Experiments have shown it to be useful in the detection of small features such as post-holes.

SOLEB, Egypt Downstream from Third Cataract, the Temple of Amenophis III (Dynasty XVIII) was built in honour of Amun and the King's own cult. Amenophis was anxious for himself to be deified as a 'living image.' Together with his wife, queen Tiye – for whom he built temple nearby – he was patron of the deities of the region. Amenophis IV – Akhenaten respected his father's desire and is shown offering to him. Other reliefs in the temple

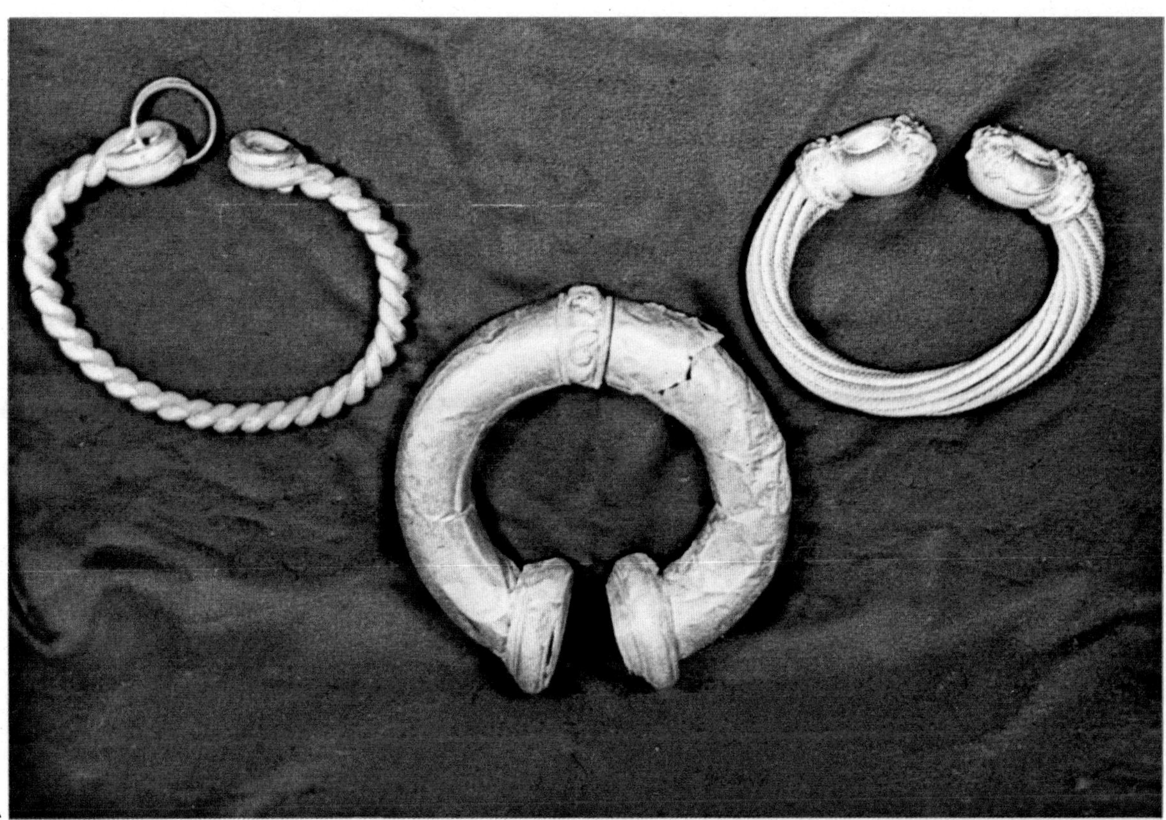

▲

celebrate Amenophis III's jubilee festival. Two majestic lions (now in the British Museum) of red granite, recumbent with paws crossed – one completed during reign of Tutankhamun – were set up as guardians of temple.

SOLIFLUXION This phenomenon usually occurs in PERIGLACIAL areas where the ground only thaws to a depth of a metre or less every summer. In such areas the upper layer of the soil becomes a liquid mud and where there is sufficient slope (2° or more) this mud, and any inclusions, will move downhill over the frozen subsoil. Material that has been moved in such a way is characteristically unsorted and contains clay, gravel and rock fragments. Good examples of solifluxion debris are the Coombe Rock deposits of the chalklands of southern England.

SOLO MAN The fossilized remains of portions of 11 skulls and 2 tibia found near the river Solo in Java, and dating to the Late PLEISTOCENE period. It is still uncertain whether these specimens, discovered between 1931 and 1941, actually represent HOMO SAPIENS or should be otherwise classified.

SOLUTREAN An Upper PALAEOLITHIC culture of France and Spain, dating 19–17,000 BC. In its later stages it is characterized by very fine flint spear points, ARROWHEADS and knives. At the TYPE-SITE (Solutré, near Macon) remains of some 6000 horses were found at the bottom of a cliff, suggesting they had been stampeded over by hunting groups. The Solutrean is succeeded by the MAGDALENEAN.

SOMERSET LEVELS A low-lying area between the Polden and Wedmore hills where marshy conditions led to the growth of peat. Permanent settlement was only possible on small 'islands' of sand or clay, e.g. MEARE island. Peat cutting has led to the discovery of ancient wooden trackways crossing the wet areas. The earliest tracks are Neolithic, *c* 2800 BC onwards. These are simple pathways: transverse timbers of birch covered with bundles of brushwood and held down by pegs. Conditions became drier after this, and there was no need for trackways until *c* 1000 BC when more flooding occurred. The trackways are dated by the help of POLLEN ANALYSIS, RADIOCARBON DATING and tools found near them.

■ **SOUNION, Greece** A beautifully positioned DORIC temple (built 444–440 BC) dedicated to Poseidon, overlooking the sea south of Athens. The ancient town is not visible.

SOUTH INDIAN MEGALITHS A rather generalized term for a complex of different burial rites in the south Indian Iron Age, which often but not always involved large stones. The main recurring burial forms are urn burial, in a small pit, of bones from which the flesh had been removed (excarnation); legged sarcophagi, often with an animal's head; pit grave circles with the body exposed on a bier in a large open pit surrounded by a circle of stones; various CISTS, sometimes with port-holes and sometimes compartmented; small rock-cut chambers. There are also rows of standing stones. Despite the diversity of burial types, some features are shared. All are accompanied by pottery, especially BLACK-AND-RED WARE, often in large quantities. Almost all graves contain some iron, including flat axes, sickles, spears and horse equipment. Identical iron objects are found up to 600km apart, suggesting they are the work of a tightly-knit group of craftsmen. These graves show a

combination of indigenous Copper Age elements and intrusive, especially INDO-EUROPEAN, features. Iron in the Deccan seems to date from *c* 1100–1050 BC, a date close to that of the introduction of iron in the north, which indicates a rapid southward movement of the techniques of iron-working if not of the iron-workers themselves.

SOUTHWESTERN TRADITION Cultures in Arizona, New Mexico, south Utah, Nevada, Colorado and west Texas down into north-west Mexico with an economy based initially on hunting and gathering, and which later evolved into food production based on the cultivation of maize, beans and squashes (*see* BAT CAVE; TEHUACAN). The tradition emerged *c* 100 BC–AD 400, developing from the local COCHISE culture of the earlier DESERT tradition. Characteristic artefacts include small arrowheads, grinding equipment, baskets, cotton textiles and pottery within the contexts of settled villages and large towns. Settlements are characterized by pit-houses, above-ground adobe and stone houses and later by PUEBLOS. The occasional presence of ceremonial platform and temple architecture indicates influences from MESOAMERICA. *See also* ANASAZI, HOHOKAM, MOGOLLON.

SPARTA, Greece The great rival and opponent of ATHENS in the Peloponnesian War (5th century BC). Very little of its archaeology is known. Its classical remains show that the Spartans had little interest in public buildings. More is known of the Roman city when Sparta was quite prosperous.

● **SPEAR THROWER [New World atlatl]** A device for improving the force behind a thrown spear, which acts by increasing the effective length of the throwing arm. The spear is lodged against a hook at the end of the thrower. It first appears in Upper PALAEOLITHIC contexts.

▲ **SPHINX** A natural crag at GIZA was transformed into a lion's body with King's head – 57m long by 20m high. It represents the pharaoh CHEPHREN (Dynasty IV), traces of paint still surviving on the face, wearing the royal NEMES and protective snake goddess. The strength of the lion, endowed with the divinity of the sun-god, emphasises Chephren as guardian of his pyramid complex. A small temple contemporary with Chephren is in front of the sphinx.

In the New Kingdom the Sphinx was taken to be the god Harmakhis (Horus in the Horizon), an aspect of the sun-god.

The earliest recorded sand-clearing operation (the last one occurred just before World War II during the excavations of Selim Hassan) was by Tuthmosis IV (Dynasty XVIII, New Kingdom) whose STELA tells how he received the instructions in a dream.

SPIRIT CAVE, Thailand An important site in north-west Thailand where excavations on the face of a limestone cliff have been undertaken since 1965. The discoveries have major implications for traditional ideas about cultural development in prehistoric south-east Asia, especially when combined with evidence for early metal-working at NON NOK THA in north-east Thailand. Previous concepts of south-east Asia as a passive rather than innovative area are now being re-assessed. Material from Spirit Cave spans the period 10,000–*c* 5600 BC. The stone tools of the lower levels are of HOABINHIAN type, though they continue throughout

the deposits. Distinctively new elements appearing by 6000 BC include early examples of partially-polished rectangular stone adzes and ground slate knives. (Similar knives, used for harvesting, have been recorded in modern use from island south-east Asia.) This date also marks the first appearance of pottery at the site. As the date of the pottery is close to 7000 BC, it ranks early among examples of pottery known archaeologically. Finishes include cord-marking, burnishing, and incised, comb-like patterns; clearly it is a developed style, with its origins still further back in time.

Of special significance are plant remains from throughout the deposits which were retrieved from sifted soil. The carbonized or desiccated remains include such edible plants as pepper, cucumber, butternut, bottle gourd, Chinese water-chestnut, pea and bean; candlenut may have been used for lighting, and betel as a stimulant. The sample is relatively small, and it is not yet known whether any of the species represent early horticultural activity, or were gathered wild. It has however been suggested that certain of the plants indicate plant exploitation beyond simple gathering.

Animal bones, most in very fragmentary condition, were retrieved throughout the sequence. Among them are specimens of bats, rats, birds, primates, shell-fish, deer, pigs and cattle, indicating the exploitation of a range of environmental niches. The pig may have been domesticated. Quantities of bamboo, mainly in the form of charcoal though also from uprights in front of the shelter, suggest that bamboo may have been culturally important, possibly widely used for implements no longer preserved.

■ **SPLIT, Jugoslavia** This modern town is built on the remains of a Roman palace of Diocletian who retired there after renouncing his emperorship in AD 305. The palace is large and almost square (208 × 195m). Diocletian's living quarters overlooked the sea from a magnificent verandah. Behind were his official buildings, his mausoleum (now the cathedral) and quarters for his retainers and bodyguard.

SRIVIJAYA The maritime empire based at Palembang, south-east Sumatra. After a series of wars with surrounding kingdoms of the archipelago for control of the Malacca and Sundra Straits, the empire fell in the 13th century AD. Srivijaya is the earliest such empire in island south-east Asia which is well documented: 7th-century Chinese visitors describe the Buddhist nature of the kingdom, and its overseas commercial enterprises. Among the goods exported were sandalwood, cloves and camphor. Srivijaya sent ambassadors to China, bearing exotic gifts including parrots and dwarfs, and in the 8th century the Chinese emperor conferred a title on the king.

STANEGATE This began as the road built under AGRICOLA, running between the Tyne and the Solway, with forts at Carlisle, CORBRIDGE, and possibly Vindolanda. It appears to have formed the northern frontier of Britain at the very beginning of the 2nd century AD, when from four to six more forts were constructed, supplemented by fortlets (e.g. at Haltwhistle Burn); but with the construction of HADRIAN'S WALL, the Stanegate forts were evacuated. North of the Stanegate are signal stations at Pike Hill and Walltown Crags, but the date of these is not certain.

STANWICK, Yorkshire A large, complex HILLFORT or OPPIDUM dating from the 1st century AD. It was mentioned by TACITUS and was probably the base of Venutius, Queen

Cartimandua's consort, in the northern resistance against the Romans. Occupation at Stanwick ended with the defeat of Venutius by AD 74. A large hoard of four sets of horse trappings, like those from the nearby ARRAS graves, dated to mid 1st century AD was found close to the hillfort.

STAR CARR, Yorkshire A waterlogged site near Scarborough, chosen for excavation (1945–51) with the aim of finding MESOLITHIC flint-work and organic remains stratified together. The results were highly significant. An Early MAGLEMOSEAN brushwood platform on the edge of a lake was uncovered, together with copious evidence for an antler-working industry, mainly involving the production of barbed HARPOON points. Other animal products included mattock-heads of elk antler, bone needles and SCRAPER-like tools, and a remarkable group of as many as 20 frontal parts of Red deer stag skulls with the antlers still attached. They had been carefully lightened by hollowing the bone, and this, together with holes drilled through the skull, suggest they were worn by members of the hunting group, possibly as part of a hunting ceremony. Wooden finds from the site included rolls of birch-bark (possibly a source of resin or pitch) and a canoe paddle. Among the unworked animal bones were the remains of a domestic dog. The settlement has been seen as a winter camp of a group moving from place to place with the seasons.

STARČEVO, Yugoslavia One of a group of related Early Neolithic cultures in south-eastern Europe, the others being Karanovo in Bulgaria and Kremikovci in Macedonia; Körös in Hungary and Cris culture in Romania; and pre-SESKLO in Greece. They date from the 6th to 4th millennium BC. These cultures, all with basically similar range of artefacts, were the first to practise farming in the area they covered (*see* LINEAR POTTERY and IMPRESSED WARE cultures, for central and south-western Europe respectively). Sheep and goats were often important, although sometimes cattle took precedence and wild animals were commonly still hunted. Cultivated crops included wheat and barley.

Although the domesticated plants and animals (except perhaps cattle) were presumably introduced into Europe from the Near East, indicating an actual movement of people, from the earliest settlements there is a break with the type of building construction found in Asia. Flat-roofed houses packed together with common walls changed to small, one-roomed free-standing structures with gabled roofs: the change was at least partly dictated by the very different climate. On the other hand, unlike those of the more northerly Linear Pottery cultures, the settlements were still permanently fixed, so that large mounds or TELLS could develop. Karanovo itself, in east Bulgaria, is one such mound; ARGISSA, Greece, is another.

STEINHEIM, Germany The site where a human skull was found in 1933, near Stuttgart. The skull's heavy brow ridge has encouraged comparisons with NEANDERTHAL man, but its principal resemblances are now thought to lie with the SWANSCOMBE remains. Its evolutionary position has been variously described as ancestral to both Neanderthal and modern man; as ancestral to modern man alone, while Neanderthal man is seen as representing a separate line; and as one of a range of variable populations of early hominids in the Middle PLEISTOCENE. The skull is of Mindel–Riss date (*see* GLACIATIONS).

STELA (Egyptian) Basically an ancient Egyptian stone memorial of funerary nature with inscriptions and scenes to forestall any lack of food or drink offerings for the dead person. The shape is usually tabloid or rectangular with a curved top or cornice. In Old Kingdom MASTABAS the chapel contained stela depicting the tomb-owner before a table full of slices of bread, and was inscribed with requests for abundance of victuals, the name of deceased and his titles. In Middle Kingdom many stelae were left as miniature cenotaphs at ABYDOS. Above the set formula to obtain (via pharaoh and gods) a constant supply of necessary offerings, there were often two amuletic eyes (representing the eyes of the falcon-god Horus) enabling visual contact by the deceased with the outside world. A few stelae have the deceased's career and important historical information, e.g. Tjetji's stela (British Museum) recording territorial expansion of one of Theban rulers just prior to reunification of Egypt in Dynasty XI. In late New Kingdom an interesting series of stelae belonged to workmen on the royal tombs living at Deir el-Medina – including scenes of the deified pharaoh Amenophis I (Dynasty XVIII) and his mother.

Pharaohs set up commemorative stelae as public mementos to achievements, e.g. in Dynasty XVIII:

(1) Tuthmosis III stela on bank of Euphrates during Middle-Eastern campaigns.

(2) Tuthmosis IV stela between front paws of SPHINX at Giza after it was cleaned from desert-sands as a result of a dream in which the sphinx complained of negligence.

(3) Amenophis IV-Akhenaten boundary stelae limiting the extent of new capital at Amarna.

STELE [plural stelae] A single slab of stone fashioned into uniform rectangular shape set upright into the ground and frequently bearing elaborate carved decoration and inscriptions.

STEPHENS, John Lloyd (1805–52) An American explorer who was amongst the first to see and describe many of the MAYA CEREMONIAL CENTRES, now so well known. Between 1839 and 1842, he published popular writings on the subject of his travels and impressions of the Maya civilization.

Main books: *Incidents of Travel in Central America* (1841); *Incidents of Travel in Yucatan* (1843).

●**STEP PYRAMID, Egypt** Situated on the plateau at Saqqara, this pyramid complex has been frequently investigated and excavated since the nineteenth century. It was the tomb of King Zoser of Dynasty III, designed by his architect IMHOTEP, whose name appears on the base of a statue. The tomb may have started as an ARCHAIC MASTABA for Zoser's predecessor but Imhotep turned it into the six-step structure–a change involving about one million tonnes of stone. The final plan gave original measurements for the pyramid of 121 m × 109m at the base and 60m in height. The burial chamber is of red granite and 11 underground galleries served as tombs for Zoser's relatives. Some rooms had blue FAIENCE tiles imitating palace matting decorations. Near the funerary temple attached to the pyramid was a serdab (cubicle) containing a powerful sculpture of Zoser looking out onto the whole complex.

STEP PYRAMID COMPLEX, Egypt A defensive wall with dummy gateways carved in the limestone enclosed the

whole rectangular area (544m × 277m). In the entrance colonnade IMHOTEP imitated in stone the architecture of his secular environment – twelve ribbed columns are 'transformed' palm trunks. In the enclosure are buildings for Zoser's coronation festival (known as the Heb Sed) which the King's spirit could use for the rest of time. The southern tomb with its frieze of cobras and imitation brickwork in stone possibly contained the King's viscera removed during mummification, or symbolized Zoser's cenotaph at ABYDOS. The Houses of the North and South, representing a united Egypt had columns symbolising national plants attached to their façades.

STILL BAY A Stone Age culture of the savannah and grassland of southern and eastern Africa, perhaps surviving up to 8000 BC. The composition of its stone industry reflects its open environment.

▲ **STIRRUP SPOUT** A pouring device in the form of a hollow stirrup-shaped ceramic tube with each end opening into the body of a bottle shaped vessel and with one single spout arising vertically from the top of the arch. This form was especially popular in ancient PERU. ▶

STOA This Greek word is applied to a covered colonnade or portico. Often two-storeyed affairs in AGORAS, they acted as covered markets and meeting places. Good examples are the stoas at Assos and the rebuilt Stoa of Attalos in ATHENS.

STONEHENGE, Amesbury, Wiltshire Like AVEBURY, Stonehenge sits in a landscape exceptionally rich in burial ■ mounds. The monument that now exists is the product of a long and complicated development, still not worked out in full detail. *C* 2500 BC, a circular bank and external quarry ditch about 100m across were dug, as were the 56 AUBREY holes (named after their discoverer) just inside the bank. Only one major stone was present at this stage, the 'Heel Stone'. GROOVED Ware was associated with this construction. In the second phase (Stonehenge II) a double circle of 82 'bluestones' was erected. The stones had been transported some 400km from the Prescelly Mountains in south Wales. At the same time, the Avenue, a pair of parallel banks and ditches running down to the river Avon 1km to the east, was constructed. The entrance through the bluestone circles was directed at the position of the sun on the horizon on midsummer day: the well-known astronomical alignment of Stonehenge had been initiated. Before long however, these stones were removed and a more ambitious programme begun. ▶

First, in about 2000 BC, some 80 SARSEN stones, weighing up to 50 tonnes each, were put in place. These stones were carefully shaped (by hammering with stone mauls) so that the horizontal slabs, as much as 7m above the ground, tongued into their supporting uprights. The unit of two uprights and a bridging stone is called a 'trilithon', a word coined by STUKELEY in the 18th century. A circle of standing sarsens carrying a continuous lintel enclosed a U-shaped arrangement of free-standing trilithons, the trilithon horseshoe. Soon after, an oval of about 20 bluestones was set up. Outside the sarsen structure, 59 holes in two concentric rings were dug (the 'Y' and 'Z' holes); before anything was put in them, plans again changed and the bluestone oval was dismantled in favour of a horseshoe and circle, bringing the monument to its present state (bar

■

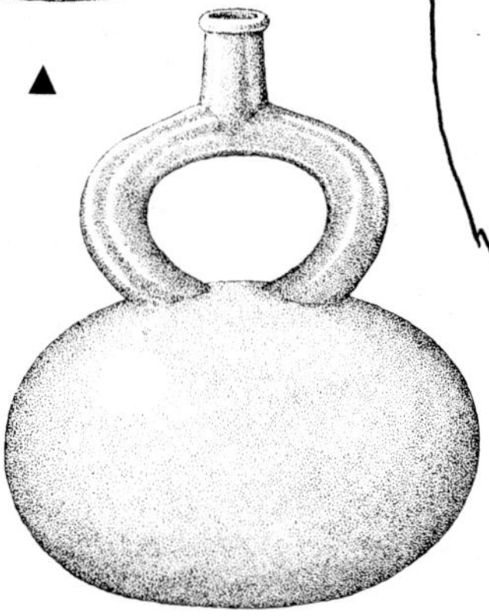

▲

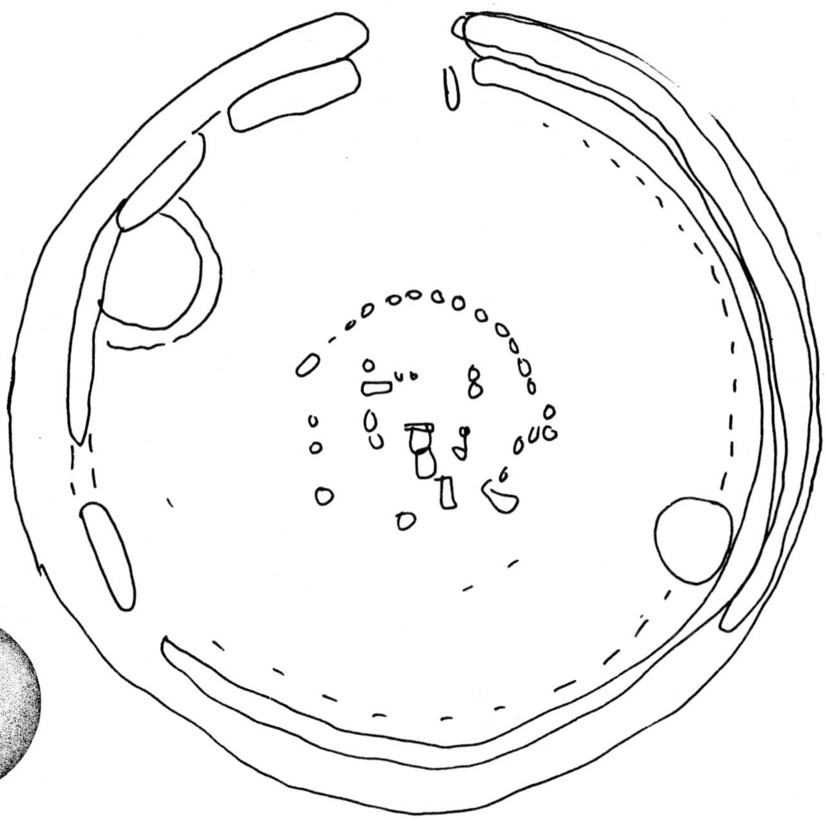

■

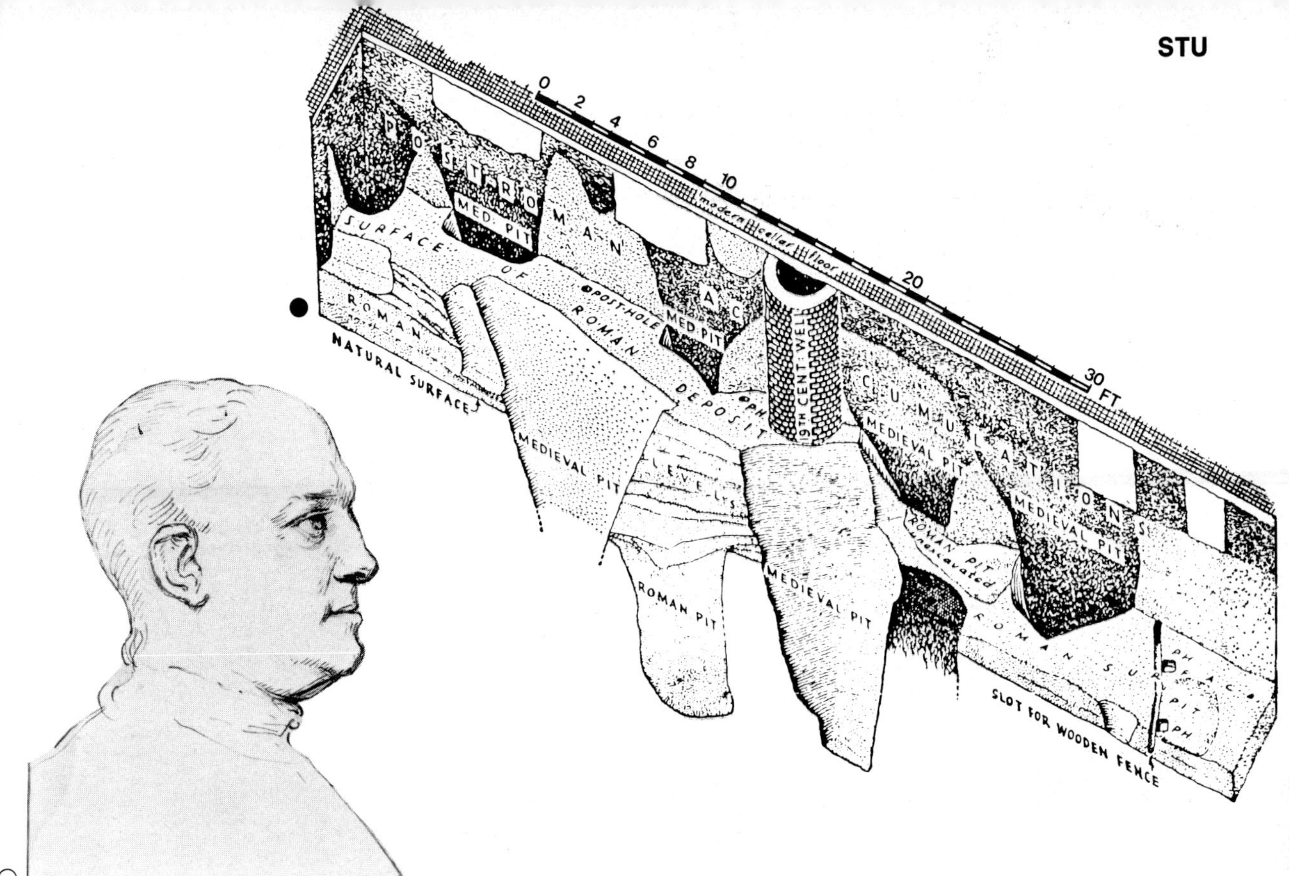

dilapidation). The final stages in the history of Stonehenge were probably contemporary with the WESSEX CULTURE. It was once thought that the monument was MYCENAEAN-inspired, or even designed, but while it is admittedly unique in north-west Europe, it is equally out of place in a Mycenaean context. Carpentry techniques are used in the mortice and tenon construction of the sarsen trilithons, suggesting that similar monuments existed in wood – WOODHENGE could have been one such. Thus Stonehenge is best seen as the most elaborate, and imperishable, of a whole series of ceremonial structures that could be found in neolithic Britain. Interestingly enough, it does not appear to have been set out with as much precision as some superficially much less impressive stone circles.

The ancient Druids are not known to have had any connection with Stonehenge.

STORAGE PIT IRON AGE sites in Britain and on the Continent are riddled with pits, probably used originally for grain storage and later filled with rubbish or the occasional burial. Modern experiments, e.g. at BUTSER HILL, have shown that unparched grain will keep for over six months with a high germination level and low insect and mould damage. In Britain, storage pits are common south of the Midlands, but the climate and soil types north of this are unsuitable for storage underground. Similar storage pits were used by many prehistoric communities in the Old and New worlds.

STRATIGRAPHY The first principle of archaeological excavation, stratigraphy is a science borrowed from geology. It concerns the relationships of different layers and other deposits, and depends upon the axiom that any layer which overlies another must have been deposited later than that which is under it: note that this does not imply that everything in an upper layer must be later in date than everything in a lower layer. The principle is extended to include such features as pits, ditches, etc, which must necessarily be later than the strata through which they cut. The stratigraphy of particular sites is often very complex, and the archaeologist must learn to distinguish between the slight differences of colour or texture which demarcate the layers, and to interpret them by means of sections.

STRIGIL A curved instrument of metal, U-shaped in section, with which Romans would scrape their skins in the baths, having anointed themselves with oil, to remove dirt. Strigils are sometimes found or depicted chained to a small oil-flask.

STUKELEY, William (1687–1765) One of the best of the early British antiquaries. His accurate records of pre-Roman field monuments in Britain, e.g. in *Itinerarium Curiosum* (1725), are extremely valuable historically, particularly for their illustrations. Unfortunately he was obsessed by classical references to the DRUIDS, and attributed STONEHENGE and AVEBURY to them in *Stonehenge, a Temple Restored to the Druids* (1740). This misled archaeologists for several generations.

STUPA An Indian funerary monument associated with holy men, in particular the BUDDHA. The main elements are a dome surmounted by a balustrade and umbrella, resting on a drum which is surrounded by a railing with gateways. The railings and gateways generally bear scenes from the life of Buddha and his former incarnations (JATAKA

STORIES). Like much Indian stone architecture, it copies the design and details of a wooden structure. *See also* AMARAVATI, BHARHUT, SANCHI.

SUB-ATLANTIC
see POSTGLACIAL PERIOD

SUB-BOREAL
see POSTGLACIAL PERIOD

SUE POTTERY This Japanese high-quality wheel-made grey-ware was mass-produced during the TOMB PERIOD, usually for aristocratic funerary use. Ornamentation is generally sparse. The first Japanese glazes appear on this pottery. Sue pottery is thought to have been introduced from Korea by Chinese workmen. *See also:* HAJI POTTERY.

SULTAN, Tell es-
see JERICHO

SUMER Southern Mesopotamia between BABYLON and the Persian Gulf. It was in this area that Near Eastern civilization first began *c* 3500 BC. Excavations at UBAID, URUK and JEMDAT NASR have shown the development of wealth, administration and architecture which, together with writing, made civilization possible. The need for large-scale organization for IRRIGATION and solving problems of flood and drought management are thought to have stimulated this development. The growing complexity of the temple building is seen at ERIDU. The best glimpse of life as it must have been in Sumer during the third millennium is seen on the Standard of UR (British Museum), found in the Royal Cemetery. The battle scene portrays the Sumerian warrior with helmet and battle axe assisted by battle wagons drawn by teams of onagers (wild asses). War was made from time to time between the city-states which constituted Sumer. Each city-state was a political and religious unit having a king and a patron deity. In peace-time most civil organization was by the priests at the temple where the god was held responsible for the condition of the area. Sumer ended in anarchy about 2000 BC, largely due to outside pressure of the Elamites (*see* SUSA) and AMORITES.

SUSA, Iran TELL by the river Karkeh in south-west Iran, excavated since 1897. The earliest settlement in the 4th millennium can be distinguished by elegant painted beakers. The early inhabitants lived in similar fashion to the people of Mesopotamia at UBAID, URUK, JEMDAT NASR and in early dynastic UR. As the Elamite capital, Susa was an important city. Twice the Elamites extended their influence over the Mesopotamian plains, the first time overthrowing the third dynasty of Ur *c* 2000 BC, and then in the 13th century BC when they fought as far as BABYLON. The latter period was prosperous and enabled King Untash Gal to build a second capital, Choga Zanbil, a little distance to the south. Excavations there in 1951–62 found a well-preserved ZIGGURAT, temples, palaces, a reservoir and city walls. Many treasures such as the stele of HAMMURAPI were taken from Babylon at this time to Susa. They are now in the Louvre, Paris. The ASSYRIANS captured Elam *c* 640 BC and destroyed Susa by fire. *C* 520 BC DARIUS rebuilt Susa magnificently. The city surrendered to ALEXANDER *c* 330 BC, after which it fell to the PARTHIANS, SASSANIANS and finally the Moslems under whom it declined to a village.

▲

■

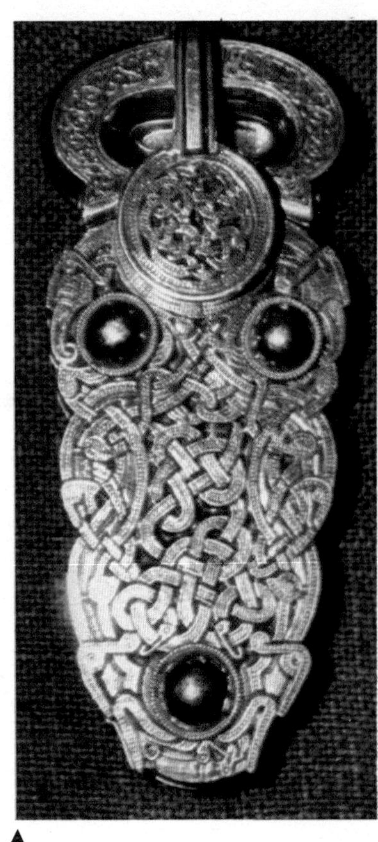

▲

SUTTON HOO, Suffolk Excavated in 1939, this is the most spectacular find ever made in Anglo-Saxon archaeology. A clinker-built ship 29m long was found under a BARROW by the river Deben near Woodbridge. It was a rowing boat with 38 oars; there was no mast or sail. Unlike the OSEBERG and GOKSTAD ships the wood was not preserved. All that remained were thousands of clench nails and timber impressions on the sand. A burial chamber amidships contained many treasures: a sword with jewelled pommel and scabbard, a shield with bird and dragon mounts and a helmet, all with gold and garnet decoration, were imported from Sweden. There were 19 pieces of English-made goldwork, including the great gold ▲ buckle covered with ribbon INTERLACE picked out with NIELLO, a purse lid with CLOISONNÉ gold, garnet and MILLEFIORI work, a pair of polychrome shoulder clasps, and other smaller jewelled mounts. Much domestic equipment and many lesser weapons were also found, as was a stringed musical instrument (lyre) placed inside an Alexandrian bronze bowl. Two unique pieces of royal regalia, a whetstone with decorated terminals and a 'standard' are the strangest objects. Many pieces of silver were imported from the Mediterranean, including a great ■ BYZANTINE dish, a large fluted bowl, a ladle and cup, and a nest of 10 hemispherical bowls. A pair of silver spoons with 'Saul' and 'Paul' inscribed in Greek on them appear to be symbols of Christianity. Most important of all the finds for dating purposes were the 37 Merovingian gold coins (*tremises*) in the purse. Numismatists agree that the deposition must date somewhere about AD 625. There was no trace of a body in the chamber or elsewhere in the mound, which, with the Christian symbolism of the spoons, has been held by some to show that the cenotaph commemorates king Raedwald of EAST ANGLIA, who lapsed from Christianity and died 625.

SWANSCOMBE, Kent The site of a series of quarries in the Thames river gravels, where three fragments of a human skull were found in the 1930s, with Middle ACHEULEAN artefacts. The remains are thought to be similar to the broadly contemporary skull from STEINHEIM.

SWIDDEN
see SLASH-AND-BURN

SWIDERIAN CULTURE Named after the location of Swidry Wielkie (near Warsaw, Poland), this is a late glacial hunter-fisher group of the eastern north European plain. Now referred to as the Swidry–Chwalibogowice group, the flint industries are distinguished by tanged points. *See* AHRENSBURGIAN; HAMBURGIAN.

SWORD A long thrusting or slashing weapon, usually double edged. It was a major weapon in Europe from its introduction in the Late BRONZE AGE until the 18th century AD. The earliest swords in Britain were imported from Europe in the URNFIELD period, *c* 11th century BC. The Rixheim swords had rod tangs; the slightly later Erbenheim leaf-shaped swords were flange hilted. Various local copies were made of these bronze swords. HALLSTATT swords are divided into the straight-sided short Gundlingen types (used by cavalry), and long leafshaped Mindelheim swords; the latter were of bronze or iron. A late Bronze Age iron sword was found at LLYN FAWR. By 600 BC bronze swords were replaced throughout Europe

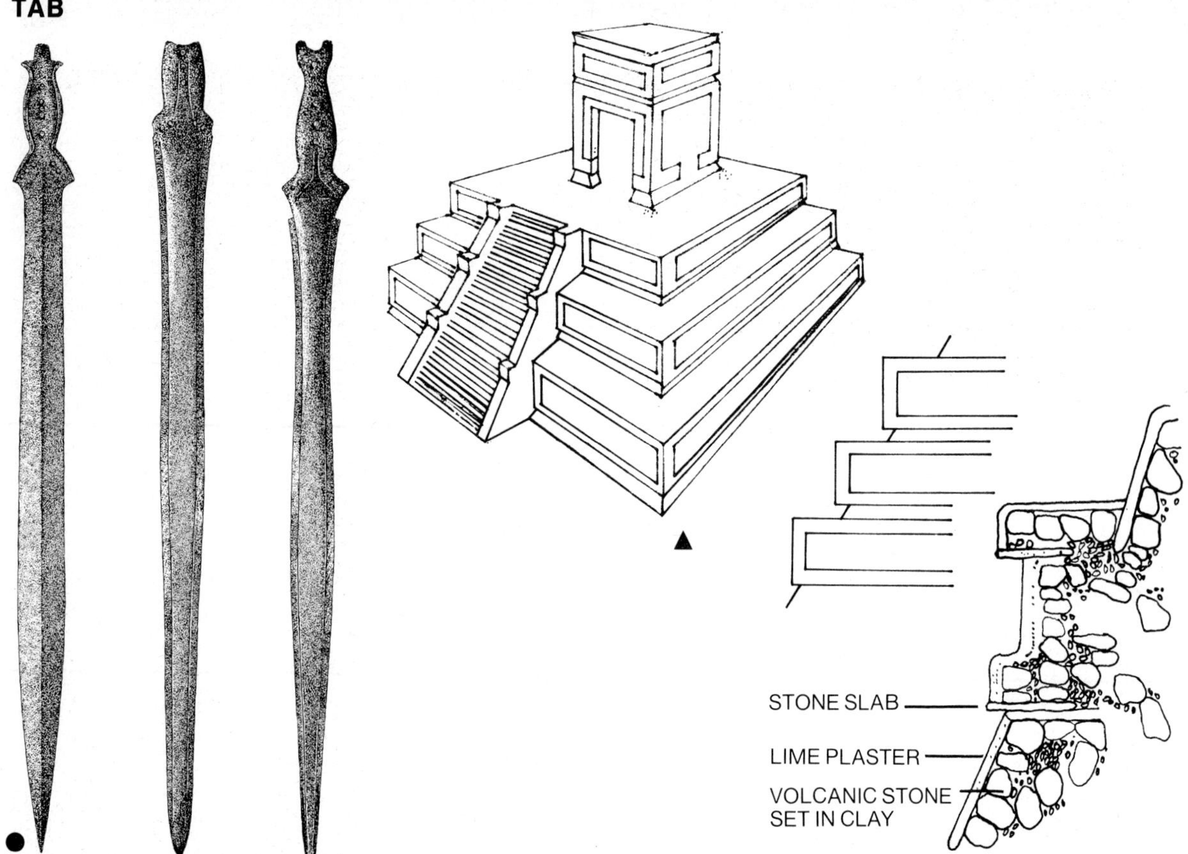

● by iron weapons, from the 2nd century BC made by specialist schools of armourers centred in Switzerland.

TABLET A smooth piece of clay on which CUNEIFORM script was inscribed. They vary in size from 10mm square to about 0.5m by 0.3m, although the most popular size is that which is easily held in the hand. All faces were inscribed. In the Near East, legal documents were often enclosed in a clay envelope on which the text was repeated together with seal impressions of the witnesses to the contract. Longer inscriptions were written on clay prisms or cylinders. Sun-dried clay tablets were also used in MINOAN Crete and MYCENAEAN Greece (*see:* LINEAR A and LINEAR B WRITING).

TABON CAVE, Philippines This site, part of the Tabon Caves complex of the south-west coast of Palawan Island, has yielded an Upper PALAEOLITHIC flake industry beginning before 40,000 BC, and continuing into the post-PLEISTOCENE period. Finds from the habitation levels almost entirely comprised flakes made of chert, a raw material common in the river beds near to the cave. Uniface CHOPPERS and hammerstones for stone-working were found, in addition to utilized flakes, waste flakes, and rare examples of flakes with secondary retouching; waste flakes constituted the largest category of stone found, and attest to the cave's use as a workshop. Animal bones were mainly of birds, bats and small mammals; only one extinct form (a deer) was identified. Skeletal remains of HOMO SAPIENS, representing at least three indviduals, have been estimated to date to *c* 20,000 BC, although they came from disturbed levels. Numerous jar burials, as well as finds such as jade and stone beads, bracelets, glass beads, and bronze, are thought to date from *c* 200 BC to AD 500.

TACITUS, Cornelius (AD 55–120) One of the most distinguished of the Roman historians, whose works have proved of great value to archaeologists and ancient historians alike. His *Histories* cover the period between Nero and Domitian; the period between Augustus and Nero was to have been described in his *Annals*, but most of this work has been lost. He wrote also a biography of his father-in-law, AGRICOLA, and a description of the German barbarians, the *Germania*. The general theme of his writings, even at such an early date, is one of decline and of the decay of traditional Roman virtues. He was a great influence on the historian Gibbon.

TACLLA [or foot plough]
see INCA

TADMOR
see PALMYRA

▲ **TALUD-TABLERO** The architectural principle for the construction of PYRAMIDS and PLATFORM MOUNDS in a series of panels and slopes. It was a diagnostic feature of TEOTIHUACAN building.

TAMPANIAN The Malayan form of the CHOPPER-CHOPPING TOOL complex of the Lower PALAEOLITHIC tradition.

TANIS, Egypt Important capital city in eastern Nile delta, now devastated by earthquakes and floods but only surpassed by THEBES in excavated statuary. The Hyksos rulers brought statues (especially sphinxes) of Middle Kingdom date to embellish Tanis which they had made

their power-base (known as Avaris). Tanis' zenith was during the Late New Kingdom when Ramesses II in particular built large temples. For some Egyptologists, Tanis is the Royal Residence, Pi-Ramesses, others preferring the nearby palace at Qantir. The excavations of the French archaeologist Montet revealed the royal necropolis of some rulers of Dynasties XXI–XXII – one of the most spectacular finds of the century in Egypt, especially the silver coffin and granite sarcophagus of Psussenes I.

TAPLOW, Buckinghamshire Before the discovery of SUTTON HOO this inhumation burial in BARROW contained the richest grave goods known from the pagan Anglo-Saxon period. A superb glass beaker, gold belt fittings, a pair of gold shoulder clasps and a large drinking-horn with decorative mounts were among other less spectacular finds. The metal-work from Taplow is particularly interesting because it contains both ANIMAL ORNAMENT and INTERLACE designs, i.e., it was made during the fusion periods of Salin's Style I and Style II.

TARA, Co. Meath The most famous HILLFORT in Ireland. It is an oval enclosure surrounded by a ditch and palisade. Like other Irish sites it was built around an older burial CAIRN. Within the hillfort are two circular RATH enclosures. Tara is historically well documented from *c* the 3rd century AD. It was the seat of the Ui Neill kings, a dynasty of overlords who claimed to rule Ireland but were dominant only in the north. The high kingship remained at Tara until AD 1002, when the kings were overthrown.

TARDENOISIAN A MESOLITHIC culture reaching from northern Europe south through Spain into north Africa. In south-west France it succeeded the SAUVETERRIAN. In north Europe (but not Britain, which was by then separated from the continent by the Channel), Tardenoisian sites are commonly found in areas of sandy soils. It lasted until the arrival of the earliest farmers, and in its later stages is associated with domesticated animals (*see* CUZOUL). Broadly Tardenoisian are a few remarkable burial groups. These include many bodies in the middens along the Tagus valley in Portugal, and 23 individuals in 10 graves on the island of Téviec off the coast of Britanny. At Ofnet in Bavaria a total of 33 human skulls were found in two adjacent pits. The culture is named after La Fère-en-Tardenois, Aisne, in northern France, the site of discoveries in 1896.

■ **TARQUINIA, Italy** The ETRUSCAN city of Tarquinia, originally on the coast, now lies a short distance inland from the present Mediterranean shoreline and is some 90km north-west of Rome. Before the Etruscan period the site of Tarquinia was occupied by a VILLANOVAN settlement of which four major cemeteries have been discovered. The Etruscan period at Tarquinia started by the second half of the 8th century BC and continued until, in 308 BC, the city submitted to Rome. Tarquinia is most famous for its wealth of important tombs, many of them richly decorated with wall paintings. In one of the tombs (the Bocchoris) an inscribed vessel of Egyptian FAIENCE of *c* 700 BC was discovered. Other tombs, particularly important for their artistic detail include the Tomb of the Augurs, the Tomb of the Triclinium and the Tomb of the Barons.

TARRAGONA, Spain A Roman town on the Mediterranean coast and capital of the province of Tarraconensis.

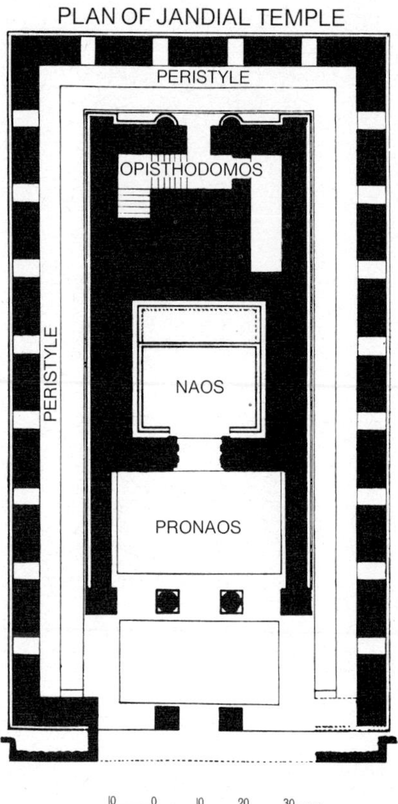

Started as a native town, it was captured by the Romans during the wars of the 3rd century BC and became a COLONIA under Caesar in the 40s BC. Not much is known of it until its sack by the Suebi and FRANKS in the mid 3rd century AD. It is now modern Tarraco. The upper part of the town was the town centre with temples, BASILICA, FORUM, CIRCUS and theatre. The amphitheatre survives near by, and was used by the Arabs for bull-fights in the 7th century AD. It now has a Romanesque church in the centre of the arena.

● **TAXILA, Pakistan** This site (near Rawalpindi) was one of the two main cities of Gandhara (*see* CHARSADA). It falls into three phases of development. The Bhir mound, an irregular jumble of houses, probably dates from the 5th century BC, on the basis of coin finds, which are the main dating evidence at Taxila. It was occupied throughout the MAURYAN era, but was probably abandoned before the Indo-Greek period. The second city, Sirkap, was built by the Indo-Greeks *c* 175 BC, and was a true Hellenistic city with a regular grid of streets defended by a stone wall with square bastions. Small STUPAS occur along the main road; these shrines continued in use even after Sirkap was abandoned. By the mid 1st century BC, Sirkap was under the rule of the KUSHAN emperors, who moved the site of their city *c* AD 100 to near-by Sirsukh. This was destroyed *c* AD 500 probably by the White Huns. Outside the city area further architectural remains are known: the Dharmarajikastupa, possibly of AŚOKAN date, rebuilt under the ▲ Kushanas, and the Jandial temple, a building closely following the classic Greek pattern but probably a PARTHIAN fire temple. During the period of the Bhir mound Taxila had close ties with Central India, shown, for example, by the presence of Mauryan coinage. But even in this period Taxila was in close contact with the ACHAEMENID empire and drew many influences from the west, While the city of Sirkap flourished, trade with the west, and especially with Rome, increased; unlike the regular utilitarian trade in the south, Taxila seems to have imported mainly luxury items on a casual basis. Finds include glassware, gems, bronze and gold statuettes, etc. The unique combination of Indian and foreign elements present in Taxila and Gandhara led to the rise of the GANDHARAN ART style. *See also* SILVER BAR COINS.

TAYACIAN Originally a term used to describe a lower PALAEOLITHIC flint industry, recognized at La Micoque, Tayac, Dordogne. The industry was without HANDAXES, and consisted of thick, irregularly shaped flakes with inconsistent RETOUCH and wear-marks indicating heavy use. It was allied to the CLACTONIAN. It has since been recognized outside France (e.g. in Spain and north Africa) and in periods of widely differing dates, so that 'Tayacian' has become more a technological than a cultural label. It is also used to refer to disturbed ASSEMBLAGES.

TEHUACAN VALLEY Puebla, Mexico A dry region in the highland basin which has yielded important evidence on the evolution of agriculture and the rise of civilization in Mesoamerica. Occupation in the valley goes back to before 10,000 BC when men hunted large game animals such as the horse, and pronghorn antelope – now extinct in the area – with spear points of finely flaked stone. During the later stages of development tool types and equipment changed to accommodate the growing emphasis on plant foods. At first these were wild, but as men increasingly experimented,

genetic changes occurred to give rise to crops now regarded as domesticated. The most important of these are maize, beans and squash upon which the success of the later large civilizations depended. Some of the first plants to be domesticated were the gourd, avocado and chile pepper, all of which were grown widely by 5000 BC. Maize underwent the most spectacular changes in its relationship with man. Controversy revolves around the origins of this crop. Some botanists believe that its ancestor is the wild grass *teosinte*; others think it developed from an ancestral wild maize which is now extinct. Pottery appears in the Purron phase *c* 2300 BC when the first semi-permanent hamlets and villages were in existence and agriculture is well attested. The Mesoamerican cultural tradition emerged here by the 1st millennium BC with the building of temple mounds and PYRAMIDS and other important traits which accompany a civilization (*see* MESOAMERICA). *See also* BAT CAVE for early maize.

TELL The name given to mounds in the Near East which have built up over many years from an accumulation of debris. Sites strategically situated with good water supply are occupied for long periods of time. When buildings are constructed of MUD-BRICK it is normal to simply level a collapsed structure and build on the remains, rather than salvage the clay. In this way the tell slowly rises. Tell (or 'tal') is Arabic and has equivalents in Turkish ('Hüyük') and in Persian ('tepe').

TELLO, Julio Cesar (1880–1947) With UHLE and KROEBER he was a pioneer in Peruvian archaeology, excavating at the PARACAS cemeteries and at PACHACAMAC. He was one of the first people to study the culture of CHAVÍN.

TENOCHTITLAN, Mexico Founded in AD 1345, the capital city of the AZTECS was built on a group of swampy islets in the middle of lake Texcoco in the valley of Mexico. It was connected to the mainland by three causeways and surrounded on its perimeter by CHINAMPAS, while aqueducts brought fresh water into the city. Tenochtitlan was beseiged for 90 days and eventually fell to the Spanish in 1521 when it was razed to the ground save for a few surviving buildings.

■ **TEOTIHUACAN, Mexico** One of the largest urban and ceremonial sites in the New World. At its height around 500 AD, Teotihuacan stretched for over 20 square km and had an estimated population of 100–200,000 persons. The whole city is planned to a central grid and orientated to a north–south axis, matching the central ceremonial structures which are disposed along the 3km Avenue of the Dead. To its north end lies the PYRAMID of the Moon, commanding the entire length of the Avenue, and on the east side lies the mighty Pyramid of the Sun 60m high by 210m broad at the base, which was even larger in its original form. At the southern end, near its intersection with the main east–west street, lies the Ciudadela with the Temple of Quetzalcoatl and the Great Compound, which was possibly a market area. Between these and all around lie temples, sunken courts, PLAZAS, palaces and the countless apartment-like dwellings of the townsfolk. Teotihuacan can be seen to dominate the religious and political scene of Mesoamerica as far away as the Gulf coast, Guatemala and even the Maya region at such sites as EL TAJIN, KAMINAL-JUYU and TIKAL through the spread of certain distinctive traits, characteristic of the city. The most important of these are TALUD-TABLERO architecture, pottery with shapes

such as candeleros, floreros and slab-leg cylindrical tripod vessels, and the depiction of important deities like the rain god TLALOC and the almost universal QUETZALCOATL. The presence of Mexican warriors carved onto stela 31 at Tikal in the Maya lowlands indicates that the influence from Teotihuacan was not necessarily peaceful. About 200 years before the end of the Classic Period, Teotihuacan suffered severe depopulation and was finally burned about AD 750, the reasons for which are unknown. Leadership passed to other local and powerful centres like CHOLULA.

TEPEXPAN, Lake Texcoco, Valley of Mexico Fossil man site of the late Pleistocene Upper Becerra deposit *c* 8000 BC. The skeleton is probably female and measures about 1.55m tall. It was buried with the legs flexed. The skeleton is characteristically of the AMERINDIAN physical type. *See also* SANTA ISABEL IZTAPAN.

TERP Artificial mounds made by the FRISIANS in the Low Countries to raise their settlements above flood level. Some *Terpen* built in the 3rd century BC continued in use until the medieval period. At sites such as Ezinge preservation of organic material, especially wood and leather, is very good. Timber longhouses with wattle animal stalls have been found with walls standing 50cm or more high provide much information about the everyday life of the pre-Roman Iron Age and MIGRATION PERIOD.

● **TERRACOTTA** A low-grade earthenware made of clay fired at a fairly low temperature (about 750°C) to give a soft finish. It is found commonly between the NEOLITHIC and ROMAN periods, being much used for figurines as well as for lamps.

TERRAMARA CULTURE A Bronze Age CULTURE in the Po valley, Italy, along the line of the Apennine foothills. The villages were artificially built up by as much as 4m to raise the settlements above flood plain level. The archaeological deposits are black and organic, hence the name *terra mara* ('black earth'). Both the metalwork and the CREMATION burials (in URNFIELD cemeteries) are very similar to the Urnfield settlements in Hungary. It is probable that immigrants from Hungary founded the Terremare sites. *See also* PESCHIERA.

TERRA SIGILLATA
see SAMIAN WARE; ARRETINE WARE

TERRET One of two bronze rings fixed upright on the CHARIOT rail or yoke of a draught horse, through which the driving reins pass. Many of the CELTIC terrets were extremely ornate.

TETRARCHY A system of government of the Roman empire introduced by Diocletian in the 3rd century AD. The empire having become unwieldy, he divided it into two, and created an 'Augustus' for both the Eastern and the Western halves. Each Augustus had a deputy, entitled 'Caesar', who would succeed him as well as helping him during his lifetime: hence inscriptions which refer to four Emperors (AVGGGG). The reform probably did much to postpone the breakdown of the empire: it did not, however, solve the thorny problem of the succession.

THEATRE A building for dramatic performances, a standard feature of Greek and Roman cities. Greek theatres were usually sited with a hillside as a base for tiers

of seats; the stage was open and the auditorium enclosed some two-thirds of a circle. The seating of Roman theatres was built up on a substructure and enclosed a semi-circle; behind the stage there was usually a stage building, often elaborately embellished with columns and niches, so that the whole auditorium was enclosed.

THEBES, Egypt Greek name loosely applied to the district in southern Egypt containing major temples to the state-god Amun and the necropolis of the pharaohs and their funerary complexes. Ancient Egyptians called it Waset (Sceptre). From a relatively obscure group of villages, it began its rise to supreme metropolis and religious capital with re-unification of Egypt under Dynasty XI. From Dynasty XVIII onwards, its local god Amun became King of all the gods – his temples adorned with impressive pylons, halls and columns, his priesthood wealthy from donations by the pharaohs. Despite massive destruction during Assyrian invasion (665 BC) pharaohs and Roman emperors continued adding to the city of Amun. For Eastern Thebes *see also* KARNAK, LUXOR. For Western ■ Thebes *see also* COLOSSI OF MEMNON, DEIR EL-BAHRI, DEIR EL-MEDINA, MEDINET HABU, RAMESSEUM, SHEIKH ABD EL-QURNA, TUTANKHAMUN, VALLEY OF THE KINGS, VALLEY OF THE QUEENS.

THERA, Greece An island in the Aegean Sea, famous for its volcano, which *c* 1450 BC exploded with a force greater than Krakatoa. Crete bore the brunt of the explosion, and the MINOAN culture there seems to have been destroyed. Akrotiri, a Minoan colony on Thera, was buried by the blast. *See also* ATLANTIS.

THERMOLUMINESCENT DATING Pottery contains minute proportions of radioactive elements which emit alpha particles. The alpha particles in turn release electrons from other elements which then become trapped in a slightly different way. When the pottery is heated to a considerable temperature the electrons are released and emit energy in the form of light. This phenomenon is utilized in thermoluminescent dating. The specimen is heated, and the emitted light measured. The rate of alpha particle production is then calculated, as is the ability of the pottery to trap the electrons released. From this information can be calculated the date of the firing of the pot. At present the method is usually accurate only to within 10 per cent of the calculated date.

THERMOREMANENT MAGNETISM
see ARCHAEOMAGNETISM

THETFORD, Norfolk First mentioned in the Anglo-Saxon Chronicle in AD 870, Thetford is the only Anglo-Saxon town with any substantial archaeological evidence. It was a new foundation by the ANGLES, and probably grew from a small trading settlement along the banks of the river Ouse. By the mid 10th century the town possessed a mint, was the seat of a bishop, and was one of the largest towns in the country. GRUBENHÄUSER with 2 posts were excavated in the town south of the river, possibly indicating pagan occupation. Several buildings dated to 9–12th centuries have been found on either side of the river. They are large rectangular structures up to 36m long; some have cellars. In the 11th century the town shifted site to the north of the river. There is no apparent street plan, but perhaps some zoning of industrial belts. One major product was hard,

grey, wheel-thrown pottery known as Thetford ware and exported all over eastern England.

THIN SECTIONING A technique used principally for examining stone, pottery and wood. A small section of material is cut from an artefact and ground down until it becomes translucent. In this condition it may be studied under a microscope, using light transmitted through the sample. Individual minerals can be identified in stone and pottery. Thin sectioning may be used to group together artefacts, such as stone axes according to their mineral composition, and has enabled groups to be assigned to geological sources and even individual rock deposits. Thin sections in wood are cut rather than ground, and are used to identify the tree from which it came.

● **THOMSEN, Christian (1788–1865)** The first curator of the National Museum of Denmark. Before its opening in 1819 he classified the collection of antiquities, dividing it for convenience into objects of stone, metal and pottery. He devised the THREE-AGE SYSTEM, deciding that a Stone Age came before a Bronze and Iron Age. He thus introduced the idea of time and sequence into prehistory; previously all pre-Roman objects were classed together. The theory of the Three Ages was published in his *Guide Book to Nordic Antiquity* (1836), although it was not accepted for another ten years.

THOTH Ancient Egyptian moon-god with main cult centre at HERMOPOLIS, although his origins probably lie in the Delta. His manifestations are the ibis or baboon. His province seems to have been mainly intellectual, he being the god who invented HIEROGLYPHS and who controlled divisions of time. Naturally enough scribes looked to him as their personal god. In the BOOK OF THE DEAD we see Thoth as an ibis recording the verdict of the weighing of the heart, and it is up to him to ensure that the examination has been properly conducted, sitting as a baboon on the top of the scales. His Egyptian role as god of wisdom is hardly reflected in the identification by the Greeks (based on one of his lesser functions) of Thoth with their messenger god Hermes. In the world's creation Thoth as an ibis lays the egg from which the sun-god emerges (*see* OGDOAD).

THREE AGE SYSTEM The chronological division of the prehistoric period into a sequence of three epochs or 'ages'. The term was first used by THOMSEN in 1819 for the periods when stone, bronze, and iron respectively were the principal materials used for tools. More recently a short COPPER AGE has been inserted by some scholars between the Stone and Bronze Ages. The Stone Age was originally divided into the PALAEOLITHIC period (or 'Old Stone Age', characterized by tools of chipped stone), and the NEOLITHIC period ('New Stone Age', with polished stone tools and a knowledge of farming). A MESOLITHIC stage is often inserted between Palaeolithic and Neolithic. The dates of these periods vary in different parts of the world.

THULE An ESKIMO culture which had spread across much of north Alaska, Arctic Canada and Greenland by *c* AD 1000 and was directly antecedent to historic and modern Eskimo groups in the area.

TIAHUANACO, Bolivia Located on the shores of lake Titicaca at an altitude of 3900m Tiahuanaco was a capital of one of the two great empires in the Middle Horizon

■

Period (*see* PERU; HUARI). Much of the city's nucleus was constructed prior to the beginning of the Middle Horizon in AD 600, but such important edifices as the great stone PLATFORM MOUND called the Acapana, and the Gateway of the Sun appear at the beginning of the period. Although Tiahuanaco influenced a wide area including the southern highlands of Peru and Bolivia, and the Far South Coast down to northern Chile, it does not seem to have been an empire based on military conquest like its neighbour Huari, but rather a religious and economic phenomenon like Chavín (*see* CHAVÍN DE HUANTAR). It seems to have been the birthplace for the themes central to Middle Horizon iconography such as the gateway god, the figure represented on the Gateway of the Sun. These main ideas were transmitted to Huari in the south central highlands of Peru from where they were widely disseminated.

TIEN CULTURE The late Bronze Age culture of the Lake Tien area of Yunnan, China, as epitomized by the site of SHIH-CHAI-SHAN, dating to the last few centuries before Christ.

▲ **TIKAL, Guatemala** One of the largest and best known of the MAYA CEREMONIAL CENTRES, situated in the rainforests of the north-east Petén. It reached its peak development *c* AD 550 when population estimates reach 45,000 persons and the site covered 123 square km. Most of the main buildings are constructed of limestone rubble and mortar faced with stone. The central area comprises five great PYRAMID temples with many palaces, STELAE altars, shrines and BALL COURTS. The East and West PLAZAS together with the North and Central Acropolis contain some of the most important structures and richest burials, whilst the two main pyramids – the Temple of the Giant Jaguar and the Temple of the Masks – rise to a height of 160km. Tikal has Preclassic origins (*see* MESOAMERICA); the earliest stela on the site dates to AD 292. Tikal maintained its optimum size and prestige until the 9th century when there is a noticeable decline, and by the 10th century all the major ceremonial structures had been abandoned.

■ **TIMBER-LACED RAMPARTS [timber-framed or box ramparts]** A technique used in the defence works of European HILLFORTS and OPPIDA from the 10th century BC; the earliest timber lacing in Britain is *c* 670 BC at Dinorben, Denbighshire. The ramparts consist of earth and/or stone walls reinforced with timbers, laid either horizontally, or vertically set into the wall; or laid in a box formation. The MURUS GALLICUS and VITRIFIED FORTS were adaptations of the widespread technique. Timber-lacing tended to be abandoned in the 1st century BC, sometimes with the adoption of GLACIS defences.

TIMGAD, Tunisia A Roman colony in north Africa founded *c* 100 BC to control a frontier area. Its plan is remarkable, being originally absolutely square (which betrays its military origins). It is one of the best-preserved Roman towns in existence with a TRIUMPHAL ARCH, THEATRE, colonnaded streets and nearly all the rigidly square houses still visible.

TIRYNS, Greece This famous MYCENAEAN fort dates from early Bronze Age times *c* 2200 BC. The main palace was constructed inside a wall of enormous 'Cyclopean' masonry *c* 1400 BC. It is in many ways one of the most perfect Mycenaean remains, yet was probably subordinate

to MYCENAE itself. The fort is uncovered and visible together with many of the internal royal apartments. The walls have tunnels under them to reach water during sieges.

TLALOC The Mexican rain god worshipped by the AZTECS, with antecedents stretching back possibly to the Preclassic OLMEC and IZAPAN traditions, where they can be seen to have a parallel development into the long-lipped MAYA CHACS. The later examples were depicted with a fringe about the mouth and large goggle eye pieces.

TLAPACOYA, Mexico Near Mexico City. The site is dated *c* 19,000 BC, earlier than TEPEXPAN and SANTA ISABEL IZTAPAN. The remains consist of hearths, animal bones and stone tools fashioned from the local andesite and from imported quartz, obsidian and basalt. There is also an important Preclassic occupation (*see* MESSOAMERICA).

● **TLATILCO, Mexico** A modern brick-yard covering an ancient cemetery, where several hundred burials of the Preclassic period (*see* MESOAMERICA) have been uncovered. Some of these graves show marked OLMEC influence; others have different pottery types and numerous distinctive figurines representing long-lasting central Mexican tradition which continued at such sites as El Arbolillo and Zacatenco.

TOLLUND, Denmark A fen where the well-preserved body of an Iron Age man was discovered in 1950. He wore a leather cap and belt, and had a leather noose around his neck; he had been hung. Various other BRONZE AGE and Iron Age bog bodies have been found, many of which died violently – Grauballe man for example died of a slit throat. Some of the bodies may have been sacrifices to the gods (*see* CELTIC ART; GUNDESTRUP). The stomach contents of both Tollund and Grauballe man consisted of vegetarian gruels, perhaps ritual meals. *See also* PAZYRYK.

TOLTEC NAHUA-CHICHIMEC peoples of the early Post-classic period (*see* MESOAMERICA) who invaded Mexico from the north-western frontier of Mesoamerica early in the 10th century AD and founded their capital at TULA in 968. These Toltecs seem to have introduced the worship of QUETZALCOATL on a wide scale, for numerous depictions of this deity are found associated with Toltec culture, whilst the ruling faction at Tula or Tollan bears this name. Legend records that in 987, Topiltzin, the ruler and priest of Quetzalcoatl and champion of peace, was deposed and exiled by the priest and followers of the god of night Tezcatlipoca who favoured war and human sacrifice. This coincides with the archaeologically demonstrated appearance of Toltec peoples in CHICHÉN ITZÁ, led by Kukulcan (which is also translated as feathered serpent). The Toltecs are best known for their introduction of militarism and human sacrifice, exemplified in the appearance of *tzompantlis* – skull-racks associated with the cult of the severed head, scenes of human sacrifice and the depiction of warriors resplendent in armour carrying weapons. Their art style is predominantly stiff and heavy, as demonstrated by the great Atlantean stone warriors at Tula, similar smaller stone carvings and CHACMOOLS. The Toltecs imported Fine Orange and PLUMBATE wares. During this period, metallurgy was introduced into Mesoamerica. The Toltec period was a time of power and plenty during which the boundaries of civilized Mesoamerica were extended to their maximum northern limit.

The Chalchihuites culture represents the northern limit of pronounced Mesoamerican influence. The fall of Tula in 1156 heralded troubled times when severe droughts in marginal areas caused northern CHICHIMEC groups to move south in search of new lands, disrupting the settled communities in their path. Toltec power became increasingly fragmented and weak; different communities founded independent centres, merging culturally with both old and newer elements in Mexico eventually to lose their identity. The purest Toltec group remained the lineage at Culhuacan with whom later tribes like the AZTECS wished to identify to underline their rise to power.

TOMB OF TI, Egypt One of the finest MASTABA tombs at SAQQARA, belonging to a court-official (Dynasty V) responsible for two pyramids and a sun temple at ABUSIR. MARIETTE first excavated the tomb. From a pillared hall, an underground passage led to the burial chamber. There was also a corridor to the offering chamber, with a serdab (cell with slit at eye level for statues of Ti to observe rituals). Low reliefs show in observant detail Old Kingdom activities, e.g. stages from tree-trunk to boat with workers adeptly using axes, adzes and clubs; goats both enticed and beaten to tread sown seed into soil; a new born calf carried by a boy across a stream watched anxiously by its mother; Ti supervising in safety the lassoing and spearing of hippopotami.

▲ **TOMB PERIOD** The protohistoric period of Japan, also known as the Kofun culture, which followed the YAYOI period *c* AD 300. It was at this point that mounded, monumental tombs (Kofun) were constructed. The tombs number at least 10,000 and suggest where the centres of power were at the time. The mounds were of varied shapes; some are round and others of 'keyhole' plan, a design apparently reserved for important rulers. The largest, NINTOKU TOMB near Osaka, covers approximately 35 hectares, necessitating vast labour forces and great organization for its construction. The highly-organized society was stratified, with large clans under the divine rule of the emperors, and trade guilds carrying hereditary positions embracing the workers and restricting their freedom. The mounted warriors of the time made extensive use of iron for their arms and armour. With the dead buried in the tumuli of the elite were symbols of wealth such as precious stones (including MAGATAMA), mirrors, and objects such as swords, horse-trappings, pottery and at times Chinese imports. HANIWA models were ceremonially placed around the tombs. Pottery was of high quality, with SUE pottery generally reserved for the funerary use of the aristocrats, and HAJI ware for domestic use, especially by the common people. During this period Chinese writing was imported by Korean scholars and adapted in Japan, along with some other features of those two cultures. By the 7th century, Buddhist influence had re-channelled customs, and temples, rather than elaborate tombs, were erected.

TORC (or torque) A neck ring of bronze or gold, often spirally twisted, worn by CELTIC leaders as a mark of distinction, although the type was known in the European Bronze Age. BOUDICCA is said to have gone into battle wearing one of gold. Gods are often shown in CELTIC ART wearing torcs.

TORO, Japan Extensive agricultural village site of the mid to late YAYOI period. Excavations revealed 11 dwellings, 2

raised store-houses, plans of ricefields, and remains of numerous artefacts, including many wooden implements.

TOU WAN
see HAN DYNASTY

TOWN PLANNING, Greek and Roman As early as the mid 7th century BC new Greek colonies in southern Italy and Sicily gave scope to enterprising architects to experiment with orthogonal, rectilinear town planning at Megara Hyblaea and probably elsewhere. Similar schemes were effected at Smyrna in Ionia, in Asia Minor, and later (during the 6th and 5th centuries BC) at AGRIGENTO, Metapontum, Selinus, Heraclea, further north at Naples and PAESTUM; and also in the ETRUSCAN towns of MARZABOTTO, near Bologna, and Capua. When Rome came in the same way, through dynamic expansion, to found military colonies at, for example, Alba Fucens, OSTIA and Cosa, the same tradition of Greek surveying was drawn on. As the Republic and then the Empire expanded, the models of this tradition which could be seen to have worked in Italy and in the HELLENISTIC kingdoms of the Middle East were applied all over the West. The many new foundations in areas with no urban tradition were sited with an eye to good communications, and proximity to good land, river crossings and harbours. The bare essentials of water supply and drainage, street layout and some form of civic nucleus, usually a FORUM, were provided. Houses and shops were left to develop from private enterprise; the wealth that was generated, in time, led to the public buildings that were typical of Roman towns: basilicas, temples, amphitheatres, theatres and baths. Initial flexibility, although on a sound basis, combined with local architectural traditions and allowed for a wide range of individuality in town plans. In the Roman East there was less scope for new foundations and it was more a case of adapting Hellenistic developments. Roman technology secured the popularity of the bath building, and the axiality of monumental Roman architecture fitted with the Hellenistic tradition of scenic architecture. Again, the individuality allowed by Roman planning saw features like the colonnaded street and fountain buildings proliferate in the East, whereas the amphitheatre and basilica never became popular.

● **TRAJAN'S COLUMN** A marble column, 30m high, erected in AD 113 to commemorate the victories of the Emperor Trajan in Dacia (modern Romania) and to serve as a tomb for himself and his wife. It was a principal feature of his new FORUM and was decorated with a continuous spiral band of reliefs illustrating his campaigns.

TRANCHET A cutting edge formed by the removal of a FLAKE at right angles to the main axis of a stone tool. Tranchet axes, which could be continually resharpened by the removal of such flakes, are characteristic of the MESOLITHIC period. Tranchet (transverse or chisel-ended) arrowheads are found in both Mesolithic and NEOLITHIC contexts. Their purpose was to stun or cut rather than to penetrate, and they were used especially to hunt birds. The arrowheads differ from tranchet axes in that the operative edge is formed by the edge of a flake or BLADE, and is not produced by a 'tranchet blow'.

TREE RING DATING
see DENDROCHRONOLOGY

▲

TRELLEBORG, Holland Situated in Zealand on a headland between two rivers, Trelleborg was an important military and naval base AD 975–1050. The fortress consisted of two sections, a main enclosure circular in plan and surrounded by a strong rampart, and an outer defence-work beyond this on the landward side. The site was planned with great precision, laid out on prepared ground in standard units of measurement based on the Roman foot. Inside the main enclosure two streets crossed at right angles in the centre, leading to four gates at the cardinal points. In each quarter of the circle four houses were arranged in squares, making a total of sixteen. The halls had bowed long walls and straight ends, with doors in the gable-ends. Internally they were divided into three parts, a central living area with a hearth, and two lateral smaller chambers, perhaps for storage purposes. Between the inner and outer ramparts thirteen other similar houses were set radially. Near the eastern gate a cemetery of about 150 graves contained the remains of men aged 20–40 years, but few women and children. Other very similar fortresses have been found at Aggersborg and Fyrkat in Denmark.

TREPANNATION [or Trephination] The practice of removing a section of bone from the skull during life. The patient frequently survived, as can be seen by the healing of the cut bone.

TREPHINATION
see TREPANNATION

TREWHIDDLE, Cornwall In 1774 a hoard of silver objects and coins was found in this mine working near St Austell. The coins are PENNIES dated AD 872–5. The silver mounts from a great drinking horn are decorated in the 'Trewhiddle style', an English fusion of Style I ANIMAL ORNAMENT and Style II INTERLACE, which was first identified here. Rare ecclesiastical objects were also found; the only surviving Anglo-Saxon chalice, 13cm high and of plain silver, and a unique scourge of plaited silver wire.

▲**TRIER, Germany** A Roman town on the river Mosel. A fort was built there in the time of AUGUSTUS, and it is possible that the plan of the streets was also laid out in this period: expansion took place after the first bridge was built by CLAUDIUS. It became in the 4th century the northern capital of the Empire but was destroyed in the 5th century. The basilica is preserved as a Christian church, and is perhaps the finest in Europe. Other notable buildings include a lavish set of baths, the Porta Nigra, a HORREA, and a double church of the 4th century.

TRIPOLYE A late NEOLITHIC and ENEOLITHIC culture in the forest steppe zone of the Ukraine, dating from *c* 3000 BC and earlier. While its material culture differs from that of the more westerly LINEAR POTTERY cultures, it shares with them the long-house. A typical Tripolye settlement consists of 30 to 50 such houses, and is sometimes defended. From the beginning, a few copper and gold objects are found.

TRISOV, Czechoslovakia A CELTIC OPPIDUM of the 1st century BC. The walls are of stone reinforced with vertical timbers, not a MURUS GALLICUS as with many other oppida. The site was chosen for its defensive potential (it has cliffs on one side and marsh on the other), and because of near-

● 

▲ 

■ 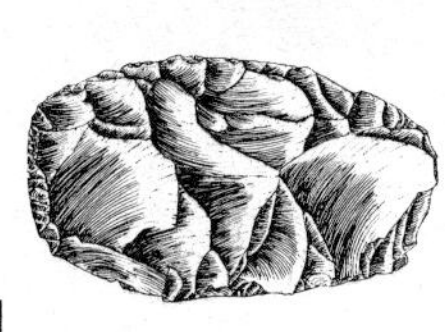

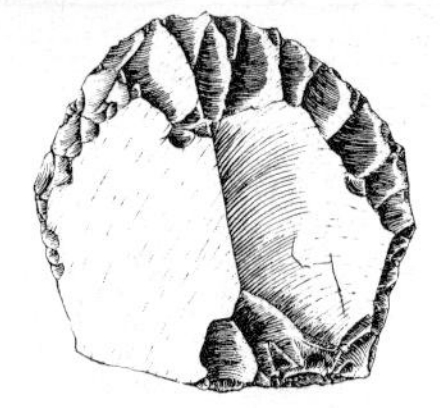

by deposits of iron ore and graphite. Pottery containing graphite was manufactured here and exported, even as far as MANCHING in Germany.

● **TRIUMPHAL ARCHES** Roman triumphal arches were built, usually crowned with a statue, in honour of individuals, towns, divinities and later the emperor from the 2nd century BC onwards. They evolved from plain, single passage arches to arches with one main passage, two side passages and much architectural and relief decoration. They were always prominent urban features, often in the FORUM.

TROY
see SCHLIEMANN

TULA [Legendary Tollan] Capital of the TOLTECS in the State of Hidalgo on the northern borders of Mesoamerica founded early in the Postclassic period (*see* MESOAMERICA) and destroyed in 1156. The ruling deity was QUETZALCOATL the feathered serpent, depictions of which appear everywhere. One of the main structures is the Temple of Quetzalcoatl on the PYRAMID of Tlahuizcalpantecuhtli, ▲ where giant warriors in stone 4m high once supported the roof with their heads; before the stairway stands the remains of a colonnaded hall – typical Toltec architecture which appears also at CHICHÉN ITZÁ.

■ **TULA ADZE** Known mainly from central Australia, these chisel-like implements are characteristcally step-flaked with an undercut edge, a generally obtuse angle and rather broad shape, with a plain striking platform. Modern examples of these stone tools are known to undergo modifications to re-sharpen them as use progressed; employed in cutting, shaping, scooping or incising by hand, they are also adapted, with resin, for mounting on SPEAR-THROWERS. They have been found in some archaeological contexts of the third millennium BC, while at KENNIFF CAVE their certain identification is placed in the second millennium BC. INGALADDI ROCK SHELTER has produced numerous specimens. Though similar forms have occasionally been noted in island south-east Asia, it so far seems that the tula adze is actually a distinctively Australian form.

TUMULUS The Latin word for a BARROW or burial mound of any date.

TUNA EL-GEBEL, Egypt Vast Graeco-Roman necropolis near the cult-centre of THOTH at HERMOPOLIS. Extensive subterranean galleries contained countless mummified baboons and ibises – sacred to Thoth. Traces of a palm garden suggest a reservation or rearing ground for the sacred creatures – watered by a huge two-storey brick well. Lefebvre excavated the hybrid tomb of Petosiris, a high-ranking priest and bureaucrat. Built during the period that marked the end of the Egyptian dynasties and the advent of ALEXANDER bringing Greek rule, the tomb contained a colourful mixture of Egyptian themes and HELLENISTIC decoration (especially in clothes and hairstyles). The sarcophagus is a masterpiece, with inlaid hieroglyphs of glass.

TURA QUARRIES, Egypt With those at Masara, the Tura quarries were the principal source on the east bank of Nile of limestone used in the necropolis of the capital MEMPHIS.

The quality of the stone added gleam and finish when casing or lining tombs. The labour force in the quarry was a highly organized unit of specialized workmen under senior officials. Inscriptions in the quarries from Middle Kingdom onwards record the names of pharaohs commissioning limestone-extraction.

TURF LINE Where an ancient land surface has been buried by an earthwork or other large deposit, the original turf is often preserved as a thick, dark line. This material can be very useful in studies of the ancient environment, by POLLEN ANALYSIS or other means. *See also* BURIED SOIL; ENVIRONMENTAL ARCHAEOLOGY.

TURKEY
see ANATOLIA

● **TUTANKHAMUN** The discovery in 1922 of his tomb in Valley of the Kings, Western Thebes, by Howard CARTER (on excavation financed by Lord Carnarvon) is a rare and, to date, unmatched example of treasure of incalculable worth rewarding an archaeologist's tenacity.

Tutankhamun, last royal-blood pharaoh of Dynasty XVIII died at about 19 years old in 1352 BC – close study of his head neither confirms nor disproves possibility of unnatural death. He was buried in a tomb originally planned for his vizier. The paintings were of unexceptional quality but interesting for their subject matter – burial procession and ceremonies (e.g. Vizier Ay performing the Opening the Mouth ritual). Carter was disappointed when he discovered that the tomb had been robbed in antiquity, but only a few objects were removed before the tomb was resealed by the necropolis police and then hidden for almost 3000 years by rubble and the huts of workers on a tomb of a later pharaoh (Ramesses VI).

After initial excitement, Carter and his colleagues meticulously photographed the tomb-contents, carried out conservation work, and removed items to Cairo Museum. Many objects are unique. The craftsmanship in metal, wood and stone is exceptional.

The Burial Chamber was almost filled by a nest of four gilded shrines representing a jubilee-festival kiosk (6m long), two Southern sanctuary replicas and one Northern sanctuary replica. These covered a quartzite sarcophagus containing three coffins in human form. The inner coffin was of solid gold and weighed 134kg. Over the King's face was a sensitive gold mask inlaid with lapis lazuli. The jewellery (pectorals, collars, bracelets and rings) mainly has designs which are of religious significance, such as the scarab beetle propelling the sun around the sky, but there are also some amusing earrings with duck's heads on bodies of the vulture goddess. On his gold-leaf wooden throne, colourfully inlaid, Tutankhamun is shown in his palace being affectionately perfumed by his queen.

TYPE-FOSSIL A particular artefact regarded as peculiar to a named archaeological CULTURE or INDUSTRY. The name of the culture may derive from the type-fossil – e.g. Beaker culture (*see* TYPE-SITE). The concept was developed in geology, where certain fossil plants or animals are used to date specific strata.

TYPE-SITE The name of a particular location has frequently been adopted as the label for an archaeological CULTURE or INDUSTRY. The type-site may have been chosen because of its representative finds, buildings etc, or because it has been extensively explored. It sometimes happens that a type-site turns out to be different from most of the other sites of the culture or industry of which it is supposedly 'typical' (this is commonly when the site was one of the earliest of its kind to have been discovered); but the name usually stays. *See* TYPE-FOSSIL.

TYPOLOGY Archaeological typology involves the study of change in the form of particular artefacts so as to arrange them in a chronological sequence. MONTELIUS worked out the basic principles in the late 19th century, and referred to the survival of stylistic features of horse-drawn coaches in railway carriages to illustrate his argument. Supported by STRATIGRAPHY, typology soon came to provide the spine of prehistoric chronology in the Old World. This role is now increasingly being taken on by RADIOCARBON dating, which is not susceptible to the subjective judgements for which typological sequences have been criticized.

TYRE
see PHOENICIANS

UAXACTUN, Guatemala Important MAYA CEREMONIAL CENTRE in the lowland forests of the Petén region. A stele with a date of AD 328 bears the second earliest Long Count (*see* CALENDAR) date in the Maya region and the site is one of the earliest in the Petén. A Classic (*see* MESOAMERICA) period building has a fine fresco of a ceremonial procession.

UBAID, Iraq The site of Al Ubaid is 7km from UR. It has given its name to a culture of about 4000 BC found during excavations 1919–24. The Ubaid culture replaces the HALAF culture in the north and later develops into the civilization of SUMER. Pottery is buff in colour and decorated with simple designs in black or brown. Houses were probably similar to the dwellings, made from reeds and coated with mud, of the modern inhabitants of the marshes. Further north, buildings were made of mud-brick. The remains of boats, nets and slings indicate that the economy was based on fishing and hunting.

UGARIT [modern Ras Shamra], Syria A site on the north coast excavated since 1929. Although the site has been inhabited since *c* 6000 BC, excavations have concentrated on the large city of 1900–1200 BC date, from which two temples, a palace, the fortifications and numerous houses have been uncovered. A number of archives of CUNEIFORM TABLETS are the most important finds. Various languages and scripts are represented, including a local ALPHABET. Religious epics, administrative documents and school texts are in the archives. A kiln full of TABLETS was found. One was a reply to a foreign king who had requested military aid: the king of Ugarit explains that his own navy and army are elsewhere and that he himself has been raided. Ugarit was destroyed by the Sea People before the kiln was fired and the letter sent. *See also* BAAL.

UHLE, Max (1856–1944) An important pioneer in South American archaeology whose work contributed to the basic chronological framework only superseded recently by modern research. He was one of the first explorers in this area to apply modern scientific archaeological techniques of STRATIGRAPHIC excavation and the seriation of finds through TYPOLOGICAL studies. Much of his work was carried out on the Coast of Peru, where he excavated at the site of PACHACAMAC and also MOCHICA and CHIMU sites. He extended his research into the highlands of Peru and Bolivia, visiting TIAHUANACO and travelling up into Ecuador and down into Chile.

UJJAIN, India One of the sixteen MAHAJANAPADAS, situated in central India. The BLACK-AND-RED WARE period, from 750 BC, has iron from the beginning, also mud houses and a massive rampart. PAINTED GREY WARE was also found. The period 500–200 BC is marked by NORTHERN BLACK POLISHED WARE associated with bone arrowheads, inscribed seals, coins and terracottas. A tiled workshop for making beads and arrowheads was found. *See also* ARYANS; GANGES CIVILIZATION.

UMAYYADS
see OMAYYADS

UMM el-QAAB, Egypt Site at Abydos in Upper Egypt. The name is Arabic for 'Mother of pots' because of a mound of pottery sherds left by visitors erroneously supposing they were seeing the grave of the god OSIRIS. In fact the site is a cemetery of the Archaic period. Royal monuments were among hundreds of graves, first excavated by the French archaeologist Amélineau. These were underground rectangular constructions of mud brick – sometimes with granite paving. Some were burnt, all violated. Royal STELAE and sealings gave names of early pharaohs. PETRIE's work here marked a great improvement in techniques and systematic surveying of sites. The main result was an increase in royal names of Archaic period, e.g. Djet, Den, Peribsen. Whether SAQQARA's archaic mastabas contained royal corpses while Abydos monuments are cenotaphs is not universally agreed.

ÚNĚTICE [Aunjetitz] An Early Bronze Age culture centred on Czechoslovakia and dating from *c* 2000 to 1600 BC. The majority of finds come from the CREMATION cemeteries; few settlement sites are known. The knowledge of copper was probably introduced by the BEAKER people, and in the Únětice phase bronze and gold metallurgy quickly became highly organized. There were skilled craftsmen and good supplies of raw materials from the Transylvanian mountains. Únětice metal products were exported over a wide area, in particular pins and AXES, and the bronze HALBERD which was developed here. The later Únětice was contemporary with the Early Bronze Age WESSEX CULTURE in Britain, and certain similarities can be seen between the two, in particular rich graves and wide trading connections. The graves contain amber imported from northern Europe; and Wessex graves have FAIENCE beads similar to those in the Únětice area.

UNIVALLATE Having only one rampart and/or ditch. Used particularly of HILLFORT defences.

UR [modern Tell el-Muqaiyar], Iraq A site by the river Euphrates. Excavation was directed by WOOLLEY 1922–34 and concluded with his spectacular find of the Royal Cemetery. The kings and queens of *c* 2900–2700 BC were buried with much of their wealth together with their servants. A second period of splendour began when Ur-Nammu founded the third dynasty *c* 2100 BC. A

large ZIGGURAT and a complex of temples and palaces testify to the richness of this period. Although Ur was destroyed by the Elamites (*see* SUSA) *c* 2000 BC it was soon rebuilt with spacious buildings. It was from here that Abraham journeyed. Ur was finally deserted in the 4th century BC after a long period of decline.

URAEUS Emblem of a cobra poised to strike, worn on forehead of deities, pharaohs and queens in Ancient Egypt. Personification of Wadjet (Edjo) major goddess of Northern Egypt whose cult centre was at Buto. Aggressive protectress of the pharaoh as ruler over Lower Egypt. Also manifestation of the scorching ferocity in the eye of the Sun-god. Statues show variety in the way it coils back across the head. The Sudanese pharaohs (Dynasty XXV) wear two juxtaposed uraei.

URARTU
see HURRIANS

URNFIELD CULTURES A group of BRONZE AGE cultures sharing a common burial practice of urned CREMATIONS in large cemeteries. The Urnfield period is noted for its beaten bronze metalwork, particularly helmets, and for the widespread occurrence of FIBULAE; these gradually replaced the earlier UNETICE pins. The Urnfield period lasted from *c* 1300 to 800 BC, though in Germany and France it continued until the 6th century BC. Iron had already made its appearance by the beginning of the HALLSTATT phase.

URUK [Biblical Erech, modern Warka], Iraq A site in southern MESOPOTAMIA 55km north-west of UR. It was a major-city state in SUMER and its earliest levels contain the development of that civilization through a period called after the name of this site. The Uruk culture of *c* 3500–3000 BC can be distinguished by the appearance of undecorated wheel-made pottery in a greater variety of shapes than the preceding UBAID culture. Buildings become considerably larger and were sometimes decorated with cone mosaic in which terracotta cones with painted heads were pressed into the mud plaster of the outside wall. The CYLINDER seal superseded the stamp seal, and the beginning of WRITING is seen during this period in the form of pictographic TABLETS. Later Uruk was a powerful city. GILGAMESH was its fifth king and its temples and ZIGGURAT indicate its religious importance. Although it lost its supremacy to Ur in about 2100 BC, Uruk continued to be an important city until it was destroyed by the SASSANIANS *c* AD 250.

UXMAL, Mexico A late Classic MAYA CEREMONIAL CENTRE in the Puuc Hills, north Yucatan, important for its elaborate relief mosaic facades. The ceremonial structures are typical of the Puuc architectural style, the most important of these being the 'Nunnery' quadrangle and the huge 'Governor's Palace'. Stone panels and friezes depict the long-nosed rain-god CHAC, serpent heads and otherwise mainly geometric motifs.

VAISALI, India Vaisali in north Bihar was the birthplace of Mahavira, the founder of the Jain religion. The earliest occupation was from this period (6th century BC) and contains iron and NORTHERN BLACK POLISHED WARE, which continues in the following period, 300–150 BC, when structures and a brick rampart were built. *See also* GANGES CIVILIZATION.

▲

VAL CAMONICA, Italy A valley in the Alps containing hundreds of rock carvings, dating from the Bronze Age to the medieval period. Drawings include human figures, animals, weapons, ploughing scenes, and abstract designs (e.g. sun symbols).

▲ **VALLEY OF THE KINGS, Western Thebes, Egypt.** Dominated by the summit known as el-Qorn (the Horn). Tombs of pharaohs from Dynasties XVIII to XX were cut into the mountainside. Despite efforts of the necropolis police, the tombs were pillaged in antiquity. There are PAPYRI recording a pharaonic trial of tomb robbers. The usual tomb plan consists of corridors, antechamber and pillared burial chamber. Wall decoration takes the form of pictures and texts to help the king in the underworld. Sixty-two tombs have been discovered in the east and west wadis of the royal necropolis. The tomb of Sethos I (Dynasty XIX) is one of the most outstanding discoveries made by BELZONI in 1817. Scenes, over 100m long, show Sethos before deities. His alabaster sarcophagus was removed to London, and his excellently preserved mummy (found in a cache at DEIR EL-BAHRI) was taken to Cairo. *See* TUTANKHAMUN.

VALLEY OF THE QUEENS, Western Thebes, Egypt. Burials (discovered mainly by Museum of Turin excavations under Schiaparelli) for royal ladies of Dynasties XIX–XX. Many tombs were unfinished or ruined. Princes dying young were also buried here. The best decorated tomb, and most elaborate belongs to Queen Nefertari, wife of Ramesses II (Dynasty XIX) – but conservation is a problem because of underground damp which is seriously affecting polychrome reliefs. Themes are funerary, such as the queen being taken by ISIS to the beetle-headed sun-god, or offering to OSIRIS.

VALLUM In general, a term used to denote a bank and rampart, e.g. in a HILL-FORT; in particular a large ditch, about 3m in depth and about 6m in width, along the south side of HADRIAN'S WALL. On each side of the ditch, separated by a broad berm (open space), is a substantial, turf-revetted bank. The Vallum appears to have been constructed some little time after the Wall itself. A lightly-metalled road, perhaps for patrols, runs along the south berm. The function of the Vallum is not clear, but it may have been a line of demarcation of the military zone. At the time of the construction of the ANTONINE WALL, the Vallum was deliberately breached by causeways at close intervals.

VANDALS Originating in eastern Germany, the Vandals took part in the great migrations of the 5th century AD. They passed rapidly through Gaul and Spain leaving little trace, and moved into north Africa. Led by Geiseric they took CARTHAGE and Hippo, then the intellectual centres of the world. Their importance was out of all proportion to their numbers since they controlled the vital grain and oil reserves of the Mediterranean. After raids on the Italian coast, Justinian made several attempts to recapture Carthage and re-establish the Roman empire in north Africa. Although his troops eventually succeeded under Belisarius, the Vandal occupation had changed the whole pattern of trade routes in Europe, and the Moslem expansion soon closed down what few remained.

VARVE DATING Varves are layered sediments found in PERIGLACIAL lakes. They are formed by the annual

deposition of sand and clay material washed into the lakes by summer meltwater from ice sheets. The varves vary in thickness as the amount of meltwater varies from year to year. Varve dating involves the establishment of a sequence of varves which date from the present day back into the PLEISTOCENE. The method used is similar to that used in DENDROCHRONOLOGY. Newly found deposits can be dated by comparing their varve patterns to the master pattern of varve fluctuations already established.

VEDAS A series of hymns composed by the ARYANS in the 2nd and 1st millennia BC, though not committed to writing until 14th century AD. The earliest is the RIGVEDA centred in north-west India; in the later Vedas the focus shifts to the Ganges indicating a movement eastwards. Although primarily religious, the Vedas include considerable information on the way of life of the Aryans. *See also* GANGES CIVILIZATION; PAINTED GREY WARE.

VENTRIS, Michael (1922–56) Famous for his decipherment of LINEAR B in 1952 when he showed it to be a hieroglyphic form of Greek, thus extending the language back by 700 years. He worked as an architect but was helped in his solution by his wartime code-breaking work. *Documents in Mycenaean Greek* (with John Chadwick) was published shortly after his death in a road accident in 1956.

VÉRTESSZÖLLÖS, Hungary A travertine quarry near Budapest which has produced an OLDOWAN-type pebble tool industry dating from the Mindel interstadial (*see* GLACIATION). These tools may therefore be contemporary with the ABBEVILLEAN elsewhere. The implements are notable for their small size, from 10mm–60mm long – a possible explanation being the lack of suitable raw material. Fragments of burnt bone provide one of the earliest indications of the use of fire by man.

● **VERULAMIUM, Hertfordshire** A Roman town near St Albans which was founded next to a BELGIC settlement in Prae Wood. After early military occupation by the river the town was established as a MUNICIPIUM in AD 50. Sacked by BOUDICCA in 60–61, the town did not recover until the 70s when a FORUM and BASILICA in Italian style were built. Its richest period was in the 2nd century with some stagnation in the 3rd century and recovery in the 4th. Occupation of the town continued well into the 5th century and there is no evidence of SAXON attack. Visible remains are some of the walls (3rd century), the theatre and several private houses. The near-by town of St Albans was founded on the spot of the reputed martyrdom of St Alban *c* 304.

VETERA
see XANTEN

VETULONIA The Etruscan city of *Vetluna*, now known as Vetulonia, lies about 20km from the coast near Grossetto, Italy. Some remains of city walls and houses survive but it is most noted for its vast cemeteries, the grave goods from which date from the 8th–6th centuries BC.

▲ **VIA APPIA** One of the best-known Roman roads, running south from Rome via Capua to Brindisi. Started in 312 BC, it reached Brindisi in 246 BC. The terminus is marked by two columns erected by Trajan in AD 117.

▲

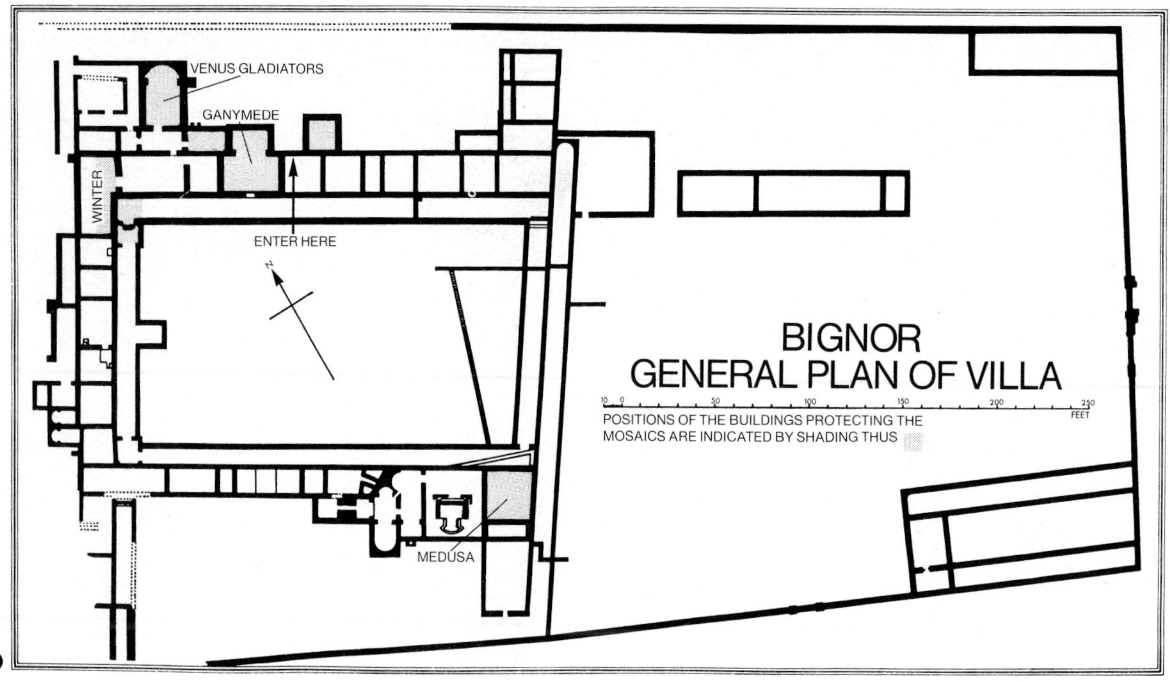

VICUS, Peru Locality in the upper Piura valley on the far north coast best known for its NEGATIVE PAINTED pottery in modelled forms typical of the north coast and highlands areas. *See also* MOCHE; RECUAY.

VICUS, (plural vici) The smallest self-administering unit in a Roman province, usually a large village or small town; it could, however, be a sub-division for purposes of administration of a larger unit. The COLONIA of LINCOLN is mentioned as having several *vici*. Smaller CIVITAS capitals might form a single vicus. In military areas, particularly along HADRIAN'S WALL and the STANEGATE, civilian vici are known to have existed close to, and perhaps largely dependent upon, the military settlements. Some British vici may have been promoted to the status of MUNICIPIA.

VIHARA An Indian monastery (generally Buddhist) developed from the arrangement of hermits' huts round a central space. Rock-cut examples comprise a square central hall enclosed on three sides by cells with the fourth a doorway with portico and verandah. Often there are two storeys with a barrel roof. *See* ROCK-CUT ARCHITECTURE.

VIKINGS The name given to the peoples living in Scandinavia AD 800–1100. They were pirates and raiders operating along the whole of the western European coast, great seamen and navigators who built splendid ships such as those found at OSEBERG and GOKSTAD. Theirs was a barbaric, heroic society which produced epic poetry, an elaborate cosmology, fine weapons, metal-work and wood-carvings. A strong colonizing impulse led to the settlement of eastern Europe by the Swedes who were trading along the Dnieper route to BYZANTIUM and the East. Towns such as NOVGOROD were set up where Scandinavian and SLAV culture intermingled. The first westward raids are recorded in AD 793 when LINDISFARNE was sacked. These Vikings came mainly from Norway, and settled in the Western Isles of Scotland, the Isle of Man and the Irish coast around Dublin. In the 10th century ICELAND, Greenland and VINLAND were colonized. Warriors from Denmark attacked England and the Channel ports such as HAMWIH, QUENTOVIC and DORESTAD, and eventually settled in England in the DANELAW area. The Vikings were international traders, and set up marts at BIRKA, HEDEBY and KAUPANG where goods from the Baltic were exchanged for Eastern and European items.

VILLA A Roman farm, although the term is also customarily used to denote the main farmhouse building. Although villas are known with, for instance, mining industries attached to them, the vast majority depended upon agriculture. They vary very considerably in scale, from a simple range of rooms and a few hectares, as at Ickleton, to palaces with large estates, as at FISHBOURNE or MONTMAURIN. Moderately prosperous villas usually have a comfortable suite of rooms, bath house (often heated by HYPOCAUSTS) and one or more MOSAIC floors, as well as the outbuildings necessary to the working life. The ground plans of the main buildings develop loosely from simple aisled corridors to winged ranges around courtyards. With their mosaics, wall-paintings and statuary, the richer villas contain many gems of Roman art. The villa as an economic unit was self-sufficient and very efficient: it is likely that the whole of particularly fertile areas was occupied by villa estates. *See also* BIGNOR; CHEDWORTH; HADRIAN'S VILLA; WOODCHESTER.

VILLANOVAN An advanced Iron Age culture which flourished from the 9th century BC on the west coast of Italy, north of Rome. Most of the information about the culture comes from cemeteries like Villanova and TARQUINIA, although some occupation material was found at Veii and Luni. The graves contain CREMATIONS in urns, in an URNFIELD cemetery. The grave goods are extremely wealthy, possibly reflecting the Villanovan success in trading. From the 7th century BC, the Villanovans were dominated by the ETRUSCANS, and later still by ROME.

VINČA, Jugoslavia A large TELL on the banks of the Danube near Belgrade. At the base of the settlement mound are STARČEVO layers. These are followed by a series of deposits relating to the various later NEOLITHIC and ENEOLITHIC Vinča cultures.

VINDONISSA, Switzerland This legionary fortress, founded *c* AD 16, was the base for the 13th Legion until AD 45–6, thereafter for the 21st Legion, the 'Plunderer'. This legion's violent behaviour towards the locals caused its transfer in AD 69 and the 11th Faithful Claudian Legion took its place. The fortress was abandoned *c* AD 100 because it was too far from the frontiers. The civil population remained outside the fort, though was housed inside from *c* AD 260 after barbarian attacks. A lot of the fort has been excavated but little remains to be seen.

VINLAND According to early Icelandic records, Leif Eriksson left Greenland in AD 992 with 35 men to settle and explore land sighted by Bjarni Herjolfsson in 986. The first landfall was called *Helluland* (Stoneland), the second *Markland* (Forestland) the third *Vinland* (Wineland), where there was abundant timber, fish and vines. Eriksson wintered there, and returned to Greenland. Serious attempts at colonization were later made by Karlsefni and others, but failed because of the great distance from their home country. It is certain that the men of Greenland discovered a non-arctic part of the mainland of the American continent *c* 1000, but precisely which part is uncertain. Excavations at L'Anse au Meadow in northern Newfoundland revealed several objects of VIKING type and the remains of a turf-walled house RADIOCARBON dated to the late 10th century.

VISIGOTHS Moved from the eastern homelands of the GOTHS, the Visigoths entered Europe as Imperial Federates employed in Aquitaine against Attila the HUN and his attacks on Gaul in AD 451. They rounded on their employer and moved into southern France and into Spain. By *c* 550 AD they completely controlled south and central Spain. Unlike the other barbarian kingdoms of the 5th and 6th centuries, they renounced their heretical Arian Christianity, rejoined the Roman church, and were able to remain on friendly terms with the Roman empire. The Visigothic domination of Spain lasted until early in the 8th century when the first onslaught of Arab invasion was felt. Like the OSTROGOTHS their material culture was heavily influenced by both Mediterranean classicism and Germanic art styles which they shared with the FRANKS.

VITRIFIED FORTS Iron Age HILLFORT defences in Scotland were often TIMBER-LACED stone ramparts, which had been burnt after construction. It is difficult to know if the firing was deliberate, but at times the heat was so intense that the rock melted and fused, i.e. vitrified.

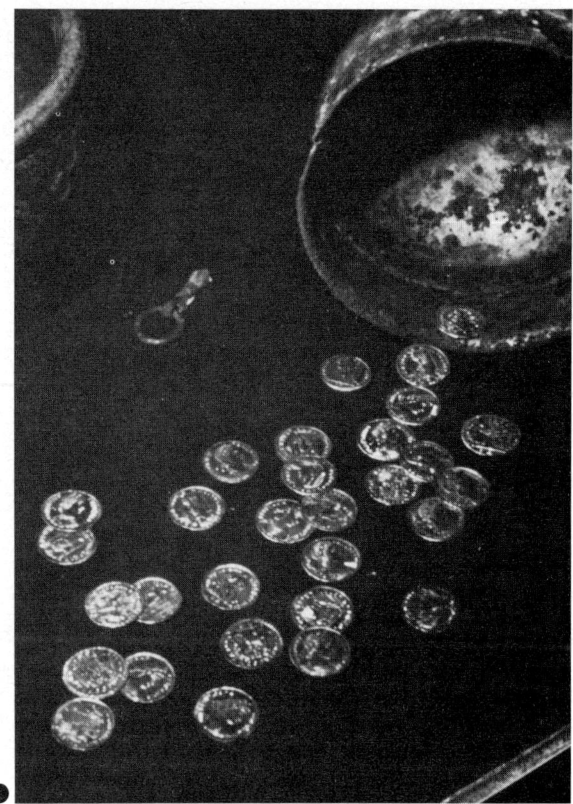

VIX, France The HALLSTATT burial of a woman. Dating to *c* 500 BC, the burial was in a timber mortuary house under a mound, with a bronze-decorated waggon. This mode of burial spread across Europe under the influence of CIMMERIAN horsemen; Vix contained some of the characteristic harness types. (*see also* DEJEBJERG.) The grave goods at Vix were very rich and many were imports from Greece and ETRUSCAN Italy. Especially important was the enormous Greek bronze krater or vessel for mixing wine. Many of the objects were associated with the wine trade which ran up the Rhône valley from the Mediterranean. The Mont Lassois hillfort associated with the Vix burial is in the centre of a very rich area, and trade in wine to the rest of Europe was probably controlled from this centre. *See also* HOHMICHELE.

VOLSINII, Italy The site of Volsinii, anciently considered to be the centre of Etruria, was usually thought to correspond with modern Bolsena which stands at the north-east corner of lake Bolsena. Although the ACROPOLIS is surrounded by strong walls of the ETRUSCAN period, there are no extensive cemeteries associated with the site and it is possible that Etruscan Volsinii may in fact have been on the site of modern ORVIETO. Volsinii was sacked by Rome in 265 BC and the populace evicted. It is thought that Orvieto therefore represents Etruscan Volsinii while Bolsena represents the city occupied during the Roman period.

VOLTERRA, Italy This ETRUSCAN city lies about 70km south-west of Florence on a hilltop overlooking the valley of the river Cecina. As with many Etruscan cities, Volterra started life as a VILLANOVAN settlement and occupation has continued to the present day. The best-preserved monuments are the city wall and the Porta dell'Arco (with heads of Etruscan deities). The cemeteries are noted for the alabaster cinerary urns with high relief decoration; the archaic sculptured stelae and the painted vases of the 3rd and 4th centuries BC are also notable.

WALDALGESHEIM, Germany A LA TÈNE chariot burial dating to *c* 400 BC. A male was buried with a CHARIOT, bronze harness and a bronze jug; laid across him was a female burial accompanied by gold ornaments. Both the jug and the ornaments were decorated in the abstract Waldalgesheim style of CELTIC ART. It has been suggested that all objects of Waldalgesheim type were made by a single school of craftsmen, and exported across Europe from a centre in the Rhineland.

WATERLOGGING Many of the most important archaeological finds of organic materials (notably wood) have been preserved in waterlogged conditions. Although such materials usually decay after burial, thorough saturation with water excludes air and thus helps to prevent bacteriological deterioration. Major sites with waterlogged materials include STAR CARR and the SOMERSET LEVELS. Viking ships such as those found in Roskilde Fjord, Denmark, were preserved in this way. Waterlogged material, although apparently robust, is usually very much degraded and will shrink and lose its shape if allowed to dry out too quickly. Chemical treatment is needed to prevent total disintegration.

● **WATER NEWTON, Cambridgeshire** This Romano-British town was the ancient Durobrivae, on the London–Lincoln road (ERMINE STREET). It is situated in the

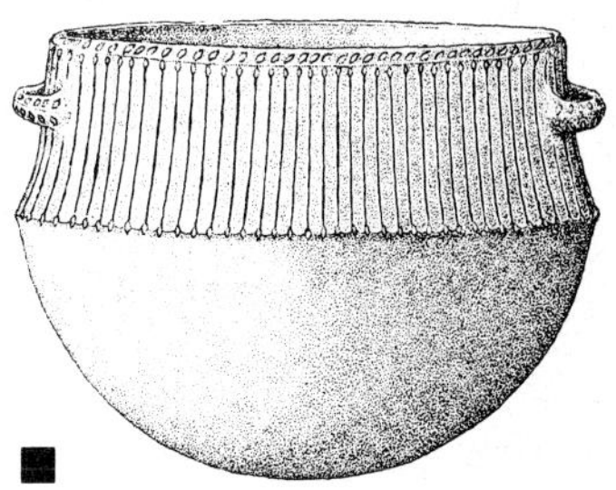

clay-rich Nene Valley and was a centre for pottery production. Originating with military potters of the 1st century AD, the industry grew so that by the early 3rd century it dominated most of the English fine pottery industry with COLOUR-COATED WARE. The finest period of production was the 4th century. A hoard of the earliest known Christian silver was found here in 1975.

WATLING STREET A Roman road running from London to Wroxeter in Shropshire and thence to Wales. It was an Imperial post-road and had posting stations on it, e.g. Wall, Mancetter, High Cross. The name of the road is ANGLO-SAXON and the road itself served as the frontier between SAXONS and DANES in the 8th century.

WESSEX The kingdom of the West Saxons, centred in the 6th century AD on the upper Thames valley, which expanded south and west. After early domination by MERCIA and much raiding by the Danes, Wessex rose to power in the 9th century under Egbert and ALFRED. It eventually became the nucleus of a unified England with a national capital at WINCHESTER.

WESSEX CULTURE A localized culture of the early Bronze Age, centred on Wiltshire, with outliers in Dorset, Devon, Cornwall, Sussex and the upper Thames valley. There are no settlement sites of this period, and the cultural definition is based on a series of distinctive graves and their contents. The many rich graves of Wessex type are all under BARROWS, sometimes with a wooden dug out coffin. Wessex I (from *c* 1650–1500 BC) is characterized by INHUMATION, grooved bronze daggers of BUSH BARROW type and amber spacer beads. The cremation graves like CAMERTON and SNOWSHILL graves of Wessex 2 period (1500–1350 BC) contain ogival bronze daggers and FAIENCE. In both periods gold ornaments and objects like ▲ the RILLATON cup are common, displaying the wealth of the Wessex aristocracy. Trade with areas outside Britain is shown by substantial imports of amber from Scandinavia (*see* HOVE CUP), and faience beads from central Europe or the MYCENAEAN area. Many objects at one time thought to be imports from Mycenae were probably made locally or imported from the UNETICE culture in Hungary. There were certainly contacts with Britanny, where a similar aristocracy with rich graves had developed.

WESTERN NEOLITHIC In most areas where they are found, including central and northern France and the British Isles, the Western Neolithic cultures represent the first communities to practise an agricultural economy. ■ They include the WINDMILL HILL culture in Britain, the CHASSEY culture in France and the CORTAILLOD culture in Switzerland. On the Mediterranean coast of France and Spain, the Chassey and ALMERIAN cultures respectively succeeded earlier Neolithic groups (*see* IMPRESSED WARE cultures), as did the LAGOZZA culture of north Italy. These cultures are distinguished from the other major NEOLITHIC groups of Europe principally by their pottery, which normally consists of simple round-based vessels, lacking any elaborate painted or incised linear decoration. *See also* FUNNEL BEAKER; LINEAR POTTERY cultures.

○ **WEST KENNET, Wiltshire** The largest CHAMBER TOMB in England and Wales, about 4km south of the ceremonial centre at AVEBURY. From the finds inside the tomb (including PETERBOROUGH WARE, GROOVED WARE and ▶

BEAKERS) it is apparent that it was in use for over 1000 years. When finally closed with a SARSEN stone weighing 50 tons, it contained the scattered remains of 40 to 50 people. Using bones from this and similar tombs, it has been estimated that the typical life-span in Neolithic Britain was 30 years, slightly more for men and slightly less for women.

WEST STOW, Suffolk An early Anglo-Saxon village has been extensively excavated at this site. It was occupied for most of the 5th and 6th centuries AD, and was composed of six HALLS each with one or more GRUBENHÄUSER near by. The halls are substantial post-built structures without aisles or internal divisions. The pit-houses contain much domestic and industrial debris; there is much evidence from the large number of sheep bones and the numerous spindle-whorls, loomweights and bone combs that wool-weaving was particularly important in the economy. The halls and others structures appear to have been laid out with reference to a much-used central area which was kept clear. BUCKELURNEN and other early pottery types have been found. *See also* MUCKING.

● **WHEELER, Sir (Robert Eric) Mortimer (1890-1976)** Wheeler believed passionately in bringing the past to life. This belief spurred him on to spend his long professional career in popularizing archaeology. He earned his reputation as the founder of modern archaeology through his development of new archaeological techniques, and the exemplary reports he wrote of all his excavations. He introduced new techniques of excavation by areas laid out in neatly parcelled squares which were readily controllable and which made the recording of finds and stratigraphy much more accurate. His experience of excavation ranged from his early years on Roman sites in Wales, via Iron Age and Roman Britain, to India, where he was Director-General of Archaeology from 1944 to 1950. Whilst in India he uncovered the prehistory of the great Indus Valley civilization and also the evidence for extensive trade between Rome and the Mediterranean and India. He recognized the value of films in introducing archaeology to a mass audience, and film of his excavations at VERULAMIUM (St Albans) in the 1930s is amongst the earliest archaeological film available. In the late 1950s and early 1960s his participation in the television quiz game 'Animal, Vegetable, Mineral?' brought him nationwide recognition and acclaim as the TV Personality of the Year. The high and continuing popular interest in archaeology in Britain may be said to date from this period and his personal projection of the subject. Throughout his life honours were bestowed upon him and he held various archaeological Chairs. His major works include: *Archaeology from the Earth* (1954); Research Reports for the Society of Antiquaries on his excavations at *Lydney* (1932), *Verulamium* (1936), *Maiden Castle* (1943), *Stanwick Fortifications* (1954), *Hill-forts of Northern France* (1957); *The Indus Civilisation* (1953, 1962, 1968); *Rome Beyond the Imperial Frontiers* (1954); *Roman Art and Architecture* (1964), etc. *Still Digging* (1955) and *My Archaeological Mission to India and Pakistan* (1976) are autobiographies.

WILSFORD SHAFT, Wiltshire A BARROW here was excavated by Ashbee in 1960–62, and proved to be the conical top of a Bronze Age shaft, 30m deep and 2m wide, cut into the chalk. It was perhaps a well. The bottom was waterlogged, preserving organic remains such as beetles, moss, rope and wooden vessels.

● 

▲ 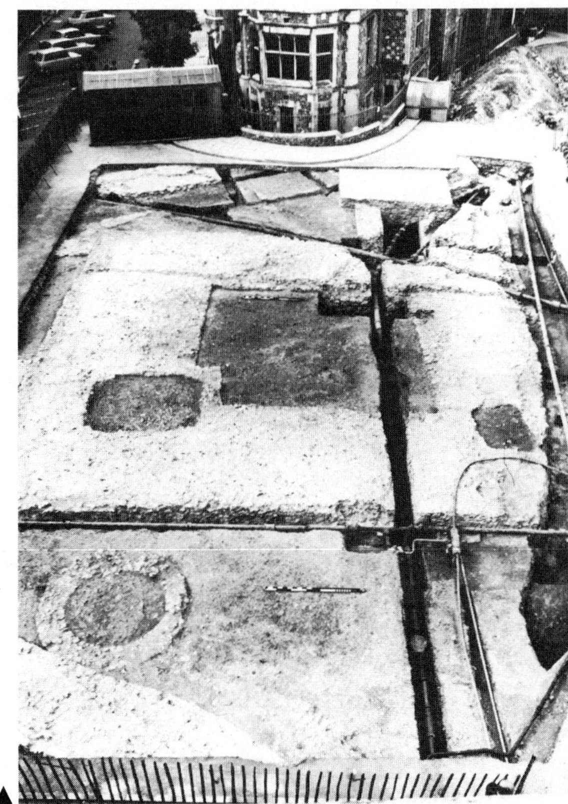

WILTON A MICROLITH-using culture of eastern and southern Africa, contemporary with the SMITHFIELD culture. Some Wilton artefacts are probably associated with rock-paintings. It has been suggested that the later Wilton people were Bushmen, presently confined to the Kalahari.

▲ **WINCHESTER, Hampshire** The capital city of WESSEX and later, under ALFRED and his successors, the capital of England in 9th–11th centuries AD. Located on the site of Roman *Venta Belgarum*, the early SAXON occupants did not adopt the existing street plan but created a new lay-out for the comparatively luxurious houses of members of the royal court. Winchester was also a centre of ecclesiastical power; a bishopric was created in the 7th century from which grew a great cathedral complex. The recent excavations have shown that it was essentially an administrative centre rather than mercantile or industrial town. Those functions were performed by HAMWIH.

WINDMILL HILL The most northerly WESTERN NEOLITHIC culture, originally called the Primary Neolithic culture of Britain, to distinguish it from the later Secondary Neolithic culture which referred to those native MESOLITHIC communities which adopted the new farming economy (*see* PETERBOROUGH WARE). From *c* 4000 BC, NEOLITHIC settlers brought sheep, cattle and domesticated cereals from across the Channel, and began to take part in communal activities such as the digging of flint mines and the erection of long earthen burial mounds. Typical settlements are surrounded by complicated shallow ditch systems (*see* CAUSEWAYED CAMP). The ditches were frequently re-dug, suggesting that the sites may have been periodically occupied, possibly by communities practising a cyclic SLASH-AND-BURN farming system comparable to the LINEAR POTTERY cultures (*see* BYLANY). Unlike the latter, however, evidence for substantial houses is lacking. It has recently been suggested that the term Windmill Hill culture should be replaced by the more general Earlier Neolithic, thus adopting a classification scheme of the type first propounded by MONTELIUS. Windmill Hill, near Avebury in Wiltshire, is one of the best known causewayed camps, and has given its name to the culture as a whole.

WISCONSIN GLACIATION The final PLEISTOCENE glacial stage in north America which began *c* 70,000 BC and ended after 9000 BC. Wisconsin correlates with the final glaciation of northern Europe. During this period, sea levels were considerably lower leaving a broad bridge of land in the Bering Straits between north Siberia and Alaska across which the first colonists of America passed.

WOODCHESTER, Gloucestershire One of the largest of Britain's Roman VILLAS, part of a cluster of rich 4th century villas in the Cotswolds. Its chief interest (exposed to public view every decade or so) is the vast MOSAIC, 15m square, of Orpheus playing his lyre to the beasts.

WOODHENGE, Wiltshire Named by its excavators after STONEHENGE, some 3km to the south-west, Woodhenge consists of six concentric rings of post-holes surrounded by a ditch in which was found GROOVED WARE. It has been claimed that each was set out from points on a Pythagorean triangle. Whatever the case, Woodhenge was certainly sited with greater care than a structure of similar size at the nearby DURRINGTON WALLS.

WOODLAND TRADITION Cultures evolving out of the ARCHAIC Tradition in the Eastern Woodlands of north America *c* 1000 BC whose economy was based on farming supplemented by hunting, fishing and collecting. Artefacts include stemmed or notched spear points, polished stone axes and adzes for wood-working, pottery vessels and figurines. Settlements were semi-permanent villages and camps and one of the most distinguishing features are the large mortuary mounds often containing rich offerings. (*See* ADENA; HOPEWELL; POVERTY POINT.) By AD 700, the Woodland gave way to the MISSISSIPPI Tradition in the Mississippi and parts of the Ohio and Missouri valleys, although in the more peripheral areas of the eastern USA, the Woodland Tradition persisted down into early historic times.

▲ **WOOLLEY, Charles Leonard (1880–1960)** Leonard Woolley is best remembered for his excavations at UR (1922–34) and Alalakh where he recovered the history of a little-known kingdom which flourished in the second millennium BC. He also excavated at Al UBAID, CARCHEMISH, Buhen and Tell el-AMARNA.

Main books: *A Forgotten Kingdom* (1953); *Excavations at Ur* (1954–76).

● **WORSAAE, J. J. A. (1821–85)** An enthusiastic and experienced Danish excavator and collector of antiquities, who was made first inspector of Danish monuments in 1847 by the king. He promulgated the THREE AGE SYSTEM, and in his book *Prehistory of Denmark* (1842) applied THOMSEN's chronology with great success to sites as well as to objects. He travelled widely in Europe and wrote many articles on European prehistory.

WRIST CLASPS Two pairs of small bronze plates of elaborate hook and eye form are often found in Dark Age female graves in EAST ANGLIA. They are normally placed near the wrist and are thought to have been sewn to each part of a tunic cuff and then linked together to form a fastening. Wrist clasps seem, from their distribution, to have been an exclusively ANGLIAN artefact.

WRITING The facilities of recording and communication provided by writing are essential to the organization basic to civilization. The earliest form of recording is picture writing (pictograms). The ideogram where one sign is equivalent to one word (as in Chinese) is the simplest form of this. Such a system requires many thousand ideograms. HIEROGLYPHICS and CUNEIFORM scripts use a more sophisticated procedure to make words from a number of signs; several hundred may be needed. LINEAR A and B and HURRIAN have signs which stand for a syllable, and only about 80 signs are required. The final development is the ■ ALPHABET. The illustration shows two ASSYRIAN scribes recording booty from a captured city; the first is incising a TABLET in AKKADIAN, a cuneiform script and the second is writing on parchment in Aramaic, an alphabetic script.

WROXETER (Viriconium), Shropshire A Roman fortress and town in the Severn valley. The fortress was founded *c* AD 60 to house the Fourteenth Legion and was later occupied by the Twentieth Legion. An important civil settlement grew up by the fortress, and is being extensively excavated. The FORUM was built *c* 129, and a large bath-house a little later. A larger forum of the late 2nd century was destroyed about a century later by a fire which affected

much of the town. There is some evidence for the sack of the town in the late 4th century.

XANTEN, Germany The site of a Roman COLONIA, founded by Trajan in AD 100. It is near the legionary fortress of Vetera, founded under Augustus and occupied until AD 70 (when it was moved a few miles away to a now-flooded site). This legionary fortress is double – for two legions – and large parts have been excavated. The fort was divided in two with one legion and all the buildings that go with it on each side. The headquarters was shared. The later colonia has also been excavated in part and has recently had a complete geophysical survey. It is the second-largest town on the Rhine after Cologne. The colony was sacked in the 3rd century, was rebuilt in the 4th century by Julian and continued to the end of the century. Subsequent FRANKISH occupation was outside in the cemeteries. Visible remains today include the amphitheatre and other buildings in the process of being uncovered.

XOCHICALCO, Morelos, Mexico An important fortified site of the early Postclassic period (*see* MESOAMERICA), constructed at the end of the Classic on a steep terraced hill defended by a series of walls and moats. The principal monument is the PYRAMID surmounted by walls and bearing carved reliefs and feathered serpents. It is one of the earliest fortified sites in Precolumbian Mexico.

X-RAY FLUORESCENCE Used in the study of the composition of metals and ceramics. The specimen to be analysed is bombarded with X-rays, and the fluorescence thus produced is examined spectrographically. Elements present can be identified by their characteristic spectra.

YAHYA, Tepe, Iran A TELL site. Excavations undertaken since 1967 show that the site was inhabited from the 5th millennium BC until the SASSANIAN period. A tablet inscribed with proto-Elamite writing and dated *c* 3500 BC is a very early example of WRITING. The main importance of the site is its position on the trade route between India and SUMER. Steatite was mined nearby and formed one of the many commodities Elam (*see* SUSA) traded with Sumer.

● **YANG-SHAO** A major Neolithic culture of north China centred on the middle course of the Yellow River, taking its name from a site in Honan. Traces of the Yang-shao culture first appear before 5000 BC, and continue for approximately 2000 years. More than 1000 sites have been attributed to this period. These early farmers cultivated mainly the cereal millet, and used stone tools such as polished axes, reaping knives, hoes, spades and grinding stones. Large communal houses may indicate cooperative agriculture. Pig, dog and sometimes cattle, sheep and goat were domesticated, deer and antelope commonly hunted, and fishing was practised. Textiles were fashioned with the aid of bone needles and spindle-whorls, and there is a suggestion that silkworms were raised. Hand-made red and black painted pottery was characteristic, in addition to a simpler red or grey ware. Basketry must have been highly developed, for a variety of cord and mat impressions in pottery have been discovered (*see* PAN-P'O). *See also* LUNG-SHAN; PAN SHAN.

▲ **YAYOI** The Japanese cultural stage which succeeded the JOMON in the 3rd century BC. The Yayoi period was one of advanced rice-growing techniques, and thus heralded the beginning of intensive agriculture in Japan. In addition,

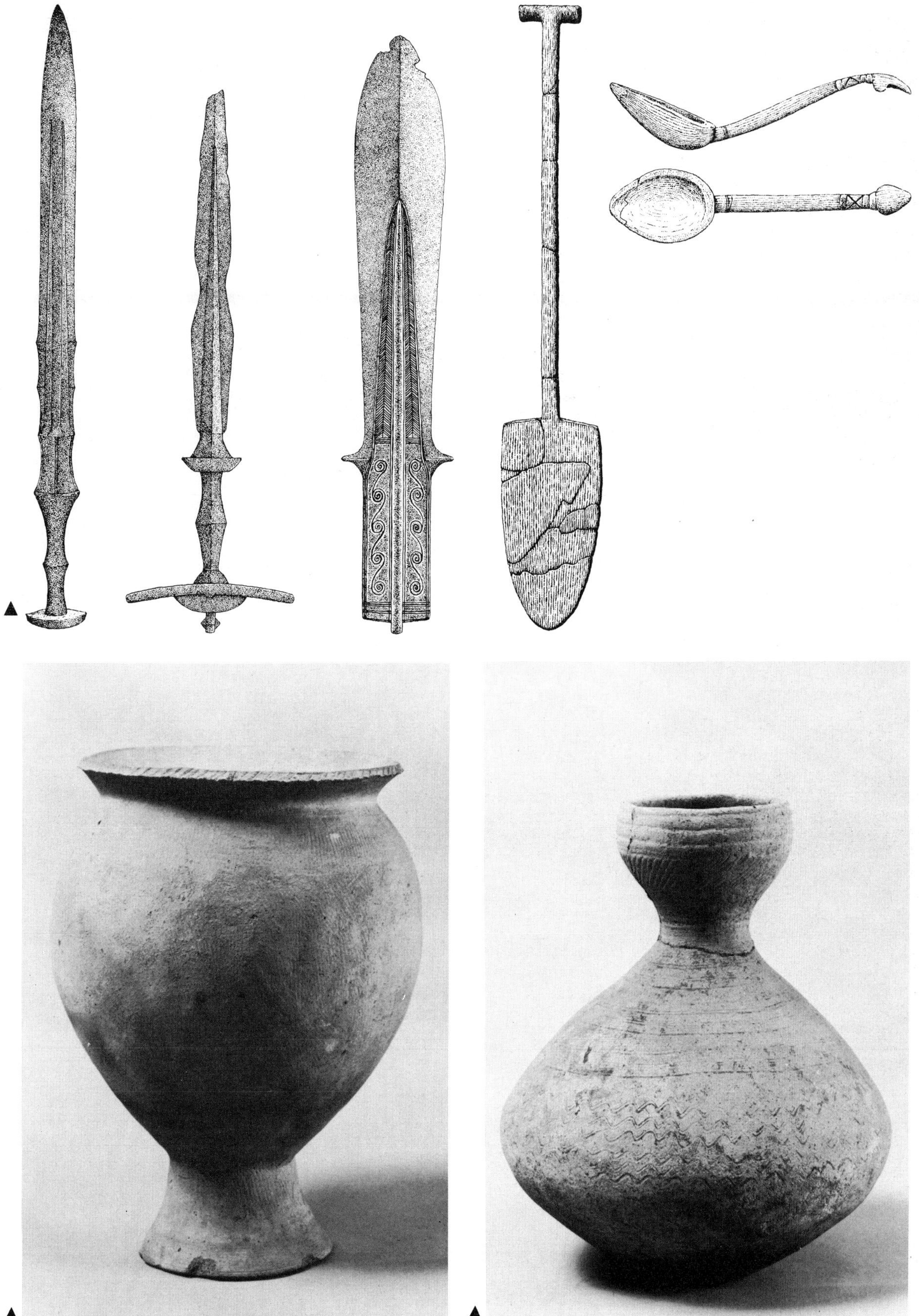

bronze- and iron-working began during this period. These innovations are thought to have come from China or Korea. Bronzes were often ceremonial in nature. Iron is found only on occasion in this period, and generally as a farming or household aid. It was to be used more widely in the protohistoric TOMB PERIOD which followed. At some Yayoi sites numerous bronze objects such as coins and mirrors of the Chinese HAN dynasty are found. The Yayoi made their own distinctive variations of cast bronze types such as large bronze bells, and weapons such as swords, spears and halberd-blades. The skills involved in these activities point to an economy with specialists working under the wealthy, whose graves contain jewellery, mirrors and weapons. The villagers lived in round or oblong dwellings of thatch-covered wooden posts and beams, with raised store-houses for grains. Excavations at the settlement site of TORO give a picture of the layout of these communities, their relationship to the irrigated rice-fields, and their equipment. Among the implements found here were the ubiquitous stone rice-reaper, wooden looms, and clogs for crossing the marshy fields. Household utensils as well as many agricultural tools seem to have been made generally of wood, especially oak and cedar. Woven hemp textiles have been found in burial jars, a form of interment sometimes made in CISTS or DOLMENS. The patterns of society begun in this era set the pattern for the even greater organization of the protohistoric TOMB PERIOD.

YAZILIKAYA
see HITTITES

YEAVERING, Northumberland The royal site in NORTHUMBRIA, called by BEDE 'Ad Gefrin', has been totally excavated and shown to consist of three main building phases under the greatest of the Northumbrian kings of the 7th century AD. The first phase was begun *c* 600 under Aethelfrith and enlarged by Edwin. After a fire of 632 it was rebuilt only to be reburnt by Penda, King of MERCIA, and reconstructed by Oswiu who reigned 654–70. The principal building is a massive royal HALL 27m long, with two side aisles and a screened-off room at the east end. The walls were of large squared timbers set in a foundation trench and externally buttressed along one side. There are several other halls on the site, one of which may have been a pagan temple later converted into a Christian church after the visit of PAULINUS in 627. A unique feature at Yeavering is a fan-shaped meeting place with banked seats and a platform with a screen behind it as a central focal point. Yeavering is important not only for its securely dated place in Northumbrian history and archaeology, but because it illustrates the kind of palace complex which may have been occupied at this time in EAST ANGLIA by the king whose treasure was found at SUTTON HOO. *See also* CHEDDAR.

YEMEN The area in south-west Arabia well known as the home of the Queen of Sheba, who visited King Solomon. The Yemen's wealth depended until recently on the trading of spices, gold, precious stones and the valuable frankincense (of which it had a monopoly). The mountainous terrain gave the inhabitants of the area security and isolation. Agriculture was carried on with the aid of irrigation, water obtained by diverting the flooded wadis with massive dams, such as the one found at Marib. Only a small amount of excavation has been completed. A large temple about three miles from Marib was found to have casemate fortification walls. The buildings at Marib were

▲ 

constructed with stone and were laid out with a definite plan. The south gate at Timna was found to be made of massive stone blocks, while the city walls were of rubble.

YIN
see SHANG DYNASTY

● **YORK, Yorkshire** The Roman *Eboracum*, and the administrative and military capital of northern Britain. It began as a fortress for the Ninth Legion *c* AD 71, and a civil settlement soon sprang up around it; at an unknown date this settlement was granted the status of COLONIA, and by the beginning of the 3rd century Eboracum was the administrative capital of Britannia Inferior. (Britain north of the Wash-Severn line). It became a centre of learning, of mosaic art and jet carving, but kept its primarily military importance, as is attested by the reconstruction of the defences in *c* AD 300. The Emperor SEVERUS and his family lived at York for some years after 208. The episcopacy of York had been established by 314. During the early Middle Ages, York became an important settlement of the VIKINGS. Some of the Roman defences still stand, capped by medieval masonry.

ZAPOTEC A people who occupied most of Oaxaca, ▲ Mexico, and whose main capital was at MONTE ALBAN. There is an unbroken stylistic continuity from historic times back to the Preclassic period (*see* MESOAMERICA); the date of the emergence of the Zapotec culture seems to be *c* 300 AD. In the late Postclassic, much of the area was taken over by the MIXTECS, spreading south and east from the Mixteca Alta. Both groups managed to maintain substantial independence from AZTEC dominion.

ZAWI CHEMI SHANIDAR, Iraq A settlement of *c* 9000 BC. The significance of the site lies in the animal bones, of which 8 out of 10 are from sheep (and more than half of these are from lambs). Such a large proportion of young animals would never be found in a natural living population, so it has been suggested that the sheep were domesticated. An alternative, and perhaps more likely, interpretation is the people were herding wild sheep. Whichever view is correct, the evidence for some form of sheep management is clear, and at a very early date.

ZIGGURAT The name given to the artificial towers found in most principal cities of SUMER, BABYLONIA and ASSYRIA. In addition to the remains such as those of Choga Zanbil (*see* SUSA), ancient writings and drawings refer to them. The Biblical tower of Babel (Genesis 11) is one probable reference. The reconstruction of the Ziggurat at UR gives an idea of their appearance. On top of a series of platforms is a temple building to which access may be gained by a stairway. The temple was the earthly residence of the patron deity of the city. The walls of each platform were painted and it is probable that trees grew on the terraces; this may explain the 'Hanging Gardens of Babylon'.

ZINJIRLI [Sinjirli], Turkey A TELL in southern Anatolia excavated by the Germans 1888–92. It was important during the HITTITE empire, after whose downfall it became an independent city-state called Sam'l. In the 7th century BC it became part of ASSYRIA before it was abandoned. The city walls were found in plan to form a circle 700m in diameter. In the centre of the city, the fortified citadel contained two palaces freely decorated with RELIEFS.

Regional Index

This index is intended to be a guide to the sites of all periods in each country; only sites given individual entries in the text are shown. The maps are necessarily of small scale and it is possible to give only the approximate position of each site; for the exact position, reference should be made to the more detailed maps in the body of the text.

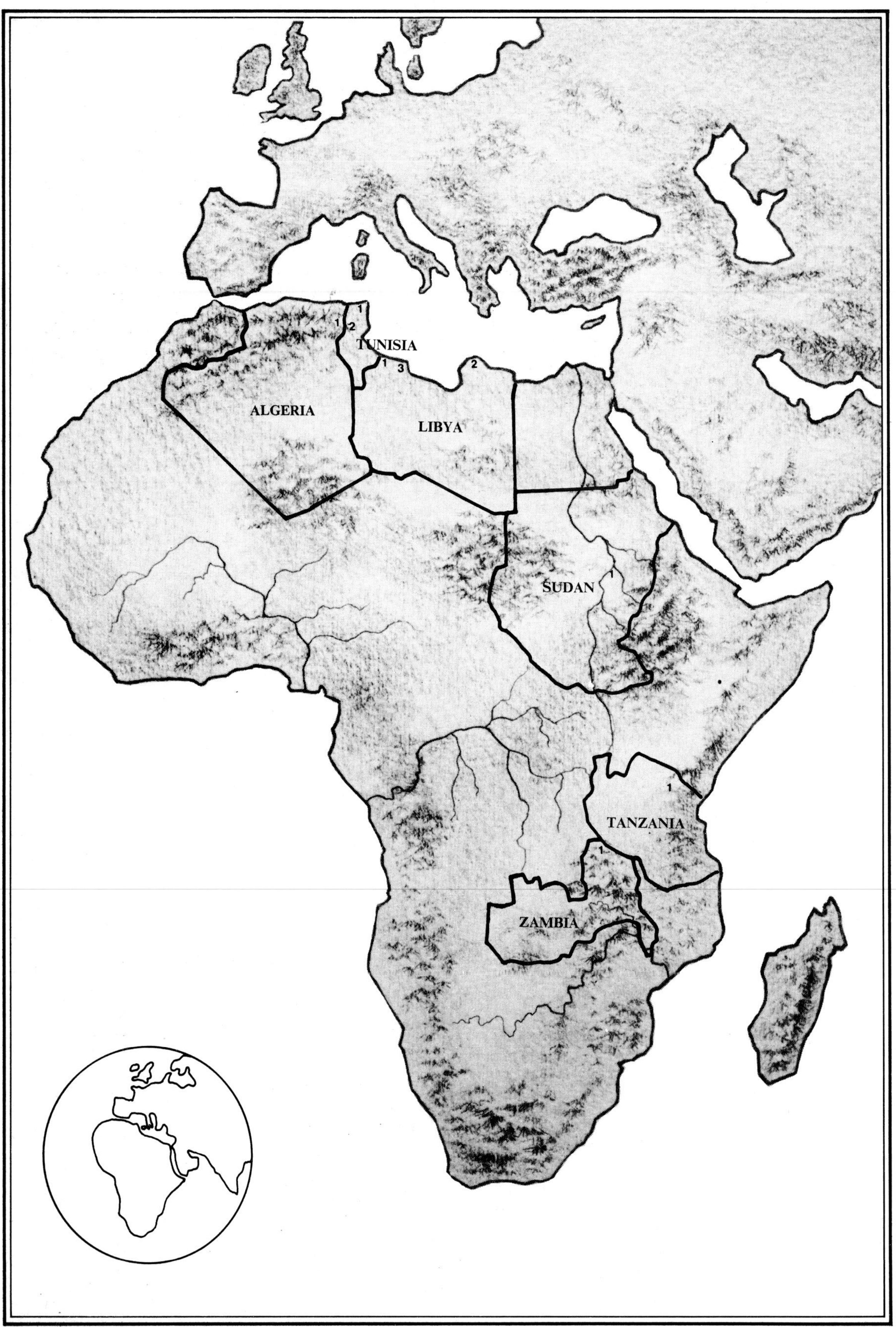
TUNISIA
ALGERIA
LIBYA
SUDAN
TANZANIA
ZAMBIA
1
2
1
1
3
2
1
1
1

AFRICA

ALGERIA
1 Lambaesis

LIBYA
1 Sabratha
2 Haua Fteah
3 Leptis Magna

SUDAN
1 Meroe

TANZANIA
1 Olduvai Gorge

TUNISIA
1 Carthage
2 Timgad

ZAMBIA
1 Kalambo Falls

EUROPE

AUSTRIA
1 Carnuntum
2 Hallstatt

CZECHOSLOVAKIA
1 Bylany
2 Třisov
3 Dolní Věstonice

DENMARK
1 Gundestrup
2 Dejbjerg
3 Tollund
4 Egtved
5 Trelleborg
6 Hedeby

FRANCE
1 Quentovic
2 Paris
3 Carnac
4 Vix
5 Grand Pressigny
6 Lezoux
7 Lascaux
8 Abri Pataud
Combe Grenal
Cromagnon
9 Lugdunum
10 Cuzoul
11 La Graufesenque
12 Pont du Gard
13 Montmaurin
14 Nemausus
15 Glanum
16 Arles
17 Entremont
18 Roqueperteuse
19 Massilia
20 Le Vallonet
21 Forum Julii

GERMANY
1 Hedeby
2 Xanten
3 Neuss
4 Cologne
Köln-Lindenthal
5 Mainz
6 Waldalgesheim
7 Trier
8 Steinheim
9 Klein Aspergle
10 Michelsberg
11 Manching
12 Heuneberg
Hohmichele

GREECE
1 Salonika
2 Nea Nikomedia
3 Argissa
4 Sesklo
5 Nicopolis
6 Delphi
7 Sounion
Athens
8 Corinth
9 Olympia
10 Mycenae
11 Epidaurus
12 Tiryns
13 Lerna
14 Delos
15 Sparta
16 Pylos
17 Rhodes
18 Thera
19 Knossos
20 Mallia
21 Phaistos

HOLLAND
1 Dorestad

HUNGARY
1 Vértesszöllös

ITALY
1 Val Camonica
2 Peschiera
3 Aquileia
4 Este
5 Ravenna
6 Grimaldi
7 Marzabotto
8 Volterra
9 Arezzo
10 Vetulonia
11 Perugia
12 Chiusi
13 Orvieto
14 Tarquinia
15 Volsinii
16 Cerveteri
17 Rome
18 Ostia
19 Cumae
20 Herculaneum
Pompeii
21 Paestum
22 Agrigento

JUGOSLAVIA
1 Vinča
2 Lepenski Vir
3 Split

NORWAY
1 Oseberg
2 Gokstad
3 Kaupang

POLAND
1 Biskupin

SPAIN
1 Altamira
2 Leon
3 Numantia
4 Segovia
5 Ampurias
6 Alcantara
7 Tarragona
8 Merida
9 Gades
10 Los Millares

SWEDEN
1 Birka

SWITZERLAND
1 Augst
2 Vindonissa
3 La Tène

TURKEY
1 Byzantium
Constantinople
2 Alaca Hüyük
3 Kültepe
4 Pergamum
5 Sardis
6 Catal Hüyük
7 Karatepe
8 Zinjirli
9 Carchemish
10 Hacilar
11 Ephesus
12 Aphrodisias
13 Alalakh

USSR
1 Novgorod

NORWAY
DENMARK
HOLLAND
GERMANY
FRANCE
SWITZERLAND
AUS
SPAIN
ITALY

USSR
POLAND
CHOSLOVAKIA
HUNGARY
AVIA
GREECE
TURKEY

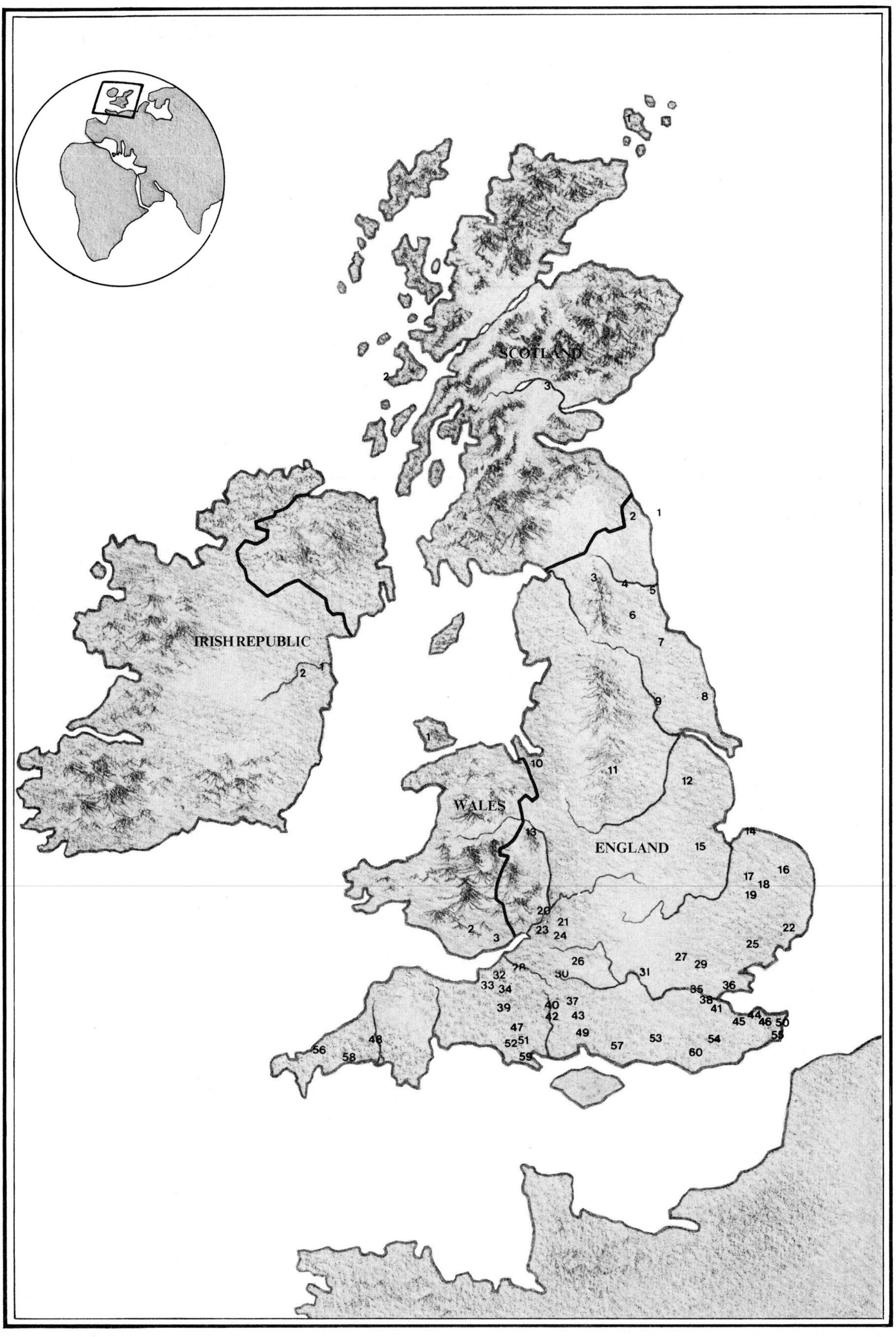
SCOTLAND
IRISH REPUBLIC
WALES
ENGLAND

THE BRITISH ISLES

ENGLAND
1 Lindisfarne
2 Yeavering
3 Housesteads
4 Corbridge
5 Jarrow
6 Heathery Burn
7 Stanwick
8 Star Carr
9 York
10 Chester
11 Benty Grange
12 Lincoln
13 Wroxeter
14 Snettisham
15 Water Newton
16 Caistor by Norwich
17 Grimes Graves
18 Thetford
19 West Stow
20 Gloucester
21 Chedworth
22 Sutton Hoo
23 Woodchester
24 Cirencester
25 Camulodunum
26 Rams Hill
27 Ivinghoe Beacon
28 Bath
29 Verulamium
30 Avebury
Silbury Hill
West Kennet
Windmill Hill
31 Taplow
32 Cheddar
33 Somerset Levels
34 Meare
Glastonbury
35 London
36 Mucking
37 Little Woodbury
38 Swanscombe
39 Cadbury
40 Bush Barrow
Durrington Walls
Stonehenge
Woodhenge
41 Lullingstone
42 Wilsford Shaft
43 Winchester
44 Faversham
45 Aylesford
46 Canterbury
47 Hod Hill
48 Rillatton
49 Hamwih
50 Richborough
51 Cerne Abbas
52 Maiden Castle
53 Bignor
54 Piltdown
55 Dover
56 Gwithian
57 Fishbourne
58 Trewhiddle
59 Kimmeridge
60 Itford Hill

IRISH REPUBLIC
1 Knowth
2 Tara

SCOTLAND
1 Maes How
Skara Brae
2 Iona
3 Inchtuthill

WALES
1 Llyn Cerrig Bach
2 Llyn Fawr
3 Caerleon

THE FERTILE CRESCENT

CYPRUS
1 Salamis
2 Enkomi
3 Khirokitia

EGYPT
1 Rosetta
2 Alexandria
3 Sais
4 Tanis
5 Bubastis
6 Heliopolis
7 Giza
8 Helwan
9 Saqqara
10 Memphis
11 Dashur
12 Lisht
13 Meidum
14 Faiyum
Hawara
Lahun
15 Abusir
16 Oxyrhynchus
17 Beni Hasan
18 Hermopolis
Tuna el-Gebel
19 Amarna
20 Abydos
Umm el Qaab
21 Dendera
22 Nagada
23 Deir el Bahri
Deir el-Medina
Karnak
Luxor
Medinet Habu
Thebes
Sheikh Abd el Qurna
24 Armant
25 El Kab
26 Hierankonpolis
27 Aswan
28 Philae
29 Beit el-Wali
Kalabsha
30 Abu Simbel
31 Ballana
Buhen
32 Soleb

IRAN
1 Hissar
2 Sialk
3 Behistun
4 Susa
5 Yahya

IRAQ
1 Shanidar
Zawi Chemi Shanidar
2 Khorsabad
3 Nineveh
4 Nimrud
5 Hassuna
6 Jarmo
7 Nuzi
8 Assur
9 Eshnunna
10 Khafajah
11 Jemdat Nasr
12 Babylon
13 Nippur
14 Lagash
15 Uruk
16 Ubaid
17 Ur
18 Eridu

ISRAEL
1 Hazor
2 Mount Carmel
3 Megiddo
4 Khirbet Kerek
5 Beth Shan
6 Farah
7 Samaria
8 Caeserea
9 Jericho
10 Jerusalem
11 Gezer
12 Lachish
13 Qumran
14 Beer Sheba
15 Arad

JORDAN
1 Ghassul
2 Beidha
3 Petra

LEBANON
1 Byblos

PERSIAN GULF
1 Bahrain

SYRIA
1 Halaf
2 Brak
3 Ugarit
4 Hama
5 Kadesh
6 Mari
7 Palmyra
8 Damascus

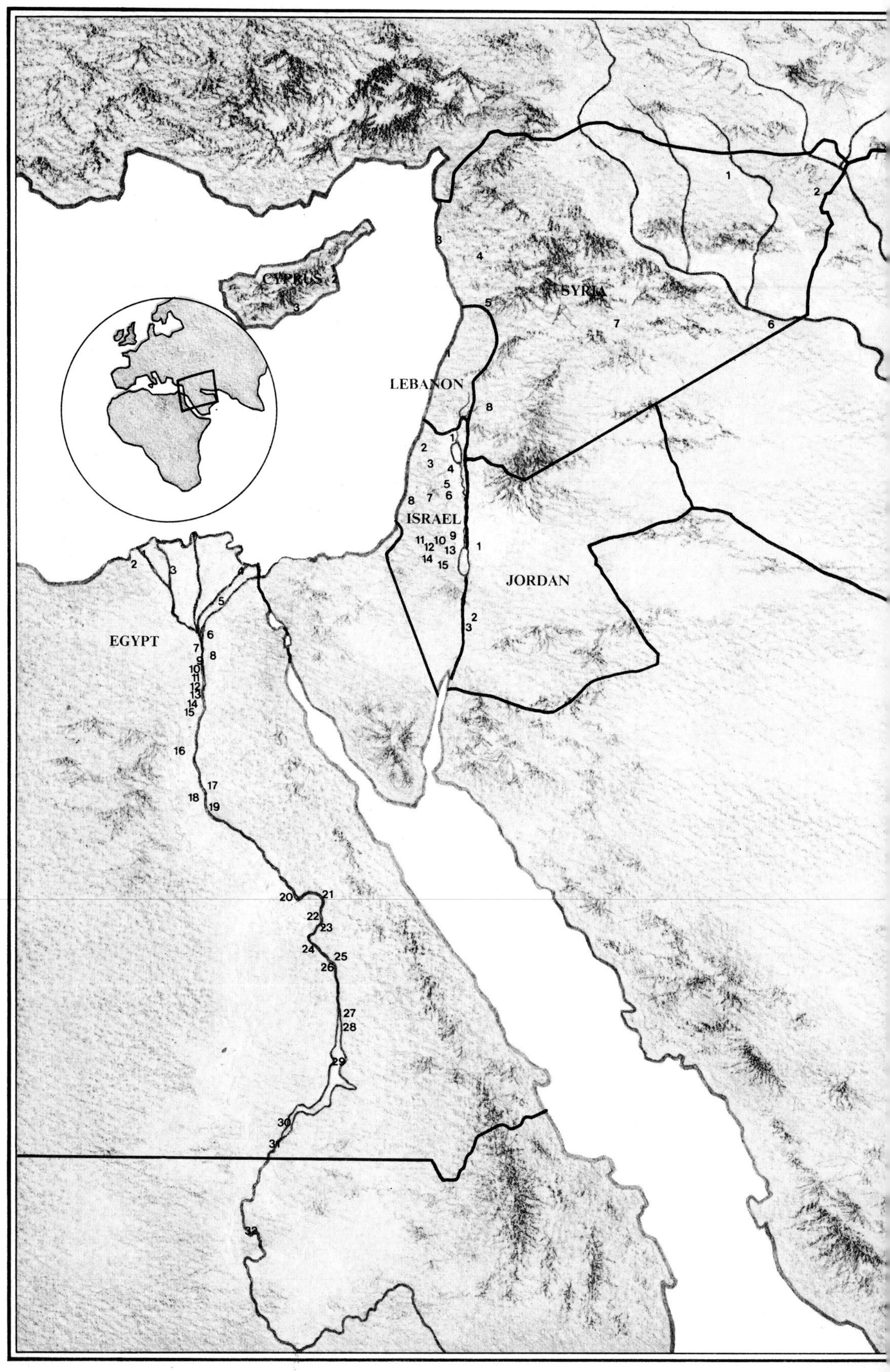

CYPRUS
SYRIA
LEBANON
ISRAEL
JORDAN
EGYPT

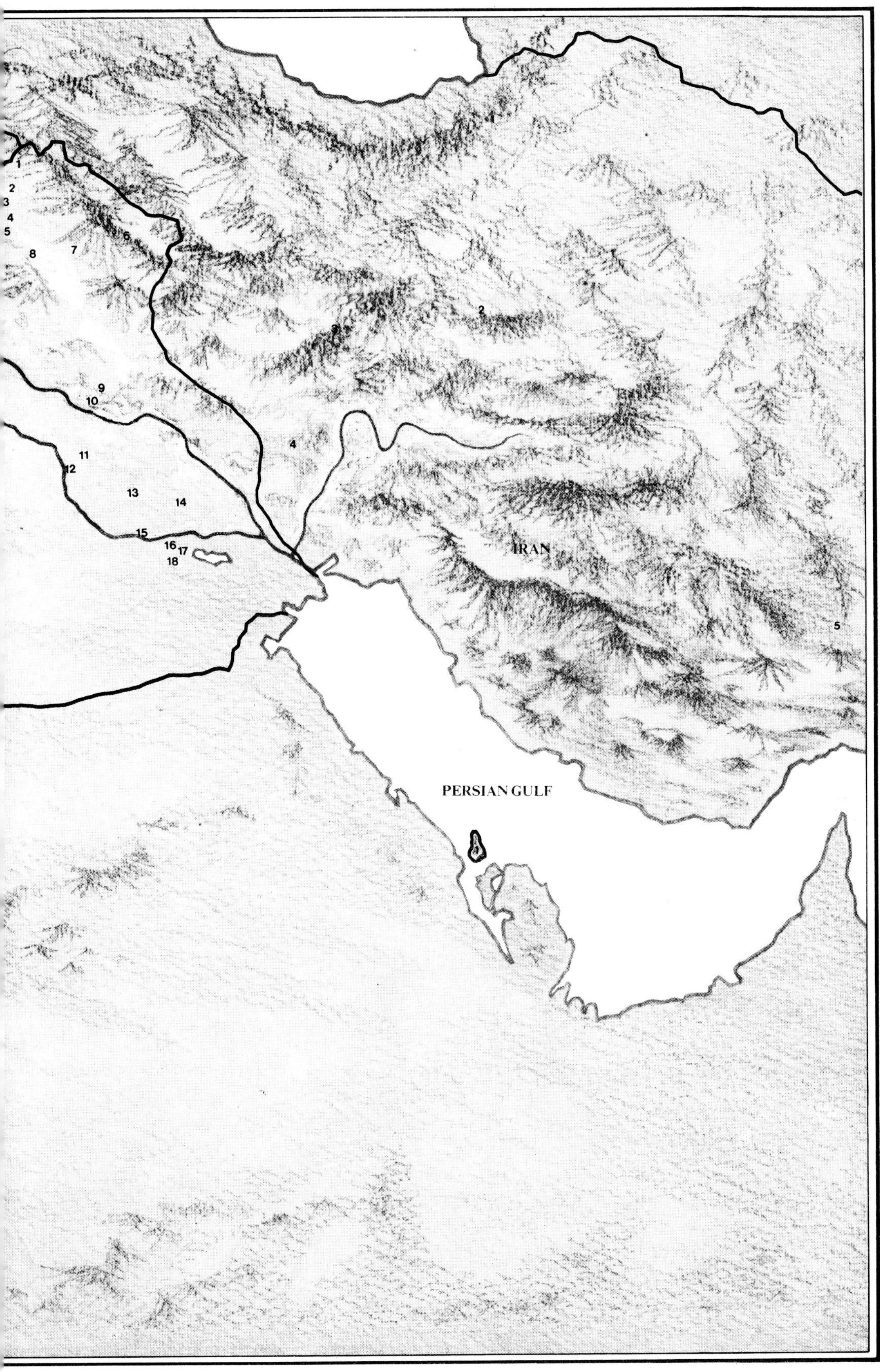

IRAN
PERSIAN GULF

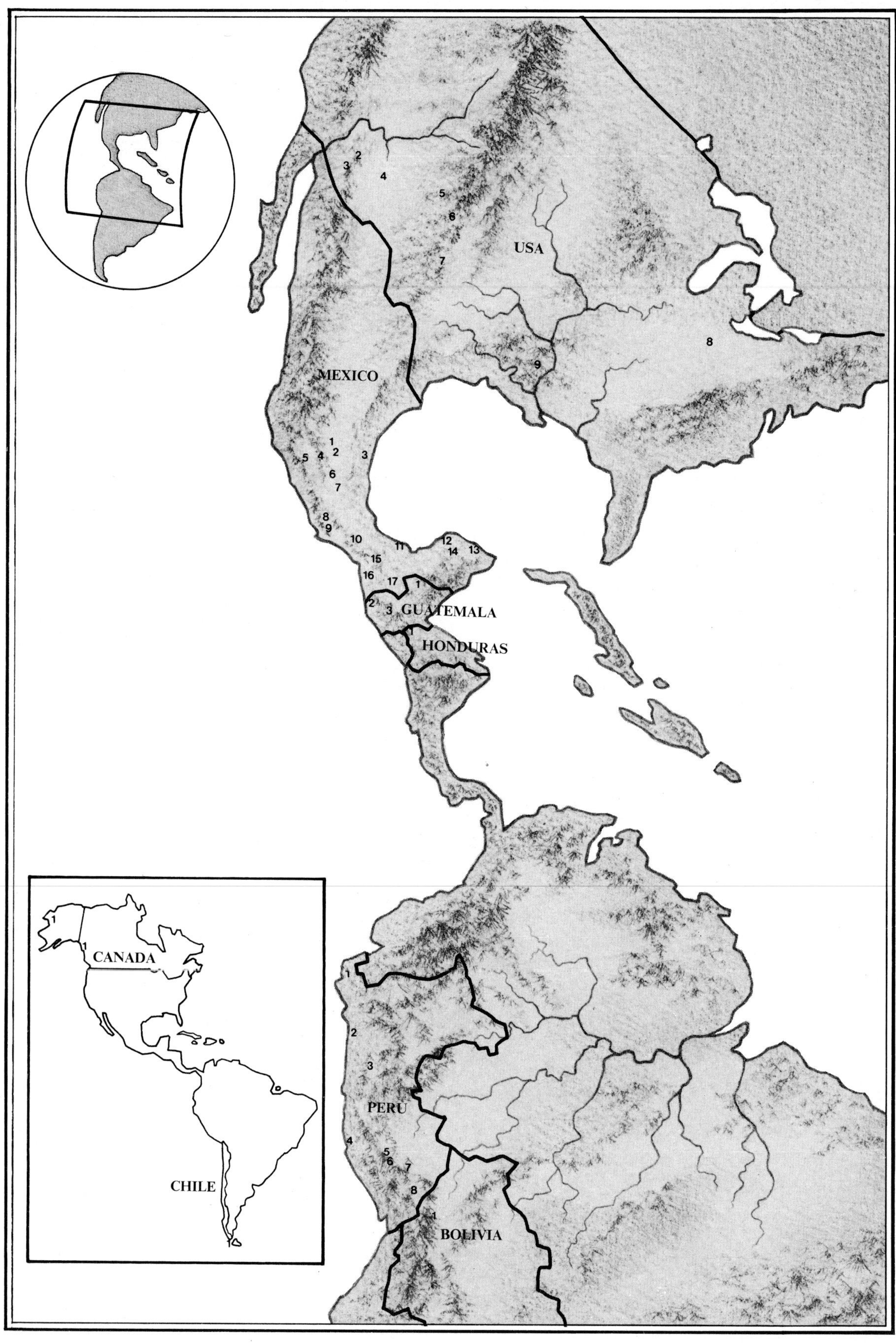

USA
MEXICO
GUATEMALA
HONDURAS
PERU
BOLIVIA
CANADA
CHILE

THE AMERICAS

BOLIVIA
1 Tiahuanaco

CANADA
1 Old Crow Flats

CHILE
1 Fell's Cave

GUATEMALA
1 Tikal
Uaxactun
2 Ocos
3 Kaminaljuyú

HONDURAS
1 Copan

MEXICO
1 Tula
2 Teotihuacan
3 El Tajín
4 Santa Isabel Iztapan
Tepexpan
Tenochtitlan
Tlapacoya
Tlatilco
5 Xochicalco
6 Cholula
7 Tehuacan Valley
8 Monte Alban
9 Mitla
10 San Lorenzo Tenochtitlan
11 La Venta
12 Uxmal
13 Chichen Itza
14 Mayapan
15 Palenque
16 Izapa
17 Bonampak

PERU
1 Vicus
2 Huaca Prieta
3 Chavín de Huantar
4 Pachacamac
5 Aya Cucho
6 Huari
7 Machu Picchu
8 Pucara

USA
1 Cape Krusenstern
Ipiutak
Onion Porterage
2 Snaketown
3 Casa Grande
4 Bat Cave
5 Sandia Cave
6 Folsom
7 Blackwater Draw
8 Adena
9 Poverty Point

THE FAR EAST

AUSTRALIA
1 Oenpelli
2 Kennif Cave
3 Ingaladdi
4 Lake Menindee
5 Lake Mungo
6 Kow Swamp
7 Devon Downs
8 Green Gully
9 Koonalda Cave

AFGANISTAN
1 Baglan
2 Begram
3 Hadda

CAMBODIA
1 Angkor

CHINA
1 Peking
2 Chou K'ou Tien
3 Anyang
4 Cheng Chou
5 Loyang
6 Pan P'o
7 Yang Shao
8 Pan Shan
9 Shih Chai Shan

INDIA
1 Rupar
2 Hastinapura
3 Kalibangan
4 Atranjikhera
5 Sankisa
6 Vaisali
Patna
7 Rajagriha
8 Rajghat
Sarnath
9 Bodh Gaya
10 Kaushambi
11 Bhar Hut
12 Sanchi
13 Ujjain
14 Lothal
15 Sisupalgarh
16 Broach
17 Amaravati
18 Arikamedu

INDONESIA
1 Gua Lawa

JAPAN
1 Iwajuku
2 Natshushima
3 Toro
4 Nintoku
5 Fukui Cave

MALAYSIA
1 Gua Cha
2 Gua Kechil

NEPAL
1 Lumbini
2 Kapilavastu

NEW GUINEA
1 Kafia Vana

PAKISTAN
1 Charsada
2 Taxila
3 Harappa
4 Mohenjo-Daro
5 Kot Diji
6 Amri
7 Barbaricum

PHILLIPINES
1 Tabon Cave

SARAWAK
1 Niah

THAILAND
1 Ban Chieng
2 Spirit Cave
3 Non Nok Tha
4 Chansen
5 Sai Yok
6 Ban Kao

USSR
1 Pazyryk

VIETNAM
1 Dong Son
2 Oc Eo

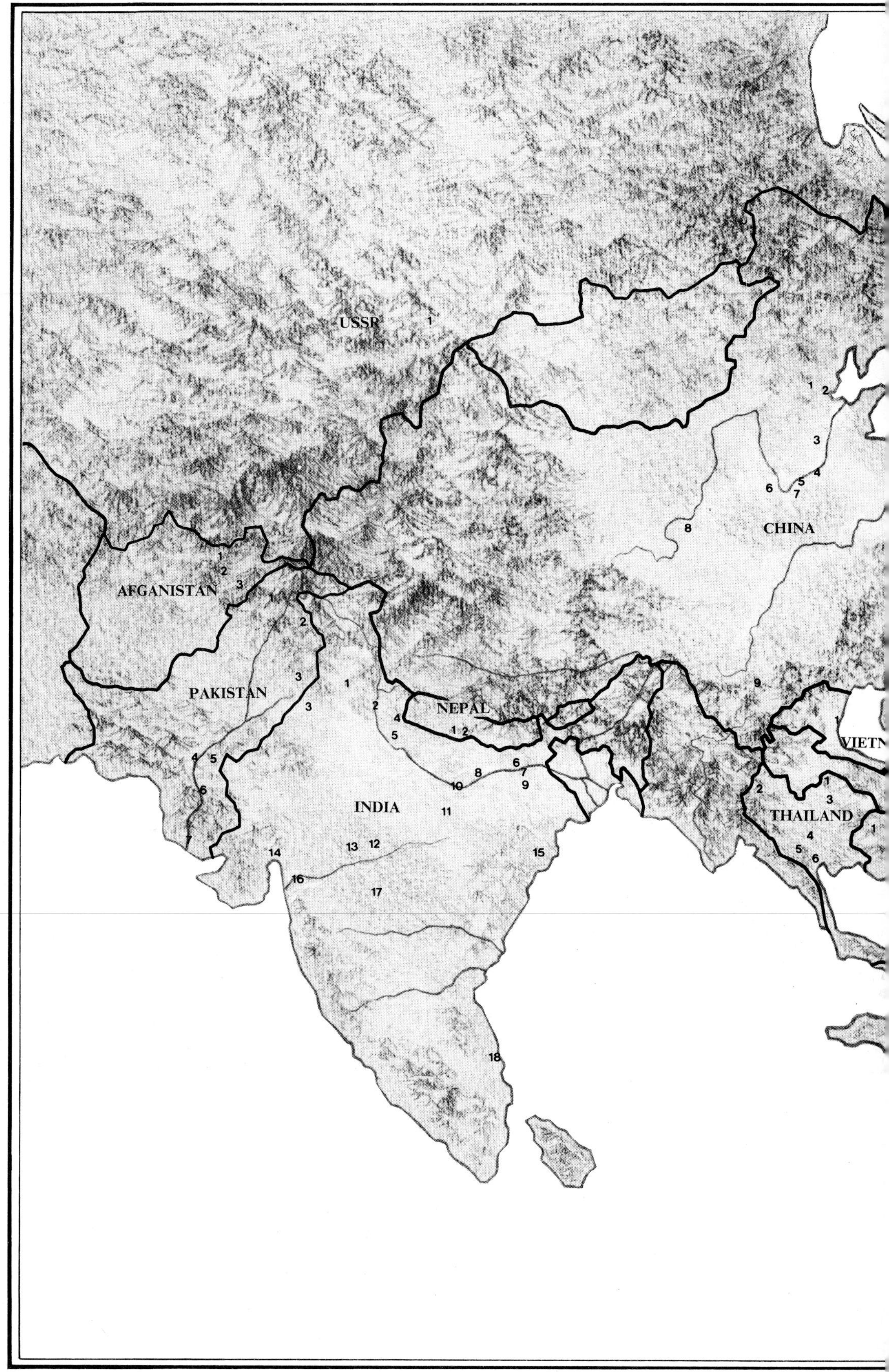
USSR
CHINA
AFGANISTAN
PAKISTAN
NEPAL
INDIA
THAILAND

AN
1
2
3
4
5
PHILLIPINES
SARAWAK
AYSIA
INDONESIA
NEW GUINEA
AUSTRALIA
1
2
3
4
5
6
7
8
9